Lecture Notes in Computer Sc

Commenced Publication in 1973
Founding and Former Series Editors:
Gerhard Goos, Juris Hartmanis, and Jan van Leeuwen

T0238180

Editorial Board

David Hutchison
  Lancaster University, UK
Takeo Kanade
  Carnegie Mellon University, Pittsburgh, PA, USA
Josef Kittler
  University of Surrey, Guildford, UK
Jon M. Kleinberg
  Cornell University, Ithaca, NY, USA
Friedemann Mattern
  ETH Zurich, Switzerland
John C. Mitchell
  Stanford University, CA, USA
Moni Naor
  Weizmann Institute of Science, Rehovot, Israel
Oscar Nierstrasz
  University of Bern, Switzerland
C. Pandu Rangan
  Indian Institute of Technology, Madras, India
Bernhard Steffen
  University of Dortmund, Germany
Madhu Sudan
  Massachusetts Institute of Technology, MA, USA
Demetri Terzopoulos
  New York University, NY, USA
Doug Tygar
  University of California, Berkeley, CA, USA
Moshe Y. Vardi
  Rice University, Houston, TX, USA
Gerhard Weikum
  Max-Planck Institute of Computer Science, Saarbruecken, Germany

Awais Rashid   Mehmet Aksit (Eds.)

Transactions on Aspect-Oriented Software Development I

 Springer

Volume Editors

Awais Rashid
Lancaster University
Computing Department
Lancaster, LA1 4YR, UK
E-mail: awais@comp.lancs.ac.uk

Mehmet Aksit
University of Twente
Department of Computer Science
Enschede, The Netherlands
E-mail: aksit@ewi.utwente.nl

Library of Congress Control Number: 2006921902

CR Subject Classification (1998): D.2, D.3, I.6, H.4, K.6

LNCS Sublibrary: SL 2 – Programming and Software Engineering

ISSN   0302-9743
ISBN-10   3-540-32972-2 Springer Berlin Heidelberg New York
ISBN-13   978-3-540-32972-5 Springer Berlin Heidelberg New York

This work is subject to copyright. All rights are reserved, whether the whole or part of the material is
concerned, specifically the rights of translation, reprinting, re-use of illustrations, recitation, broadcasting,
reproduction on microfilms or in any other way, and storage in data banks. Duplication of this publication
or parts thereof is permitted only under the provisions of the German Copyright Law of September 9, 1965,
in its current version, and permission for use must always be obtained from Springer. Violations are liable
to prosecution under the German Copyright Law.

Springer is a part of Springer Science+Business Media

springer.com

© Springer-Verlag Berlin Heidelberg 2006
Printed in Germany

Typesetting: Camera-ready by author, data conversion by Scientific Publishing Services, Chennai, India
Printed on acid-free paper   SPIN: 11687061   06/3142   5 4 3 2 1 0

Editorial

Welcome to the first volume of *Transactions on Aspect-Oriented Software Development*. Aspect-oriented methods, tools and techniques are gaining in popularity due to their systematic support for modularizing broadly scoped properties, the so-called *crosscutting concerns*, in software systems. Such crosscutting concerns include security, distribution, persistence, mobility, real-time constraints and so on. As software systems become increasingly ubiquitous, mobile and distributed, the modular treatment of such crosscutting concerns also becomes critical to ensure that software artifacts pertaining to such concerns are reusable, evolvable and maintainable. This modular treatment of crosscutting concerns by aspect-oriented techniques is not limited to code level. In fact, aspect-oriented techniques cover the software life cycle, handling crosscutting concerns in requirements, architecture, design, code, test cases, system documentation, etc.

The aspect-oriented software development community is growing fast, with an increasing number of researchers and practitioners across the world contributing to the development and evolution of the field. The community launched its own conference in 2002, which has since been held with great success on an annual basis. Recent reports from Burton and Gartner groups have put aspect-orientation on the *plateau of productivity* on the evolution cycle of new technologies. One of the key indicators of the maturity of a field is the availability of high quality research of an archival nature. The launch of *Transactions on Aspect-Oriented Software Development*, therefore, signifies a key milestone for the maturity of work in this area. The journal is committed to publishing work of the highest standard on all facets of aspect-oriented software development techniques in the context of all phases of the software life cycle, from requirements and design to implementation, maintenance and evolution. The call for papers is open indefinitely and potential authors can submit papers at any time to: taosd-submission@comp.lancs.ac.uk. Detailed submission instructions are available at: http://www.springer.com/sgw/cda/frontpage/ 0,,3-164-2-109318-0,00.html. A number of special issues on current important topics in the community are already in preparation. These include special issues on AOP systems, software and middleware; AOP and software evolution; dynamic AOP, and Early Aspects. Calls for such special issues are publicized on relevant Internet mailing lists, Web sites as well as conferences such as the Aspect-Oriented Software Development conference.

The articles in this volume cover a wide range of topics from software design to implementation of aspect-oriented languages. The first four articles address various issues of aspect-oriented modeling at the design level. The first article, "Assessing Aspect Modularizations Using Design Structure Matrix and Net Option Value", by Lopes and Bajracharya, proposes a methodology and a tool to show how aspects can be beneficial as well as detrimental to a certain design. The second article, "Modularizing Design Patterns with Aspects: A Quantitative Study", by Garcia et al., analyzes and compares the aspect-oriented and object-oriented implementations of design patterns with respect to quality values such as coupling and cohesion. The article "Directives for Composing Aspect-Oriented Class Models", by Reddy et al., proposes models for expressing aspect-oriented and non–aspect-oriented properties of systems and defines techniques to compose these models together. In the article "Aspect Categories and Classes of Temporal Properties", Shmuel Katz defines a method for classifying aspects with respect to their temporal properties so that application of aspects in a system can be better understood and analyzed.

The following four articles discuss various programming language issues. The article "An Overview of CaesarJ", by Aracic et al., gives an overview of the CaesarJ programming language, which aims at integrating aspects, classes and packages so that large-scale aspect components can be built. In the article "An Expressive Aspect Language for System Applications with Arachne", Douence et al. motivate the applicability of the Arachne language in improving systems written in the C language, where system dynamicity and performance play an important role. Monteiro and Fernandes define in their article, "Towards a Catalogue of Refactorings and Code Smells for AspectJ", a catalogue that helps in detecting aspects in object-oriented programs and in improving the structure of extracted aspects within the context of the AspectJ language. The final paper in the language category is "Design and Implementation of An Aspect Instantiation Mechanism" by Sakurai et al. It proposes association aspects as an extension to AspectJ for flexible descriptions of aspects whose instances are associated with more than one object.

The final article in this volume, "abc: An Extensible AspectJ Compiler", by Avgustinov et al., describes a workbench for implementing aspect-oriented languages, so that easy experimentation with new language features and implementation techniques are possible.

The inception and launch of *Transactions on Aspect-Oriented Software Development* and publication of its first volume would not have been possible without the guidance, commitment and input of the editorial board and the reviewers who volunteered time from their busy schedules to help realize this publication. We thank them greatly for their help and efforts. Most important, we wish to thank authors who have submitted papers to the journal so far. The journal belongs to the community and it is the submissions from the community that are at the heart of this first volume and future volumes of *Transactions on Aspect-Oriented Software Development*.

Awais Rashid and Mehmet Aksit
Coeditors-in-chief

Organization

Editorial Board

Mehmet Aksit, University of Twente
Don Batory, University of Texas at Austin
Shigeru Chiba, Tokyo Institute of Technology
Siobhán Clarke, Trinity College Dublin
Theo D'Hondt, Vrije Universtiteit Brussel
Robert Filman, Google
Shmuel Katz, Technion-Israel Institute of Technology
Gregor Kiczales, University of British Columbia
Karl Lieberherr, Northeastern University
Mira Mezini, University of Darmstadt
Ana Moreira, New University of Lisbon
Linda Northrop, Software Engineering Institute
Harold Ossher, IBM Research
Awais Rashid, Lancaster University
Douglas Schmidt, Vanderbilt University
David Thomas, Bedarra Research Labs

List of Reviewers

Jonathan Aldrich
Joao Araujo
Elisa Baniassad
Lodewijk Bergmans
Lynne Blair
Paulo Borba
Silvia Breu
Johan Brichau
Shigeru Chiba
Ruzanna Chitchyan
Siobhán Clarke
Yvonne Coady
Wesley Coelho
Maja D'Hondt
Theo D'Hondt
Pascal Dürr
Ulrich Eisenecker
Tzilla Elrad
Eric Ernst
Robert France
Alessandro Garcia
Andy Gokhale
Jeff Gray

Jean-Marc Jezequel
Joerg Kienzle
Micheal Kircher
Barbara Kitchenham
Shriram Krishnamurthi
Ramnivas Laddad
Karl Lieberherr
Roberto Lopez-Herrejon
David Lorenz
Hidehiko Masuhara
Marjan Mernik
Mattia Monga
Ana Moreira
Juan Manuel Murillo
Gail Murphy
Harold Ossher
Klaus Ostermann
Andres Diaz Pace
Monica Pinto
Ragghu Reddy
Christa Schwanninger
Domink Stein
Stan Sutton

John Grundy
Charles Haley
Stephan Hannenberg
Jan Hannemann
Wilke Havinga

Wim Vanderperren
Kris de Volder
Robert Walker
Nathan Weston
Jianjun Zhao

Table of Contents

Assessing Aspect Modularizations Using Design Structure Matrix and Net Option Value[*]

Cristina Videira Lopes and Sushil Krishna Bajracharya

Department of Informatics,
Donald Bren School of Information and Computer Sciences,
University of California, Irvine
{lopes, sbajrach}@ics.uci.edu

Abstract. The design structure matrix (DSM) methodology and the net option value (NOV) model have been used before to show how aspects can add value to a design. Following an in-depth analysis of that study, this paper demonstrates how aspects can be beneficial as well as detrimental. The structural transformations involved in aspect modularizations are carefully analyzed in the context of DSMs. This analysis exposes the unique *reversion* effect on dependencies that aspect modules are known for. To capture that effect within the NOV model, we extend its original set of six modular operators with an additional *reversion* operator. Using a design case study, its NOV worksheet and NOV experiments' curves are presented to show a simulation of the evolutionary patterns of modules, including aspect modules. These patterns show how subtle dependencies, or the lack of them, bring down, or up, the value of an existing design. Based on the observations made in this case study, preliminary design guidelines for aspects are formulated.

Keywords: Aspect-oriented programming and design, modularity, design space matrix, net option value.

1 Introduction

Software design is a complicated process that tries to balance several factors, some of them contradictory. Bad design decisions can have disastrous consequences. Therefore, whenever new design concepts are proposed, they must be carefully assessed, so that their scopes of appropriate applicability can be identified. Such is the case with aspect-oriented design. To do that, one needs to use appropriate assessment methods. Conventional techniques for evaluating software design are based on metrics, quality attributes and heuristics [14, 17, 35]. While they can be useful for a posteriori analyses, they are not thought of for assessing the design options at certain decision points. But in the case of aspects, one needs to be able to assess when an aspect modularization is more beneficial than its nonaspectual alternatives.

---

[*] This work has been supported in part by the National Science Foundation's grant no. CCF-0347902.

A. Rashid and M. Aksit (Eds.): Transactions on AOSD I, LNCS 3880, pp. 1–35, 2006.
© Springer-Verlag Berlin Heidelberg 2006

This paper presents a case study where several object-oriented and aspect-oriented design variants for a software application are compared and analyzed in depth using a new methodology. This methodology uses the design structure matrix (DSM) as a design representation and net option value (NOV) as an analytical model. The paper explores this new methodology for assessing design options, and at the same time, it demonstrates how aspect-oriented modularization can cause beneficial as well as detrimental effects in an existing object-oriented design.

DSM, also known as design space matrix or dependency structure matrix, is an analysis and design tool used in various engineering disciplines [1, 15, 38, 40]. In its simplest form, a DSM is an adjacency matrix representation of the dependencies between design elements. The idea of using DSMs to model complex systems was first introduced by Steward [40]. DSMs are widely used in system design, independent of NOV. Various analysis techniques, metrics and tools have been developed that are based on DSMs. MacCormack et al. present an empirical study that compares the structure of large-scale complex software (Linux and Mozilla) using DSM-based metrics [28]. A commercial tool for analyzing software architecture based on DSMs has been developed by Lattix [2]. These related works demonstrate the applicability of DSMs in analyzing large software systems.

NOV is a model for evaluating modular design structures based on the economic theory of real options. Baldwin and Clark formulated NOV and first demonstrated its usage in analyzing design options [13] in the computer hardware industry. There are two fundamental components in Baldwin and Clark's work: (a) a general theory of modularity in design with six modular operators as sources of design variation;[1] and (b) NOV as a mathematical model to quantify the value of a modular design: the mathematical expressions for NOV tie together modular dependencies, uncertainty and economic theory in a cohesive model.

Sullivan et al. first demonstrated how the methodology using DSMs and NOV can be used in the analysis of software design [42]. Their work extends the DSM structure by introducing *environment parameters*, and applies this extended model to the design of KWIC (Keywords in Context), the program originally presented by Parnas [31]. Using NOV analysis they showed how information-hiding design is superior to the protomodular one. Information hiding is achieved by defining appropriate interfaces as *design rules*, which facilitate future changes in the design by reducing intermodular dependencies.

DSMs and NOV have also been used in analyzing aspect-oriented modularization [26]. This was the first work that looked into a new form of modular construct, *Aspect* [22], in addition to the conventional constructs for creating independent modules with representations for data structure, interface and algorithm.

In the context of the prior work mentioned above, namely [26, 42], the contributions of this paper are as follows:

---

[1] The six modular operators are: (i) splitting, (ii) substitution, (iii) augmenting (augmentation), (iv) exclusion, (v) inversion, and (vi) port(ing).

– The paper provides examples that give insights on the correlation between module dependencies and the benefits/disadvantages of aspects, using a realistic case study.
– Based on the detailed analysis of the design evolution of the case study, preliminary guidelines for aspect-oriented design are presented.

In addition, the work presented in this paper is one of the most detailed applications of NOV to software design to this date (late 2005). It explores the applicability of NOV in evaluating software design options and exposes limitations that need to be further resolved. In the context of NOV, a new modular operator for aspects is defined that has been named *reversion*.

The paper is organized as follows. The software application used as the case study is described in Sect. 2. Further detail on DSMs as applied to this paper is given in Sect. 3. The process of exploring design variants for the case study is detailed in Sect. 4. This starts with studying a third-party application to identify the design parameters within it. These parameters are changed to obtain a design for a new application which is further modified to obtain rest of the variants, the last two being the results of aspect modularization (Sects. 4.3–4.7). Each of these design changes is described in terms of one or more of the six modular operators from the NOV model. A new modular operator called *reversion* is formulated in Sect. 5 based on the structural changes that aspects bring in and the effect they have on module dependencies. Section 6 summarizes the mathematical model of NOV and details all the assumptions made about the NOV parameters for the case study in this paper. Section 7 discusses the NOV analysis of the case study, and, based on several observations, it formulates preliminary aspect-oriented design guidelines. Section 8 describes the limitations of the analysis, the open issues in using NOV to evaluate software design and further work we intend to pursue. Section 9 concludes the paper.

2   Case Study

The case study used throughout the paper is a Web application that uses Web services to meet most of its functional requirements. The application, *WineryLocator*, uses Web services to locate wineries in California. This section describes what the application is about and how is it structured.

A user can give a point of interest in California as a combination of street address, city and zip code. The address need not be exactly accurate. Once this information is given, the user is either presented with a list of matching locations to his/her criteria or is forwarded to another page if the given address uniquely maps to a valid location in California. Once the application gets a valid starting point, the user then can select preferences for the wineries. Based on the preferences and the starting point, the application generates a route for a tour consisting of all the wineries that match the criteria. The result is a set of stops in the route and a navigable map. From the result the user can also get driving directions.

2.1   Functional Decomposition

With the functionality described above, the following types of services are needed:

Finding Accurate Locations (List). A service that takes an incomplete description of a location and returns exact/accurate locations that match the description.

Getting List of Wineries. A service that returns a list of all the wineries around the vicinity of the user's starting point. The user must be able to filter (her) his selection according to the different criteria (s)he wanted regarding the wineries to be visited.

Getting Wineries Tour. Once an accurate starting point is obtained, we need to get a set of wineries around that starting location. This further breaks down as:

- Getting all the winery stops and information that form a tour
- Getting a map for the tour that constitutes the wineries
- Navigating the map that highlights the tour with appropriate marks and supports basic operations like panning and zooming

Driving Directions. Given a route made up of locations, we need a set of driving directions to visit all the destinations in the tour.

We use an existing application for MapPoint Web services [8] called *Store-Locator*,[2] developed by SpatialPoint [9], as our starting design so that we can make changes in it to get *WineryLocator*. StoreLocator is similar in many ways to WineryLocator. Given a starting point of interest, StoreLocator displays several matching locations. Once the user picks the starting location, it generates a navigable map and a list of all coffee stores close to that starting location within a radius specified by the user. The user then can click on each store to get driving directions from the start location.

Hence, as far as the functionalities are concerned, only two changes need to be made in StoreLocator to get WineryLocator: (i) replace the coffee store search with winery search, and (ii) present the user with a tour including the start location and all the wineries, unlike a list of directions from the start location to a selected store in StoreLocator.

In order to locate points of interest, such as coffee stores or wineries, MapPoint allows their service users to either use an already available *datasource* or upload new geographic data as a custom datasource. To bring out more opportunities for design changes, we substitute this functionality from MapPoint by our own Web service *WineryFind*, which provides a list of wineries around a vicinity of an exact start location. WineryFind also allows the users to set their search criteria by giving different preferences related to wines and wineries.

Table 1 shows the mapping of core application functionalities to the available Web services. The implementation was done in Java, using Apache AXIS [7] as well as the SOAP [43] toolkit to access the Web services.

---

[2] Available online at http://demo.mappoint.net.

Table 1. Mapping tasks to services

Task	Services	Providers	Method Signatures *
Finding set of exact locations	FindService	MapPoint	`FindResults findAddress (FindAddressSpecification)`
Getting wineries matching criteria	WineryFind	Local service we developed	`Destination[] getLocationsByScore (WinerySearchOption)`
Generating route from the tour given set of destinations	RouteService	MapPoint	`Route calculateSimpleRoute (ArrayOfLatLong, String /*dataSourceName*/, SegmentPreference)`
Getting a map representing a route/tour. Also, navigating the map	RenderService	MapPoint	`ArrayOfMapImage getMap(MapSpecification)`
Getting driving directions	RouteService	MapPoint	can be obtained from a `Route` object

* Showing only the most relevant methods in format - **return_type Web_service_function_name (input_parameter_type)**. The types shown in the list represent the classes in Java that map to the types defined in the MapPoint object model. These classes were autogenerated by the tool WSDL2Java, which is a part of the Apache AXIS toolkit [7].

2.2   Subsidiary Functions

Besides the main functionalities that WineryLocator offers to its end users, we consider two subsidiary functions the application needs to provide. These subsidiary functions, which are not directly visible to the users, are as follows: (1) *Authentication:* Before using any of the MapPoint services the application needs to provide a valid credential (username and password) to it. This credential does not come from an end user, but is managed by the application service provider. MapPoint uses the HttpDigest authentication mechanism for this. (2) *Logging:* A logging feature is introduced in the system as a nonfunctional (subsidiary) requirement to trace all the calls made to the Web services. Such a feature is useful in many scenarios that require maintaining statistics about the access to the Web services within the application. This feature can simply be implemented by tracing every call to a Web service in the system.

3   Representing Design Structures with DSM

Figure 1 depicts the design of StoreLocator in a DSM. Before presenting the design evolution from StoreLocator to WineryLocator in DSMs, we first describe some fundamental design concepts presented by Baldwin and Clark in [13], focusing primarily on software.

			1	2	3	4	5	6	7	8	9	10	11
<EP>	< service > MapPoint	1	*										
	< API > Apache AXIS	2		*									
	< API > Servlet	3			*								
	HttpSessionBindingListener	4				X	*						
<DR>	MapPoint Design Rules	5	X	X			*						
<AM>	StoreLocator	6					X	*					
	HttpSessionStoreLocator	7		X		X		X	*				X
<AC>	< jsp > locate	8			X		X		X	*	X		
	< jsp > display	9			X		X		X	X	*	X	
	< jsp > directions	10			X		X		X	X		*	
	< DD > web.xml	11	X	X	X								*

Fig. 1. DSM for StoreLocator

3.1 Elements of Modular Design in Software

In this paper, interpretation of the terms like modularity, architecture and hierarchy remains the same and as generic as that originally presented by Baldwin and Clark [13]. Almost all of the constituents of design that make up their theory can be seen in the designs for StoreLocator and WineryLocator. We briefly summarize the definitions of the core elements from [13], as they are seen in the examples presented in this paper. All the definitions and vocabulary borrowed from [13] are shown in *italics* below.

1. *Design: Design* is defined as *an abstract description of the functionality and structure of an artifact.* Representations such as software architectures [33, 39] design models in UML or source code fit this definition.
2. *Hierarchies:* The notion of hierarchy concurs with the one defined by Parnas [32]. A module A is dependent on module B if A needs to know about B to achieve its function, i.e., if B is visible to A.
3. *Medium* for expressing design: A designer expresses the basic structure and configuration of design elements with a *medium* (s)he chooses to work with. Examples are Architecture Description Languages (ADLs) for software architecture [30], UML for object-oriented modeling and Java for program design (code). Media are among the highest parameters in the design hierarchy.
4. *Design parameters—the elements of design:* Parameters are the attributes of the artifact that govern the variation in design. Choosing new values for parameters gives new design options. Java is used as the primary medium to express all the design variants presented in this paper, so the basic structural constructs like classes, objects, attributes, methods and packages all could be seen as the design parameters. In the examples, we remain at the granularity of classes and interfaces.
5. *Module:* Structural elements that are strongly connected are grouped together as a module. Modules adhere to these three fundamental characteristics [13]:

(a) *Modularity increases the range of manageable complexity.*

(b) *Modularity allows different parts of a design to be worked on concurrently.*

(c) *Modularity accommodates uncertainty.*

While identifying modules in a design, we follow these principles listed above. A module can also be characterized by the set of tasks it performs. A module's *task* is equivalent to an operation or a service it provides.

6. *Modular operators:* Baldwin and Clark define design evolution as a value-seeking process, with the six modular operators as *sources of variation.* We discuss our design changes and map them to one or more of these six modular operators.

7. *Abstraction: Abstraction hides the complexity of the element.* As a measure to reduce the complexity of design parameters, we represent complex modules (made up of further submodules) as a single parameter, as long as the details inside need not be revealed. An example of this in our models is treating a Web service as a single parameter.

   Following the definitions for design parameters, module and abstraction, three interchangeable terms can be used to refer to the individual elements that constitute a design: (i) *design elements,* (ii) *design parameters* and (iii) *modules.* For example, if we have a module composed of a set of simpler modules, the latter can be considered as the design parameters of the former. But both are design elements, too. Thus, we use these three terms interchangeably without the loss of generality.

8. *Interface and design rules:* Making changes in modules that have highly interdependent structures often requires endless tweaking as the designer tends to get lost in the cyclic side effect one module has on others. To avoid such cycles, decisions common to modules that are unlikely to change are factored out as design rules. These design rules constitute the interfaces that designers use to connect modules with each other.

9. *Architecture:* provides a *framework that allows for both independence of structure and integration of function.* In our designs, frameworks for enabling enterprise computing capabilities, such as J2EE [11], and APIs (Application Programming Interfaces), such as Java Servlet [10] (also a part of J2EE), are considered architectures.

3.2   Categories of Design Parameters

We categorize the modules in the DSMs based on our ability to change them:

External Parameters. These are the parameters that cannot be modified and that are taken for granted from some external providers. These parameters might be replaceable with similar parameters providing same functionality. External services, imported libraries and frameworks fall under this category. External parameters usually bring their own set of design rules into the application.

Extending DSMs with *environment parameters* was a major enhancement made to DSMs [42]. We take *external parameters* to be a particular category of *environment parameter* as they have similar characteristics.

Design Rules. Parameters used as the interface between modules and that are less likely to be changed are design rules. Design rules can either be imported from external parameters or designed specifically for the application.

Application (functional) Modules. Functional units in the system that perform application-specific task(s) are categorized as *application modules*.

Subsidiary Modules. We further classify modules that contribute to subsidiary or secondary functionalities as *subsidiary modules*. If a module performs both application-specific tasks as well as subsidiary tasks, it is treated as an *application module*.

Application Controller. These are mostly connector modules, as they use the design rules as interface to access the functionalities provided by the application modules, "gluing them up" in an application, and serving the end users. We also put configuration modules such as *deployment descriptors* in this category as they contribute in assembling modules, even though they do not directly serve the end users of the system.

We believe most of the modules in modern applications fall into one of the above categories. Furthermore, most of the development task in today's applications lies within mapping application-specific requirements to the imported functionalities from external modules.

3.3   Conventions for DSMs

Figure 1 shows the DSM for StoreLocator. The DSMs have been constructed as normally is done [1, 13, 38, 42]. All the design parameters are arranged in row–column form, with marks in those cells where we need to show the interdependencies between the parameters. We have adopted the simplest form of showing interdependencies, by putting an "X" mark in the relevant cell.

The DSMs and the design parameters roughly match the application structure, but there is not an exact one-to-one mapping from the elements in a DSM to the syntactic constructs in the program. The parameters we have shown are semantic, rather than syntactic objects that occur to a designer's mind. However, all of the parameters, excluding the external ones, can be mapped to any one of these: Java classes or interfaces, aspects written in AspectJ [3], or XML deployment descriptor files. In short, a DSM presents an abstract view of module dependencies in an application.

Clustering and *partitioning* are two standard DSM operations to get a modular or a *protomodular* [13] structure from an otherwise unmodularized DSM. The elements in our DSMs are taken from a ready-made application, StoreLocator. Thus, each DSM already has a basic modular structure, and the DSM operations do not have a very significant role in our process. The only explicit clustering done in the DSMs is the categorization of the parameters into the categories listed in Sect. 3.2. The following list describes the graphical and visual clues present in our DSMs:

1. The leftmost (first) column in the DSM is used to label the clusters of parameters. This clustering is based on the classification presented in Sect. 3.2.
2. The second column lists the name of all the design parameters.
3. The third column assigns numbers to all these parameters for easy reference. The rest of the columns constitute the matrix showing dependencies. The topmost row resembles the parameters by the numbers as assigned in the third column.
4. In the matrix area (fourth column onwards), thick solid borders in the cells set the boundary for modules, dark dashed lines set boundaries for the interaction areas between different categories of modules (for example, between design rules and external parameters) and light dotted lines are markers for individual cells.
5. Shaded groups of cell(s), enclosed within a dark border, represent a group of parameters (or a single parameter) that we treat as individual modules for NOV analysis.
6. We use a descriptive text inside a pair of opening and closing angular bracket (e.g., $< DR >$) for two purposes: (i) in first column to abbreviate the category name and (ii) in second column as a stereotype to mark the special connotation some design parameters bear. Table 2 lists all such stereotypes we have used.

Table 2. Labels used in DSMs and hierarchy diagrams (HD)

Labels	Meaning	Used in
Medium	As defined in Sect. 3.1	HD
Architecture	As defined in Sect. 3.1	HD
API	Application Programming Interface	HD, DSM
porting tool	Translation tool used to convert artifacts produced in one medium to another	HD
service	Remote Web service	HD, DSM
DD	Deployment descriptor	HD, DSM
JSP	Java server pages	HD, DSM
Aspect	A modular unit representing a crosscutting concern	HD, DSM
Design Rules	Java server pages	HD, DSM
EP	External parameters	DSM
DR	Design rules	DSM
AM	Application modules	DSM
AC	Application controller	DSM
SM	Subsidiary modules	DSM

3.4   Design Hierarchy Diagrams

Figure 2 depicts the *design hierarchy diagram* (or simply, hierarchy diagram) of StoreLocator. Hierarchy diagrams and DSMs model the same structure and information about dependencies among design elements. A hierarchy diagram is a dependency graph of all the parameters in a design. A parameter in a hierarchy diagram has two set of connections: connections from above, to those parameters it depends on, and connections from below, to those parameters that depend on it.

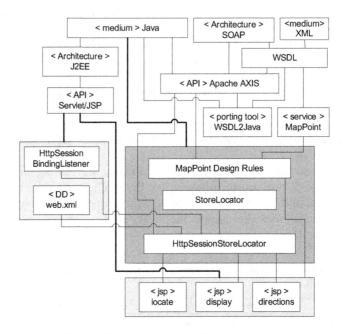

Fig. 2. Hierarchy diagram for StoreLocator

To avoid line cluttering in the hierarchy diagram we have omitted a few dependencies from Fig. 2.[3] Furthermore, we group some related parameters into large boxes, and show their common dependency with other parameters using the box that encloses them. We label, or stereotype, special elements in hierarchy diagrams (as in the DSMs). These labels are listed in Table 2.

Even though all the designs for StoreLocator and WineryLocator are discussed using DSMs, hierarchy diagrams are introduced in this section for two reasons. First, we want to show all the higher level elements in the design that remain the same across all design variants (Fig. 2). Elements such as Java, XML, SOAP, WSDL and WSDL2Java remain unchanged in all the design variants.[4] Thus, Fig. 2 serves as a contextual view of the architecture of *StoreLocator*, which is the starting point of our design exploration. Second, hierarchy diagrams are also used to depict the effect of different modular operators on existing designs (Sect. 5).

---

[3] The DSM for StoreLocator in Fig. 1 shows these excluded dependencies.
[4] These design elements are discussed in Sect. 4.2.

4   Analyzing Design Evolution with DSMs

4.1   Design Goals for WineryLocator

StoreLocator serves as the right design to start our analysis. We derive several design variants for WineryLocator, starting from StoreLocator, which gradually fulfill the following design goals:

1. Identifying separate functional units as application modules so that we can plug in our own Web service, providing winery information between the several functionalities offered by the MapPoint Web services.
2. Decoupling the application controller from MapPoint's design rules.
3. Defining a set of simple, yet sufficient design rules for our application that allows us to have different implementation of application controller modules; for example, to switch from Web-based to a GUI application based on Java Swing.
4. Being able to replace each of the application modules with an alternative implementation with the least possible side effects to the other modules.

With the required background and conventions we now discuss the different design variants.

4.2   Identifying Basic Design Elements

The DSM in Fig. 1 is the starting point for our design exploration. These diagrams were created after understanding the code structure of StoreLocator and the design rules of MapPoint. The list below enumerates all the design parameters and their role in the initial design of StoreLocator shown in Figs. 1 and 2.

1. *MapPoint design rules:* These constitute the classes and methods as defined in the MapPoint object model [4], which are used to access and interact with its services. The porting tool *WSDL2Java*, part of the *Apache AXIS* toolkit [7] for Web services, generates all these required classes in Java from the description of the Web services expressed in XML as a *WSDL* (Web Services Description Language) [44] file.
2. *StoreLocator:*[5] This is an application module implemented as a Java class. It handles the mapping of the application tasks to the services available from MapPoint by providing methods that take user inputs as parameters and call the appropriate service methods to list starting locations. It also provides access to the list of stores, maps, map navigation functions and driving directions. This StoreLocator module uses MapPoint's classes as parameters in its helper methods.

---

[5] The name of this module is same as the application. Whenever this distinction is not clear from the context, we explicitly specify whether we are referring to the application or to this module.

3. *HttpSessionStoreLocator:* Since a valid credential comprising a user name and a password needs to be provided to MapPoint before using any of its services, the module StoreLocator is extended as a class *HttpSessionStoreLocator* that adds the authentication capability. There are no design parameters in the Mappoint object model that reflect this authentication mechanism because MapPoint relies on HttpDigest authentication. This authentication mechanism is a part of the XML-based communication protocol that Web services use. The AXIS toolkit [7], which implements such protocol, injects parameters that support such protocol-specific tasks in the *MapPoint design rules* during the process of generating them. Consequently *HttpSessionStoreLocator* depends on the Apache AXIS API to submit the authentication credentials to MapPoint as the parameters related to authentication come along with Apache AXIS. This is a subtle dependency, as the otherwise unnecessary detail has to be known to understand the full working of this authentication mechanism.

4. *HttpSessionBindingListener:* This is an interface defined in the Java Servlet API [10]. *HttpSessionStoreLocator* implements this interface and provides methods that are called by the servlet container whenever an object of *HttpSessionStoreLocator* is brought into a session. In this way the servlet container can provide the values for the "username" and "password", configured in the *deployment descriptor* of the application, to *HttpSessionStoreLocator.*

5. *web.xml:* is the *deployment descriptor* of the application and stores configuration information like user name/password values and URLs for accessing the Web services. These values are passed into *HttpSessionStoreLocator* through the methods it implements from HttpSessionBindingListener.

6. *Application controller* modules (JSPs, Deployment Descriptor): *locate* takes the information on starting location, presents the matching list and picks a starting address. It links to *display* for rest of the functionalities. *display* presents the user with the matching store locations and also a navigable map with the stores highlighted. *display* takes the information on a particular store to be visited and links to the *directions* page that displays the driving directions from the start address to the store selected in *display.*

Most of the external parameters are omitted in the DSMs as the application modules do not directly depend on them. Since the changes we make are concentrated within the application, this omission does not affect the comprehensibility of design evolution.

The hierarchy diagram in Fig. 2 shows all the external parameters in the StoreLocator. The dependencies among these external parameters show how *porting* [13] works at a higher level, enabling the interoperability of externally implemented services with a custom application and how external design rules can be imported in applications. Most of these external parameters remain unchanged in all of the design variants we discuss.

4.3 First Version of WineryLocator After Performing Splitting and Substitution on StoreLocator

Figure 3 shows the DSM for the first version of WineryLocator we obtained from StoreLocator. A new set of design rules, *WineryFind Design Rules* $(F.3, P.7)$[6] have been imported into the application for using the services provided by the *WineryFind* Web service $(F.3, P.2)$. The *StoreLocator* module (F.1,P.6) along with *HttpSessionStoreLocator* $(F.1, P.7)$ have been split, resulting in five parameters $(F.3, P.8$ through 12). The application controller modules have been substituted and augmented with a new module *searchWinery* $(F.3, P.14)$. The design changes listed in Table 3 describe all the splitting, substitution and augmentation made from Fig. 1 to Fig. 3.

			1	2	3	4	5	6	7	8	9	10	11	12	13	14	15	16	17
External Parameters		< service > MapPoint	1	*																
		< service > WineryFind	2		*															
		< API > Apache AXIS	3			*														
		< API > Servlet	4				*													
		HttpSessionBindingListener	5				X	*												
<DR>		MapPoint Design Rules	6	X		X			*											
		WineryFind Design Rules	7		X	X				*										
Application Modules		AddressLocator	8						X		*									
		AuthAddressLocator	9			X		X			X	*								X
		WineryFinder	10							X			*							
		RouteMapHandler	11						X					*						
		AuthRouteMapHandler	12			X		X						X	*					X
Application Controller		< jsp > startWineryFind	13				X		X			X				*	X			
		< jsp > searchWinery	14				X		X	X			X			X	*	X		
		< jsp > tour	15				X		X						X	X		*	X	
		< jsp > directions	16				X		X							X			*	
		< DD > web.xml	17	X	X	X	X													*

Fig. 3. DSM for WineryLocator application after splitting and substituting the modules in StoreLocator

4.4 Introducing Subsidiary Functionality with Augmentation

We get to the design in Fig. 4 by adding a logging feature to the first version of WineryLocator shown in Fig. 3. We introduce a new module *WebServicesLogger* $(F.4, P.8)$ that is responsible for logging the access of Web services and maintaining any pertaining statistics. $(F.4, P.9)$, $(F.4, P.11)$ and $(F.4, P.12)$ are the three modules that access the Web services. All the calls to the Web services within these modules need to be traced and linked to *WebServicesLogger* $(F.4, P.8)$ to maintain the log.

4.5 Setting Application-Specific Design Rules for WineryLocator

The design of WineryLocator in Fig. 4 is functionally complete, in the sense that it fulfills all the functional requirements that we had set for WineryLocator

---

[6] From here on, we refer to figures by "F" and parameters by "P" for brevity. With this convention we can refer to any nth parameter in a Fig. m as $(F.m, P.n)$.

Table 3. Changes made in StoreLocator for the first version of WineryLocator

StoreLocator (*Old*)	WineryLocator (*New*)	*Changes*
Figure 1 (DSM)	Figure 3 (DSM)	StoreLocator application modified as WineryLocator application
StoreLocator ($F.1, P.6$)	AddressLocator ($F.3, P.8$), WineryFinder ($F.3, P.10$), RouteMapHandler ($F.3, P.11$)	The composite functionality of StoreLocator module has been split into ($F.3, P.8$) that locates an accurate starting address, ($F.3, P.10$) that generates list of wineries (this enabled the substitution of "store search" with "winery search") and ($F.3, P.11$) that generates maps and routes.
HttpSessionStoreLocator ($F.1, P.7$)	AuthAddressLocator ($F.3, P.9$), AuthRouteMapHandler ($F.3, P.12$)	Splitting of ($F.1, P.6$), led to the splitting of ($F.1, P.7$) into ($F.3, P.9$) and ($F.3, P.12$). This split was necessary to carry on the authentication feature ($F.1, P.7$) provided to ($F.1, P.6$) into the newly created modules ($F.3, P.9$) and ($F.3, P.12$).
Locate ($F.1, P.8$)	StartWineryFind ($F.3, P.13$)	($F.1, P.8$) substituted by ($F.3, P.13$), both provide an equivalent functionality.
— —	SearchWinery ($F.3, P.14$)	($F.3, P.14$) is a new module that helps users to specify criteria for refining winery search; this functionality was absent in StoreLocator (addition of this module can be taken as augmentation).
Display ($F.1, P.9$)	Tour ($F.3, P.15$)	($F.3, P.15$) presents the user with list of wineries and a navigable map that constitutes a tour.
Directions ($F.1, P.10$)	Directions ($F.3, P.16$)	($F.3, P.16$) presents the user with detailed driving directions for a tour of all the wineries, whereas ($F.1, P.10$) presents the directions from a start location to a destination.

in Sect. 2. But it lacks the design goals listed in Sect. 4.1. We introduce a new set of design rules for WineryLocator to decouple the application controller modules from MapPoint's design rules. This allows us to move MapPoint and WineryFind Design rules to the *external parameters* category. These new design rules are specific to WineryLocator and are independent of the MapPoint and WineryFind design rules.

			1	2	3	4	5	6	7	8	9	10	11	12	13	14	15	16	17	18
External Parameters	< service > MapPoint	1	*																	
	< service > WineryFind	2		*																
	< API > Apache AXIS	3			*															
	< API > Servlet	4				*														
	HttpSessionBindingListener	5				X	*													
<DR>	MapPoint Design Rules	6	X		X			*												
	WineryFind Design Rules	7		X	X				*											
<SM>	WebServicesLogger	8								*										
Application Modules	AddressLocator	9						X		X	*									
	AuthAddressLocator	10					X			X	X	*								X
	WineryFinder	11							X	X			*							
	RouteMapHandler	12						X		X				*						
	AuthRouteMapHandler	13					X			X				X	*					X
Application Controller	< jsp > startWineryFind	14					X	X			X					*	X			
	< jsp > searchWinery	15					X	X	X		X					X	*	X		
	< jsp > tour	16					X	X						X			X	*	X	
	< jsp > directions	17					X	X						X				X	*	
	< DD > web.xml	18	X	X	X	X														*

Fig. 4. DSM for WineryLocator with logging feature after augmentation

Five new parameters ($F.5, P.8$ through 12) are introduced as application design rules for WineryLocator. The application controller modules ($F.5, P.19$ through 22) use these application design rules as interfaces to the application modules ($F.5, P.14$ through 18). Table 4 lists the role of the newly introduced design rules through the tasks they model.

Table 4. Application-specific design rules for WineryLocator

Design Rules	ID	Models
startAddress:Address	$(F.5, P.8)$	Starting location users provide and select
matches:Address[]	$(F.5, P.9)$	Collection of address matches for the starting location
WinerySearchOption	$(F.5, P.10)$	Preferences for winery search
Tour	$(F.5, P.11)$	Tour representation for all wineries visit including a representation for map
MapOperation	$(F.5, P.12)$	Standard map operations users perform

4.6 Applying Aspect-Oriented Modularization

We use the two forms of modularization that Aspects[7] provide to reduce the dependencies among the modules (application and subsidiary) in the design for WineryLocator in Fig. 5. We perform aspect-oriented modularization for two of WineryLocator's features:

---

[7] Although we conceive these modularizations with AspectJ in mind, any aspect-oriented framework providing *Pointcut-Advice* and *Introduction* can be used for this purpose.

Category	Module	#	4	6	1	2	3	5	7	8	9	10	11	12	13	14	15	16	17	18	19	20	21	22	23
External Parameters	< service > MapPoint	4	*																						
External Parameters	< service > WineryFind	6		*																					
External Parameters	< API > Apache AXIS	1			*																				
External Parameters	< API > Servlet	2				*																			
External Parameters	HttpSessionBindingListener	3				X	*																		
External Parameters	MapPoint Design Rules	5	X		X			*																	
External Parameters	WineryFind Design Rules	7		X	X				*																
Design Rules	startAddress : Address	8								*															
Design Rules	matches : Address [ ]	9									*														
Design Rules	WinerySearchOption	10										*													
Design Rules	Tour	11											*												
Design Rules	MapOperation	12												*											
<SM>	WebServicesLogger	13													*										
Application Modules	AddressLocator	14						X		X	X				X	*									
Application Modules	AuthAddressLocator	15				X	X									X	*								X
Application Modules	WineryFinder	16							X			X	X		X			*							
Application Modules	RouteMapHandler	17						X				X	X	X	X				*						
Application Modules	AuthRouteMapHandler	18				X	X												X	*					X
Application Controller	< jsp > startWineryFind	19				X				X	X							X			*	X			
Application Controller	< jsp > searchWinery	20				X				X	X								X		X	*	X		
Application Controller	< jsp > tour	21				X							X	X						X		X	*	X	
Application Controller	< jsp > directions	22				X							X									X		*	
Application Controller	< DD > web.xml	23	X	X	X	X																			*

Fig. 5. DSM for WineryLocator after introducing application-specific design rules

1. *Logging:* Using the *Pointcut-Advice* mechanism [29], we remove the dependencies that modules $(F.5, P.14)$, $(F.5, P.16)$ and $(F.5, P.17)$ have on module $(F.5, P.13)$. We add a *Logging* aspect $(F.6, P.22)$ that captures the calls to the Web services directly from the design rules for MapPoint $(F.6, P.6)$ and WineryFind $(F.6, P.7)$. The logging aspect, module $(F.6, P.22)$, hooks these calls with the module WebServicesLogger $(F.6, P.21)$.

2. *Authentication:* We use *Introduction*, also known as the *open-class* mechanism [29], to inject the authentication-specific functionality into the application modules $(F.6, P.13)$ and $(F.6, P.8.15)$. This adds another aspect, *Authentication* $(F.6, P.23)$, in the final design.

With this modification, all the design goals set for WineryLocator have been achieved.

4.7   Localizing Method Calls from JSP Pages in an Aspect

The *Application Modules* in previous designs (in particular, Figs. 5 and 6) mainly have two parts: (i) a visible interface, methods that the JSP pages call to use the functionality supported by these modules, and (ii) a hidden implementation, all the machinery that is needed to map the public interface to external services via design rules. The latter includes some helper methods and additional code that is hidden from the client modules.

As a final experiment in WineryLocator's design, it is remodularized one last time by defining a new aspect module called *JSPConnections*. The role of this aspect is to encapsulate all the visible operations (i.e., public methods) in the

Fig. 6. DSM for WineryLocator after aspect-oriented modularization

Fig. 6 — DSM matrix (columns 1–23):

Group	Element	#	1	2	3	4	5	6	7	8	9	10	11	12	13	14	15	16	17	18	19	20	21	22	23
External Parameters	< service > MapPoint	1	•																						
	< service > WineryFind	2		•																					
	< API > Apache AXIS	3			•																				
	< API > Servlet	4				•																			
	HttpSessionBindingListener	5					•																		
	MapPoint Design Rules	6	X		X			•																	
	WineryFind Design Rules	7		X	X				•																
Design Rules	startAddress : Address	8								•															
	matches : Address [ ]	9									•														
	WinerySearchOption	10										•													
	Tour	11											•												
	MapOperation	12												•											
Application Modules	AddressLocator	13						X		X	X				•										
	WineryFinder	14							X			X	X			•									
	RouteMapHandler	15						X					X	X			•								
Application Controller	< jsp > startWineryFind	16				X				X	X				X			•	X						
	< jsp > searchWinery	17				X				X		X				X		X	•	X					
	< jsp > tour	18				X							X	X		X	X	X	X	•	X				
	< jsp > directions	19				X							X					X			•				
	< DD > web.xml	20	X	X	X	X																•			
Subsidiary Modules	WebServicesLogger	21																					•		
	< Aspect > Logging	22						X	X														X	•	
	< Aspect > Authentication	23				X		X							X	X					X				•

Fig. 7. DSM for WineryLocator after localizing method calls from JSP pages in an aspect

Fig. 7 — DSM matrix (columns 1–15, 24, 16–23):

Group	Element	#	1	2	3	4	5	6	7	8	9	10	11	12	13	14	15	24	16	17	18	19	20	21	22	23
External Parameters	< service > MapPoint	1	•																							
	< service > WineryFind	2		•																						
	< API > Apache AXIS	3			•																					
	< API > Servlet	4				•																				
	HttpSessionBindingListener	5					•																			
	MapPoint Design Rules	6	X		X			•																		
	WineryFind Design Rules	7		X	X				•																	
Design Rules	startAddress : Address	8								•																
	matches : Address [ ]	9									•															
	WinerySearchOption	10										•														
	Tour	11											•													
	MapOperation	12												•												
Application Modules	AddressLocator	13						X		X	X				•											
	WineryFinder	14							X			X	X			•										
	RouteMapHandler	15						X					X	X			•									
	< Aspect > JSPConnections	24								X	X	X	X	X	X	X	X	•								
Application Controller	< jsp > startWineryFind	16				X				X	X				X			X	•	X						
	< jsp > searchWinery	17				X				X		X				X		X	X	•	X					
	< jsp > tour	18				X							X	X		X	X	X	X	X	•	X				
	< jsp > directions	19				X							X					X	X			•				
	< DD > web.xml	20	X	X	X	X																	•			
Subsidiary Modules	WebServicesLogger	21																						•		
	< Aspect > Logging	22						X	X															X	•	
	< Aspect > Authentication	23				X		X							X	X						X				•

Application Modules that are called from the JSPs. This results in a new design as shown in Fig. 7. For this remodularization, all the public methods from the *Application Modules* (*F.7, P.*13 through 15) are moved into the *JSPConnections* aspect (*F.7, P.*24). This aspect uses Introduction to inject all the removed methods in the respective *Application Modules*.

This change makes *JSPConnections* (*F.7, P.*24) dependent on the rest of the *Application Modules* (*F.7, P.*13 through 15) and on the *Design Rules* (*F.7, P.*8 through 12). Since *JSPConnections* now holds all the methods that the JSP pages use, it too belongs to the *Application Modules* category. Although the clients (JSP pages, *F.7, P.*16 through 19) are unaware of the presence of the aspect *JSPConnections* (*F.7, P.*24), they directly depend on it, as the methods that these clients expect to be in the *Application Modules* now reside in the aspect.

5   Effect of Aspects on Dependencies

Separating interface from implementation is a common practice in software design that concurs with the notion of design rules and hidden modules. But the consequence of this separation technique is that the *client modules* need to be linked to the *server modules* (those that implement the interfaces) in some way. (To prevent any confusion we refer to these *server modules* as *providers* and *client modules* simply as *clients*.)

Different strategies exist to resolve these dependency issues between *providers* and *clients*. Fowler discusses these in some depth in [18] and [19], where he introduces *dependency injection* as one of the solutions. Dependency injection relies on *Assembler* modules that are responsible for connecting the client modules with implementation, thus clients become virtually independent on implementation, they just *see* the interface. Assembler modules lie lowest in the hierarchy.

Aspect-oriented modularizations, especially those involving Introduction, are similar to the dependency injection technique. However, they can add subtle dependencies that affect the evolution of the system. We discuss those in this section.

5.1   Structural Transformations

The hierarchy diagrams in Figs. 8–10 show the effects that aspects have on module dependencies. In these figures the direction of the large arrows indicate the design change after introducing aspects. Figure 8 models the design change that was made to perform aspect-oriented modularization to logging. Figure 9 models the design change for the authentication aspect, and Fig. 10 shows two possible dependency models for the *JSPConnections* aspect in the final version of WineryLocator.

In the case of modularizing authentication using Introduction (from Fig. 5 to Fig. 6), the client modules do not directly need, or more precisely *expect*, the parameters in the provider modules that were captured by the aspect. But in the case of *JSPConnections* (Fig. 7), the parameters that were extracted out from the providers and localized in the aspect are the parameters that the client modules

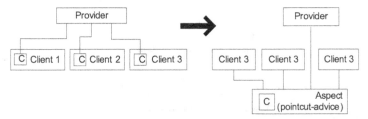

Fig. 8. Effect of the logging aspect on dependencies. The logging aspect includes pointcut-advice elements only. "C" represents common points in clients accessing the providers. (Direction of the *arrow* shows the change after applying aspect-oriented modularization).

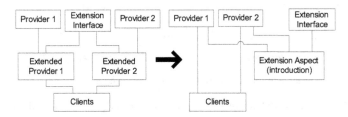

Fig. 9. Effect of the authentication aspect on dependencies. The authentication aspect includes introduction.

(JSP pages) directly use and expect from the provider modules. Once the aspect is implemented, this dependency from clients to the parameters captured inside aspects has to be somehow reflected in the new design. Two alternative design options that resemble the case of implementing *JSPConnections* are shown in Fig. 10. Alternative 2 in Fig. 10 models the DSM in Fig. 7.

With these observations we can say that good aspect modularization eliminates the dependencies *clients* have on *providers* by introducing aspects as new modular structures. Aspects depend on (or see) these *clients* and *providers*, and are responsible for providing connections between them. In cases where aspect modularization introduces additional dependencies (such as between clients and aspects) the effect may be detrimental.

5.2   Inversion vs. Reversion

The structural changes introduced by aspect-oriented modularizations are similar, but not identical, to Baldwin and Clark's *inversion* operator. Inversion has two major effects, namely (i) it captures common elements hidden inside the modules, and (ii) puts them above the existing modules as architectural modules, thus changing the *levels* of the modules and dependency relationships between them. A simple example of inversion is shown in Fig. 11.

Both inversion and aspect-oriented modularization involve capturing common parameters and moving those common parameters to a single module, creating a new level in the hierarchy. However, aspect-oriented modularization introduces

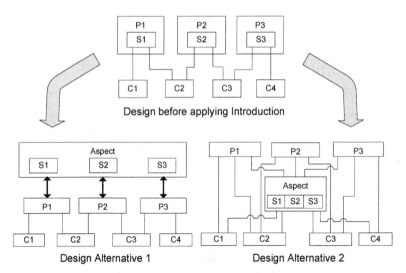

Design alternatives for localizing services using Introduction

Fig. 10. Effect of the JSPConnections aspects on dependencies. The JSPConnections aspects include introduction. Here, Px = provider, Sx = visible services offered by providers, and Cx = clients (x = 1, 2 or 3). *Bidirectional arrows* represent two-way dependencies.

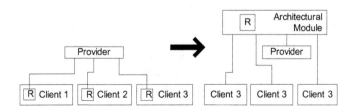

Fig. 11. The effect of inversion. "R" represents redundant parameters/code in clients that is moved to Architectural module after inversion.

modules (aspects) that depend on existing modules, whereas inversion introduces modules on which existing modules are dependent. This makes aspect-oriented modularization a new operator, which we call *reversion*.

5.3   Design Rules for Aspects

Figures 8–10 are three variations of Pointcut-Advice and Introduction mechanisms. Particularly, in these figures we do not see what the visible design rules for aspects are. In both cases aspects depend on *clients* or/and *providers*.

In Fig. 8 a small box labeled as C denotes the common points in *clients* accessing the *providers*. C is moved into the aspect after aspect-oriented modularization, and it represents two things: (i) interfaces that a *provider* provides,

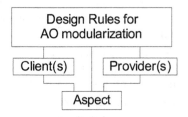

Fig. 12. Design rules for aspect-oriented (AO) modularization

and (ii) points in *clients* that access such interfaces. A typical way to design aspects following this process (as in AspectJ) is to capture these points as *join-points* (for example, the method names a *provider* provides and the method names of *clients* that access the *provider*), which need to be *advised*. Such join-points constitute C, and, in a way, become design rules for the aspect. Defining design rules for aspects implies making such joinpoints explicit. Just as architectural modules emerge after sustaining a considerable design evolution, an aspect-oriented design would also result in well-defined design rules for aspect-oriented modularization, as in the structure shown in Fig. 12. This notion of design rules for aspects, which was first raised in an earlier work [26], is critical for avoiding unforeseen addition of dependencies after aspect modularizations. One of the reasons that we encounter detrimental dependencies from modules to aspects (as in Fig. 10) is due to the lack of standard design rules to which clients, providers and aspects can conform.

6   Quantitative Analysis with Net Option Value

This section presents the quantitative analysis of the various design options for WineryLocator starting from StoreLocator. The analysis is based on a generic expression for NOV [13]. This generic expression for evaluating the option to redesign a module is represented mathematically as shown below.

$$V = S_0 + NOV_1 + NOV_2 + ... + NOV_n, \tag{1}$$

$$NOV_i = max_{ki}\{\sigma_i n_i^{1/2} Q(k_i) - C_i(n_i)k_i - Z_i\}, \tag{2}$$

$$Z_i = \sum_{j-sees-i} cn_j. \tag{3}$$

Below we present a brief explanation of mathematical model for NOV as given in [13].

- V denotes the value of a system.
- S_0 is the value of the system with no modular structure, which can be normalized to 0.
- NOV_i is the NOV for ith module, taken as the maximum return value possible out of k design experiments on the ith module.

- $(\sigma_i n_i^{1/2} Q(k_i))$ represents the expected benefit to be gained from the ith module. This value is assumed to be the expected value of a random variable with a normal distribution having a variance of $\sigma_i^2 n_i$.
  - σ_i is the *technical potential* of the module.
  - $Q(k)$ is the expected value of the best k independent trials from a standard normal distribution for all positive values in the distribution.
- $(C_i(n_i))$ represents the cost of running a design experiment on the ith module. Mathematically the cost of an experiment is a function of the module's complexity. Thus,
  - $(C_i(n_i)k_i)$ is the cost of running k experiments on the ith module.
  - If N represents the total complexity of a system, then n_i, the complexity of the ith module, would be given as m_i/N , where m_i is the ith module's contribution to N.
- (Z_i) is the visibility cost, the cost to replace the ith module.
  - Mathematically, $Z_i = \sum_{j-sees-i} c_j n_j$. It sums up the cost to redesign each jth module containing n_j parameters that depends on (*sees*) the ith module.
  - c_j is the redesign cost per parameter for the jth module.

6.1   NOV for Aspect-Oriented Modularization (Reversion)

Based on the discussion of inversion vs. reversion presented in Sect. 5.2, Table 5 presents a model for the NOV of aspect-oriented modularization, comparing it with NOV for inversion. Baldwin and Clark have defined NOV expressions for all their six modular operators. However, for the purposes of this paper, in evaluating the design options, we have not used these individual expressions. We believe further work is needed for these individual NOV expressions to be directly used in evaluating various forms of fine-grained design changes made in software. Instead, we use the generic expression for NOV (discussed earlier in this section) that is applicable to any modular design.

Table 5. NOVs for inversion (NOV_{inv}) and reversion (NOV_{rev})

NOV_{inv}	$=$	Option value of architectural module
	$-$	Cost of designing architectural module
	$-$	Option value lost in hidden modules' experiments
	$+$	Cost savings in hidden modules' experiments
	$-$	Costs of visibility
NOV_{rev}	$=$	Option value of aspect module (aspects and design rules for aspects)
	$-$	Cost of designing aspects and design rules for aspects
	$-$	Option value lost in scattered code's experiments in hidden modules
	$+$	Cost savings in scattered code's experiments in hidden modules
	$-$	Costs of visibility of modules on design rules for aspects

6.2   Assumptions for NOV Analysis

The main objective behind the NOV analysis in this paper is to compare the difference between the values of the different designs, rather than to assess the individual worth of the design in terms of a market value. We believe our assumptions give consistent values for comparing the different designs.

We omit *external parameters* as modules for NOV analysis because they are not subjected to further experimentation. We treat all parameters under *design rules* as a single module. All other design parameters are treated as individual modules. Our assumptions for rest of the parameters are given below.

Redesign Cost Per Parameter (c_i). We assume the redesign cost of a single module to be 1 (following [13]).

Technical Potential (σ) of a Module. A fundamental relation between the technical potential σ and cost c for (re)designing individual modules comes from the *break-even* assumption of one experiment on an unmodularized system [13]. This assumption says that in an unmodularized system (or a system with only one module), $\sigma N^{1/2}Q(1) - cN = 0$. With this relation we can assume the maximum value for $\sigma = 2.5$, as we have assumed c_i, redesign cost of a single module to be 1 and $Q(1) = 0.4$.

Estimating the technical potential of a module has been identified as the most difficult task in NOV analysis [12, 26, 42]. Simple heuristics has been used to calculate the technical potential for the modules in *StoreLocator* and *WineryLocator* [26]. But, such heuristics lacks proper validation and is based on a set of design constraints to be enforced in the case studied. Since we lack the basic historical data for the designs presented in this paper we simply choose the technical potential of all the modules in our designs to be 2.5. *Design Rules* and *web.xml* are two exceptions. The *design rules* are kept fixed in all given designs so, we can assign them a technical potential of 0. The parameter *web.xml* is merely a configuration file, and since it is not subjected to any design experiment we assign it a technical potential of 0, too.

Module Complexity (n_i). A module's complexity is proportional to its tasks [13]. Table 6 lists the number of visible tasks that each module exposes to its prospective clients or users. These tasks do not account for the internal tasks that a module hides from others. We add a baseline value of 1 to the task numbers for each module to account for such hidden tasks. This convenient assumption leads to a nonzero value to the three *application modules* (AddressLocator, WineryFinder and RouteMapHandler) in the final design (Fig. 7) as all the tasks that resided in these modules (in earlier designs) are moved into the aspect *JSPConnections*.

Finally, to calculate the complexity of individual modules we assume N, the complexity of the whole design, to be the total tasks (visible tasks + 1) performed by all the modules in the system. We calculate the complexity of a module by dividing the total number of tasks it performs by N.

Table 6. Task list used to calculate the complexity (n_i) of individual modules. (# denotes number of externally visible (public) tasks. * denotes the modules from the last design shown in Fig. 7)

Design parameter	Tasks	#
ExternalParameters	–	0
DesignRules (StoreLocator)	Provide structures that model start location, address matches, directions and map	4
DesignRules (WineryLocator)	Provide structures that model start location, address matches, winery search option, tour and map	5
StoreLocator	Locate addresses, list stores, provide maps, map navigation, provide directions	5
HttpSessionStoreLocator	Authentication	1
locate	List location, specify starting address	2
display	List store, map, map navigation	3
directions	List directions	1
Web.xml	Application configuration	1
AddressLocator	List locations	1
AuthAddressLocator	Authentication	1
WineryFinder	List wineries, provide options for wineries selection	2
RouteMapHandler	Generate maps, provide navigation, list directions	3
AuthRouteMapHandler	Authentication	1
startWineryFind	List location, specify starting address	2
searchWinery	Set winery search options	1
tour	List wineries, map, map navigation	3
directions	Present directions	1
WebServicesLogger	Implement logging	1
Logging (Aspect)	Provide logging	1
Authentication (aspect)	Authentication	1
AddressLocator*	List locations	0
WineryFinder*	List wineries, provide options for wineries selection	0
RouteMapHandler*	Generate maps, provide navigation, list directions	0
JSPConnections*	Generate maps, provide navigation, list directions	6

7   Observations

The result of the NOV analysis is shown in Table 7. The NOV increased with each of the subsequent designs, except the final one, where the NOV went down. The last three columns give a comparison of the relative changes in NOVs of each design with respect to a particular design. The last column (I_4) shows the relative changes in NOV with respect to the earliest complete version of

WineryLocator (Fig. 4). In other words, it compares the NOV of the last four designs that are functionally equivalent, in terms of the visible tasks they perform. This means that the differences in the NOVs in this column are entirely due to remodularizations: introduction of an additional layer of design rules (Fig. 5), aspect-oriented modularizations for logging and authentication (Fig. 6), and localization of the public methods from the *Application Modules* into the aspect *JSPConnections* (Fig. 7).

The results clearly indicate that the introducing Design Rules (OO modularization, Fig. 5) adds more value to the existing design (Fig. 4). Separating logging and authentication using aspects (Fig. 6) enhances the existing OO design (Fig. 5). However, isolating the public methods from the *Application Controllers* in an aspect is detrimental (Fig. 7). In fact, the use of aspects in this last case lowers the value of the design with respect to all comparisons we make (Table 7, last row).

We provide some insight on these design consequences in the following sections. A closer look at the NOVs of all the modules for different experiments gives more insight on the effect aspects have on the value of the overall design.

Table 7. NOVs for different design options. Here, I_c = cumulative increase in value, I_3 = net increase in value with respect to WineryLocator (Fig. 3), I_4 = net increase in value with respect to WineryLocator with logging (Fig. 4).

Design	Fig.	NOV	I_c (%)	I_3 (%)	I_4 (%)
StoreLocator	1	1.05	NA	NA	NA
WineryLocator	3	2.87	172.20	NA	NA
WineryLocator with Logging	4	3.07	6.99	6.99	NA
WineryLocator with design rules for application	5	3.13	1.92	9.04	1.92
WineryLocator with Aspects	6	3.34	6.58	16.21	8.62
WineryLocator with aspect *JSP-Connections*	7	2.68	-19.65	-6.63	-12.73

7.1 NOV Worksheet

Figure 13 is the NOV worksheet that details the complete calculation of NOV for the last three designs; Fig. 6 (AO-Design), Fig. 5 (OO-Design) and Fig. 7 (AO-Design). Along with all the parameters of NOV, the worksheet shows the simulated value of each kth experiment for each parameter in all three designs. These values are shown in the 11 columns corresponding to the 11 values of k (second row). These 11 columns can be taken as the evolutionary simulation of experiments on the individual parameters of the given designs. In short, they depict the *evolutionary patterns* of individual modules.

We can see that for all the modules with nonzero σ the value of experiments increases until a break-even point is reached. All these break-even points have been highlighted with a shaded cell and solid borders. Experiments after this break-even point result in declining returns for investment. Experiments lower

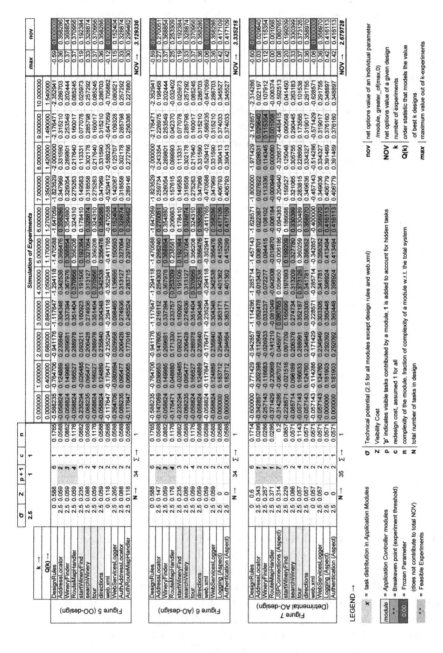

Fig. 13. NOV worksheet showing calculations for last three design variants

than the threshold values are labeled feasible, indicating that further experiments (increasing k) will keep the value increasing until the experiment threshold.

With the visual cues for feasible experiments and the experiment threshold in the NOV worksheet, we can see that both AO-Design and OO-Design have the same evolutionary pattern (all the modules reach experiment threshold after the same number of experiments). However, they differ in terms of the value each module contributes to the total NOV. In OO-Design authentication modules contribute less than in the AO-Design. Also, the value of *AddressLocator* goes down in AO-Design compared to the OO-Design.

The Detrimental AO-Design has a different evolutionary pattern compared to the other two designs. Particularly the *Application Modules* (AddressLocator, WineryFinder and RouteMapHandler) have a wider range for feasible experiments. This might seem beneficial (as a sign of more opportunities to experiment) but, this is, in fact, a consequence of bad design. The values for the experimental thresholds for these modules are very low compared to the ones in the earlier two designs (OO/AO-Design). This indicates that this design might lead to experiments on modules that are nonprofitable and result in very low value. The Detrimental AO-Design also introduces a new parameter, JSPConnections, which has the highest complexity (that is, provides a lot of functionality) but contributes very little to the overall NOV of the design. This, again, is an indicator of a bad design.

7.2   NOV Curves

Figure 14 shows the option values of each module in the last four designs. Each curve represents the variation of NOV of a module for 11 different experiments [13]. The highest peak in each curve denotes the value a module contributes to the NOV of the overall design. Sum of all the peak values of all the curves give the NOV.

We can see the same evolutionary pattern we observed in the NOV worksheet using NOV charts too. The charts show that NOV curves for the designs in Fig. 4 (WineryLocator with MapPoint design rules) and Fig. 5 (WineryLocator with application design rules) are almost identical. Design in Fig. 6 (AO-Design) is slightly different from Figs. 4 and 5. In the curves for Fig. 6 we can see that one of the curves goes above 0.4, and there is only one curve that lies below 0.2, compared to curves for Figs. 4 and 5 that have two curves below 0.20. This indicates how aspect modularization leads to a better design in Fig. 6.

The NOV curves for the design in Fig. 7 are strikingly different from rest of the curves. We see many curves starting below 0 for lower values of k. This indicates that these modules need more experiments before they reach the threshold (maximum value) they offer. Two of the modules hardly contribute to the total NOV (AddressLocator and RouteMapHandler). Almost half of the curves lie below 0.2, and the curve for JSPConnections reaches its threshold too early, without contributing much to the total NOV. All this indicates how the new aspect modularization in Fig. 7 affects the evolution pattern of all the modules and brings down the NOV of the entire design.

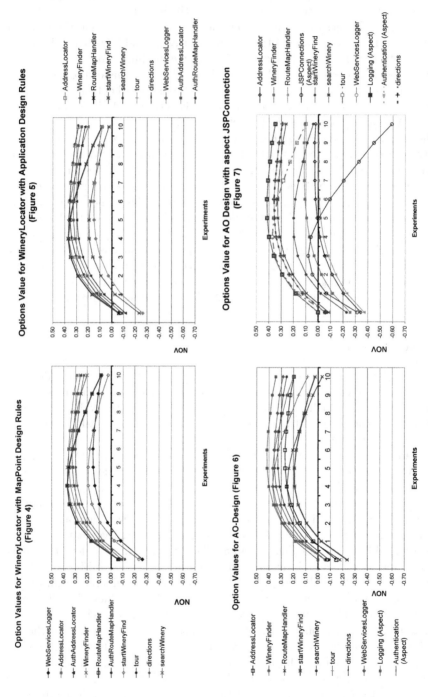

Fig. 14. Charts showing the effect of aspect-oriented modularization on option values

In [26] we observed how additional design constraints inhibit the evolution of existing modules. In particular, the various assignments for σ that captured the design heuristics about not all modules being equal caused the curve for *WebServicesLogger* stay below zero in all designs.

We can see that after aspect-oriented modularization the NOV curves for existing *Application Modules* (such as *RouteMapHandler*) go down. The increase in overall NOV for WineryLocator after aspect-oriented modularization is due to the NOV of newly introduced aspects, *Logging* and *Authentication*.

7.3   Towards Formulating Design Guidelines for Aspects

In light of the preceding observations made in the NOV worksheet and the NOV curves, we can now formulate the following preliminary guidelines for using aspect-oriented modularizations:

- *An aspect modularization adds value to the existing design if the parameters captured by aspects can be hidden from the existing parameters.*

  The case of modularizing logging with aspects clearly presents this case. In the design given in Fig. 5, the *Application Modules* ($F.6, P.14, 16, 17$) depend on *WebServicesLogger* ($F.5, P.13$). These dependencies are eliminated in Fig. 6 as the aspect *Logging* ($F.6, P.22$) hides the module *WebServices-Logger* ($F.6, P.21$) from the application modules ($F.6, P.13$ through 15). This is one of the primary factors that increased the NOV value of the aspect-oriented design (Fig. 6) in our case study.
- *An aspect modularization can be harmful when aspects enforce additional dependencies from the rest of the parameters to the aspects.*

  The final design (Fig. 7) in the case study illustrates this guideline. The aspect *JSPConnections* ($F.7, P.24$) introduces four new dependencies in the design in Fig. 7, which are largely responsible for bringing down the NOV of this design.

These two basic guidelines can inform designers for making decisions about aspect-oriented designs. The variations in design options we have considered and the results obtained from NOV attest to these guidelines. They also conform to a generally acceptable notion about dependencies and design quality.

8   Limitations and Future Work

Three problem areas need to be addressed before adopting NOV as a practical tool to assess design options in software. First, there is the question about the validity of the NOV model itself as it applies to software. Second, it would be very useful to be able to combine the NOV of modular operators instead of always computing the NOV of the whole design. Finally, the validity of the assumptions can also be questioned. We discuss these below.

8.1   Applicability of NOV

The first problem is about some of the simplifying assumptions in the NOV model, such as the linearity in summing up the NOV of a design and assumptions about the probabilistic relationship that simulates the module evolution. We have taken these assumptions as they are, and an elaborate discussion of these is beyond the scope of this paper. However, an implicit assumption about the visibility cost in NOV needs some clarification.

In all our designs, we have prepared the DSMs showing only the direct dependencies between design parameters. We do not include transitive dependencies in the DSMs. This has a serious implication on calculating visibility cost. The visibility cost in the NOV ($Z_i = \sum_{j-sees-i} cn_j$), described earlier in Sect. 6, only considers the direct dependents of a module. This means that, by modeling only the direct dependencies and using Baldwin and Clark's definition for visibility cost, we are considering that the ripple effects due to any change in a given module will be compensated in its direct dependents, and thus those changes will not be allowed to propagate further down the dependency tree. A naive way of accounting the ripple effects on all the dependents is to build higher order matrices that show both direct and transitive dependencies and calculate the visibility cost on such a matrix. Another approach might be to modify the definition of the visibility cost itself such that it follows the dependencies until it hits all terminal dependents. However, if we need to capture all such possibilities this naive approach will not be sufficient. Since we are using the programming model as the design space, with constructs like classes and methods as design parameters, we need a deeper understanding about how these dependencies propagate along different relations. For example, in Fig. 5 *startWineryFind* depends on *AuthAddressLocator* because of *usage*, while AuthAddressLocator depends on AddressLocator because of *inheritance*. We need to further investigate how to account for transitive operations on different relations such as these.

In a recent work, Cai and Sullivan have proposed a formal theory for modeling and analysis of design [16]. Their approach seems feasible for a tractable reasoning of design alternatives at a higher level of abstraction. It takes away some of the fuzziness such as the problem of properly reasoning about the transitive operation on two (or more) different relationships.

8.2   Modular Operators and Special NOV Expressions

Our analysis of NOV for the various designs is based on the general expression to calculate NOV of a modular design rather than the NOV expressions for the individual operators. We followed this approach because we still need to have a precise understanding about how a NOV for a design change resulting in a different dependency structure, other than the modular operators model, should be expressed in terms of these individual NOV for the operators. For example, we cannot exactly pick which operator models the design change we presented in Sect. 4.5 (from Fig. 4 to Fig. 5). We can treat it as a refinement of *inversion*, which previously had created the *design rules* in Figs. 3 and 4, but accurate evaluation cannot be done without a precise NOV expression that models this change in the design. Such problems arise as we move into finer granularity of design changes and thus need to investigate the feasibility of modeling and evaluating finer design changes with Baldwin and Clark's theory (for example, various forms of small and big refactorings [20]). We need to understand how far (or deep) we can go with these basic operators, and in particular with NOV, in considering fine-grained design changes in software.

8.3   Assumptions About the NOV Parameters

The assumptions made in Sect. 6.2 directly follow convenient conventions that are borrowed from Baldwin and Clark's original work [13], for example, the assumption about redesign cost being 1 for all modules and the definition for complexity. Also, earlier heuristics for calculating the technical potential lack formal or empirical verification [26]. Standard techniques to estimate parameters for NOV and richer models for NOV for software are issues of further research in this field.

Some of the open questions about NOV have been discussed in [12]. Empirical validation of the assumptions made about NOV parameters has been proposed as a possible approach in seeking answers to such questions. In particular, some preliminaries on measuring the technical potential of a module are given.

Despite of these limitations we are positive about the reliability of NOV results under the influence of varying assumptions for its parameters. Two NOV analyses have been done with the same case study; the one in this paper and in an earlier work [26]. These analyses use two different techniques for assigning value to σ, the technical potential of a module. Both strategies show that logging and authentication aspects are beneficial (from design in Fig. 5 to Fig. 6) whereas the *JSPConnections* aspect is detrimental to *WineryLocator*'s design (from design in Fig. 6 to Fig. 7). This result has been summarized in Table 8, which shows how the NOV result varies with two different assumptions about σ. The exact NOV values are different with these two different assumptions for σ. But, the values themselves are consistent in indicating whether the design is good (value increase) or bad (value decrease). Alternative approaches for measuring the values of NOV parameters can be found in existing literature [41, 42].

Table 8. NOVs for different design options with two different measurement strategies for σ

NOV for design shown in Fig. →	3	4	5	6	7
Using the measurement heuristics for σ from [26]	1.38	1.41	1.59	1.76	1.73
With σ assumed to be 2.5 for all modules (see Sect. 6.2)	2.87	3.07	3.13	3.34	2.68

8.4   Future Work

In this paper we have only considered two aspect-oriented techniques, Pointcut-Advice and Introduction. We intend to investigate the structure of dependencies and modularity in several existing models for representing aspects, using techniques and theories presented in related works, such as [5, 21, 24, 29, 37].

Some of the major recent efforts in aspect-oriented software development that are relevant and seem promising in contributing to further solve some problems we have identified are given below.[8]

1. *Symmetric models for AOP* that provide a unified approach for implementing advice implementations and classes, and decouple aspect implementation from binding, have potentials in allowing designers to express uniform design rules both for aspects and base classes. Some of the recent works in this area are [6, 27, 34].
2. *Principles of aspect modularization:* Other related works put forward some principles and mechanisms to identify and implement standard interfaces in aspects [23, 25, 41]. We believe these efforts will contribute greatly in identifying the standards for *Design Rules* for AO modularization (see Fig. 12).
3. *Classification system for aspects:* Rinard et al. have presented a classification system for aspects [36]. Although we have not yet incorporated such a classification, we believe it is critical to account for such differences that various types of aspects have on design. One possible way to account for such differences is to assign different *weights* to dependencies in the DSMs.

We believe these research efforts will contribute in discovering standard techniques to define design rules for aspects and help us understand the implications these design rules have on the overall value of an aspect-oriented design.

We observed that it is tedious and error-prone to work with DSMs and NOV analysis without proper tool support. We believe DSM can be implemented as an interactive and direct manipulation tool for software design. We intend to look into the issues of scalability and possibilities for alternative representations of design in DSM. We also plan to incorporate advanced features of DSMs such as numerical DSMs with dependencies classified according to their strength and modeling software with various types of DSMs using component-based and team-based DSMs [1, 15]. With these, we intend to investigate whether DSM can be further extended as a tool for real software practitioners and designers.

We are currently investigating modular dependencies based on the true nature of aspects. With a rigorous analysis based on: (i) what form of aspect is used, (ii) where the aspect is applied (or, how it relates to other existing modules), and (iii) how the aspect is applied (such as various kinds of joinpoints/pointcuts), we can augment a model like net option value, for example, by providing a classification scheme for assigning values for the strength of dependencies. We believe such efforts would lead us to a more accurate evaluation and analysis of aspect-oriented designs.

---

[8] This is not an exhaustive and complete list, but represents some of the recent works that we have come across that complement the work presented in this paper.

9   Conclusion

Originally conceived as a modularity mechanism, aspects bring powerful possibilities whose deep implications in an existing design cannot be fully known without a rigorous analysis. We have presented a case study that illustrates the consequences that aspects have on modular design evolution using the NOV model. In particular, the evolutionary patterns of modules using the NOV worksheet and NOV curves provide insights on the role that aspects play on the evolution of other modules in the system. These patterns help in understanding how subtle dependencies due to aspects bring down the value of an existing (good) design. Based on this, we formulated basic guidelines on aspect design that say that aspects should hide design parameters from other modules and aspects should avoid enforcing additional dependencies from the rest of the parameters.

It should be noted that NOV is just one model to do assessments like these, and there might exist other forms of analysis techniques for designs that would complement NOV or address different issues than NOV does. A natural extension to the manual work presented here would be to implement these analysis techniques in design tools. This would greatly simplify analysis and make evaluating individual alternatives feasible.

The example we have used in this paper is relatively complex. However, it is rather small in comparison to real industrial software that ranges in millions lines of code. It is imperative to gain experience in using NOV with such systems to understand its applicability in analyzing complex design options.

We believe that a deeper look into the problems we have identified will provide a scientific basis for making design decisions that go beyond intuitions. This will lead to a clear understanding of using aspects that will open doors for their widespread adoption.

References

[1] Tutorials and resources on DSM, http://www.dsmweb.org. Cited 20 September 2005
[2] Lattix Web site. http://www.lattix.com. Cited 20 September 2005
[3] AspectJ project Web site. http://www.aspectj.org. Cited 20 September 2005
[4] MapPoint Object Model, http://msdn.microsoft.com. Cited 20 September 2005
[5] Concern Manipulation Environment (CME). http://www.eclipse.org/cme. Cited 20 September 2005
[6] AspectWerkz, http://aspectwerkz.codehaus.org. Cited 20 September 2005
[7] The Apache Foundation. Apache AXIS, http://ws.apache.org/axis. Cited 20 September 2005
[8] MapPoint Web services. http://www.mappoint.com. Cited 20 September 2005
[9] Spatialpoint. http://www.spatialpoint.com. Cited 20 September 2005
[10] Sun Microsystems. Java Servlet Specification. http://java.sun.com/products/servlet. Cited 20 September 2005
[11] Sun Microsystems. J2EE, Java 2 Enterprise Edition Specification. http://java.sun.com/j2ee. Cited 20 September 2005

[12] S.K. Bajracharya, T.C. Ngo, and C.V. Lopes. On using net options value as a value based design framework. In: *EDSER '05: Proceedings of the Seventh International Workshop on Economics-Driven Software Engineering Research*, ACM, New York, pp. 1–3, 2005

[13] C.Y. Baldwin and K.B. Clark. *Design Rules Vol. I, The Power of Modularity.* MIT Press, Cambridge, MA, 2000

[14] J.K. Blundell, M.L. Hines, and J. Stach. The measurement of software design quality. *Ann. Softw. Eng.*, 4:235–255, 1997

[15] T.R. Browning. Applying the design structure matrix to system decomposition and integration problems: a review and new directions. *IEEE Transactions on Engineering Management*, 48:292–306, 2001

[16] Y. Cai and K.J. Sullivan. A value-oriented theory of modularity in design. In: *Proceedings of the 7th International Workshop on Economics-Driven Software Engineering Research (EDSER) at ICSE'05*, 2005

[17] N. Fenton and S.L. Pfleeger. *Software Metrics 2nd edn.: A Rigorous and Practical Approach*, PWS, Boston, MA, 1997

[18] M. Fowler. Inversion of control containers and the dependency injection pattern. http://www.martinfowler.com/articles/injection.html

[19] M. Fowler. Module assembly. *IEEE Software*, 21(2):65–67, 2004

[20] M. Fowler, K. Beck, J. Brant, O. Opdyke, and D. Roberts. *Refactoring: improving the design of existing code.* Object Technology Series. Addison-Wesley, 1999

[21] W.H. Harrison and H.L. Ossher. Member-group relationships among objects. IBM Technical Report RC22048, 2002

[22] G. Kiczales, J. Lamping, A. Mendhekar, C. Maeda, C. Lopes, J.-M. Loingtier, and J. Irwin. Aspect-oriented programming. In: M. Akşit and S. Matsuoka (eds.) *11th Europeen Conf. Object-Oriented Programming, LNCS Vol. 1241*, Springer, pp. 220–242, 1997

[23] G. Kiczales and M. Mezini. Aspect-oriented programming and modular reasoning. In: *ICSE '05: Proceedings of the 27th International Conference on Software Engineering*, ACM, New York, pp. 49–58, 2005

[24] K. Lieberherr, D. Lorenz, and M. Mezini. Programming with Aspectual Components. Technical Report NU-CCS-99-01, College of Computer Science, Northeastern University, Boston, MA, 1999

[25] C.V. Lopes. On the nature of aspects: Principles of aspect-oriented design. In: *ACM Transactions of Software Engineering.* Under Review

[26] C.V. Lopes and S.K. Bajracharya. An analysis of modularity in aspect oriented design. In: *AOSD '05: Proceedings of the 4th International Conference on Aspect-Oriented Software Development*, ACM, New York, pp. 15–26, 2005

[27] C.V. Lopes and T.C. Ngo. The Aspect markup language and its support of Aspect plugins. ISR Technical Report UCI-ISR-04-8, 2004

[28] A. MacCormack, J. Rusnak, and C. Baldwin. Exploring the structure of complex software designs: An empirical study of open source and proprietary code. Harvard Business School Working Paper Number 05-016, 2004

[29] H. Masuhara and G. Kiczales. Modeling crosscutting in aspect-oriented mechanisms. In: *ECOOP 2003–Object-Oriented Programming 17th European Conference*, Springer, pp. 2–28, 2003

[30] N. Medvidovic and R.N. Taylor. A classification and comparison framework for software architecture description languages. *IEEE Trans. Softw. Eng.*, 26(1):70–93, 2000

[31] D.L. Parnas. On the criteria to be used in decomposing systems into modules. *Commun. ACM*, 15(12):1053–1058, 1972

[32] D.L. Parnas. On a "Buzzword": Hierarchical structure. In: *Software Pioneers: Contributions to Software Engineering*, Springer, New York, pp. 429–440, 2002

[33] D.E. Perry and A.L. Wolf. Foundations for the study of software architecture. *SIGSOFT Softw. Eng. Notes*, 17(4):40–52, 1992

[34] H. Rajan and K.J. Sullivan. Classpects: unifying aspect- and object-oriented language design. In: *ICSE '05: Proceedings of the 27th International Conference on Software Engineering*, ACM, New York, pp. 59–68, 2005

[35] A.J. Riel. *Object-Oriented Design Heuristics*. Addison-Wesley Longman, Boston, MA, 1996

[36] M. Rinard, A. Salcianu, and S. Bugrara. A classification system and analysis for aspect-oriented programs. In: *SIGSOFT '04/FSE-12: Proceedings of the 12th ACM SIGSOFT Twelfth International Symposium on Foundations of Software Engineering*, ACM, New York, pp. 147–158, 2004

[37] M.P. Robillard and G.C. Murphy. Concern graphs: finding and describing concerns using structural program dependencies. In: *Proceedings of the 24th International Conference on Software Engineering (ICSE-02)*, ACM, New York, pp. 406–416, 2002

[38] D. Sharman and A. Yassine. Characterizing complex product architectures. *Systems Engineering Journal*, 7(1):35–60, 2004

[39] M. Shaw and D. Garlan. *Software Architecture: Perspectives on an Emerging Discipline*. Prentice-Hall, 1996

[40] D.V. Steward. The design structure system: A method for managing the design of complex systems. *IEEE Transactions on Engineering Management*, 28:71–74, 1981

[41] K. Sullivan, W.G. Griswold, Y. Song, Y. Cai, M. Shonle, N. Tewari, and H. Rajan. Information hiding interfaces for aspect-oriented design. *ESEC/FSE 05 (April)*

[42] K.J. Sullivan, W.G. Griswold, Y. Cai, and B. Hallen. The structure and value of modularity in software design. In: *Proceedings of the 8th European Software Engineering Conference Held Jointly with 9th ACM SIGSOFT International Symposium on Foundations of Software Engineering*, ACM, New York, pp. 99–108, 2001

[43] W3C, SOAP (Simple Object Access Protocol) version 1.2 specification. http://www.w3.org/TR/soap12. Cited 20 September 2005

[44] W3C, Web Services Description Language (WSDL). http://www.w3.org/TR/wsdl. Cited 30 September 2005

Modularizing Design Patterns with Aspects:
A Quantitative Study

Alessandro Garcia[1], Cláudio Sant'Anna[2], Eduardo Figueiredo[2], Uirá Kulesza[2],
Carlos Lucena[2], and Arndt von Staa[2]

[1] Lancaster University, Computing Department, InfoLab 21,
Lancaster - United Kingdom
garciaa@comp.lancs.ac.uk
[2] PUC-Rio, Computer Science Department, LES, SoC+Agents Group,
Rua Marques de São Vicente, 225 - 22453 - 900, Rio de Janeiro, RJ, Brazil
{claudios, emagno, uira, lucena, arndt}@inf.puc-rio.br

Abstract. Design patterns offer flexible solutions to common problems in software development. Recent studies have shown that several design patterns involve crosscutting concerns. Unfortunately, object-oriented (OO) abstractions are often not able to modularize those crosscutting concerns, which in turn compromise the system reusability and maintainability. Hence, it is important verifying whether aspect-oriented approaches support improved modularization of crosscutting concerns relative to design patterns. Ideally, quantitative studies should be performed to compare OO and aspect-oriented implementations of classical patterns with respect to fundamental software engineering attributes, such as coupling and cohesion. This paper presents a quantitative study that compares Java and AspectJ solutions for the 23 Gang-of-Four patterns. We have used stringent software attributes as the assessment criteria. We have found that most aspect-oriented solutions improve separation of pattern-related concerns, although only four aspect-oriented implementations have exhibited significant reuse. This paper also discusses the scalability of the analyzed solutions with respect to separation of concerns, and the determination of a predictive model for the modularization of design patterns with aspects.

1 Introduction

Since the introduction of the first software pattern catalog containing the 23 Gang-of-Four (GoF) patterns [9], design patterns have quickly been recognized to be important and useful in real software development. A design pattern describes a proven solution to a design problem with the goal of assuring reusable and maintainable solutions. Patterns assign roles to their participants, which define the functionality of the participants in the pattern context. However, a number of design patterns involve crosscutting concerns in the relationship between the pattern roles and participant classes in each instance of the pattern [15]. The implementation of the pattern roles often crosscuts several classes in a software system. Moreover, recent studies [11, 12, 15] have shown that object-oriented (OO) abstractions are not able to isolate these pattern-specific concerns and tend to lead to programs with poor modularity. In this context, it is important to systematically verify whether aspect-oriented approaches

A. Rashid and M. Aksit (Eds.): Transactions on AOSD I, LNCS 3880, pp. 36–74, 2006.
© Springer-Verlag Berlin Heidelberg 2006

[22, 33] support improved modularization of the crosscutting concerns relative to the patterns.

To the best of our knowledge, Hannemann and Kiczales [15] have developed the only systematic study that explicitly investigated the use of aspect-oriented programming (AOP) to implement classical design patterns. They performed a preliminary study in which they developed and compared Java [20] and AspectJ [2] implementations of the GoF patterns. Their findings have shown that AspectJ implementations improve the modularity of most patterns. However, these improvements were based on some attributes that are not well known in software engineering, such as composability and (un)pluggability. This study has also not investigated the scalability of both object-oriented and aspect-oriented solutions. Moreover, this study was based only on a qualitative assessment and empirical data is missing. To solve this problem, this previous study should be replicated and supplemented by quantitative case studies in order to improve our knowledge body about the use of aspects for addressing the crosscutting property of design patterns.

This paper presents quantitative assessments of Java and AspectJ implementations for the 23 GoF patterns. Our study is based on well-known software engineering attributes such as separation of concerns, coupling, cohesion and size. We have found that most aspect-oriented solutions improved the separation of pattern-related concerns. In addition, we have found that:

(i) The use of AOP helped to improve the coupling and cohesion of some pattern implementations.

(ii) The "aspectization" of design patterns reduced the number of attributes of 10 patterns, and decreased the number of operations and respective parameters of 12 patterns.

(iii) Only four design patterns implemented in AspectJ have exhibited significant reuse.

(iv) The relationships between pattern roles and application-specific concerns are sometimes so intense that it seems not trivial to separate those roles in aspects.

(v) The use of coupling, cohesion and size measures was helpful to assist the detection of opportunities for aspect-oriented refactoring of design patterns.

We have also analyzed the influence of AspectJ solutions on inheritance coupling. In addition, we discuss the scalability of both aspect-oriented and object-oriented solutions, and the determination of a predictive model for the aspectization of design patterns. As each design pattern usually has different variants and is heterogeneously instantiated through distinct applications [9], we also present some discussions about the particularities of the AspectJ implementations of the patterns used in this study. This information is useful to any software engineer, specially those who wish to replicate our experiment. Finally, we summarize how the findings of our study confirm or contradict the claims presented in the Hannemann and Kiczales' work [15].

The remainder of this paper is organized as follows. Section 2 presents our study setting, while giving a brief description of Hannemann and Kiczales' study. Section 3 presents the study results with respect to separation of concerns, and Sect. 4 presents the study results in terms of coupling, cohesion and size attributes. These results are interpreted and discussed in Sect. 5, in which a broader analysis is drawn. Section 6 introduces some related work. Section 7 includes some concluding remarks and directions for future work.

2   Study Setting

This section describes the configuration of our empirical study. As this study is directly related to Hannemann and Kiczales' work, the goals and conclusions of that study are presented in Sect. 2.1. Section 2.2 uses the Mediator pattern to illustrate the crosscutting property of some design patterns. Section 2.3 introduces the metrics used in the evaluation process, and Sect. 2.4 describes our assessment procedures.

2.1 Hannemann and Kiczales' Study

Several design patterns exhibit crosscutting concerns [15]. In this context, Hannemann and Kiczales (HK) have undertaken a study in which they have developed and compared Java [20] and AspectJ [2] implementations of the 23 GoF design patterns [9]. They claim that programming languages affect pattern implementation. Hence it is natural to explore the effect of aspect-oriented programming (AOP) techniques on the implementation of the GoF patterns. For each of the 23 GoF patterns, they developed a representative example that makes use of the pattern and implemented the example in both Java and AspectJ.

Design patterns assign roles to their participants; for example, the Mediator and Colleague roles are defined in the Mediator pattern. A number of GoF patterns involve crosscutting structures in the relationship between roles and classes in each instance of the pattern [15]. For instance, in the Mediator pattern, some operations that change a Colleague must trigger updates to the corresponding Mediator; in other words, the act of updating crosscuts one or more operations in each Colleague in the pattern.

Two kinds of pattern roles are identified in the HK study, which are called *defining* and *superimposed* roles. A defining role defines a participant class completely. In other words, classes playing a defining role have no functionality outside the pattern. The unique role of the Façade pattern is an example of defining role. A superimposed role can be assigned to participant classes that have functionality outside of the pattern. An example of superimposed role is the Colleague role of the Mediator pattern, since a participant class playing this role usually has functionality not related to the pattern. These kinds of roles are used by the authors to analyze the crosscutting structure of design patterns.

In the HK study, the goal of the AspectJ implementations is to modularize the pattern roles. The authors have reported that modularity improvements were reached in 17 of the 23 cases, and 12 aspect-oriented pattern implementations resulted in improved reuse. The degree of improvement with AOP has varied according to each pattern implementation. The next section discusses these improvements and crosscutting pattern structures in terms of the Mediator pattern.

2.2 Example: The Mediator Pattern

The intent of the Mediator pattern is to define an object that encapsulates how a set of objects interact [9]. The Mediator pattern defines two roles, Mediator and Colleague, to their participant classes. The Mediator role has the responsibility for controlling and coordinating the interactions of a group of objects. The Colleague role represents the objects that need to communicate with each other. Hannemann and Kiczales [15] present a simple example of the Mediator pattern in the context of a Java Swing application. In such a system the Mediator pattern is used to manage the communication between two kinds of graphical user interfaces components. A Label class plays the Mediator role of the pattern, and a Button class plays the Colleague role.

Figure 1 depicts the class diagram of the OO implementation of the Mediator pattern. The interfaces GUIMediator and GUIColleague are defined to realize the roles of the Mediator pattern. Specific application classes must implement these interfaces based on the role that they need to play. In the example presented, the Button class implements the GUIColleague interface. The Label class implements the interface GUIMediator in order to manage the actions to be executed when buttons are clicked. Figure 1 also illustrates how the OO implementation of the Mediator pattern is spread across the code of the application classes. The shadowed attributes and methods represent code necessary to implement the Colleague role of the Mediator pattern in the application context.

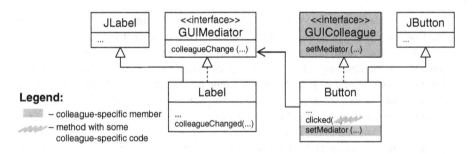

Fig. 1. The OO design of the mediator pattern

Figure 2 illustrates the source code of the Button class. The necessary elements to implement the Colleague role are shadowed. The Button class implements the GUIColleague interface (line 2), defines an attribute to reference a mediator (line 3), and implements the respective setMediator() method (lines 5–7). Moreover, the clicked() method of the Button class defines the functionality to communicate with the mediator (line 20).

In their study, Hannemann and Kiczales identified the generic part of several design patterns and isolated their implementation by defining "abstract reusable aspects". These aspects are reused and extended in order to instantiate the pattern for a specific application. In the AspectJ solution of the Mediator pattern, for example, the code for implementing the pattern is textually localized in two categories of aspects: (i) the MediatorProtocol abstract aspect that encapsulates the common part to all potential instantiations of the pattern, and (ii) concrete extensions of the abstract aspect that instantiate the pattern for specific contexts.

```
01 public class Button extends JButton
02                      implements GUIColleague {
03    private GUIMediator mediator;
04
05    public void setMediator(GUIMediator mediator) {
06      this.mediator = mediator;
07    }
08
09    public Button(String name) {
10      super(name);
11      this.setActionCommand(name);
12      this.addActionListener( new ActionListener() {
13        public void actionPerformed(ActionEvent e) {
14          clicked();
15        }
16      });
17    }
18
19    public void clicked() {
20      mediator.colleagueChanged(this);
21    }
22 }
```

Fig. 2. The Button class of the OO implementation

Figure 3 presents the reusable MediatorProtocol abstract aspect. Code related to the Colleague role is shadowed. Both roles are realized as protected inner interfaces named Mediator and Colleague (line 3 and line 7, respectively). Concrete extensions of the MediatorProtocol aspect assign the roles to particular classes. Implementation of the mapping from Colleague to Mediator is realized using a weak hash map that stores for each colleague its respective mediator (line 9). Changes to the Colleague–Mediator mapping can be realized via the public setMediator() method (lines 16–18). The MediatorProtocol aspect also defines an abstract pointcut named change and an abstract method named notifyMediator(). The former specifies points in the execution (joinpoints) of colleague objects where a communication with the mediator object needs to be established. The latter defines the functionality to be executed by a Mediator object when a change to a Colleague occurs. These abstract elements must be concretized by the MediatorProtocol subaspects. Finally, the communication protocol between Mediator and Colleague is implemented by an after advice (lines 22–24) in terms of the change pointcut and the notifyMediator() method.

As we can see, in the AspectJ implementation of the Mediator pattern, all code pertaining to the relationship between Mediators and Colleagues is moved into aspects. In this way, code for implementing the pattern is textually localized in aspects, instead of being spread across the participant classes. Moreover, the abstract aspect code can be reused by all pattern instances.

```
01 public abstract aspect MediatorProtocol {
02
03   protected interface Mediator { }
04
05   protected abstract void notifyMediator(Colleague c, Mediator m);
06
07   protected interface Colleague { }
08
09   private WeakHashMap mappingColleagueToMediator = new WeakHashMap();
10
11   private Mediator getMediator(Colleague c) {
12     Mediator mediator = (Mediator) mappingColleagueToMediator.get(c);
13     return mediator;
14   }
15
16   public void setMediator(Colleague c, Mediator m) {
17     mappingColleagueToMediator.put(c, m);
18   }
19
20   protected abstract pointcut change(Colleague c);
21
22   after(Colleague c): change(c) {
23     notifyMediator(c, getMediator(c));
24   }
25 }
```

Fig. 3. The MediatorProtocol aspect

2.3 The Metrics

In our study, a suite of metrics for separation of concerns, coupling, cohesion and size [29] was selected to evaluate Hannemann and Kiczales' pattern implementations. These metrics have already been used in five different studies [8, 10, 11, 19, 31], where the measures have been proved to be effective quality indicators. Most of them have been automated in our own measurement tool [7]. This metrics suite was defined based on the reuse and refinement of some classical and OO metrics [5, 6]. The original definitions of the OO metrics [5] were extended to be applied in a paradigm-independent way, thereby supporting the generation of comparable results. The metrics suite also encompasses new metrics for measuring separation of concerns [10, 29]. Table 1 presents a brief definition of each metric and associates them with the attributes measured by each one.

The separation of concerns metrics measure the degree to which a single concern in the system maps to the design components (classes and aspects), operations (methods and advices), and lines of code. The more directly a concern maps to the design and code elements, the fewer elements are affected by the concern, and the better modularized the system is. The suite is composed of three metrics for separation of concerns: (i) concern diffusion over components (CDC), (ii) concern diffusion over operations (CDO), and (iii) concern diffusion over lines of code (CDLOC).

In order to better understand these metrics, consider the OO example of the Mediator pattern, shown in Fig. 1 (Sect. 2.2). In that example, there is code relative to the Colleague role in the GUIColleague interface and in the shadowed methods of the Button class. In other words, the Colleague concern is implemented by one interface and one class. Therefore, the value of the CDC metric for this concern is two. Similarly, the value of the CDO metric for the Colleague role is three, since this concern is implemented by the one method of the GUIColleague interface and the two shadowed methods of the Button class. Figure 2 shows the shadowing of the Button class in detail.

The CDLOC metric allows us to measure the number of transition points for each concern through the lines of code. A transition point is the place in the code where there is a "concern switch". CDLOC is measured by shadowing lines of code in the application classes related to the specific concern that you are interested in investigating. After that, it is necessary to count the number of transitions points through the source code of every shadowed class. In the example presented in Fig. 2, the Button class was shadowed in order to make it possible to measure the value of CDLOC for the Colleague concern. The value of CDLOC is four in that case, since that is the number of transition points through the source code of the Button class.

Table 1. The metrics suite

Attributes	Metrics	Definitions
Separation of concerns	Concern diffusion over components (CDC)	Counts the number of classes and aspects whose main purpose is to contribute to the implementation of a concern and the number of other classes and aspects that access them
	Concern diffusion over operations (CDO)	Counts the number of methods and advices whose main purpose is to contribute to the implementation of a concern and the number of other methods and advices that access them
	Concern diffusion over LOC (CDLOC)	Counts the number of transition points for each concern through the lines of code. Transition points are points in the code where there is a "concern switch"
Coupling	Coupling between components (CBC)	Counts the number of other classes and aspects to which a class or an aspect is coupled
	Depth inheritance tree (DIT)	Counts how far down in the inheritance hierarchy a class or aspect is declared
Cohesion	Lack of cohesion in operations (LCOO)	Measures the lack of cohesion of a class or an aspect in terms of the amount of method and advice pairs that do not access the same instance variable
Size	Lines of code (LOC)	Counts the lines of code
	Number of attributes (NOA)	Counts the number of attributes of each class or aspect
	Weighted operations per component (WOC)	Counts the number of methods and advices of each class or aspect and the number of its parameters

Our suite also includes two metrics for assessing coupling from different viewpoints: coupling between components (CBC) and depth of inheritance tree (DIT). Coupling among system components has long been regarded as a major contributor to the system complexity. Coupling is an indication of the strength of interconnections between the components in a system. Highly coupled systems have strong interconnections, with program units largely dependent on each other. Excessive coupling is not desirable, since it is detrimental to modular design. CBC is defined for a component (class or aspect) as a tally of the number of other components to which it is coupled. DIT is concerned with inheritance coupling. DIT is defined as the maximum length from a node to the root of the tree. It counts how far down the inheritance hierarchy a class or aspect is declared. DIT is an extension of the traditional OO metric [5] with the same name that also considers the inheritance between aspects [10, 29].

The suite of metrics encompasses one metric for cohesion, called lack of cohesion in operations (LCOO). This metric measures the lack of cohesion of a component by counting the amount of method/advice pairs that do not access the same instance variable [10, 29]. A low LCOO value indicates high closeness on the relationships between internal component operations (i.e., high cohesion), which is a desirable situation. On the other hand, low-cohesive components suggest an inappropriate design, because each of them involves the encapsulation of unrelated module entities, which should not be kept together in the same modular unit[3].

The software size measures the length of a software system's design and code [6]. Size metrics are concerned with different perspectives of the system size. The metrics suite encompasses three size metrics: (i) lines of code (LOC), (ii) number of attributes (NOA), and (iii) weighted operations per component (WOC). In general, the higher the size, the more complex the system is. LOC counts the lines of code in the system implementation, while NOA captures the number of attributes in each aspect or class. WOC measures are obtained by counting the number of parameters of the operation. The metric treats advice and methods of aspects in the same way that the corresponding OO metric [5] treats methods of classes.

2.4   Assessment Procedures

Replication of software engineering experiments is one of the main mechanisms to enable us to improve our understanding of existing techniques. In our study, we have used the same Java and AspectJ implementations of the HK study so that we could explicitly correlate our empirical results with the ones from this previous study. The AspectJ implementations basically followed the strategies described in [15], where abstract reusable aspects (Sect. 2.2) were defined when possible. It was not particularly feasible to define a reusable aspect for the patterns Abstract Factory, Factory Method, Template Method, Builder, and Bridge; aspects were used to isolate the pattern roles while providing support for multiple inheritance, which is not supported in Java. The Façade implementations are the same in AspectJ and Java.

As Hannemann and Kiczales have mostly chosen the default version of the patterns, no major decisions needed to be taken in the Java implementations of the patterns since the pattern implementations are already explicitly documented in the GoF book. This procedure was important to guarantee that the Java versions were good enough to enable fair comparisons with the AspectJ counterparts. The only major change done in both implementations of the patterns was that abstract classes defined in the patterns were replaced with interfaces, as often happens in realistic applications. The idea is to allow the business classes to extend application-specific abstract classes in addition to the interfaces of the pattern. In few cases, they have chosen specific variants of the patterns in the Java implementations, but the design differences with respect to the main version of the pattern are also documented in the GoF catalogue. In addition, the AspectJ solutions implemented those same variants. The implementation of nondefault versions of the patterns only happened in two cases: the Singleton pattern (variant exploring specialization of singletons), and the Adapter pattern (variant called *Object Adapter* [9]). Refer to [1, 15] for further details about the design pattern implementations, and respective decisions and constraints.

In order to compare the two implementations of the patterns, we had to ensure that both versions of each pattern were implementing the same functionalities. Therefore, some minor modifications were realized in the original code [1] of the patterns. Examples of such kinds of changes were: (i) to add or remove a functionality – a method, a class or an aspect – in the aspect-oriented (or object-oriented) implementation of the pattern in order to ensure the equivalence between the two versions. We decided to add or remove a functionality to the implementation by evaluating its relevance for the pattern implementation. Another kind of change was (ii) to ensure that both versions were using the same coding styles.

Afterwards, we changed both Java and AspectJ implementations of the 23 GoF patterns to add new participant classes to play pattern roles. For instance, in the Mediator pattern implementation, four classes playing the role of Colleague were added, as the `Button` class in Fig. 1 (Sect. 2.2); furthermore, four classes playing the role of Mediator were added, as the `Label` class in Fig. 1. These changes were introduced because the HK implementations encompass few classes per role (in most cases only one). Hence we have decided to add more participant classes in order to investigate the pattern crosscutting structure and the scalability of both OO and AO solutions. Table 2 presents the superimposed roles of each studied pattern and the participant classes introduced to each pattern implementation example. Finally, we have applied the chosen metrics to the changed code. We analyzed the results after the changes, comparing with the results gathered from the original code (i.e., before the changes).

In the measurement process, the data was partially gathered by the CASE tool Together 6.0 [34]. It supports some metrics: LOC, NOA, WOC (WMPC2 in Together), CBC (CBO in Together), LCOO (LOCOM1 in Together) and DIT (DOIH in Together). The data collection of the separation of concerns metrics (CDC, CDO and CDLOC) was preceded by the shadowing of every class, interface and aspect in both implementations of the patterns. Their code was shadowed according to the role of the pattern that they implement. Like the HK study, we treated each pattern role as a concern, because the roles are the primary sources of crosscutting structures. Figures 2 and 3 exemplify the shadowing of some classes and aspects in both Java and AspectJ implementations of the Mediator pattern by considering the Colleague role of this pattern. After the shadowing, the data of the separation of concerns metrics (CDC, CDO, and CDLOC) was manually collected.

Table 2. The design patterns, their superimposed roles and the respective changes

Design patterns	Superimposed roles	Introduced changes
Abstract Factory	–	4 Factories
Adapter	Adaptee	4 Adaptee methods
Bridge	–	2 Abstractions and 2 implementors
Builder	–	4 Builders
Chain of Responsibility (CoR)	Handler	4 Handlers
Command	Commanding, Receiver	4 Commands and 2 invokers
Composite	Composite, Leaf	2 Composites and 2 leafs
Decorator	Component	4 Decorators
Façade	–	No change
Factory Method	–	4 Creators
Flyweight	Flyweight	4 Flyweights
Interpreter	–	4 Expressions
Iterator	Aggregate	2 Iterators and 2 aggregates
Mediator	Mediator, Colleague	4 Mediators and 4 colleagues
Memento	Originator	2 Mementos and 2 originators
Observer	Subject, Observer	4 Observers and 4 subjects
Prototype	Prototype	4 Prototypes
Proxy	Proxy	4 Proxies and 2 real subjects
Singleton	Singleton	4 Singletons and 4 subclasses
State	Context	4 States
Strategy	Context	4 Strategies and 4 contexts
Template Method	AbstractClass, ConcreteClass	4 Concrete classes
Visitor	Element	4 Elements and 2 visitors

3   Results: Separation of Concerns

This section and Sect. 4 present the results of the measurement process. The data have been collected based on the set of defined metrics (Sect. 2.3). The goal is to describe the results through the application of the metrics before and after the selected changes (Sect. 2.4). The presentation of the measurement outcomes is broken into two parts. This section focuses on the analysis of to what extent the aspect-oriented (AO) and object-oriented (OO) solutions[1] provide support for the separation of pattern-related concerns. Section 4 presents the results with respect to coupling, cohesion and size. The discussion about the interplay among all the results is concentrated in Sect. 5. Section 5 also presents other relevant discussions, such as the relationships between our study's results and the conclusions obtained in the HK study.

Graphics are used to represent the data gathered in the measurement process. The resulting graphics present the gathered data *before* and *after* the changes applied to the pattern implementation (Sect. 2.4). The graphic Y-axis presents the absolute values gathered by the metrics. Each pair of bars is attached to a percentage value, which represents the difference between the AO and OO results. A positive percentage means that the AO implementation was superior, while a negative percentage means that the AO implementation was inferior. These graphics support

---

[1] From herein, we will use the terms "aspect-oriented solutions" and "object-oriented solutions" to refer to, respectively, the Aspect solutions and Java solutions.

an analysis of how the introduction of new classes and aspects affect both solutions with respect to the selected metrics. The results shown in the graphics were gathered according to the pattern point of view; that is, they represent the tally of metric values associated with all the classes and aspects for each pattern implementation.

For separation of concerns, we have verified the separation of each role of the patterns on the basis of the three metrics defined for this purpose (Sect. 2.3). For example, the isolation of the Mediator and Colleague roles was analyzed in the implementations of the Mediator pattern, while the modularization of the Context and State roles was investigated in the implementations of the State pattern. According the data gathered, the investigated patterns can be classified into 3 groups. Group 1 represents the patterns that the aspect-oriented solution provided better results (Sect. 3.1). Group 2 represents the patterns in which the OO solutions have shown as superior (Sect. 3.2). Group 3 involves the patterns in which the use of aspects did not impact the results (Sect. 3.3).

3.1 Group 1: Increased Separation

The first group encompasses all the patterns that aspect-oriented implementations exhibited better separation of concerns. This group includes the following list of 14 patterns: Decorator, Adapter, Prototype, Visitor, Proxy, Singleton, Mediator, Composite, Observer, Command, Iterator, CoR (Chain of Responsibility), Strategy and Memento. This list is decreasingly ordered by the measures for separation of concerns, starting from the design pattern that presents the best results for the aspect-oriented solution, the Decorator pattern.

Figures 4 and 5 depict the overall results for the AO and OO solutions based on the metrics. The figures only present a representative set of the patterns in this group. Note that the graphics present the measures before and after the execution of the changes. Figure 4a presents the CDC results, i.e., to what extent the pattern roles are isolated through the system components in both solutions. Figure 4b presents the CDO results, the degree of separation of the pattern roles through the system operations. Figure 5 illustrates the CDLOC measures – the tally of concern switches (transition points) through the lines of code.

Most of these graphics show significant differences in favor of the aspect-based solutions. These solutions require fewer components and operations than OO solutions to express these concerns. In addition, they require fewer switches between role concerns, and between role concerns and application concerns. An analysis of Figs. 4 and 5 show that the best improvements come primarily from isolating the pattern roles into the aspects. For example, the definition of the Component role required eight classes, while only two modular units were necessary to encapsulate this concern before the changes (Fig. 4a). It is equivalent to 67% in favor of the AO design for the Decorator pattern. In fact, most superimposed roles were better modularized in the AO solution, such as Mediator (8 against 2), Colleague (7 against 3), and Handler (9 against 3). The results were similar when analyzing separation of concerns over operations (Fig. 4b) and lines of code (Fig. 5). In addition, we can also observe that good results are achieved on the modularization of some defining roles, such as Decorator.

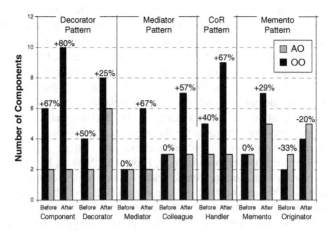

(a) Concern diffusion over components

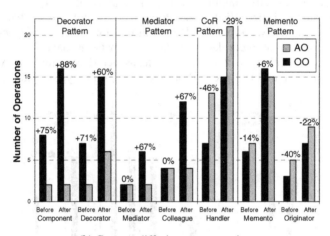

(b) Concern diffusion over operations

Fig. 4. Separation of concerns over components and operations (Group 1)

After a careful analysis of Figs. 4 and 5, we come to the conclusion that after the changes most AOP implementations isolated the roles 25% or higher than the OO implementations. There are some cases where the difference is even more striking — the superiority of AOP exceeds 70%. In some cases, such as the Colleague role, the AO solution is even better before the incorporation of new components. This problem happens in the OO solution because several operation implementations are intermingled with role-specific code. For example, the code associated with the control and coordination of the interobject interactions (Mediator pattern – Sect. 2.2) is amalgamated with the basic functionality of the application classes. It increases the number of transition points and the number of components and operations that deal with pattern-specific concerns.

The results also show that the overall performance of the AO solutions gradually improves as new components are introduced into the system. It means that as more components are included into an OO system, more role-related code is replicated through the system components. Thus a gradual improvement takes place in the AO solutions of the patterns. The series of small introduced changes (Sect. 2.4) affects negatively the performance of the OO solution and positively the AO solution. The changes lead to the degradation of the OO modularization of the pattern-related concerns. This observation provides evidence of the effectiveness of AO abstractions for segregating crosscutting structures for the patterns in this group.

Among the list of 14 patterns mentioned above, the first six are the patterns that achieved the best results: Decorator, Adapter, Prototype, Visitor, Proxy and Singleton. These patterns have several similar characteristics. They presented superior results for the AO solution both before and after the introduced changes. This means that the AO implementations of these patterns are superior even in simple pattern instances, i.e., circumstances where there are few application classes playing the pattern roles. In fact, the role-specific concerns are easier to separate in these patterns because the AspectJ constructs directly simplify the implementation of most of these patterns, namely Decorator, Adapter, Visitor and Proxy. As a result, the implementation of these patterns completely disappears [15], requiring fewer classes and operations to address the isolation of the roles. All these six patterns have another common characteristic: they either involve no reusable aspect (Decorator and Adapter) or involve very simple reusable aspects (Prototype, Visitor, Proxy, Singleton).

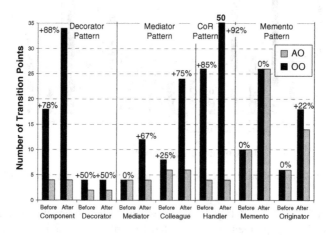

Fig. 5. Concern diffusion over LOC (Group 1)

The Decorator pattern is the representative of this kind of patterns in Figs. 4 and 5. Note that the AO solution for this pattern exhibits meaningful advantages on the modularization of both roles from all the perspectives: numbers of components (CDC), operations (CDO) and transition points (CDLOC). One additional observation is that these numbers remain unaltered as the change scenarios are applied to the AO implementation. For example, the absolute number of operations and components for specifying the Component role is the same before and after the scenarios in the AO design. The changes do not affect the measures. It demonstrates how well the AO abstractions localize these pattern roles. In addition, after the scenarios are applied, the absolute difference on the measures between AO and OO implementations tends to be higher in favor of the AO solutions than before the change scenarios.

The following five patterns in Group 1 – Mediator, Composite, Observer, Command and Iterator – expressed similar results. They manifested improved separation of concerns only after the introduced changes. In general, the use of aspects led to inferior or equivalent results before the application of the changes, but led to substantially superior outcomes after the changes. It happens because the AO implementations of these patterns involve generic aspects that are richer; they encapsulate more operations and LOC than the simple reusable aspects defined for the four patterns mentioned before in this group. In this way, the benefit of improved locality is observed in the AO solutions of these patterns only when complex instances of the patterns are used. The more pattern code can be captured in a reusable aspect, the less has to be duplicated in the participant classes.

The Mediator pattern represents these five patterns in Figs. 4 and 5. Note that after the changes, the isolation of the Mediator and Colleague roles with aspects was 60% higher than the OO solution for all the metrics. This is an interesting fact given that in these cases the values were equivalent in both OO and AO solutions before the implementation of the changes. The definition of the Colleague role required 12 classes, while only four aspects were able to encapsulate this concern. This result was similar in the other four patterns, i.e., absolute number of components (CDC) did not vary after the modifications in the AO solutions. This reflects the suitability of aspects for the complete separation of the roles associated with the five patterns. When new classes are introduced, they do not need to implement pattern-related code.

Finally, there were three AO solutions in this group (CoR, Strategy, and Memento) that, although provided overall improvements in the isolation of the roles, presented some negative results in terms of a specific measure. Figures 4 and 5 illustrate two examples: CoR and Memento. The AO implementation of CoR has fewer components (Fig. 4a) and transition points (Fig. 5) both before and after the changes. However, it has more operations involved in the implementation of the pattern role (Fig. 4b). The AO solution of Memento isolates well the Memento role for most the metrics (CDC and CDO). However, although the implementation of the Originator role with aspects led to fewer transition points (Fig. 5), the same observation does not happen to number of operations and components (Fig. 4).

3.2 Group 2: Decreased Separation

The second group includes design patterns in which AO implementations exhibited decreased separation of concerns. This group includes six patterns, namely Template Method, Abstract Factory, Factory Method, Bridge, Builder and Flyweight. In fact, the AspectJ implementations of the first five are mainly meant to explore AOP as an alternative solution to multiple inheritance, replacing abstract classes with interfaces and thereby increasing implementation flexibility [15]. Figure 6 depicts the CDC, CDO and CDLOC measures of separation of concerns for the pattern implementations in this group.

Although some measures presented similar results for the OO and AO solutions of these patterns, several measures presented differences in favor of OO implementations. As the pattern roles are already nicely realized in OO, these patterns could not be given more modularized aspect-oriented implementations. Thus the use of aspects does not bring apparent gains to these pattern implementations regarding to separation of concerns. On the contrary, the OO implementations, in general, provided better results, mainly with respect to the CDC measures (Fig. 6a).

The main reason for this result is that all the patterns in this group, except the Flyweight, are structurally similar: they have an additional aspect to replace the

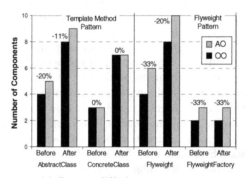

(a) Concern diffusion over components

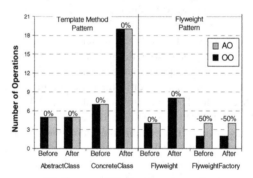

(b) Concern diffusion over operations

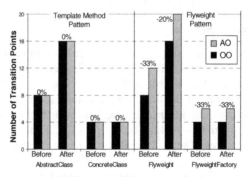

(c) Concern diffusion over LoC

Fig. 6. Separation of concerns (Group 2)

abstract class mentioned in the GoF solution by interfaces without losing the ability to associated (default) implementations to their methods [15]. For example, the Template Method pattern has an additional aspect that attaches the template method and its implementation to a component that plays the AbstractClass role, thereby allowing it to be an interface. Although this kind of aspects makes the patterns more flexible, it does not improve the separation of the pattern-specific concerns.

The Flyweight pattern is an exception in this group. The OO design provided better results than the AO design for all the measures. The superiority of the OO solution reaches 33% for most of the measures. It happens because the AO solution does not help to separate a crosscutting structure relative to the pattern roles. In fact, the classes playing the Flyweight role are similar in both implementations. The aspects have no pointcuts and advices, and the generic `FlyweightProtocol` aspect could be implemented as a simpler class. As a result, the additional components and operations introduced by the AO solution decreases the separation of concerns since the roles implementation are scattered over more design elements.

3.3 Group 3: No Effect

This group includes three patterns: Façade, Interpreter, and State. Overall, no significant difference was detected in favor of a specific solution; the results were mostly similar for the AO and OO implementations of these patterns. The AO and OO implementations of the Façade pattern are identical. There were some minor differences, as in the State pattern, but they were irrelevant (less than 5%). The outcomes of this group were highly different from the ones obtained in Group 1 (Sect. 3.1) because the OO implementations of the patterns do not exhibit significant crosscutting structures. The role-related code in these patterns affects a very small number of methods.

4 Results: Coupling, Cohesion and Size

This section presents the coupling, cohesion and size measures. We used graphics to present the data obtained before and after the systematic changes (Sect. 2.4), similarly to the previous section. The results represent the tally of metric values associated with all the classes and aspects for each pattern implementation, except the DIT metric. The DIT results represent the maximum value of this metric through the whole pattern implementation. In other words, it represents the higher inheritance depth achieved in a given AspectJ or Java implementation. The patterns were classified into five groups according to the similarity in their measures.

4.1 Group 1: Better Results for AO

The first group includes the Composite, Observer, Adapter, Mediator and Visitor patterns, which presented meaningful improvements with respect to the attributes coupling, cohesion and size in the AO solution. In some cases, the improvement was higher than 50%. Figure 7 shows the graphics with results for the Mediator and Visitor patterns, which represent this group.

In the AO implementation of the Mediator pattern, the major improvements were achieved in the CBC, LCOO, NOA and WOC measures. The use of aspects led to a 17% reduction of CBC in relation to the OO design. This occurs because the Colleague classes are unaware of the Mediator class in the AO design (Sect. 2.2), while in the OO implementation each Colleague holds a reference to the Mediator. Thus, all the Colleague classes are coupled to the Mediator class. In the same way, the AO implementation of the Visitor pattern led to a 32% reduction after the changes. The reason is that the Visitor classes are coupled to all the Element classes in the OO implementation. These couplings are not necessary in the AO solution.

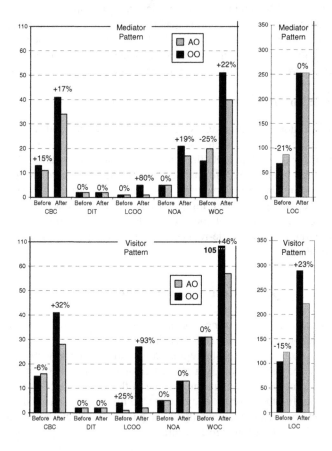

Fig. 7. The Mediator and Visitor patterns: coupling, cohesion and size (Group 1)

Note that inheritance was not affected by the use of aspects. The OO solution of the Mediator pattern used the interface implementation to define the Colleague and Mediator participants. The AO solution is based on specialization to define a concrete Mediator protocol (Sect. 2.2). As a result, the DIT was two for both solutions.

The AO solution was superior to the OO solution in terms of cohesion. The cohesion in the AO implementation was 80% higher than in the OO implementation because the Colleague and Mediator classes in the OO solution implement role-specific methods, which, in turn, are not related to the main functionality of the classes. An example is the setMediator() method, which is part of the Colleague role and is responsible for setting the Mediator reference (see Fig. 1). The AO design localizes these methods in the aspects that implement the roles, increasing the cohesion of both classes and aspects. Likewise, the OO solution of the Visitor pattern has a method defined in the Element classes to accept the Visitor objects. This method is not related to the main functionality of the Element classes and, therefore, does not access any attribute of these classes. In the AO solution, this method is moved to the aspect. Consequently, the cohesion of the Element classes in the OO implementation is inferior to the classes in the AO solution.

The number of attributes and weight of operations in the OO implementation of the Mediator pattern were, respectively, 19% and 22% higher than in the AO code after the introduction of new components. In the OO solution, each Colleague class needs both an attribute to hold the reference to its Mediator and a method to set this reference. These elements are not required in the Colleague classes of the aspect-oriented solution, because only the aspect controls the relationship between Colleagues and Mediators. A similar benefit was reached in the AO implementation of the other patterns in this group.

The coupling, cohesion and size improvements in the aspect-oriented solutions of the patterns in this group are directly related to the achieved separation of concerns for them (Sect. 3.1). The enhanced isolation of the pattern implementations directly contributed to (i) reduce the number of LOC, operations and attributes; (ii) improve the module cohesion by disentangling pattern-related concerns; and (iii) achieve reduced coupling (Fig. 7). For instance, as previously explained in this section, the coupling, cohesion and size of the Mediator pattern are improved because the pattern roles are better isolated in aspects and not spread over several classes. A similar result occurs in the other four patterns. For instance, in the Visitor pattern, the AO implementation solves the problem of code replication related to the implementation of the method that accepts the Visitor classes in every Element class. Hence after the changes the OO implementation had 23% more LOCs, and an inferior coupling in 46% (Fig. 7).

4.2 Group 2: Better Results for AO in Most Measures

This group encompasses the patterns in which AO solutions produced better results in most of the measures except in one metric. This group includes the Decorator, Proxy, Singleton and State patterns. The measures gathered from implementations of the Decorator, Proxy, Singleton were mostly similar. The AO implementation of these patterns showed improvements related to all metrics except the CBC metric. On the other hand, the AO solution of the State pattern did not show improvements only in the number of attributes. Figure 8 presents the results of the Decorator and State patterns as representative of this group.

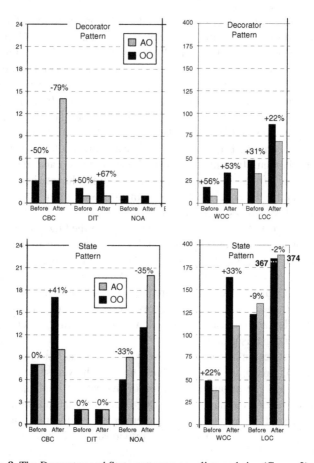

Fig. 8. The Decorator and State patterns: coupling and size (Group 2)

The AO implementations of the Decorator, Singleton and Proxy patterns manifest similar benefits to the patterns of Group 1 (Sect. 4.1). That is, the improvement in the separation of the pattern-specific code (Sect. 3.1) conducted to improvements in other attributes, such as, cohesion and size. However, as shown in Fig. 8 for the Decorator pattern, the CBC measures were inferior in the AO implementation: 50% and 79% before and after the changes, respectively. This problem occurs in the Decorator pattern because one of the Decorator aspects has to declare the precedence among all the Decorator aspects. Therefore, it is coupled to all the other aspects. In the Singleton pattern, there is an additional aspect per Singleton class. The coupling between the aspects and the Singleton classes increased the results of the CBC metric.

The measures concerning the State pattern provided peculiar results. Despite showing no improvements related to the separation of concerns metrics (Sect. 3.3), the AO implementation of the State pattern was superior in coupling, cohesion and weight of operations (Fig. 8). On the other hand, the OO implementation provided better results in two measures: NOA and LOC. The coupling in the OO solution is higher than in the AO solution because the classes representing the states are highly coupled to each other. This problem is overcome by the AO solution because the aspects modularize the state transitions (Fig. 9), minimizing the coupling between the pattern participants. Figure 9 shows that the coupling in the OO solution is 7 because each State class needs to have references to the other State classes.

It is important to highlight that the definition of the State pattern [9] does not specify which pattern participant defines the criteria for state transitions. In this way, it is possible to isolate the state transitions even in the Java solution by moving them from the "state" classes to the "context" class (when the criteria are fixed). However, even though it is possible to isolate the transitions in the "context object", the transitions can be, in several cases, more naturally implemented in the state classes due to a number of conditions/constraints specific to the state classes. The AspectJ solution supports an improved modularization of the state transitions in this second case.

With respect to WOC measures, the OO solution produced more complex operations because all the methods on the State classes have an additional parameter to receive the Context object in order to implement the state transition. It is not required in the AO design because a central aspect is responsible for managing the transitions between states.

From the NOA point of view, the OO design was superior because the AO design has additional attributes in the aspects to hold references to the State elements. This difference increases as new State elements are added to the system (Fig. 8). In spite of the fact that the State classes in the AO implementation have fewer lines of code, the OO implementation as a whole provided fewer LOCs. This occurs because the aspect, which manages the state transitions, has a high number of LOCs since: (i) it holds references to all the State classes, and (ii) it has one additional advice associated with methods of State classes.

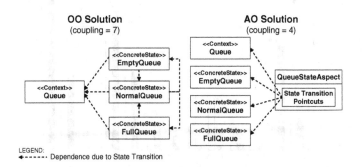

Fig. 9. Coupling in the state pattern: OO vs. AO

4.3 Group 3: Better Results for OO in Most Measures

This group includes the CoR, Command, Prototype and Strategy patterns. The measures gathered from the implementations of these patterns were similar in the sense that, in general, the OO implementations provided better or similar results. The AO solutions improved the results for only one size metric. The AO implementation of the CoR, Command and Strategy patterns required fewer attributes than the OO implementation (NOA metric), while the AO solution of the Prototype pattern involved fewer operations (WOC metric).

The CoR pattern is the representative element of this group. Figure 10 shows the results for this pattern. Note that the OO implementation had 75% more attributes than the AO implementation after the inclusion of new Handler classes. Nevertheless, the AO implementation showed inferior results concerning lines of code and weight of operations. Moreover, there was insignificant difference between the two solutions in terms of the coupling metrics (CBC and DIT).

As shown in Sect. 3.1, these patterns benefit from the AO implementation in terms of separation of concerns. However, those benefits were not sufficient to improve most of the other quality attributes. For instance, the OO implementation of the CoR pattern requires the incorporation of an attribute to hold a reference to its successor in the Handler class. In the AO implementation, the chain of successors is localized in an aspect, removing the successor attribute from the Handler classes. As a consequence, the number of attributes was lower in the AO implementation. However, the amount of additional operations required in the aspect to handle the chain of successors negatively affected the LOC and WOC measures. Furthermore, due to the coupling between the aspect and all the Handler classes, the AO solution did not provided significant improvements (CBC metric). This phenomenon also happened in the other patterns of this group. For instance, in the AO implementation of the Prototype pattern, the methods to clone the Prototype classes were localized in an aspect and not replicated in all the Prototype classes. However, this design choice was only sufficient to reduce the weight of operations (WOC metric).

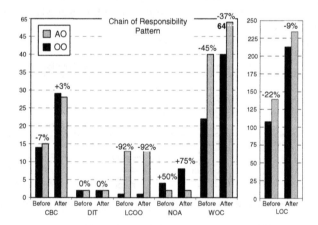

Fig. 10. The Chain of Responsibility pattern: coupling, cohesion and size (Group 3)

4.4 Group 4: Better Results for OO

The fourth group comprises the patterns that the AO implementation provided worse results related to coupling, cohesion, and size. This group includes the following list of eight patterns: Template Method, Abstract Factory, Bridge, Interpreter, Factory Method, Builder, Memento and Flyweight. The Template Method and Memento patterns represent this group in Fig. 11.

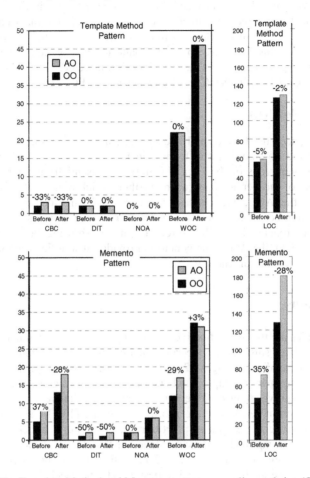

Fig. 11. The Template Method and Memento patterns: coupling and size (Group 4)

The measures of the Template Method, Abstract Factory, Bridge, Interpreter, Factory Method and Builder patterns exhibited minor differences in favor of the OO implementation. In fact, we have already mentioned in Sect. 3.2 that these patterns are already nicely realized in OO, and thus could not be given more modularized AO implementations. The AO implementation of the Template Method, for instance, showed higher coupling (33%) and more lines of code (5%) than the OO implementation. The other measures produced equal results for both solutions (see Fig. 11). This minor difference is due to the additional aspect which associates (default) implementation to the methods in the interface that plays the AbstractClass role.

The measures of the Flyweight and Memento patterns showed better results for the OO implementation. The AO implementation of the Flyweight pattern showed worse results mainly with respect to coupling. It is because an aspect is coupled to all Flyweight classes in order to introduce the Flyweight interface in them by means of the intertype declaration mechanism. The AO implementation of the Memento pattern showed the worst results when compared with the other AspectJ pattern implementations in this group. Removing the pattern-related code from the Originator classes and placing it in an aspect makes the design more complex. This is shown by the results of the CBC, DIT, WOC and LOC metric (see Fig. 11).

4.5 Group 5: No Effect

This group includes the Iterator and Façade patterns. The measures related to these patterns exhibited no significant difference in favor of a specific solution. The AO and OO implementations of the Façade pattern are essentially the same. In the AO implementation of the Iterator pattern, the method which returns a reverse iterator is removed from the Aggregate classes. These methods are localized in an aspect. However, the number of methods was not reduced since it was still necessary one method per Aggregate class. Therefore, in spite of showing better separation of concerns (Sect. 3.1), the AO implementation provided insignificant improvements in terms of coupling, cohesion and size.

5 Discussions

Empirical studies are the most effective way to supply evidence that may improve our understanding about software engineering phenomena [4, 23]. Although quantitative studies have some disadvantages [23], they are very useful because they boil a complex situation down to simple numbers that are easier to grasp and discuss. They supplement qualitative studies with empirical data. Quantitative studies investigating the implementation of design patterns as aspects are rare [15]. Most of the claims are supported by experience reports of practitioners, but there is a lack of quantitative research providing empirical evidence in favor of the claimed benefits. This section provides a more general analysis (Sect. 5.1) of the previously observed results in Sects. 3 and 4, some analysis of specific design patterns (Sect. 5.2), and discussions about the constraints on the validity of our empirical evaluation as well as lessons learned (Sect. 5.3).

5.1 General Analysis

This section presents an overall analysis of the results observed on the application of metrics for separation of concerns, coupling, cohesion and size. The general analysis also covers discussions on: the scalability of the pattern implementations (Sect. 5.1.2), the effects of the design pattern aspectization on different coupling dimensions (Sect. 5.1.4), reusability issues (Sect. 5.1.6), the interplay between these measures and a predictive model (Sect. 5.1.7), a comparative summary between this study's findings and the HK study's claims (Sect. 5.1.8), and the need for multidimensional assessments (Sect. 5.1.9).

5.1.1 Separable and Inseparable Concerns

Table 3 summarizes the findings on separation of concerns for each design pattern. This table complements the graphics presented in Sect. 3, which only shows the results for some representative patterns. The first three columns bring the gathered data for both AO and OO solutions with respect to all the three measures of separation of concerns: concern diffusion over components (CDC), concern diffusion over operations (CDO), and concern diffusion over lines of code (CDLOC). Table 3 focuses on the measures obtained after the changes (Sect. 2.4) introduced to the pattern implementations.

An additional goal of Table 3 is to provide a different perspective on the results obtained for separation of concerns. While the graphics in Sect. 3 show the measures in terms of each pattern role, Table 3 presents the values associated with the whole design pattern, i.e., the value shown in each cell represents the tally of the measures for all the roles of a design pattern. For example, consider the Mediator pattern: the graphic in Fig. 4a shows that, after the changes, the CDC measure for the Mediator role was 6 in the OO version against 2 of the AO version, and for the Colleague role was 7 in the OO version against 3 of the AO version. As a result, considering the two roles of the pattern, the final result indicates that the AO solution was superior – 5 against 13 of the OO solution, as illustrated in Table 3. This different perspective shows how the Java and AspectJ solutions were effective or not to modularize the pattern as a whole. It is worth recalling here that a higher value means that the implementation approach was inferior to modularize the pattern roles.

The last two columns of Table 3 are respectively concerned with the scalability criterion and with the indication of which implementation was superior. The scalability issue will be discussed in the next section. With respect to the last column, we have classified an AspectJ or Java solution as superior when it has achieved better results for most the measures when compared with the results of the other solution. The AspectJ solutions that achieved the best results, as discussed in Sect. 3.1, are marked with the symbol "+". The AspectJ implementations for these patterns were superior both before and after the introduced changes.

Table 3 shows that AspectJ implementations of 14 patterns have shown better results in terms of all the metrics for separation of concerns. In addition, the Java implementation of six patterns presented superior separation of roles (Sect. 3.2), and three patterns presented similar results in both implementations (Sect. 3.3). This observation provides evidence of the superior effectiveness of AO abstractions for segregating crosscutting structures relative to design patterns. Indeed, most of these results have confirmed the observations in the HK study in terms of the locality property.

However, the HK study also claimed that three additional patterns offered locality improvements in the respective AO implementations: Flyweight, State and Template Method. Our study's results somewhat contradict these claims (Table 3). The solution of patterns in Group 2 (Sect. 3.2), like Template Method, sounds to be natural in the OO fashion, and it does not seem reasonable or even possible to isolate the pattern roles into aspects. In fact, the AO solution of the Template Method is not aimed at improving the separation of the pattern roles, but increasing the pattern flexibility [15] (Sect. 3.2). The AO implementation of the Flyweight pattern is similar to the OO implementation with additional aspects that do not assist in the isolation of crosscutting pattern-specific concerns (Sect. 3.2). The separation of concerns in the AO version of the State pattern helps to separate state transitions, but the differences in the measures are not significant (Sect. 3.3).

Table 3. Overall results for separation of concerns

Design pattern	CDC		CDO		CDLOC		Scalability		Superior solution
	OO	AO	OO	AO	OO	AO	OO	AO	
Abstract Factory	14	16	35	35	34	34	No	No	OO
Adapter[#]	8	7	30	22	32	16	No	Yes	AO[+]
Bridge	12	13	24	26	16	16	No	No	OO
Builder	9	10	29	30	8	8	Yes	Yes	OO
CoR[#]	9	3	15	21	50	4	No	Yes	AO
Command[#]	17	11	23	16	38	21	No	Yes	AO
Composite[#]	18	9	149	28	70	48	No	No	AO
Decorator[#]	18	8	31	8	38	6	No	Yes	AO[+]
Façade	Same implementations for Java and AspectJ								
Factory Method	14	16	23	23	18	18	No	No	OO
Flyweight[#]	10	13	10	12	20	26	No	No	OO
Interpreter	13	13	26	26	38	38	No	No	=
Iterator[#]	10	6	20	20	18	14	No	No	AO
Mediator[#]	13	5	18	6	36	10	No	Yes	AO
Memento[#]	11	10	23	24	44	40	No	No	AO
Observer[#]	14	9	49	9	92	20	No	Yes	AO
Prototype[#]	7	3	7	2	30	8	No	Yes	AO[+]
Proxy[#]	11	11	38	19	8	2	No	Yes	AO[+]
Singleton[#]	6	6	6	1	6	2	Yes	Yes	AO[+]
State[#]	10	10	78	78	30	30	No	No	=
Strategy[#]	14	12	20	17	18	16	No	No	AO
Template Method[#]	15	16	24	24	20	20	No	No	OO
Visitor[#]	20	9	50	23	34	14	No	Yes	AO[+]
Success total	6 vs. 12		5 vs. 11		1 vs. 14		2 vs. 11		6 vs. 14

\# The design pattern contains one or two superimposed roles.
+ The AO solutions that achieved the best results.

An additional interesting observation in our study is that sometimes the pattern roles are expressed separately as aspects, but it remains nontrivial to specify how these separate aspects should be composed with the application classes into a simple manner. A lot of effort is required to compose the participant classes and the aspects that modularize the pattern roles. For example, the AO design of the Memento pattern provided better separation of the pattern-related concerns (Sect. 3.1). However, although the AO solution isolates the pattern roles in the aspects, it resulted in higher complexity in terms of coupling (CBC), inheritance (DIT) and lines of code (LOC), as described in Sect. 4.4. The same observation can be made for the Strategy and CoR patterns (Sect. 4.3). Hence, there are some cases where the separation of the pattern-related concerns leads to more complex design solutions.

The last line of Table 3 also counts how many patterns each solution was superior with respect to each metric (3 first cells), and in general terms (last cell). These values show that around 50% of the AO solutions have not shown improvements in terms of the CDO metric. In these cases, either the OO implementation required fewer operations to handle the pattern-related concerns than the AO implementation or they were similar. An analogous situation occurred in the CDC measures. The superiority of the AO solutions seems to be more compelling in the CDLOC measures: 14 against 1. The frequency of concern switches in the AspectJ implementations was drastically reduced. It means that there is a tendency on several AspectJ implementations to not reduce the number of operations implementing a concern. In general, it seems that the most recurring benefits come from *disentangling* the pattern-related concerns and other application concerns.

5.1.2 Scalability
As explained in Sect. 2.4, we changed both original Java and AspectJ implementations of the 23 patterns to investigate the scalability of those solutions to more complex instances of the patterns. In the context of this study, scalability is used to determine whether the introduction of the changes (described in Table 2) in a given implementation did not require modifying more components in that implementation than the number of elements introduced. In other words, we considered here a solution as scalable if the evolution of the implementation did not impact a number of modules that is higher than the number of modules being introduced.

We have used the CDLOC metric as the main mechanism to assess the scalability of the OO and AO versions. For example, Fig. 5 shows that the total number of concern switches for the implementation of the Mediator pattern, considering both roles before the changes, is 12 in the OO version and 10 in the AO version. After the changes, the number of switches remains 10 in the AO solution. However, it grows to 36 in the OO version, which is higher than the number of introduced changes (8 changes – i.e., 4 mediators and 4 colleagues). As a result, Table 3 indicates that the OO solution is not scalable, while the AO solution is considered scalable. In fact, the evolution of the AspectJ version occurred in a modular manner. All the separation of concerns measures, not only CDLOC, remained unaltered as the change scenarios were applied to the implementation, as illustrated in Figs. 4a, 4b and 5. The changes did not affect the measures. We have drawn a similar conclusion for the AO implementation of the Decorator pattern in Sect. 3.1; it is also ranked as scalable in opposite to the corresponding OO version.

Table 3 summarizes the scalability results for all the OO and AO solutions. Some AO solutions that were classified as superior did not achieve a good scalability. For the 14 AspectJ solutions that were considered as superior, 11 implementations were also classified as scalable. Only two Java solutions, Builder and Singleton, were effectively scalable with respect to the CDLOC measures. Although the AO solutions of the Composite, Iterator and Memento presented a better separation of the pattern roles than the respective OO solutions, they are not very scalable since they also require reasonable efforts to support the separation of the pattern roles. For instance, Fig. 5 illustrates this scalability problem for the Memento pattern. The CDLOC measures show that a number of extra changes were also required in the AspectJ version. A similar problem was detected for the Iterator and Composite. We do not extensively reproduce all the detailed measurements here. The complete description of the data gathered is available at [28].

5.1.3 Reducing Coupling and Increasing Cohesion

Table 4 summarizes the conclusions related to coupling and cohesion for each design pattern. Like Table 3, it complements the graphics presented in Sect. 4, which shows only partial results. The first two columns respectively describe the results with respect to intercomponent coupling (CBC) and inheritance-related coupling (DIT) for both AO and OO solutions. The third column presents the gathered data for the cohesion metric (LCOO). Table 4 also concentrates on the description of the measures obtained after the changes.

Table 4. Overall results for coupling and cohesion

Design pattern	CBC		DIT		LCOO		Superior solution
	OO	AO	OO	AO	OO	AO	
Abstract Factory	37	44	7	7	1	1	OO
Adapter#	5	5	2	1	–	–	AO
Bridge	17	18	2	2	0	0	OO
Builder	2	3	2	2	12	6	OO
CoR#	29	28	2	2	1	13	OO
Command#	21	34	7	7	3	4	OO
Composite#	47	23	2	2	463	82	AO
Decorator#	3	14	3	1	0	0	AO
Façade	Same implementations for Java and AspectJ						
Factory Method	22	24	2	2	3	0	OO
Flyweight#	11	17	2	2	0	1	OO
Interpreter	17	23	5	5	0	0	OO
Iterator#	12	13	2	2	0	0	=
Mediator#	41	34	2	2	5	1	AO
Memento#	13	18	1	2	0	0	OO
Observer#	45	40	2	2	80	30	AO
Prototype#	7	13	2	2	0	0	OO
Proxy#	11	39	2	2	0	0	AO
Singleton#	11	22	2	2	5	0	AO
State#	17	10	2	2	106	93	AO
Strategy#	18	32	2	2	–	–	OO
Template Method#	2	3	2	2	–	–	OO
Visitor#	41	28	2	2	27	2	AO
Success total	**15 vs. 6**		**1 vs. 2**		**3 vs. 8**		**12 vs. 9**

\# The design pattern contains one or two superimposed roles.

It is interesting to observe that the intercomponent coupling was weaker in 15 Java solutions against 6 AspectJ implementations. The DIT values were similar for both versions in most the measures. With respect to the cohesion metric, the AspectJ solutions achieved a better score: eight implementations were more cohesive against only three Java implementations. As indicated in Table 4, it was not possible to measure the cohesion of a few solutions because either there was no attribute defined in those implementations or there were modules with a single method. As explained in Sect. 2.3, our selected cohesion metric captures the closeness between internal methods by checking accesses to the same attributes. Considering all the coupling and cohesion measures, only five AspectJ solutions clearly presented weaker coupling and stronger cohesion, namely Mediator, Observer, State, Visitor, and Composite.

Finally, based on Tables 3 and 4 and on the interplay of the results in Sects. 3 and 4, we can conclude that the use of aspects provided better coupling and cohesion results for the patterns with high interaction between the roles in their original definition. In fact, the Mediator, Observer, State, Visitor and Composite patterns are examples of this kind of pattern. The Mediator pattern, for instance, exhibits high inter-role interaction: each Colleague collaborates with the Mediator, which in turn collaborates with all the Colleagues. The use of AOP was useful to reduce the coupling between the participants in the pattern and to increase their cohesion, since the aspect code modularizes the collaboration protocol between the pattern roles. Figure 9 illustrates how the aspect was used to reduce the coupling of the OO solution of the State pattern. On the other hand, the use of aspects did not succeed for improving coupling and cohesion in the patterns whose roles are not highly interactive. This is the case for the Prototype and Strategy patterns and the patterns in Group 4, presented in Sect. 4.4.

5.1.4 Inheritance Coupling: A Different Perspective

Given the results obtained from the DIT measures, which did not show considerable differences between AspectJ and Java implementations, we have decided afterwards to use another classical metric: Number of Children (NOC) [5]. This measure counts the number of modules that extends a module using inheritance. Table 5 presents the NOC measures for the OO and AO versions of all the pattern implementations. It also compares the DIT values with the NOC values.

From the NOC point of view, it is clear that the use of AO abstractions significantly reduces the use of inheritance as extension mechanism. While AspectJ solutions tend to present a stronger intercomponent coupling (Sect. 5.1.3) since they heavily rely on pointcuts and advice to support the specification of extensions and refinements to the affected modules, the Java implementations tend to present a stronger inheritance coupling. This observation motivates the need for further empirical case studies that evaluate the trade-offs of using each of these different extension mechanisms with respect to distinct quality attributes, such as understandability, reusability, maintainability, and reliability.

5.1.5 Aspects and Size Attributes

The reduction in the program size in general decreases the likelihood of developers introducing errors into the system [25]. Table 6 presents the overall results for size-related measures in terms of each pattern. Section 4 presented the size results associated with coupling and cohesion. Table 6 brings a new view for our assessment because it classifies the pattern implementations only in terms of size-related programming efforts. The columns respectively present the results with respect to number of attributes (NOA), complexity of operations (WOC) and lines of code LOC).

Table 5. Results for two inheritance-related measures

Design pattern	DIT		NOC		Superior solution
	OO	AO	OO	AO	
Abstract Factory	7	7	6	6	=
Adapter[#]	2	1	1	0	AO
Bridge	2	2	8	8	=
Builder	2	2	6	6	=
CoR[#]	2	2	7	1	AO
Command[#]	7	7	6	1	AO
Composite[#]	2	2	6	1	AO
Decorator[#]	3	1	8	0	AO
Façade	Same implementations for Java and AspectJ				
Factory Method	2	2	6	6	=
Flyweight[#]	2	2	6	7	OO
Interpreter	5	5	9	9	=
Iterator[#]	2	2	6	3	AO
Mediator[#]	2	2	10	1	AO
Memento[#]	1	2	0	3	OO
Observer[#]	2	2	10	3	AO
Prototype[#]	2	2	6	1	AO
Proxy[#]	2	2	9	6	AO
Singleton[#]	2	2	5	10	OO
State[#]	2	2	7	7	=
Strategy[#]	2	2	6	1	AO
Template Method[#]	2	2	6	6	=
Visitor[#]	2	2	10	10	=
Success total	**1 vs. 2**		**3 vs. 11**		**3 vs. 11**

The design pattern contains one or two superimposed roles.

We have found that the use of aspects has a considerable impact on the size attributes of the pattern implementations In general, the AO solutions were superior with the exception of lines of code. For 7 of the patterns, the AO solutions had fewer LOC than the OO solutions, which were superior in 14 cases. However, for these 14 implementations, the difference was not relevant in several cases. In fact, the discrepancy was evident (i.e., more than 10%) only in 1 case: the Memento pattern (Table 6). For ten of the patterns, the AspectJ implementations had fewer attributes than the Java implementations. Only one OO solution was superior in terms of NOA. For 12 of the patterns, the AO implementation reduced the number of operations and respective parameters (WOC metric). The OO implementation provided better results for seven patterns with respect to the WOC metric.

The last column of Table 6 indicates which solution was superior for each pattern considering all the three size measures. Similarly to Tables 4 and 5, we have classified an AspectJ or Java solution as superior when it has achieved better results for most the measures when compared with the results of the other solution. We have only considered that an implementation was better than the other when the difference between two values for the same metric was equal or higher than 10%. The last cell of Table 6 shows the final result: the AO solutions succeeded in ten cases against four for the OO solutions.

Table 6. Overall results for size measures

Design pattern	NOA		WOC		LOC		Superior solution
	OO	AO	OO	AO	OO	AO	
Abstract Factory	9	9	37	41	231	265	OO
Adapter[#]	3	1	34	32	67	61	AO
Bridge	1	1	40	44	156	161	OO
Builder	7	7	50	51	168	177	=
CoR[#]	8	2	40	64	213	234	=
Command[#]	6	4	26	29	198	206	=
Composite[#]	19	12	169	63	501	283	AO
Decorator[#]	1	0	34	16	88	69	AO
Façade	Same implementations for Java and AspectJ						
Factory Method	1	1	17	17	135	146	=
Flyweight[#]	7	7	30	36	119	132	OO
Interpreter	14	14	99	99	216	219	=
Iterator[#]	9	9	50	53	164	163	=
Mediator[#]	21	17	51	40	253	253	AO
Memento[#]	6	6	32	31	128	179	OO
Observer[#]	26	21	134	117	363	265	AO
Prototype[#]	6	6	38	33	142	147	AO
Proxy[#]	9	3	105	38	248	190	AO
Singleton[#]	30	26	25	21	238	251	AO
State[#]	13	20	164	110	367	374	=
Strategy[#]	5	1	62	58	251	264	AO
Template Method[#]	0	0	46	46	125	128	=
Visitor[#]	13	13	105	57	289	222	AO
Success total	1 vs. 10		7 vs. 12		14 vs. 7		4 vs. 10

\# The design pattern contains one or two superimposed roles.

5.1.6 Reusability Issues

The HK study observed reusability improvements in the AspectJ versions of 12 patterns by enabling a core part of the pattern implementation to be abstracted into reusable code (Sect. 2.2). In our study, expressive reusability was observed only in four patterns: Mediator, Observer, Composite and Visitor. These patterns were also qualified as reusable in the HK study and have several characteristics in common: (i) defined as reusable abstract aspects, (ii) improved separation of concerns (Sect. 3.1), (iii) low coupling – CBC – and high cohesion – LCOO (Sect. 4.1), and (vi) decreased values for the LOC and WOC measures as the changes are applied. Expressive reuse is evident when the extension or customization of existing components to include new functionalities requires the implementation of few lines of code, operations, attributes, classes and the like.

However, note that in our investigation the presence of generic abstract aspects has not necessarily led to improved reusability in several cases. The Flyweight, Command, CoR, Memento, Prototype, Singleton and Strategy patterns have abstract aspects and were ranked as "reusable" patterns in the HK study. In contrast, an analysis of the results presented in Sects. 3 and 4 leads to contrary conclusions for these patterns. In general, reusable elements lead to less programming effort by requiring fewer operations and lines of code to be written. However, the LOC and WOC measures of the AO implementations of these patterns were higher than in the respective OO implementations both before and after the changes. In fact, the abstract aspects associated with these patterns are very simple and do not enable a reasonable degree of reuse.

5.1.7 Superimposed Roles as a Predictive Model?

Determining when an AO technique is useful in a given context is a challenging task. The HK study has tried to establish a predictive model for helping the designers to decide when AspectJ should be used in design pattern implementations. According to this preceding study, the *presence of superimposed roles* (Sect. 2.1) seems to be a determining factor in such a decision-making process. Participant classes have their own functionalities outside the pattern scope in addition to the incorporation of pattern-related superimposed behavior. The OO version of the pattern implementation forces each of these classes to implement at least two concerns: the original responsibility and the pattern-specific behavior. The HK study claims that the AspectJ solution allows for the improved modularization of the superimposed roles.

Various flavors of our empirical study can be used to support or refute this claim, including the separation of concerns measures (Sect. 3), and the coupling, cohesion, and size measures (Sect. 4). In general, the results presented in Table 3 do not accredit this predictive model as absolute. In the table, the 17 patterns with superimposed roles are marked with "#". Some patterns that encompass superimposed roles achieved improved modularity in AspectJ implementations, namely Adapter, Decorator, Proxy, Visitor, Composite, Mediator, Singleton and Observer. Indeed, for seven of them (except the Composite and Iterator patterns), the AO solution has scaled up well (Table 3). However, seven of them did not reach convincing modularity improvements: Templated Method, Command, Flyweight, Memento, Strategy, CoR and Prototype. Moreover, the AspectJ version of the State pattern has not exhibited improved separation of concerns, when the aspectization of the Iterator pattern has presented poor coupling (CBC metric) and more complexity in the operation definitions (WOC metric). As a result, there is no evidence that the presence of superimposition should be considered as the sole determining factor to use AO abstractions to implement design patterns.

Analyzing simultaneously Tables 3 and 4 and according to the discussions in the previous subsections, it clearly seems that other important factors should be considered as part of a predictive model. Coupling and cohesion should be also considered when deciding for the aspectization of the design patterns since the more successful AspectJ implementations were the ones where there was a higher inter-role interaction (Sect. 5.1.3). The coordinated analysis of these factors would certainly result in a more consistent prediction mechanism according to our findings.

5.1.8 Comparison with the HK Study

Through the replication of case studies with similar goals, the AOSD community can build an experience factory of empirical findings. In this context, when performing systematic case studies it is important to compare the new results with those of previous studies so that we can effectively build a body of knowledge about the theme under assessment. This information is also important to researchers and practitioners who intend to replicate this experiment. This section summarizes the outcomes of our study that confirms, contradicts or refines the claims in the HK study [15]. We have focused only on three issues where there was a direct intersection in the findings:

   (i) While the HK study has found improved separation of concerns in 17 AspectJ pattern implementations, our study detected only 14 improvements (Sect. 5.1.1).

  (ii) The first study ranked 12 AspectJ solutions as reusable against 4 of this study (Sect. 5.1.6).

 (iii) The findings in this study suggest that the original prediction model, presented by the HK study, should be refined to also consider coupling and cohesion (Sect. 5.1.7).

The differences in the two studies are mainly because the HK study has used only simple pattern instances, which did not allow a clear understanding of the benefits and drawbacks of the aspect-oriented implementations. In addition, the authors took a narrow view of reusability, and the definition of the proposed predictive model was naturally biased by the role-oriented strategy that they have used to "aspectize" the design patterns.

5.1.9 Need for Multidimensional Analysis

As discussed in Sect. 5.1.7, it seems imperative to analyze other software attributes when assessing AO solutions. The HK study has centered the comparative analysis only on separation of concerns, and how the achieved separation helps to improve directly associated high-level qualities, such as (un)pluggability and composability. Lopes [24] has also carried out a case study that rests only on separation of concerns as assessment criteria. However, based on the results of this study (Sects. 3 and 4) and the discussion above, it seems clear that the analysis of other software dimensions or attributes, such as coupling and internal complexity of operations, are extremely important to compare AO and OO designs. In fact, the interaction between the aspects and the classes is sometimes so intense that the separation of aspects in the source code seems to be a more complex solution with respect to other software attributes.

5.2 Analysis of Specific Patterns

The measurements in this study were also important to assess the AO implementation of each design pattern in particular. We have found that some problems in the AO solutions are not related to the AO paradigm itself, but to some design or implementation decisions taken in the HK implementations. In this sense, quantitative assessments are also useful to capture opportunities for refactoring in AO software, for discarding a specific solution or for just clarifying important limitations of the solution. This section presents some examples of how the metrics used in this quantitative study were useful to support either the refactoring (Sects. 5.2.1 and 5.2.2) or the discarding (Sects. 5.2.3–5.2.6) of some AO solutions of the GoF patterns.

5.2.1 Prototype

The use of the selected metrics for separation of concerns was important to detect remaining crosscutting concerns relative to the design patterns. For example, the original AspectJ implementation of the Prototype pattern left the declaration of the `Cloneable` interface, which is a pattern-specific responsibility, in the description of the application-specific classes. This solution was refactored based on the use of an intertype declaration in order to improve the separation of concerns, overcoming the crosscutting problem present in the original version of the AspectJ implementation [15].

5.2.2 Chain of Responsibility and Memento

The coupling measures were also important to detect opportunities for improvements in the AO implementations. For example, the implementations of some client classes, such as in the CoR and Memento patterns, have explicit references to the aspects implementing the pattern roles that increase the system coupling. These references are used in the client classes to trigger aspect initializations. This kind of coupling is unnecessary and could be avoided. The aspects associated with these patterns could incorporate, in addition to the initialization methods in the aspects, the definition of simple pointcuts to capture the joinpoints where the initializations should be triggered. This finding was also supported by the metrics for separation of concerns.

5.2.3 Flyweight and Interpreter

The presence of several negative results can also serve as warnings of unhelpful designs. As mentioned before, the AspectJ implementation of the Flyweight pattern did not provide evident benefits. All the metrics for separation of concerns (Sect. 3.2) and almost all the metrics for coupling, cohesion and size (Sect. 4.4) supported this finding.

In the same way, the metrics did not show advantages for the AO solution of the Interpreter pattern. In fact, there is no difference between the AO and OO implementations in terms of the structure of this pattern. This claim is supported by similar results for all the metrics. There are minor differences in favor of the OO version in terms of coupling and size. This difference is caused by the use of an aspect to attach methods to the participant classes by means of the intertype declaration mechanism. However, this aspect does not change the OO structure of the pattern. It is only used to add methods in the participant classes without changing them. Therefore, the AO solution is not useful for removing pattern code from the participant classes. Actually, in this aspect code there is a comment where Hannemann and Kiczales claim that, due the very nature of the Interpreter pattern, using aspect to remove the pattern code from the participants does not work nicely [15].

5.2.4 Strategy

As stated earlier, for some patterns, the AO solution was more complex than the OO solution in terms of coupling and size. This problem occurred for the Strategy pattern and was detected with the help of the coupling between components (CBC) and lines of code (LOC) metrics. The results of these metrics showed high values for the concrete aspect used to assign the roles to the Strategy and Context classes and trigger the execution of the strategy algorithm. In order to choose what is the strategy to be executed for a given Context class, this aspect uses a sequence of "if" statements and references to all Strategy classes. This design is less flexible than the OO design since this aspect has to be changed whenever a new Strategy class is created.

5.2.5 Command

The problem of the aspect-oriented solution of the Command pattern is similar to the problem described for the Strategy pattern (Sect. 5.2.4). The aspects, which modularize pattern roles, are highly coupled to the other elements in the design. In the case of the Command pattern, a concrete aspect is coupled to all Invoker, Receiver and Command classes. As a consequence, adding new participants to an instance of the AspectJ version of this pattern requires more effort than to an instance of the Java version. This occurs because the aspect needs to be inevitably changed.

Another deficiency of the AO version of this pattern concerns to the use of parameters on the `execute()` method of the Command classes. In the AspectJ implementation, the Invoker classes are not aware of the command execution as they are in the OO implementation. Instead, the execution of the commands is triggered by the aspects. This design decision does not allow the Invokers to pass information of their context to the commands as parameters of the `execute()` method. Thus, if the Command classes need information from the context of the Invokers, this AO solution of the Command pattern should not be used.

5.2.6 Decorator

The AO implementation of the Decorator pattern showed better results for most metrics. However the inferior results obtained for the coupling between components (CBC) metric highlight an important limitation of this design. One of the Decorator aspects is coupled to all other aspects, since it determines the order in which the decorators are applied to the component by means of the `declare precedence` construct. Therefore, this aspect has to be changed whenever a new decorator is created. Besides, this design is very rigid in the sense that the decorators must be applied in the same order for every component. Hence, if it is necessary to apply decorators in different orders, this AO solution should be discarded.

5.3 Study Constraints and Lessons Learned

Concerning our experimental assessment, there is one general type of criticism that could be applied to the used software metrics (Sect. 2.3). This refers to theoretical arguments leveled at the use of conventional size metrics (e.g., LOC), as they are applied to traditional (non-AO software) development. Despite, or possibly even because of, simplicity of these metrics, it has been subjected to severe criticism [37]. In fact, these measures are sometimes difficult to evaluate with respect to a software quality attribute. For example, the LOC measures are difficult to interpret since sometimes a high LOC value means improved modularization, but sometimes it means code replication.

However, in spite of the well-known limitations of these metrics, we have learned that their application cannot be analyzed in isolation, and they have shown themselves to be extremely useful when analyzed in conjunction with the other used metrics. In addition, some researchers (such as Henderson-Sellers [16]) have criticized the cohesion metric as being without solid theoretical bases and lacking empirical validation. However, we understand this issue as a general research problem in terms of cohesion metrics. In the future, we intend to use other emerging cohesion metrics based on program dynamics.

We have also learned some lessons when using the separation of concerns metrics. We have observed that these three metrics complement each other. CDC and CDO respectively measure the number of components and operations that implement a concern. However, a concern may be spread through many classes, but may not be tangled with other concerns, since these components and operations may only implement a single concern. The isolate use of CDC and CDO are not enough to capture the noncrosscutting nature of such a concern; even worse, they will likely provide false warnings to the AO designers. In this way, CDLOC metric complements CDC and CDO metrics by measuring if the concern is tangled with other concerns. Therefore, these metrics are complementary since we need to measure both degrees of scattering and tangling in order to verify whether a concern is well modularized. In addition, CDC and CDO also complement each other because a concern may be scattered over few components but may affect many operations in those components. This situation was observed in the AO solution for the Chain of Responsibility pattern, where Handler role was implemented by few aspects but scattered over many operations, indeed, more operations than the OO solution.

The limited size and complexity of the examples used in the implementations may restrict the extrapolation of our results. In addition, our assessment is restricted to the specific pattern instances at hand. However, while the results may not be directly generalized to the context of real-world systems and professional developers, these representative examples allow us to make useful initial assessments of whether the use of aspects for the modularization of classical design patterns would be worth studying further. In spite of its limitations, the study constitutes an important initial empirical work and is complementary to qualitative work (e.g., [15]) previously performed. In addition, although the replication is often desirable in experimental studies, it is not a major problem in the context of our study due to the nature of our investigation. Design patterns are generic solutions and, as a consequence, exhibit similar structures across the different kinds of applications where they are used.

Finally, we have also learned that some problems may be directly related to the programming language used in this study. There is a pressing need to perform similar studies applying other AO programming languages, such as Hyper/J [18] and Caesar [26]. Each of these languages has different features that certainly impact on the pattern implementations with respect to the quality software attributes investigated in this quantitative study. In fact, other quantitative studies on the aspectization of design patterns are needed; for example, it would be important to investigate whether and how the AO solutions scale in real large-scale systems. In this sense, it would be possible to quantify the effects of modularizing pattern-related crosscutting concerns with aspects in systems where the pattern implementations are not simple pattern instances and are inserted in richer application contexts. In addition, it would be important to explore and assess the use of aspects when combining the use of two or more design patterns, as was done in [21] where an OO version of the Builder pattern and an AO version of the Decorator pattern were composed.

6   Related Work

There is little related work focusing either on the quantitative assessment of AO solutions in general, or on the empirical investigation of using aspects to modularize crosscutting concerns of classical design patterns. Up to now, most empirical studies involving aspects rest on subjective criteria and qualitative investigation. In a previous work [30], we have quantitatively analyzed only six patterns. The present paper presents a complete study involving all the 23 design patterns. There are some other works [13, 14, 17, 27] that investigate the interplay between aspects and design patterns. However, they focus on specific patterns and do not provide systematic quantitative assessments.

One of the first case studies was conducted by Kersten and Murphy [21]. They built a Web-based learning system using AspectJ. In this study, they discussed the effect of aspects on their OO practices and described some rules they employed to achieve their goals of modifiability and maintainability using aspects. Since several design patterns were used in the design of the system, they considered which of them should be expressed as classes and which should be expressed as aspects. They found that Builder, Composite, Façade and Strategy patterns [9] were more easily expressed as classes, once these patterns had little or no crosscutting behaviors. We have found here similar results for the Strategy, Builder and Façade patterns (Sects. 3 and 4). However, the AO implementation of the Composite pattern achieved better separation of concerns in our study.

Soares et al. [32] reported their experience using AspectJ to implement distribution and persistence aspects in a Web-based information system. They implemented the system in Java using specific design patterns and restructured it with AspectJ. They argued that the AspectJ implementation of the system bring significant advantages with the corresponding pure Java implementation.

Garcia et al. [11] have presented a quantitative study designed to compare the maintenance and reuse support of a pattern-oriented approach and an AO approach for a multiagent system. The subjects in the study used both approaches to try to modularize agent-related concerns, including autonomy, interaction, mobility, learning, adaptation and collaboration. They used an assessment framework that includes the same metrics suite used in our study. The results showed that the AO approach allowed the construction of the investigated system with improved modularization of the crosscutting agent-specific concerns. The use of aspects resulted in superior separation of the agent-related concerns, lower coupling (although less cohesive) and fewer lines of code. However, their study was also not focused on the use of aspects to isolate the crosscutting concerns relative to classical design patterns.

Zhao and Xu [35, 36] have proposed new cohesion measures that consider the peculiarities of the AO abstractions and mechanisms. Their metrics are based on a dependence model for AO software that consists of a group of dependence graphs; each of them can be used to explicitly represent various dependence relations at different levels of an AO program. Also, the cohesion measures [36] proposed by the authors are formally defined. The authors have shown that their measures satisfy some properties that good measures should have. However, these metrics have not yet been validated or applied to the assessment of realistic AO systems.

7 Conclusion

This paper presented a quantitative study comparing the AO and OO implementations of the GoF patterns. The results have shown that most AO implementations provided improved separation of concerns. However, some patterns resulted in higher coupled components, more complex operations and more LOCs in the AO solutions. Another important conclusion of this study is that separation of concerns cannot be taken as the only factor to conclude for the use of aspects. It must be analyzed in conjunction with other important factors, including coupling, cohesion and size. Sometimes, the separation achieved with aspects can generate more complicated designs. Hence, based on our analysis, many AO implementations present implementation alternatives with different tradeoffs from their OO equivalents. Also, since this is a first exploratory study, to further confirm the findings, other rigorous and controlled experiments are needed.

It is important to notice that from this experience, especially in a nonrigorous area such as software engineering, general conclusions cannot be drawn. The scope of our experience is indeed limited to (a) the patterns selected for this comparative study, (b) the specific implementations from the GoF book [9] and the HK study [15], (c) the Java and AspectJ programming languages, and (d) a given subset of application scenarios that were taken from our development background. However, the goal was to provide some evidence for a more general discussion of what benefits and dangers the use of AO abstractions might create, as well as what and when features of the AO paradigm might be useful for the modularization of classical design patterns. Finally, it should also be noted that properties such as reliability must be also examined before one could establish preference recommendations of one approach relative to the other.

Acknowledgments. We would like to thank Jan Hannemann and Gregor Kiczales for making the pattern implementations available, and Brian Henderson-Sellers and Barbara Kitchenham for the discussions on the selection of the software metrics. This work has been partially supported by CNPq-Brazil under grant No. 381724/04-2 for Alessandro, grant No. 140214/04-6 for Cláudio and under grant No. 140252/03-7 for Uirá. The authors are also supported by the ESSMA Project under grant 552068/02-0.

References

[1] Aspect-Oriented Design Pattern Implementations. http://www.cs.ubc.ca/~jan/AODPs/. Cited May 2005

[2] AspectJ Team. The AspectJ Guide. http://eclipse.org/aspectj/

[3] Basili V., Briand, L., Melo W. A validation of object-oriented design metrics as quality indicators. *IEEE Transactions on Software Engineering*, 22(10):751–761, 1996

[4] Basili V., Selby R., Hutchins D. Experimentation in software engineering. *IEEE Transactions on Software Engineering*, SE-12, 733–743, 1986

[5] Chidamber S., Kemerer C. A metrics suite for OO design. *IEEE Transactions on Software Engineering*, 20(6):476–493, 1994

[6] Fenton N., Pfleeger S. Software metrics: A rigorous practical approach. PWS, London 1997

[7] Figueiredo E., Garcia A., Sant'Anna C., Kulesza U., and Lucena C. Assessing aspect-oriented artifacts: Towards a tool-supported quantitative method. In: *QAOOSE.05: Proceedings of the 9th ECOOP Workshop on Quantitative Approaches in OO Software Engineering*, Glasgow, 2005

[8] Filho F., Rubira C., and Garcia A. A quantitative study on the aspectization of exception handling. In: *Proceedings of the ECOOP Workshop on Exception Handling in Object-Oriented Systems*, 2005

[9] Gamma E. et al. Design patterns: Elements of reusable object-oriented software. Addison-Wesley, Reading, 1995

[10] Garcia A. From objects to agents: An aspect-oriented approach. Doctoral Thesis, PUC-Rio, Rio de Janeiro, Brazil, 2004

[11] Garcia A. et al. Separation of concerns in multi-agent systems: An empirical study. In: *Software Engineering for Multi-Agent Systems II, LNCS vol. 2940*, Springer, 2004

[12] Garcia A., Silva V., Chavez C., Lucena C. Engineering multi-agent systems with aspects and patterns. *Journal of the Brazilian Computer Society*, 8(1):57–72, 2002

[13] Hachani Q., and Bardou D. On Aspect-oriented technology and object-oriented design patterns. In: *ECOOP: Workshop on Analysis of Aspect-Oriented Software*, Springer, Germany, 2003

[14] Hachani Q., and Bardou D. Using aspect-oriented programming for design patterns implementation. In: *OOIS: Workshop on Reuse in Object-Oriented Information Systems Design*, 2002

[15] Hannemann J., and Kiczales G. Design pattern implementation in java and AspectJ. In: *OOPSLA'02: Proceedings of the Conference on Object-Oriented Programming, Systems, Languages and Applications*, pp. 161–173, 2002

[16] Henderson-Sellers B. Object-oriented metrics: Measures of complexity. Prentice Hall, New Jersey, USA, 1996

[17] Hirschfeld R et al. Design patterns and aspects - Modular designs with seamless run-time integration. *3rd German GI Workshop on Aspect-Oriented Software Development*, German Informatics Association, University of Essen, Germany, 2003

[18] Hyper/J Web page. http://www.research.ibm.com/ hyperspace/HyperJ/HyperJ.htm, 2001

[19] Godil I., Jacobsen H. Horizontal decomposition of prevayler. In: *Proceedings of CASCON 2005*, Richmond Hill, Canada, 2005

[20] Java Reference Documentation. http://java.sun.com/reference/docs/index.html

[21] Kersten M., and Murphy G. Atlas: A case study in building a web-based learning environment using aspect-oriented programming. In: *OOPSLA'99: Proceedings of the Conference on Object-Oriented Programming, Systems, Languages and Applications*, 1999

[22] Kiczales G. et al. Aspect-oriented programming. In: *ECOOP'97: Proceedings of the European Conference on Object-Oriented Programming, LNCS vol. 1241*, Springer, pp. 220–242, 1997

[23] Kitchenham B. Evaluating software engineering methods and tools, part 1: The evaluation context and evaluation methods. *ACM SIGSOFT Software Engineering Notes*, 21(1):11–15, 1996

[24] Lopes C. D: A language framework for distributed programming. *PhD Thesis*, Northeastern University, Boston, USA, 1997

[25] Malaiya Y., and Denton J. Module size distribution and defect density. In: *ISSRE'00: Proceedings of the 11th International Symposium on Software Reliability Engineering*, 2000

[26] Mezini M., and Ostermann K. Conquering aspects with caesar. In: *Proceedings of the 2nd International Conference on Aspect-Oriented Software Development*, Boston, USA, 2003

[27] Miles R. AspectJ cookbook. *O'Reilly*, UK, 2004

[28] Modularizing Patterns with Aspects: A Quantitative Study. http://www.teccomm.les.inf.puc-rio.br/alessandro/GoFpatterns/empiricalresults.htm

[29] Sant'Anna C. et al. On the reuse and maintenance of aspect-oriented software: An assessment framework. In: *SBES'03: Proceedings of the Brazilian Symposium on Software Engineering*, Manaus, Brazil, pp. 19–34, 2003

[30] Sant'Anna C. et al. Design patterns as aspects: A quantitative assessment. *Journal of the Brazilian Computer Society (SBES'04 Best Paper Award)*, 10(2), Porto Alegre, Brazil, 2004

[31] Soares S. An aspect-oriented implementation method. *Doctoral Thesis*, Federal University of Pernambuco, Recife, Brazil, 2004

[32] Soares S., Laureano E., and Borba P. Implementing distribution and persistence aspects with AspectJ. In: *OOPSLA'02: Proceedings of the Conference on Object-Oriented Programming, Systems, Languages and Applications*, pp. 174–190, 2002

[33] Tarr P. et al. N degrees of separation: Multi-dimensional separation of concerns. In: *ICSE'99: Proceedings of the International Conference on Software Engineering*, pp. 107–119, 1999

[34] Together Technologies. http://www.borland.com/together/

[35] Zhao J. Towards a metrics suite for aspect-oriented software. Technical-Report SE-136-25, Information Processing Society of Japan (IPSJ), 2002

[36] Zhao J., and Xu B. Measuring aspect cohesion. In: *FASE'04: Proceedings Conference on Fundamental Approaches to Software Engineering, LNCS vol. 2984*, Springer, pp. 54–68, 2004

[37] Zuse H. History of software measurement. http://irb.cs.tu-berlin.de/~zuse/metrics/History_00.html

Directives for Composing Aspect-Oriented Design Class Models

Y.R. Reddy, S. Ghosh, R.B. France, G. Straw, J.M. Bieman,
N. McEachen, E. Song, and G. Georg

Computer Science Department,
Colorado State University,
Fort Collins, CO 80523, USA
ghosh@cs.colostate.edu

Abstract. An aspect-oriented design model consists of a set of aspect models and a primary model. Each aspect model describes a feature that crosscuts elements in the primary model. Aspect and primary models are composed to obtain an integrated design view. In this paper we describe a composition approach that utilizes a merging algorithm and composition directives. Composition directives are used when the default merging algorithm is known or expected to yield incorrect models. Our prototype tool supports default class diagram composition.

Keywords: Aspect-oriented modeling, Composition directives, KerMeta, Metamodel, EMOF, Signature, UML.

1 Introduction

Design features that address dependability concerns (e.g., security and fault tolerance concerns) may crosscut many elements of a design model. The crosscutting nature of these features can make understanding, analyzing, and changing them difficult. This complexity can be better managed through the use of aspect-oriented modeling (AOM) techniques that support separation and composition of crosscutting features [1].

In the AOM approach that we developed [1], an aspect-oriented design model consists of a primary model and one or more aspect models. An aspect model describes a feature that crosscuts the primary model. Aspect models are generic descriptions of crosscutting features that must be instantiated before they can be composed with the primary model. An integrated view of an aspect-oriented design model is obtained by composing the instantiated aspect models and the primary model. Instantiated aspect models and primary models consist of UML [2] models. Composition of the models involves merging UML models of the same types. For example, the class model in an instantiated aspect model is merged with the class model in a primary model. In previous work, a name-based composition approach was used to merge UML models [1]. Model elements with the same name are merged to form a single element in the composed model. The composition approach assumes that elements with the same name represent consistent views of the same concept. This may not always be the case. For example, consider an aspect-oriented design consisting of a primary model that describes a class representing a server that provides unrestricted access to services via operations in the

A. Rashid and M. Aksit (Eds.): Transactions on AOSD I, LNCS 3880, pp. 75–105, 2006.
© Springer-Verlag Berlin Heidelberg 2006

class, and an instantiated aspect model that describes the same server class with access control features. In this case, simple name-based merging of the two classes and the operations in them could lead to operations that are associated with inconsistent specifications (a primary model operation and its corresponding aspect model operation would have the same name but different argument lists and specifications). Often, a more sophisticated form of composition is needed to produce composed models with required properties. To meet this need we proposed the use of composition directives to ensure that the name-based composition approach produces desired results [3].

This paper extends previous work by introducing (1) a more general form of model element matching that is based on the notion of model element signatures, (2) a composition metamodel with behavioral features that specify how UML elements are composed, and (3) new forms of composition directives. In this paper we illustrate how a signature-based composition approach can be used to compose class models and describe how composition directives can be used to ensure that the composition approach produces desired results. We have developed a prototype tool that implements the class model composition behavior specified in the composition metamodel [4].

The remainder of the paper is organized as follows. Section 2 gives an overview of signature-based model composition and composition directives. Section 3 describes the composition metamodel. Section 4 describes the composition directives and provides illustrations of their use. Related work is discussed in Sect. 5, and Sect. 6 presents conclusions and plans for future work.

2   An Overview of Signature-Based Model Composition

A primary model in an aspect-oriented design model consists of one or more UML models, where each model describes a view of the core functionality. The core functionality determines the dominant structure of a design. Aspect models consist of UML model templates that describe generic forms of crosscutting features as patterns. An aspect model must be instantiated to produce a model that can be composed with a primary model. An instantiation of an aspect model, called a *context-specific aspect model*, describes the form the feature takes in a part of the design. Instantiating an aspect model involves binding the aspect model's template parameters to application-specific values.

A single aspect model may have to be instantiated multiple times for a given application. For example, consider the case where a decision has been made to make an application design fault-tolerant and highly available by replicating critical resources such as data repositories and service providers. Incorporating the crosscutting replication feature into the (primary) design model proceeds as follows:

1. An aspect model describing the replication feature for a generic resource is developed or acquired.
2. The replication aspect model is instantiated multiple times. Each instantiation is a context-specific aspect model that describes the replication feature for a specific application resource.
3. The context-specific aspect models are composed with the primary application model to produce a design in which specified resources are replicated.

In our previous work we developed a composition approach that used model element names to identify the elements that are to be merged. Model elements of the the same syntactic type and with the same name are merged to form a single model element. Naming conflicts can be avoided if there is a managed namespace from which values used to bind aspect models and to name primary model elements are obtained. We refer to such a namespace as the *application domain namespace* [1]. Unfortunately, a managed namespace is often not available in design development environments, and thus naming conflicts may occur.

2.1 Matching Model Elements Using Signatures

Name-based composition is relatively easy to implement, but as a matching criterion, it can be too permissive in some cases. For example, matching operations using only their names could lead to merging problems when the operations have incompatible return types or when the argument lists differ. Similarly, matching attributes using only their names can lead to merging problems when the types associated with the attributes are incompatible. One would like to have matching criteria that take into consideration additional properties of the elements being matched. For example, one should be able to express a matching criterion for attributes that requires matching attributes to have the same name and type. The need for finer-grained matching criteria led to the development of the signature-based composition approach described in this paper.

The signature-based composition approach merges information in model elements with matching signatures to form a single model element in the composed model. A model element's signature is defined in terms of its syntactic properties, where a syntactic property of a model element is either an attribute or an association end defined in the element's UML metamodel class. For example, *isAbstract* is a syntactic property defined in the metamodel class called `Class`. If an instance of `Class` is an abstract class then *isAbstract = true* for the class, otherwise the instance is a concrete class (i.e., *isAbstract = false*).

The signature of a model element is a collection of values for a subset of syntactic properties defined in the model element's metamodel class. The set of syntactic properties used to determine a model element's signature is called a *signature type*. For example, the signature type for an operation can be defined as a set consisting of the following properties defined in the `Operation` class: name (value is the operation's name) and `ownedParameter` (value is the collection of parameters associated with the operation). Using this signature type, the signature of an operation *update*(*x* : *int*, *y* : *int*) is the set {*update*, (*x* : *int*, *y* : *int*)}. If this signature is used to match operations, two operations match if and only if they have the same name and parameter list. If the signature type of an operation consists only of the operation name, then the signature of the operation is {*update*}. Use of this name-only signature type results in a weaker matching criterion for operations: two operations match if and only if they have the same name.

A signature type that consists of all syntactic properties associated with a model element is called a *complete* signature type. Complete signature types require that matching model elements have equivalent values for all syntactic properties (i.e., the matching elements must be syntactically identical). Complete signature types are typically used for matching contained model elements such as class attributes and operation parame-

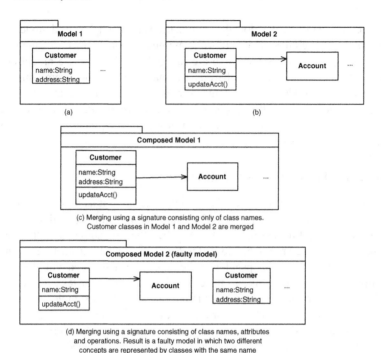

Fig. 1. An example of model element matching and merging

ters. Composite model elements that contain a variety of model elements (e.g., classes) tend to have signature types that are not complete.

If two model elements of the same syntactic type[1] have the same signature, then their properties are merged to form a single model element of that syntactic type. As an example, consider a model, *Model 1*, containing a concrete class named *Customer* with attributes *name* and, *address*, (see Fig. 1a) and another model, *Model 2*, which contains a concrete class named *Customer* with an attribute *name* and a reference to an *Account* object (see Fig. 1b). If the signature type used to compose the classes in Figs. 1a and 1b consists of the class name property and the *isAbstract* property, then the two classes match (they have the same name and they are both concrete), and their contents are merged to form a single class. The issue of merging syntactic properties that are not part of a model element's signature type arises in this case. The matching classes in this example have different attribute, operation, and association end sets. Merging the constituent model elements involves matching them using signature types defined for the elements. The constituent elements that are matched are merged in the composed model. Those elements that are not matched are included in the composed model.

The composed model shown in Fig. 1c is obtained by using complete signature types for attributes, operations, and association ends:

---

[1] The syntactic type of a model element is the class of the model element in the UML meta-model.

- The attribute *name : String* in *Model 1* and *Model 2* match and is included once in the composed model.
- The attribute *address : String* in *Model 1* does not appear in *Model 2* and thus is not matched. It appears in the composed model.
- The operation *updateAcct()* in *Model 2* does not appear in *Model 1* and thus is not matched. It appears in the composed model.
- The association and the class *Account* in *Model 2* do not appear in *Model 1* and thus are not matched. They are included in the composed model.

The use of particular signature types can lead to models that are not syntactically well-formed in some cases. For example, consider the case in which the signature type for class is defined as consisting of the following properties: Name, isAbstract, and ownedAttribute. Two classes match using this signature type if and only if they have the same name, are both abstract or are both concrete, and they have the same set of attributes and association ends. If this signature type is used to compose the class models shown in Fig. 1a and Fig. 1b, then the result is shown in Fig. 1d. The model is not well-formed because there are two classes with the same name in the same namespace.

To resolve the above problem one must understand the intent behind the signature type. If it is determined by the modeler that the signature type correctly reflects the syntactic form of classes that represent the same concept, then the problem is resolved by renaming either the *Customer* class in *Model 1* or the *Customer* class in *Model 2*. As will be described later in this paper, this can be accomplished by using a rename composition directive. On the other hand, if the modeler determines that the classes actually represent similar classes then the signature type must be changed so that the classes are matched.

2.2   Identifying and Using Composition Directives

The composition approach that we have developed utilizes a signature-based merging algorithm and composition directives. In some cases, sole use of the algorithm will produce models with undesirable properties. This is the case when the views described by the models contain inconsistent information. In some cases, the problems can be resolved by syntactically tweaking the models that are involved in the composition or by overriding some of the composition rules. Composition directives can be used for these purposes.

Figure 2 shows activities related to identifying and using composition directives. The activity diagram shows the relationship among three activities: the composition activity (*Compose aspect and Primary models*), the model analysis activity (*Analyze Composed model*), and the directives identification activity (*Identify Composition Directives*). The composition activity, *Compose aspect and Primary models*, takes in three inputs: a primary model, a nonempty set of context-specific aspect models, and a (possibly empty) set of composition directives. In this activity, the aspect and primary models are composed using the algorithm and composition directives to produce a *Composed model*. The matching and merging procedure is capable of detecting conflicting syntactic property values associated with matching model elements. For example, if two matching classes have different values for the *isAbstract* property, a conflict is flagged.

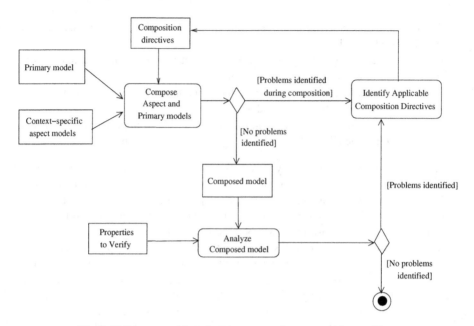

Fig. 2. Using composition directives to resolve composition problems

After composition, the composed model can be formally analyzed against desired properties (referred to as *Properties to Verify* in Fig. 2) to uncover design errors. For example, one can analyze the models against well-formedness rules to identify badly formed models, or one can analyze the models against desired semantic properties (e.g., "only the owner of a file can delete the file"). In related work, we developed a technique for uncovering semantic problems during composition [5]. In the approach, the semantic property to be verified is used in the composition process to generate proof obligations. Establishing that a composed model has the stated semantic properties requires discharging the proof obligations.

In some cases, the uncovered problems can be resolved using composition directives. In these cases an appropriate set of directives are identified and used to compose the context-specific aspect and primary models. In other cases, more substantial changes may be required. For example, it may be determined that another variant of the aspect model is needed or that the primary model has to be significantly refactored.

This paper focuses on the *Compose Aspect and Primary models* activity shown in Fig. 2. Activities related to analysis of models to uncover problems and the identification of composition directives is not within the scope of this paper.

2.3   Examples of Applying Composition Directives

Composition directives can be classified as *Model Directives* and *Element Directives*. Model directives are used to determine the order in which multiple aspect models are composed with a primary model. Element directives are used to determine how an aspect model is composed with a primary model. Element directives can be classified in terms of when they are applied in the composition process:

- *Premerge directives*: These directives are used to carry out simple modifications of the models before they are merged. For example, one can rename model elements, delete model elements, or replace model elements (delete and add model elements) in the primary or context-specific aspect models.
- *Merge directives*: These directives are used to override rules for merging model elements. For example, one can specify that a model element in one model completely replaces an element in another model.
- *Postmerge directives*: These directives are used to carry out simple modifications on the model produced after merging possibly modified primary and context-specific aspect models. The directives for renaming, adding, deleting, and replacing model elements also fall into this category.

In the remainder of this section we provide examples of composition problems that can be resolved using composition directives. It is important to note that the composition approach discussed in the following sections does not provide systematic techniques for analyzing composed models nor for identifying appropriate composition directives once problems are uncovered. As stated earlier, the merging algorithm will flag cases where conflicting syntactic properties exist for model elements that are merged. It does not, however, detect semantic conflicts that can arise as a result of inconsistent specifications of behavior or other semantic properties. Uncovering such semantic properties requires formal semantic analysis of the composed model.

Figure 3 shows a simple example of a composition that leads to a faulty composed class model. In the example, a modeler creates a primary model (see Fig. 3a) in which an output producer (an instance of `Writer`) sends outputs directly to the output device to which it is linked (instance of `FileStream`). The modeler then decides to incorporate a buffering feature into the model by instantiating a buffering aspect model. Figure 3b shows the class diagram template that is part of the buffering aspect model. The aspect model describes how entities that produce outputs (represented by instantiations of *BufferWriter*) are decoupled from output devices through the use of buffers. Template parameters are preceded by the symbol "|". The operation templates |write() in |Buffer and |BufferWriter are associated with template forms of operation specifications [1].

To incorporate the buffering feature into the primary model, the modeler must first instantiate the aspect model to produce a context-specific model. Instantiating the buffering class diagram template produces a class diagram that describes how buffering is to be accomplished in the context of the primary model. The class diagram shown in Fig. 3c is obtained from the buffering class diagram template using bindings that include the following:

```
(|Buffer<-WriterBuffer), (|Output<-FileStream), (|BufferWriter<-Writer),
(|BufferWriter::|write()<-writeLine()), (|Buffer::|write()<-writeBuff()),
(|Output::|write()<-addToStream())
```

The result of composing the class diagram shown in Fig. 3c with the primary model class diagram shown in Fig. 3a is presented in Fig. 3d. Composition is carried out by matching model elements using signatures consisting only of model element names. If the matching model elements are associated with invariants, the invariant associated

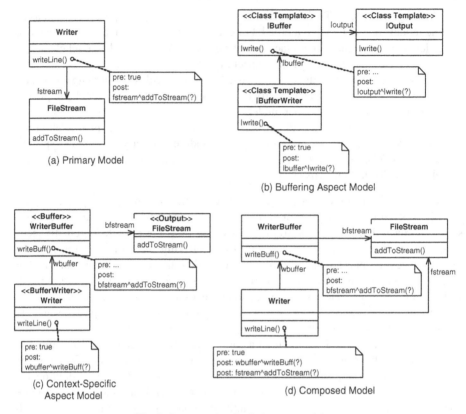

Fig. 3. An example of a faulty composition

with the merged element in the composed model is the conjunction of the invariants in the matched elements. Operation specifications, expressed as OCL pre- and postconditions, can also be merged for matching operations. The precondition of the merged operation in the composed model is the disjunction of the preconditions associated with the matching operations, and the postcondition of the merged operation is the conjunction of their postconditions.

The merging of the `writeLine()` operations in the primary and context-specific aspect models produces an operation that calls the buffer's write operation `writeBuff()` and the filestream's write operation `addToStream()`. This is not the desired result: The intent is to completely decouple `Writer` from `FileStream` using `WriteBuffer`. To resolve this problem, the following composition directives can be used:

- a premerge composition directive that removes the association between `Writer` and `FileStream` in the primary model
- a premerge composition directive that removes the operation specification associated with the `writeLine()` operation in the primary model

Once the above premerge directives are applied, the composition algorithm is used to compose the modified primary model with the context-specific aspect model.

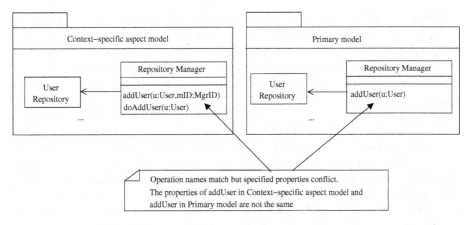

Fig. 4. Example of a property conflict

As another example, consider the partial context-specific and primary class models shown in Fig. 4. The addUser() operation in the primary model adds a user (instance of User) to a collection of users (instance of a class User Repository). The addUser() operation in the context-specific aspect model calls the doAddUser operation only when the client calling the operation is authorized to add a user. The doAddUser() operation adds a user to the collection. Using signatures that consist only of model element names, the two *Repository Manager* classes match and thus their properties are merged. During the merge of these two classes, the addUser() operations are matched and their specifications (not shown) are merged. The resulting addUser() operation specification will have a semantic conflict: The specification from the primary model allows unconditional adding of users, but the specification from the context-specific model will allow adding of users only if the operation is authorized for the client. This is an example of a *semantic property conflict*: A semantic property conflict occurs when two matching elements (elements with the same signature) are associated with conflicting semantic properties. In this example, the intent is to merge the doAddUser() operation in the context-specific aspect model with the addUser() operation in the primary model. To resolve this conflict and reflect the intent, a premerge composition directive that renames the addUser() operation in the primary model to doAddUser() can be used. After this renaming, signature-based composition will produce a composed model with the required properties.

Renaming directives can also be used to resolve *syntactic naming conflicts*. A syntactic naming conflict occurs when two or more model elements representing different concepts have the same name. This class of conflicts can be avoided by instantiating the generic aspect model such that the names do not match or by using a premerge rename directive.

In some cases, postmerge directives are needed to add or delete elements in the model produced by merging primary and context-specific aspect models to produce a model that has required properties. For example, associations may be added between a class introduced by the primary model and another class introduced by a context-specific aspect model to provide required access to behaviors defined in the classes, or they may be removed to prevent access that is to be prohibited in the composed model.

With the ability to rename, add, and remove elements comes the risk of another type of conflict: the nonexistent-reference conflict. A nonexistent-reference conflict arises when a reference in one of the models refers to an element that no longer exists, or exists under a different name. To resolve this conflict, the affected references in a model must be identified and updated. Composition directives that identify and update specified references are needed.

In an aspect-oriented model that contains multiple aspect models, different composition orderings may produce different composed models [6]. A particular ordering can lead to undesirable emergent behaviors. For example, consider an auditing feature and a password feature that are to be composed with a primary model. If the password feature is composed with the primary model before the auditing feature, then the end result could be a model in which the auditing feature captures and stores passwords. This may be an undesirable emergent behavior. Composition directives that can be used to specify the order used to compose multiple aspects with a primary model are needed.

Defining composition ordering raises another type of conflict. A cyclic-ordering conflict occurs when there is a cycle among ordering relationships defined over multiple aspects. Analysis can detect and correct ordering conflicts.

The above discussion indicates that the following list of actions should be captured by composition directives:

- creating new elements
- adding elements to a Namespace
- deleting elements from a Namespace
- changing property values of elements
- finding and changing references to specified model elements
- specifying override relationships between matching elements
- changing default composition rules
- specifying ordering relationships among multiple aspects

The above list of actions reflects our current experience and may be incomplete.

3   The Composition Metamodel

Our composition metamodel uses static and behavioral features needed to support model composition. In this paper, we describe the behavioral properties in terms of class operations and narrative descriptions of the operations. Alternatively, sequence and activity diagrams can be used to describe the interactions and activities that take place during composition.

The core part of the metamodel has been implemented using KerMeta, an open source metamodeling language developed by the Triskell team at IRISA [7]. KerMeta extends the *Essential Meta-Object Facility* (EMOF) 2.0 [8] with an action language that allows one to describe the behavior of operations associated with classes in a metamodel. KerMeta was used primarily because it is compatible with the Eclipse Modeling Framework (EMF), which allows us to use Eclipse tools to edit, store, and visualize models manipulated in our AOM approach. A more detailed description of the language is presented in [9].

EMOF 2.0 is a subset of the Meta-Object Facility (MOF) that can be used to describe metamodels using object-oriented concepts. It utilizes concepts from UML 2.0, and thus allows one to use UML tools to build metamodels. EMOF defines a class called *Object* from which all other EMOF classes inherit properties. This class contains the following operations that will be used in the composition metamodel described later in this section:

- The *getMetaClass*() operation returns the class of an object.
- The *container*() operation returns the containing parent object.
- The *equals*(*element*) operation determines if the element is equal to this instance.
- The *set*(*property, element*) operation sets the value of the property to the element.
- The *get*(*property*) operation returns a list of values or a single value depending on the multiplicity.

The *isComposite* attribute defined in the EMOF class *Property* returns true if the object is contained in the parent object. Cyclic containment is not possible, i.e., an object can be contained in only one other object. The *getAllProperties*() operation in the EMOF class called *Class* returns all the properties (including inherited properties) associated with a *Class* object.

Figure 5 shows the core part of the composition metamodel. The metamodel contains elements from the UML metamodel [2], but it differs from the UML metamodel in that it includes operations that specify composition behavior.

The core concepts shown in Fig. 5 are described below:

- **Element:** Instances of this class are model elements. *Element* is an extension of the UML metaclass, *Element*. It is extended by the operation *getMatchingElements* (*e* : *Set*(*Element*)). Operations associated with the EMOF *Object* class are also available in the *Element* class.
  - **Element::getMatchingElements():** This operation takes in a set of elements and returns a set of elements that have the same syntactic type and signature as the element that invokes it. The syntactic type check is performed by invoking the *getMetaClass*() and the *getAllProperties*() operations defined in the EMOF *Object* class. The signature is obtained using the *getSignature*() operation.
- **Mergeable:** This is an abstract class that characterizes model elements that can be merged. Examples of mergeable elements shown in the figure are instances of *Classifiers*, *Operations*, and *Models*.
  - **Mergeable::merge():** This operation merges the element with the mergeable element passed in as an operation argument. The merge method returns a new element that is the merge of the element m and the element on which the merge is called.
  - **Mergeable::sigEquals():** This operation determines whether the element's signature is equal to the signature of another element.
  - **Mergeable::getSignature():** This operation gets the signature of the element.
- **Signature:** Instances of this class are representations of signatures. Every mergeable element is associated with exactly one instance of this class.

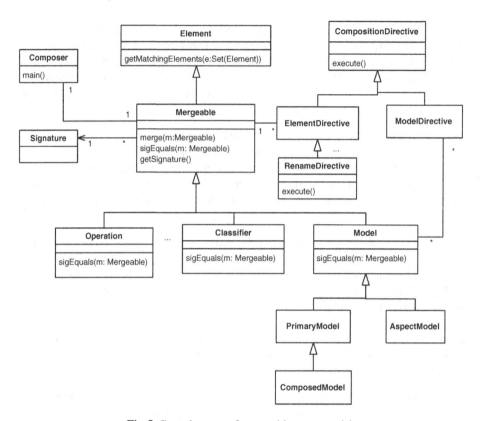

Fig. 5. Core elements of composition metamodel

The KerMeta implementation of the core parts of the composition metamodel (i.e., the metamodel obtained by excluding the *CompositionDirective* hierarchy) treats the model elements and instances of the other classes in the metamodel as objects (i.e., instances of the EMOF *Object* class). The implementation is thus written independently of model element types, and it uses reflection to obtain type information. The operations in the composition metamodel (including those defined in EMOF) were implemented using the KerMeta action language.

The model elements are merged only when they have the same syntactic type and the same signature. The *sigEquals()* operation is used to determine whether signatures of model elements are the same (see Appendix). Each model element type defines its own procedure for checking equality of signatures, that is, specializations of Mergeable can override the inherited *sigEquals()*.

Merging of two matching model elements, *e*1 and *e*2, in the absence of composition directives proceeds as follows:

– **Primitive property rule:** A primitive property is a model element property that must be associated with exactly one value. The *isAbstract* property of classes is an example of a primitive property. The primitive properties of matching elements must have the same values. If they have different values then a conflict is indicated for each conflicting value. For example, if $e1$ and $e2$ are matching classes with different values for the *isAbstract* property then a conflict is indicated.

– **Composite property rule:** This rule applies to model element properties that are associated with values that are collections of model elements. The *ownedAttribute* property of a class is an example of this kind of property. This rule has a base case part and a recursive part. The recursive part essentially applies the merge recursively to merge the constituent parts of the property that match across the encompassing two model elements. The base case part determines the stopping condition for the recursion. In what follows, the composite property is referred to as p, $e1.p$ refers to the collection of values associated with p in $e1$, and $e2.p$ refers to the collection of values associated with p in $e2$.

   • **Recursive part:** For each constituent element in $e1.p$ a search is made for a matching element in $e2.p$ (based on the signature type associated with the constituent element type). If a match is not found then the element is included in merged form of $e1$ and $e2$. If a match is found the two matching constituent elements are merged and included in the merged form of $e1$ and $e2$.

   • **Base Case part:** If two constituent matching elements, $c1$ and $c2$, are composites that consist of only one model element, q, then the following occurs. If the signatures of $c1.q$ and $c2.q$ match then $c1.q$ is merged with $c2.q$. If the signatures do not match, then a conflict is indicated. For example, if two attributes are matched using only their names, then a conflict is indicated if their types do not match.

The composition of two models (instances of *Model*) is started by calling the *merge()* operation in one of the models, using the other as an argument. The *main()* method of the *Composer* class invokes the initial merge. Since a Model is not a primitive type, its *merge()* operation will result in the merging of the matching parts of the model. The algorithm for merging elements is given in the Appendix.

Two types of composition directives are described in the composition metamodel. Element directives (instances of *ElementDirective*) are composition directives that apply to a group of elements in a single model. These directives can be used to add new elements, delete existing elements, rename elements, override elements, and replace references in a model. Model directives (instances of *ModelDirective*) are composition directives that are associated with a group of models. An example of a model directive is a composition directive that specifies the order in which aspects are composed with a primary model.

Each composition directive is associated with a behavior that implements the action associated with the directive. These behaviors are invoked by the *merge()* operations of elements before the merges of constituent properties are attempted.

The KerMeta implementation of the composition metamodel currently does not support the use of composition directives. We are now developing such support. The pre- and postmerge directives can be viewed as transformations on models and this is how they will be implemented in KerMeta (KerMeta was originally designed to support specification of model transformations).

4   Composition Directives

In this section we describe the composition directives that we have identified through application of the composition approach on small case studies (e.g., see [10, 11, 12]). The directives can be used to modify aspect and primary models, add new elements to composed models, or to override default composition rules in order to produce desired composed models. The directives that modify models can be viewed as transformations on the models. Directives that affect only aspect and primary models are applied to the models before their elements are merged. Those that add elements to composed models and those that override composition rules are applied during merging.

Each directive (except for the directives that override composition rules) is described using the following format:

- *Directive Name:* This section states the name of the directive or the form of names for a family of directives.
- *Application:* This section describes the purpose of the directives and describes the entities that the directives operate on.
- *Form:* This section describes the syntactic form of the directives.
- *Constraint:* This section gives the conditions that must hold if the directives are to have the intended effect. The constraint in this section is referred to as the directive precondition.
- *Effect:* This section describes the effect of the directives on their targets. The specification of effect is called the directive postcondition.

As indicated in the composition metamodel described in the previous section, there are two types of composition directives: element directives and model directives. The following sections describe the directives in each of these categories and give examples of their application.

4.1   Element Directives

We have identified the following element directives thus far:

- creating new model elements (a family of directives)
- adding model elements to a namespace
- removing model elements from a namespace
- changing properties (a family of directives)
- replacing references to a model element in a namespace
- overriding model elements
- overriding composition rules (a family of directives)

When an element is created by a create directive, a handle that can be used to reference the element is provided. These handles can be used in composition directives that are applied after the creation of the model elements. The names that appear on model elements in aspect and primary models serve as references to the model elements in directives. For example, an association name or a role name can refer refer to an association in a directive.

Creating new model elements.   The following describes the family of create directives.

Directive Name: **create**<metamodel class name>
The following are examples of names for create directives: **create**Association, **create**Class, where *Association* and *Class* are the names of concrete classes in the UML metamodel.

Application: The create directives are used to create new model elements (i.e., model elements that are not in the primary or aspect models being composed). In the composition metamodel, each concrete *Element* class is associated with a constructor. The create directives use these constructors to create model elements to ensure that the created elements are syntactically well-formed. The new element is not a member of any namespace when it is created.

A create directive has set of operands that determines the arguments passed to the constructors of the model elements. The operands are a set of (*property name = property value*) pairs, where the *property name* is the name of a model element property.

Form: newHandle = **create**<Element> {operands}

The following is an example of a create directive that creates a concrete class with a name "NewClass".

```
newClass = createClass {name = "NewClass", isAbstract = false}
```

The following create directives are used to create a strong aggregation relation between two existing classes: primary::UserMgmt, and aspect::UserAuth.

```
userAuthEnd = createProperty { isComposite = false, aggregation = none,
   type = aspect::UserAuth, opposite = userMgmtEnd, lower = 1, upper = 1 }

userMgmtEnd = createProperty { isComposite = true, aggregation = composite,
   type = primary::UserMgmt, opposite = userAuthEnd, lower = 1, upper = -1 }

userAuth-userMgmt = createAssociation { name = "UserAuth-UserMgmt" ,
   isDerived = false, memberEnd = [userAuthEnd,userMgmtEnd] }
```

The operands of the above directives indicate that the two association ends (property) userAuthEnd and userMgmtEnd must be created before the association userAuth-userMgmt is created. We assign the value of "-1" to upper (representing the upper limit of a multiplicity), where "-1" represents the multiplicity "*". The "[..]" notation is used to denote a collection of association ends in the **create**Association directive.

Constraint: There are no constraints for these directives.

Effect: A create directive provides a reference to a new model element that is valid. The new Element is not a member of any namespace.

Adding model elements to a namespace.

Directive Name: **add**

Application: The **add** directive is used to add a model element to a namespace in a model. It can be used to add a newly created model element (i.e., one created by a create directive) to a namespace and to add an element from another namespace into a target namespace. The latter action is needed when a model element is migrated to a new namespace in order to ensure that the composed model has required properties. Such a migration would involve removing the element from its original namespace (using the **remove** directive described later) and then adding it to the new namespace.

The **add** directive has one operand, the model element to be added.

Form: **add** `owner::elem`
In the above, the model element, `elem,` is added to the namespace, `owner.`

Constraint: The target namespace must exist, the element to be added must have a unique name within the namespace, and the element must be an instance of a concrete UML metamodel class that can be owned by the namespace.

Effect: The element is in the target namespace.

Removing model elements from a namespace.

Directive Name: **remove**

Application: The **remove** directive is used to remove a model element from a namespace. It is used when the presence of certain model elements compromises desired properties of the composed model. For example, consider a security aspect model that requires that certain associations not exist in the composed model because their presence can lead to leaks of sensitive information. The **remove** directive can remove these associations in the primary model.

Removing a composite model element involves removing all its contained parts. For example, removing an association involves removing its association end properties (but not the classes at the association ends).

Removing a model element can result in models with hanging references: References to the removed element may be present in the namespace and elsewhere (e.g., in OCL expressions) after removal. Use of the directive should be coupled with the use of other directives that take care of the hanging references. For example, one can use the **replaceOccurrences** directive to replace reference to the deleted element with references to other elements.

The **remove** directive has one operand, the model element that is to be removed.

Form: **remove** `owner::elem`
In the above, the model element, `elem,` is removed from the namespace, `owner.`

Constraint: The namespace must exist in a model. The element must be in the namespace before the directive is applied.

Effect: The element is not in the namespace.

Changing properties of model elements in a namespace.   The family of directives for changing model element properties are described below.

Directive Name: **change**<property name>
Examples of change directive names are **change**isAbstract and **change**name. The **change**name directive is written more concisely as **rename**.

Application: The **changeProperty** directive is used to change the value of a model element property. This directive can be used to force or prevent matching of model elements by changing the property values used to determine element matches. For example, in the cases where matching is based only on the names of elements, this directive can be used to rename elements so that they match or do not match.

This directive has two operands. The first is the model element with the property, and the second is the new value of the property.

In our case studies we often use this directive to rename model elements, and thus we use a more concise name for the directive: **rename**. The renaming directive is often applied to the primary model, because renaming of elements in the context-specific aspect models can also be accomplished by rebinding the (generic) aspect model.

Form: **change**<property name> owner::targetElement **to** propertyValue

In the cases where the property to be changed is a model element name one can use the form below:

rename owner::targetElement **to** newName

Constraint: The element must exist in a primary, aspect or composed model.

Effect: The specified property value in the target model element has the new value.

Replace references to a model element in a namespace.

Directive Name: **replaceOccurrences**

Application: The **replaceOccurrences** directive is used to replace references to a model element with references to another model element in a namespace. It is often used in conjunction with directives that add and remove model elements. For example, if an association that is referenced in an OCL expression is removed then one can use this directive to change the reference in the OCL expression.

The **replaceOccurrences** directive has two operands: The first is a reference to a model element, and the second is a reference to another model element.

Form: **replaceOccurrences** owner1::elem **with** owner2::replacementElem
The above states that references to elem in the namespace owner1 are to be replaced by references to replacementElem in the namespace owner2.

Constraint: There are no constraints for this directive.

Effect: All existing references to the model element owner1::elem are changed to references to the element owner2::replacementElem.

Overriding a model element.   This composition directive is similar to the override relationship proposed by Clarke et al. [13].

Directive Name: **override**

Application: The **override** directive defines an override relationship between two potentially conflicting model elements. It indicates that the properties of a model element take precedence over properties of a matching model element during composition.

When an **override** relationship is defined for two model elements, the relationship propagates to the contained model elements. The consequences of the implicit overrides may not be immediately obvious. Explicit **override** relationships should be defined for contained model elements when this is feasible and practical.

The **override** directive has two operands. The second operand is the model element that overrides the first operand.

Form: **override** `owner1::elem1` **with** `owner2::elem2`

Constraint: `owner1::elem1` and `owner2::elem2` must exist in separate models, one in a primary model, and the other in a context-specific aspect model. The two elements must match.

Effect: During composition, the properties of `elem1` are replaced by properties of `elem2`.

Overriding default composition rules. When merging matching model elements with different property values, a composition mechanism can use default rules to determine the property values that will be used in the composed model. For example, in previous work [5] we defined the following rules for combining properties with different values in matching elements:

- If two matching attributes are associated with invariants, the invariant in the composed model is the conjunction of the two invariants.
- If two matching operations have operation specifications, the composed operation has a precondition that is the disjunction of the two preconditions and a postcondition that is the conjunction of the two postconditions.
- If two associations match and their multiplicities are different, then the merged association uses the weaker multiplicity constraint at each end.

Sometimes one may want to change the default rules when composing models. For example, one may want to use the stronger multiplicity constraint at the ends of composed associations. *Override composition rule* directives are used for this purpose. In our approach, each rule is associated with a set of possible variations, and a directive for each variation is defined. For example, the association end multiplicity rule is associated with the following directive:

association end multiplicity rule `owner1::assocend1;`
   `owner2::assocend2` **stronger**

Use of this directive indicates that the stronger of the two multiplicities at the specified associations are to be used in the composed model. One can also override the rule globally using the following directive:

association end multiplicity rule stronger

For the operation specification rule we have the following directive:

operation specification rule owner1::aclass1::**PreSpec**(anoperation1),
  owner2::aclass2::**PreSpec**(anoperation2) **conjunct**

The above states that the precondition of the operation formed by merging the matching operations anoperation1 and anoperation2 is the conjunction of their preconditions. A similar directive for postconditions is also defined:

operation specification rule owner1::aclass1::**PostSpec**(anoperation1),
  owner2::aclass2::**PostSpec**(anoperation2) **disjunct**

Currently we have a very limited number of composition rules. In the cases where we do not have such rules, composition results in a conflict when the property values differ. Work on providing a small and useful set of rules and associated directives is ongoing.

4.2 Composition Examples

The following are examples of composition scenarios that require the use of directives to produce desired results. In the examples we show the effect of directives in terms of before and after diagrams. Note that the after diagrams are not the composed models: They show only the effect of the directives on the primary and aspect models.

Example 1: The faulty composition shown in Fig. 3 can be avoided by using composition directives that do the following (the aspect and primary models are shown in Fig. 6):

1. Remove the association between Writer and FileStream in the primary model: In the desired composed model, all writing to the file stream is done via the buffer. The write should not have direct access to the filestream in the composed model.
2. Remove the OCL specification for writeLine() in the primary model: The operation specification in the context-specific aspect model fully specifies the desired behavior and thus the conflicting specification in the primary model can be deleted.

The directives that accomplish the above are given below:

(1) **remove** primary::Writer::fstream
(2) **remove** primary::Writer::**Spec**(writeLine)

In the above, **Spec**(writeLine) refers to the specification associated with the operation writeLine(). Figures 6 and 7 illustrate the effect of the directives on the primary and aspect model. An "X" indicates the removal of an element.

In the example, the operation specification associated with writeLine() in the primary model contained only a statement that refers to the deleted *fstream* element. If the specification had contained additional statements that were required in the operation specification of writeLine() in the composed model, then removal of the specification

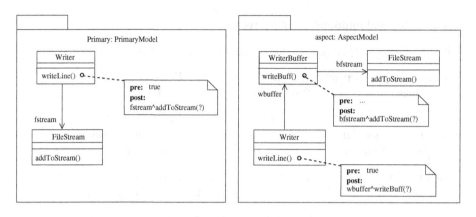

Fig. 6. Example 1. Before application of directives

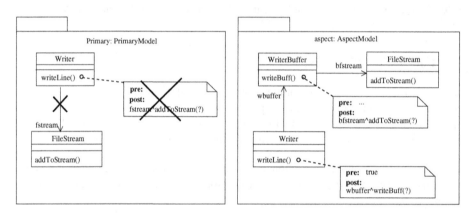

Fig. 7. Example 1. After application of remove directives

in the primary model would not give the desired result. To handle these situations, directives that replace the elements to be removed in the OCL specifications with desired elements are needed. Such directives require technology for parsing OCL expressions. A metamodel for the OCL is currently being standardized by the Object Management Group (see http://www.omg.org/uml), and it is expected that OCL parsers based on the metamodel will be developed soon after.

An alternative way to accomplish the above would be to use the **override** directive instead of the second **remove** directive, as shown below.

(1) **remove** `primary::Writer::fstream`
(2) **override** `primary::Writer` **with** `aspect::Writer`

Figure 8 illustrates the effect of the directives on the primary and aspect models.

Example 2: The following example, from France et al. [1], illustrates the use of the **create**, **add**, **remove**, and **replaceOccurrences** directives. The aspect model shown

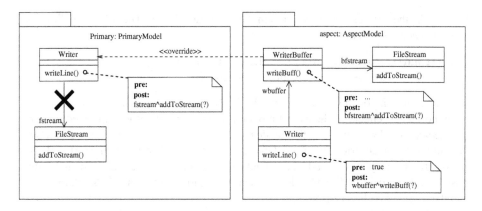

Fig. 8. Example 1. After application of remove and override directives

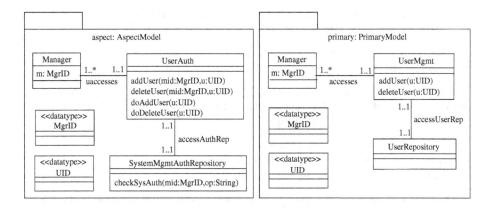

Fig. 9. Example 2. Before application of directives

in Fig. 9 presents a view in which add and delete user actions must be authorized before they are carried out. The primary model describes a view in which authorization does not occur. The objective of the composition is to produce a composed model in which the authorization behavior in the aspect is incorporated into the primary model. In Fig. 9, the UserAuth class in the aspect model performs authorization checks on clients requesting the addition or deletion of users from the system. In the composed model, Manager client must request the add and deleter user operations by calling the corresponding operations in UserAuth and should have no direct access to the UserMgmt class. To accomplish this, a directive is used to remove the accesses association in the primary model:

(1) **remove** primary::Manager::accesses

There are references to the accesses association in Manager that must be replaced or removed. In this case, references to accesses in the primary model must be changed to uaccesses in the context-specific aspect model, because all access to the operations is made via the uaccesses association in the composed model. The following directive is used to accomplish this:

(2) **replaceOccurrences** primary::Manager::accesses
     with aspect::Manager::uaccesses

The definitions of the addUser and deleteUser operations in UserAuth include an authorization check. In the aspect model, if a Manager client is authorized to carry out the add or delete action a call is made to the respective doAddUser, doDeleteUser operations. In the described composed model, the operations addUser and deleteUser in UserMgmt carry out the add and delete user actions, respectively. To make this possible a composition directive that adds an association between the UserMgmt class and the UserAuth class is used:

(3) userAuthEnd = **create**Property { isComposite = false, aggregation = none,
     type = aspect::UserAuth, opposite = userMgmtEnd, lower = 1, upper = 1 }

userMgmtEnd = **create**Property { isComposite = true, aggregation = composite,
     type = primary::UserMgmt, opposite = userAuthEnd, lower = 1, upper = -1 }

userAuth-userMgmt = **create**Association { name = "UserAuth-UserMgmt" ,
     isDerived = false, memberEnd = [userAuthEnd, userMgmtEnd] }

Once the new Association is created, we need to add it to the composed model. The composition directive that accomplishes this is given below. We reference the composed model using the name *comp*:

(4) **add** comp::userAuth-userMgmt,
     add comp::UserAuth::userAuthEnd,
     add comp::UserMgmt::userMgmtEnd

There are two options for creating a composed model in which authorized calls to addUser and DeleteUser are made: The first option is to replace the specifications of doAddUser and doDeleteUser so that they delegate the actions to the respective operations in UserMgmt using the new association. The second option is to replace the calls to doAddUser and doDeleteUser by calls to the respective operations in UserMgmt. We give the directives that accomplish the latter option below:

(5) **replaceOccurrences** aspect::UserAuth::doAddUser
         with primary::UserMgmt::addUser(),
     remove aspect::UserAuth::doAddUser,
     replaceOccurrences aspect::UserAuth::doDeleteUser
         with primary::UserMgmt::deleteUser(),
     remove aspect::UserAuth::doDeleteUser

The effect of the directives on the aspect and primary models is shown in Fig. 10. The association between UserMgmt and UserAuth exists in the composed and not in the aspect or primary models; it is shown here only to indicate that this association will exist in the composed model. The dependencies from the addUser and deleteUser operations in UserAuth indicate that they call the respective operations in UserMgmt.

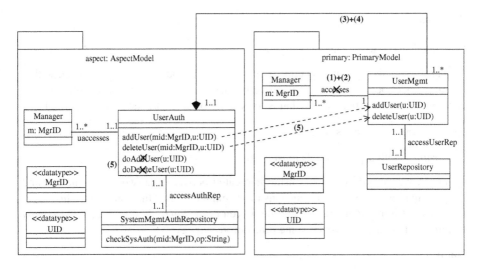

Fig. 10. Example 2. After application of directives

4.3   Combining Element Directives

The examples and the descriptions of composition directives provide some indication that use of some element directives are often coupled with the use of others. For example, removing a model element sometimes requires use of directives such as the **replaceOccurrences** directive to avoid hanging references. An overview of combined directives in the premerge, merge, and postmerge categories are given below:

Premerge combined directives: Matching directives are combined directives that force the matching of elements or disallow the matching of elements. The directives are often combinations of **changeproperty** and **replaceOccurrences** directives.

Merge combined directives: Combinations of the **override** and **replaceOccurrences** directives are often used to override rules used to merge model elements.

Postmerge combined directives: These directives are often combinations of directives for creating model elements, adding model elements to a namespace, and deleting model elements from a namespace.

The development of a library of combined directives that are based on actual use of directives on realistic projects is a major goal of our research on composition directives.

4.4   Model Directives

Model directives determine how a set of models are composed. The model directives we have identified constrain the order in which context-specific aspect models are composed with a primary model. These directives can define a weave-ordering relationships between aspect models. A weave-ordering relationship is a binary constraint that specifies an ordering between two aspect models. There are two cases: An aspect model must be composed before another, or an aspect model must be composed after another.

Precedes

Directive Name: **precedes**

Application: This directive specifies that one aspect model is to be composed with a primary model before another. This directive has two aspect models as operands. The first operand is the aspect model that is to be composed before the second operand.

Form: `former` **precedes** `latter`

Constraint: Both aspect models must exist.

Effect: A weave-ordering relationship is created between the two aspect models and added to the set of weave-ordering constraints maintained by the composer. This directive does not imply that `former` will be woven immediately before `latter`. It simply requires that `former` be woven some time before `latter`.

Follows

Directive Name: **follows**

Application: This directive specifies that one aspect model is to be composed with a primary model after another. This directive is provided only to increase the readability of composition directives. It may be interpreted as equivalent to the **precedes** directive with the operands switched. This directive has two aspect model operands. The first operand is the aspect model to be composed after the second operand.

Form: `later` **follows** `earlier`

Constraint: See **precedes**.

Effect: See **precedes**.

4.5   Weave Ordering Example

Consider the aspect design model in Fig. 11(a). There are three different aspect models and the primary model. In this example, the authentication aspect model needs to be composed before the authorization aspect model, because authorization without authentication is meaningless. Therefore, we declare the following composition directive to make the order explicit.

(1) `authentication` **precedes** `authorization`

We could have also defined a composition directive using the **follows** directive with the operands reversed to achieve the same result.

Suppose we also wish to weave the `errorChecking` aspect model last. The following composition directives accomplish this:

(2) `errorChecking` **follows** `authorization`
(3) `errorChecking` **follows** `authentication`

The result is shown in Fig. 11(b). The dependency from authentication to authorization illustrates the weave-order relationship that specifies that authentication must be woven before authorization, and the dependencies from errorChecking to each of the other aspects illustrates the two binary weave-order relationships that specify errorChecking as the last aspect to be woven.

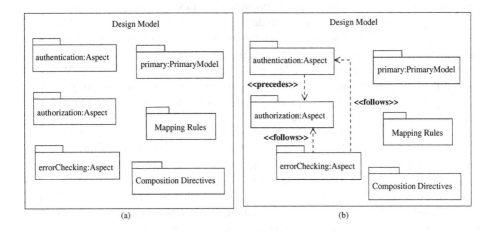

Fig. 11. Example 4. Specifying weave order

5 Related Work

A number of researchers have developed aspect-oriented software development (AOSD) approaches (e.g., see [13, 14, 15, 16, 17, 18, 19, 20]). The composition approaches used in these AOSD approaches can be categorized as *asymmetric* and *symmetric* [21]. In *asymmetric* composition, aspects and base models play clearly distinguished roles during composition. These composition approaches tend not to support composition of aspects and composition of base models. AspectJ [22] is one of the popular aspect-oriented programming languages that uses an asymmetric composition approach. In *symmetric* composition both aspect and base models are treated the same, and thus aspect and base model composition are possible. The composition approaches used in work on viewpoints [23], subject-oriented programming [24, 25], and multidimensional separation of concerns (MDSOC) [26] tend to be symmetric. This paper uses a hybrid composition approach. The (generic) aspect models are patterns that cannot be directly composed with base models, but the instantiated forms of the aspect models (i.e., context-specific aspect models) are not distinguished from the primary model during composition. The approach can be used to compose (generic) aspect models (i.e., patterns) to obtain new aspect models (e.g., see [27]) and to compose UML models. To date we have implemented the procedure for composing UML class models.

A survey of AOSD approaches can be found in Chitchyan et al. [28]. Very few approaches in the survey provide support for composing design models. At the programming level, the subject-oriented approach is closest to the approach described in this paper. In subject-oriented programming [24, 25], program elements such as classes and methods are composed by merging corresponding elements. The correspondence is established based on specified composition rules. The default correspondence is name-based, which can be altered by writing additional composition rules. The composition rules used to control this process can be classified under three categories: rules that establish correspondence, rules that control combination, and rules that control both correspondence and combination. The composition rules in subject-oriented programming are analogous to our use of signatures to determine matches and the use of directives to alter model elements and override default composition rules. Our composition approach depends on the properties specified in the signature rather than just names of model elements, primarily because not all UML model elements are named elements. We have found that name-based matching has a greater potential of producing faulty models than signature-based composition, simply because signature-based composition allows for finer tuning of matching criteria.

At the model level, a comparable AOM approach is the Theme approach proposed by Baniassad and Clarke [13, 29, 30]. In the Theme approach, a design, called a *theme*, is created for each system requirement. These themes, like context-specific aspect and primary models, are essentially design views. A comprehensive design is obtained by composing themes. Composition in the Theme approach is based on the symmetric approach used in subject-oriented programming. Composition relationships specify how models are to be composed by identifying overlapping concepts and specifying how models are integrated. Two types of integration strategies are used: override and merge. Override integration is used when existing behavior in a subject needs to be updated to reflect new requirements. Merge integration is used when subjects for different requirements are to be integrated. Operations in related subjects may need to be merged into a unified operation. Reconciliation strategies resolve conflicts between property values of corresponding subject elements. Precedence relationships, transformation functions applied to conflicting elements, explicit specification of reconciled elements, and default values may be used for reconciliation. Clarke [13] also extends the UML meta-model with the notion of *composableElements* that can be composed using a composition relationship. They have a *Match* metaclass that supports specification of matching criteria. Their matching criteria include *matchByName* and *dontMatch*. They leave the details of implementing the *matchByName* and *dontMatch* to the user of the meta-model. In this sense the metamodel describes a framework for composing UML models. In our work we have developed a more specialized metamodel that contains specifications of composition behaviors. The metamodel was designed to describe our composition approach and to guide the development of supporting tools. To validate the metamodel, we used it to develop a prototype tool for composing UML class models. The composition directives that we have developed include some that are similar to the merge and override integration strategies. The use of composition directives and signatures, as described in this paper, allows modelers to define and apply their own integration and reconciliation strategies, and thus to gain finer control over how models are composed.

Brito and Moreira describe an aspect composition process that identifies match points in a design element and defines composition rules [31]. Rules use identified match points, a binary contribution value (either positive or negative) that quantifies the affects on other aspects, and a priority for a given aspect. In the context of AOP [32], Kienzle et al. describe composition rules based on dependencies between aspects [33]. Both papers [31, 33] focus primarily on relationships that can exist between aspects. We describe the possible relationships between aspects as weave-order relationships and override relationships, but it may also be possible to use priorities and dependencies as done by Kienzle, Brito, and Moreira in our approach. In this sense, the ideas presented in their papers complement the ideas presented in this paper.

Aldawud et al. [34] propose a mechanism for composing state charts where a cross-cutting behavior is an event that triggers a state transition. The composition is specified by linking events across state diagrams. We have not considered composition of state charts in our work.

6 Conclusions and Future Work

In this paper we present a signature-based composition approach that allows one to vary how models are composed using composition directives. The signature-based approach improves upon name-based composition approaches by giving the modeler finer-grained control over the criteria used to match model elements. Composition directives give added flexibility by providing the means to alter model elements and override default composition rules to obtain desired composed models. The directives described in this paper are based on our experience with using the composition approach to compose aspects modeling security features with primary models. For example, we have applied the approach to modeling and composition of access control features such as Role-Based Access Control and Bell LaPadula schemes [5, 27, 35, 36], and for other security features [6, 37, 38, 39]. We are currently applying the techniques in a larger case study involving the development of an e-commerce system.

A composition metamodel that describes the static and behavioral properties needed to support model composition is also presented. The metamodel describes not only the static relationships among composition concepts, but also provides specifications of behaviors that are needed to support model composition using our approach. The composition metamodel describes the behavior needed to support model composition and thus can be used to guide the development of model composition tools that support the composition approach we developed. To validate the metamodel, we built a prototype tool on top of the KerMeta framework. The tool currently supports the composition of UML class models and can be extended to support additional features that appear in the composition metamodel. We are currently developing a subsystem for handling composition directives that will be plugged into the tool.

Empirical evaluation is needed to validate the composition approach in real-world design settings. Such studies can determine the amount of effort required to specify the kinds of compositions that are required in real-world designs. The studies can also be used to determine whether the composition directives match the requirements of a real project. The insights gained from the studies will be used to develop a tractable method for selecting, defining, and applying composition directives and signatures. Work in this respect could result in the specification of some common composition strategies [6] to ease the task of specifying and using composition directives.

Acknowledgment

This material is based upon work partially funded by AFOSR under Award No. FA9550-04-1-0102.

References

[1] France R.B., Ray I., Georg G., Ghosh S. An aspect-oriented approach to design modeling. *IEE Proceedings - Software*, Special Issue on Early Aspects: Aspect-Oriented Requirements Engineering and Architecture Design, 151:173–185, 2004

[2] The Object Management Group (OMG): Unified Modeling Language: Superstructure. Version 2.0, Final Adopted Specification, http://www.omg.org (2003)

[3] Straw G., Georg G., Song E., Ghosh S., France R., and Bieman J. Model composition directives. In: *Proceedings of the International Conference on the UML*, Springer, pp. 84–97, 2004

[4] Reddy R., France R.B., Ghosh S., Fleury F., and Baudry B. Model composition - A signature based approach. In: *Proceedings Aspect Oriented Modeling workshop held with MODELS/UML 2005*, Montego Bay, Jamaica, 2005

[5] Song E., Reddy R., France R., Ray I., Georg G., and Alexander R. Verifiable composition of access control and application features. In: *SACMAT '05: Proceedings of the tenth ACM symposium on Access control models and technologies*, ACM, New York, pp. 120–129, 2005

[6] Georg G., Ray I., and France R. Using aspects to design a secure system. In: *ICECCS 2002: Proceedings of the International Conference on Engineering Complex Computing Systems*, ACM, pp. 117–126, 2002

[7] TRISKELL: The KerMeta Project home page. http://www.kermeta.org (2005)

[8] OMG adopted specification ptc/03-10-04: The Meta Object Facility (MOF) Core Specification. Version 2.0. http://www.omg.org

[9] Muller P., Fleury F., and Jézéquel J. Weaving executability into object-oriented metalanguages. In: *Proceedings of MODELS/UML 2005*, Montego Bay, Jamaica, 2005

[10] Reddy Y.R., France R.B., Georg G. An aspect-based approach to modeling and analyzing dependability features. *Technical Report CS04 - 109*, Colorado State University, Fort Collins, CO, USA, 2004

[11] France R., Georg G. Modeling fault tolerant concerns using aspects. *Technical Report 02-102*, Computer Science Department, Colorado State University, Fort Collins, CO, USA, 2002

[12] Georg G., France R.B., and Ray I. Composing aspect models. In: *4th AOSD Modeling with UML Workshop*, San Francisco, CA, 2003

[13] Clarke S. Extending Standard UML with Model Composition Semantics. *Science of Computer Programming* 44, pp. 71–100, 2002

[14] Araujo J., and Coutinho P. Identifying aspectual use cases using a viewpoint-oriented requirements method. In: *Early Aspects 2003: Aspect Oriented Requirements Engineering and Architecture Design, Workshop of the 2nd Intl. Conference on Aspect-Oriented Software Development*, Boston, MA, 2003

[15] Clarke S., and Walker R.J. Composition patterns: An approach to desigining reusable aspects. In: *Proc. of 23rd Intl. Conference on Software Engineering (ICSE)*, Toronto, Canada, pp. 5–14, 2001

[16] Gray J., Bapty T., Neema S., Tuck J. Handling crosscutting constraints in domain-specific modeling. *Communications of the ACM*, 44:87–93, 2001

[17] Grundy J.C. Multi-perspective specification, design and implementation of software components using aspects. *International Journal of Software Engineering and Knowledge Engineering*, 10(6):713–734, 2000

[18] Jacobson I. Case for aspects - Part I. *Software Development Magazine*, 32–37, 2003

[19] Rashid A., Sawyer P., Moreira A., and Araujo J. Early aspects: A model for aspect-oriented requirements engineering. In: *IEEE Joint Intl. Conference on Requirements Engineering*, Essen, Germany, pp. 199–202, 2002

[20] Aksit M., Wakita K., Bosch J., Bergmans L., and Yonezawa A. Abstracting object interactions using composition filters. In: Guerraoui R., Nierstrasz O., and Riveill M. (eds.) *Proceedings of the ECOOP'93 Workshop on Object-Based Distributed Programming*, Springer, Vol. 791, pp. 152–184, 1994

[21] Harrison W., Ossher H., Tarr P. Asymmetrically vs. symmetrically organized paradigms for software composition. *Technical report*, IBM - RC22685 (W0212-147), 2002

[22] Kiczales G., Lamping J., Mendhekar A., Maeda C., Lopes C., Loingier J., and Irwin J. Aspect oriented programming. In: *ECOOP: Proc. of the European Conference on Object-Oriented Programming, LNCS vol. 1241*, Springer, pp. 220–242, 1997

[23] Nuseibeh B., Kramer J., Finkelstein A. A framework for expressing the relationships between multiple views in requirements specification. *IEEE Transactions on Software Engineering*, 20:760–773, 1994

[24] Harrison W., and Ossher H. Subject oriented programming (a critique of pure objects). In: *OOPSLA '93: Proc. of the 8th Annual Conference on Object-Oriented Programming: Systems, Languages, and Applications*, Washington, DC, pp. 411–428, 1993

[25] Ossher H., Kaplan M., Katz A., Harrison W., Kruskal V. Specifying subject-oriented composition. *Theory and Practice of Object Systems*, 2(3):179–202, 1996

[26] Tarr P., Ossher H., Harrison W., and Sutton S. N degrees of separation: Multi-dimensional separation of concerns. In: *ICSE '99: Proceedings of the 21st International Conference on Software Engineering*, pp. 107–119, 1999

[27] Ray I., Li N., Kim D.K., and France R. Using parameterized UML to specify and compose access control models. In: *IICIS 2003: Proceedings of Sixth IFIP TC-11 WG 11.5 Working Conference on Integrity and Internal Control in Information Systems*, 2003

[28] Chitchyan R., Rashid A., Sawyer P., Garcia A., Alarcon M., Bakker J., Tekinerdogan B., Clarke S., Jackson A. Survey of aspect-oriented analysis and design approaches. *Technical Report ULANC-9*, AOSD, Europe, 2005

[29] Baniassad E., and Clarke S. Theme: An approach for aspect-oriented analysis and design. In: *Proceedings of the International Conference on Software Engineering*, pp. 158–167, 2004

[30] Clarke S., and Walker R.J. Composition patterns: An approach to designing reusable aspects. In: *ICSE: The 23rd International Conference on Software Engineering*, Toronto, Canada, 2001

[31] Brito I., and Moreira A. Towards a composition process for aspect-oriented requirements. In: *Proceedings of the Early-Aspects Workshop at AOSD2002*, 2002

[32] Kiczales G., Lamping J., Mendhekar A., Maeda C., Lopes C.V., Loingtier J.M., and Irwin J. Aspect-oriented programming. In: *ECOOP '97: Proceedings of the European Conference on Object-Oriented Programming, LNCS vol. 1241*, Springer, pp. 220–242, 1997

[33] Kienzle J., Yu Y., and Xiong J. On composition and reuse of aspects. In: *Proceedings of the Foundations of Aspect-Oriented Languages Workshop*, Boston, MA, USA, 2003

[34] Aldawud O., Bader A., and Elrad T. Weaving with statecharts. In: *Workshop on Aspect-Oriented Modeling (held with AOSD-2002)*, Enschede, Netherlands, 2002

[35] Ray I., France R., Li N., Georg G. An aspect-based approach to modeling access control concerns. *Information and Software Technology* 40:557–633, 2004

[36] Ray I., Li N., France R., and Kim D.K. Using UML to visualize role-based access control constraints. In: *SACMAT: Proceedings of the Symposium on Access Control Models and Technologies*, pp. 31–40, 2004

[37] Georg G., France R., and Ray I. Designing high integrity systems using aspects. In: *IICIS 2002: Proceedings of the Fifth IFIP TC-11 WG 11.5 Working Conference on Integrity and Internal Control in Information Systems*, Bonn, Germany, 2002

[38] Georg G., France R., and Ray I. An aspect-based approach to modeling security concerns. In: *Proceedings of the Workshop on Critical Systems Development with UML*, Dresden, Germany, 2002

[39] Homb S.H., Georg G., France R., Bieman J., and Jurjens J. Cost-benefit trade-off analysis using BBN for aspect-oriented risk-driven development. In: *ICECCS: Proceedings of the 10th IEEE International Conference on Engineering of Complex Computer Systems*, 2005

Appendix

Merge Part of the Signature-Based Composition Procedure

```
**************************************************************************************
// e1 and e2 are the model elements that need to be merged
e1.merge(e2 : ModelElement)      //precondition : e1.sigEquals(e2) returns true
**************************************************************************************
result := e1.getMetaClass.new // create the merged instance in the context of e1

// Iterate on all properties of the objects to be merged.
// e1 and e2 have the same meta-class. Thus, they have the
// same set of properties.

foreach Property p in e1.getMetaClass.getAllProperties

  if type of p is primitive
  // Primitive types are basic datatypes such as string, int.
  // If an object does not have a value for a property then
       // the value val is taken from the other object and vice versa.
       // This is not a conflict.
  // If neither object has values, then val is null in the resulting
  // merged object.
     if e1.get(p) is null or e2.get(p) is null then
         result.set(p, val)
     else
         // If the values are the same then it is ok.
         // Otherwise a conflict has been detected.
         if e1.get(p) = e2.get(p) then
             result.set(p, e1.get(p))
         else
             A conflict has been detected
  else
  // Type of p is not primitive.
  // If the property refers to a single object, this is the base case.
     if the property upper bound is 1
         if e1.get(p) is null or e2.get(p) is null then
             result.set(p, val)      // val is the same as above
         else
           if sigEquals(e1.get(p), e2.get(p)) then
           // If the object e1.get(p) is contained by e1 and same for e2
```

```
// (p.isComposite=true) then the objects should be merged,
// otherwise, one is chosen.
// Either one can be chosen because they both have the same signature

        if p.isComposite is true then
            result.set(p, merge(e1.get(p), e2.get(p)))
        else
            result.set(p, e1.get(p).clone())
    else
        A conflict has been detected
else
// The property refers to a collection of objects.
// The resulting merged object should contain property values that are
    // either only in e1 or only in e2, or the merged version of objects
    // that are in both e1 and e2.
    for each value v1 in e1.get(p)
        for each matching element v2 in e2.get(p)
            if p.isComposite then
                result.get(p).add(merge(v1, v2))
            else
                result.get(p).add(v1.clone())
                if no element found
                    result.get(p).add(v1.clone())
        for each value v2 in e2.get(p)
            if NO matching element found in e1.get(p)
                result.get(p).add(v2.clone())
*************************************************************************
```

Aspect Categories and Classes of Temporal Properties

Shmuel Katz

Computer Science, The Technion, Haifa, Israel
katz@cs.technion.ac.il

Abstract. Generic categories of aspects are described, and their potential value is explained. For some categories, broad classes of syntactically identifiable temporal properties, such as safety, liveness, or existence properties, are guaranteed to hold for a system with any aspect of the category woven into it, if the property was true in the system without the aspect. Thus classes of properties preserved by the aspect are defined. Moreover, relatively simple verification techniques are shown to hold for some classes of temporal properties over systems augmented with some other categories of aspects. Verification of new properties added by the aspects is also considered. Each category is defined in terms of the semantic transformation it makes to the state graphs of underlying systems. A generic procedure to identify syntactically when an aspect belongs to a category is described and related to existing code analysis systems that use static code analysis and dataflow techniques. The definitions of categories, identification procedures, and lemmas about property classes provide the needed foundations that justify and motivate automatic code analysis modules to identify aspect categories. The categories enable simpler proofs of correctness than would otherwise be possible, and exploiting their characteristics can aid in software development.

Keywords: Aspect specification, spectative, regulative, invasive, aspect categories, dataflow analysis, aspect verification.

1 Introduction

Aspect-oriented programming seeks to isolate crosscutting concerns in aspect modules that are then woven with other aspects or with more standard object-oriented classes. Even in the earliest examples of aspects, it was clear that some were more complicated than others as far as the relation to the underlying program with which they were woven. The classic examples of logging or adding performance monitoring influence the underlying program less than aspects treating overflow of integer computations, or restricting access to some methods to favored users. In turn, those are less closely tied to the computations of the underlying program than aspects that compute and apply discount prices to an underlying online bookshop or that change the designs of buildings in an architecture support program in order to enforce handicapped access regulations.

In [27] and in some earlier works on superimpositions, spectative, regulative, and invasive types of aspects were suggested to describe categories of aspects such as those above. The *spectative* aspects only gather information about the system to

A. Rashid and M. Aksit (Eds.): Transactions on AOSD I, LNCS 3880, pp. 106–134, 2006.
© Springer-Verlag Berlin Heidelberg 2006

which they are woven, usually by adding fields and methods, but do not otherwise influence the possible underlying computations. On the other hand, *regulative* aspects change the flow of control (e.g., which methods are activated in which conditions) but do not change the computation done to existing fields, while *invasive* aspects do change values of existing fields (but still should not invalidate desirable properties).

In this paper these categories of aspects are extended and made more precise. An analysis is given of how properties are affected by aspects in each category. The classes of properties are described as those satisfying generic temporal logic formulae, and have previously been used for purposes related to refinement and proof techniques. Both the influence of the aspect on classes of properties that already were true in the underlying system, and the difficulty of verifying new properties added by the aspect are considered. The categories and lemmas enable establishing some properties automatically without expensive proofs using model checkers. For some other properties and categories the verification is not immediate, but simpler proofs of correctness can be used than would otherwise be possible. Aspect categories can aid in software development by encouraging the modularity that is identified in the categories presented here.

The view taken in this paper is of a main existing system to which one or more aspects can be applied, as in AspectJ [18]. When the entire system is considered to be a composition of aspects, as in the HyperJ approach [24], similar considerations can be applied. The implications of our results for interference among aspects are considered in Sect. 8, but otherwise the relations between a given system and a single aspect are treated. In the continuation, the system before an aspect is woven into it is termed the *original* or the *underlying* system. After an aspect has been woven into it, the result is referred to as the *augmented* system. The aspect categories are defined in terms of restrictions on the semantic changes between the state graphs of the underlying and the augmented system. These are then used to justify claims about classes of temporal logic properties. A particular aspect generally cannot be directly checked for the semantic restrictions. Instead, for most aspect languages, static analysis with dataflow techniques or a rich type system can be used to identify subsets of the categories. Here, generic dataflow techniques for identification are presented for each category, and shown to guarantee the semantic definitions. In Sect. 9, related approaches and analysis techniques are surveyed, and their connections to the categories defined here are explained. As new techniques are developed, they can be shown to identify the appropriate semantic categories, so that the associated lemmas on classes of properties will automatically hold. Thus this paper can be seen as providing a semantic foundation and implications for temporal logic properties over static analysis for aspects.

In this paper a running example is used of aspects over an underlying system that manipulates fractions, and generates and checks online exams for students with simple arithmetic exercises for fractions. In Fig. 1, the outline of this system is given, as a minimal basis on which to add aspects. The RationalExam class initiates exams, generates questions, accepts answers, and checks whether an answer is correct, all using the Rational class. The doExam method is activated externally. In later sections aspects are added to compile the results, restrict use of the system, and reduce the fractions.

```
public class Rational{
        private int        numerator       = 0;
        private int        denominator     = 1;
        public int getNumerator() {...}
        public void setNumerator(int numerator) {...}
        public int getDenominator() {...}
        public void setDenominator(int denominator) {...}
        public Rational add(Rational r) {...}
}
public class RationalExam{...
        private static String getInput() {...}
        private static Rational randomRational() {...}
        private Rational getAnswerToAddQuest(Rational r1, Rational r2) {...}
        private boolean checkAnswer(Rational answer, Rational correctresult) {...}
        public void doExam() {...}
}
```

Fig. 1. Outline of an online exam system

In order to investigate the properties of a system and categorize aspects applied to it, the systems to which aspects are woven as well as the aspects themselves will be assumed to have *specifications*. These are descriptions of the desirable properties of the system. Often the exact nature of the specifications will not need to be available, but rather the class of property described will be sufficient, e.g., safety or invariant properties. Note that specifications do not describe all properties of the system, only those seen as important and positive. Such properties should be maintained (perhaps in a modified form) even if the system is augmented with aspects, or even if an aspect is combined with other aspects. For example, if a system has been shown to properly complete each request submitted externally, and an aspect is added to monitor performance, we do not want the combined system with the aspect to occasionally crash in midtreatment of a request. In the system with fractions, a desirable invariant property might be that the denominator of every fraction is positive, and any aspects added might be expected to maintain that invariant. What can change completely are the properties of the system *not* seen in the specification. The form of such specifications using syntactic forms of temporal logic assertions is described in Sect. 2.

In general, once an aspect has been shown to belong to one of the categories described, there are various semantic implications for the properties of a system augmented with such an aspect. In the best case, classes of properties true of the underlying system can be shown to be maintained automatically in the augmented one, without further proof. In other situations, properties can be established by analyzing only the aspect code. In the worst case, the entire system must be considered, but for certain properties easier proof methods can be used. The lemmas about aspect categories and types of temporal properties are justified using a semantic view of object systems and aspects based on state graphs. In Sect. 3, this view is presented and related to other definitions of the semantics of aspects. Section 4 explains that real-time and next-state properties are not covered by the analysis framework in this paper. In Sects. 5–7, spectative, regulative, weakly invasive, and invasive categories of aspects are defined in terms of the semantic transformations of the graphs, syntactic checks are shown to guarantee aspects of the desired category, and classes of temporal properties are shown to be preserved or to be easier to prove for the category. In Sect. 8 interactions among multiple aspects are considered, Sect. 9 discusses related work, while Sect. 10 summarizes the results.

2   Temporal Logics and Classes of Properties

2.1 Specifications of Aspects

Specifications of aspects need to describe both what is assumed true of the underlying system at each joinpoint identified by the aspect (often, any object or method in the basic system to which the aspect may be applied), and, on the other hand, what is required to be true after the advice is applied, if the needed assumption indeed holds at the joinpoint. For each joinpoint and advice segment of code, the advice assumes some property of the system, and guarantees some property when it finishes (as well as possibly some properties during the aspect execution). Such an assume–guarantee structure for aspects has already been recognized [9, 27, 28] and is essential for describing the added value of an aspect. The overall properties added by the aspect can also be globally described.

Since many aspects deal with so-called nonfunctional concerns such as availability, fault tolerance, security, or persistence, explicitly providing their specifications is that much more difficult. Still, no such distinction is made here, and temporal logic can be used to specify such properties as well as functional ones. Even if some properties have not been formally expressed, for the purposes of property analysis described below, it is sufficient to identify to which well-known classes of specification properties the specific properties of interest belong, e.g., if they are invariant properties.

2.2 The Semantics of Temporal Logic

Temporal logic provides a formal notation for describing properties of execution sequences, using temporal modalities to quantify over the execution sequences and the states in them from a reference state. In the simplest version of linear temporal logic (without existence properties), G stands for "globally", i.e., from now on in the sequence of states, and F stands for "in the future", i.e., eventually there is a state. Thus an assertion $G(p => Fq)$ means that in every state, if p is true then eventually there will be another state with q. If p represents "a request has been made", while q is "a response is given", this corresponds to a specification that every request has a later response. An assertion pUq means that p will hold in all states from now on until a state that satisfies q (and there is a state satisfying q). An assertion Xp (in words: "next" p) is true in a state if p itself is true in the state immediately following. Formally, in terms of an execution sequence (a sequence of states) σ, and an index in that sequence i, we have:

- (σ, i) satisfies Gp iff $\forall j \geq i.\ p(\sigma(j))$
- (σ, i) satisfies Fp iff $\exists j \geq i.\ p(\sigma(j))$
- (σ, i) satisfies pUq iff $\exists j \geq i.\ q(\sigma(j)) \wedge \forall k.\ j > k \geq i.\ p(\sigma(k))$
- (σ, i) satisfies Xp iff $p(\sigma(i+1))$

Similar past modalities are defined symmetrically. Linear temporal logic (LTL) only has modalities defined in this format.

In branching temporal logic, such as CTL [4], there are also *path* quantifiers over all possible continuations from a state (denoted A) and some possible continuation (denoted E). Formally, such formulas are interpreted over an execution tree, i.e., a collection of execution sequences organized into a tree, where common prefixes are written once as paths from the root. When applied to systems, temporal logic formulae are interpreted over a Kripke structure semantics (see [5]) consisting of a state transition graph with nodes corresponding to the possible states reachable in executions of the system, and edges labeled by possible atomic actions of the system that transform the source state into the target. The states are labeled by values for every possible atomic assertion.

In linear temporal logic an assertion is true for a system iff it is true for every path through the Kripke structure starting at initial states, while for CTL, the formula must be true for the execution tree obtained by "unwinding" the Kripke structure. Thus an LTL assertion Gp is equivalent to a branching temporal logic assertion AGp.

2.3 Classes of Temporal Properties

Classes of temporal properties were first defined by [22] and were shown to correspond to a simple syntactic form, to a proof method, and to a complexity hierarchy. **Safety** properties hold in every state, and may relate to the history of states up to the state being considered. Such properties describe what is allowed in the system, under what conditions, and what states cannot occur. This class includes precedence properties such as "a state satisfying P is always preceded by a state satisfying Q", as well as the invariant properties described below. As shown in [22], all safety properties can be expressed as an LTL assertion of the form Gp, where p is a predicate without other future modalities, relating only to the state variables or the past history leading to the state under consideration (a past predicate). The temporal modalities needed to express such past assertions are not given here since they are not needed in the continuation.

(**Global**) **invariant** properties are true in every state (without reference to the computation history), and are the most common subclass of assertion in the class of safety properties. A weaker safety assertion common in object-oriented systems is known as a **class invariant**, and is required to be true initially, as well as before and after each method call of the class (but not while method calls are ongoing). A **partial correctness** assertion, intended to hold whenever the system terminates, is also a kind of invariant property. An invariant intended to be true at certain points, such as a class invariant or partial correctness assertion, can be transformed to a global invariant of the form "at(method call) implies p" or "at(return) implies p" instead of only asserting p at the method call or return point. Thus partial correctness and class invariants are merely special forms of global invariants.

Liveness properties are guaranteed to hold eventually for every possible execution. Example properties in this category are the successful termination of a kind of method activation, an assertion that every message sent is eventually received, or an assertion that some crucial event (e.g., a particular method call) will occur whenever some other event occurs first. Such properties always can be expressed using an eventuality (F or Until) modality not negated. Among the common combinations are Fp (to express "eventually there is a state in which p is true"), GFp (to express that p is infinitely often true in an infinite computation), FGp (to express that eventually p becomes continuously true), or various combinations of these forms.

Both safety and liveness are categories that make assertions about every possible computation of a system. In a branching temporal logic, there is an A quantifier on the outer level, and no other path quantifiers. As noted above, there are also branching temporal logic **Existence** properties that can express assertions about possible computations of a system (e.g., there is a path that reaches an interrupt). Syntactically, these are equivalent to properties with an E path quantifier not negated, relating to the existence of a computation among the possible executions of the system. There are branching time generalizations of the safety and liveness properties above that have been shown to be maintained under certain types of model abstractions [7]. Instead of writing "for every object r of a class, r.fieldname" in assertions, just the fieldname is used when clear from the context. So G(denominator >0) means that the assertion is true in every object of class Rational.

3   The Semantics of Aspects and Object Systems

3.1   Approaches to Aspect Semantics

In order to define and reason about the categories of aspects and their connections to classes of properties, the form of an object-oriented system and its semantics must be defined. There are several formal semantic definitions of aspects and aspect systems, using, e.g., denotational [32], operational (or so-called *small step* semantics) [15], process calculus [3], and functional [31] approaches. In principle, any of them could be used to justify the claims connecting categories of aspects to the correctness of types of temporal properties. Most of them assume a simplified object or functional base language, in order to concentrate on a semantic definition for the new aspect construct.

3.2   State Machine Semantics for Object Systems

Here we adopt the state graph semantic view, because it is most appropriate for verification of temporal properties, and is used by software model checkers such as Bandera [14]. This view can be seen in the UML statechart semantics, where each class is accompanied by a statechart (equivalent to a hierarchical state graph) expressing the possible states and transitions for each instance (object) of that class.

A node in the state graph of an object gives specific values to the variables, fields, and control state of that object, and the edges (transitions) describe the effect of executing an enabled step from that node. A system is then described by the cross product of the state graphs of the active objects, linked by potential method calls among them. Each object has a designated node in its state graph corresponding to the present values of the object. The cross product of these designated nodes defines a mapping that provides the present values of variables, fields, locations, and internal stacks of method activations along with identification of which actions are presently enabled in the system, for each object. This can be seen as a continuation semantics describing both the immediate values and the potential continuations for each point during an execution. For simplicity, the term *variables* is used to refer to all of the state components that are given values in each state.

The semantic meaning of a system (either underlying or augmented with aspects) at any point during its execution is defined as the expansion of the cross product of state graphs described above, to a single computation state graph, where the nodes are particular values for the existing variables at that point (what is usually called a state), and the arrows are transitions that correspond to the atomic actions of the system. Note that this does not exclude transitions that extend the state graph by adding new object occurrences, or shrink it by discarding objects that have been finished. Issues of inheritance and polymorphism can complicate the definition of the state graph, but are orthogonal to the question of adding aspects. The system and semantic state graph are often organized as a reactive system [22], where each external activation leads to a finite computation corresponding to a transaction. A maximal sequence of states in the graph from an external activation to a rest state is known as a *trace*. Although such a state graph may have an infinite number of states (if there are variables with infinite domains, such as the integers), abstraction techniques can be used to create finite-state versions that are used in model-checking.

3.3   Aspect Semantics as State Graph Transformations

An aspect declaration and its binding (known as *weaving*) to an underlying system define   *joinpoints* or events of the underlying system where the aspect is to be activated and aspect code (known as *advice*) is to be executed. The joinpoints are described syntactically using *pointcut* declarations. Semantically, the weaving of an aspect to a system transforms the graph of the original system to that of the augmented one. Thus the semantics of an aspect is defined as a transformer of state graphs: given the graph of the underlying system, it yields the graph of the augmented one. Note that this semantics is neutral about how aspects and weaving are actually implemented in an aspect language: systems that in-line aspect code, those that capture events and transfer control at run time, as well as languages with other known implementation techniques, are all equally valid.

When an aspect is woven, for each joinpoint in the original system, a transition to the beginning of the state machine of the corresponding advice is added. The transitions and states generated by applying the aspect advice code are part of the subgraph following the joinpoint transition. However, note that objects of the original system not related to the joinpoint continue to have enabled operations that can be interleaved with those of the aspect code, and that appear in the state graph of the augmented system as transitions from states generated by aspect operations (or as separate components that have an implicit cross product of local states).

The semantic picture is clearly influenced by whether the aspect code is intended to interrupt the underlying system *before*, *after*, or *around* an event of that system.

(Note that the terminology of AspectJ is used here, although other aspect languages have similar ideas.) If the aspect advice code is intended to execute *before* the event that defines the occurrence of a joinpoint, then the transition to the advice code is from the state before the transition corresponding to the joinpoint event, and the joinpoint event transition itself is removed at that point, to be inserted later where the aspect advice completes. The intention is that the code of the underlying program will be continued after the advice completes, but it is not at all clear that the continuation is from the local state that previously held before that continuation. Thus the issues raised by where to reconnect are discussed as the types of aspects are examined in greater detail. The considerations for an aspect intended to occur *after* an event defined by a pointcut are similar, with the transition to the beginning of the advice state graph added from the state after the event in the underlying system. When the *around* option is used and the *proceed* statement occurs in the advice, it is equivalent to a *before* advice, followed by an *after* advice. When *proceed* does not occur, the advice does not continue from the point in the code at which it was interrupted, so there is no return arrow at all.

A fragment of a generic state graph of an underlying system is seen in Fig. 2a, where x represents the state of the original system, while the augmented graph after weaving an aspect before the P transition is seen in Fig. 2b. As will be shown later, assuming that w is local to the aspect, the situation described is typical of a spectative aspect because the x component is not changed by the aspect transitions, and the P transition at the end of the aspect transitions reconnects to the same state as in the original, if we ignore w. Note that in this example, there are no independent objects

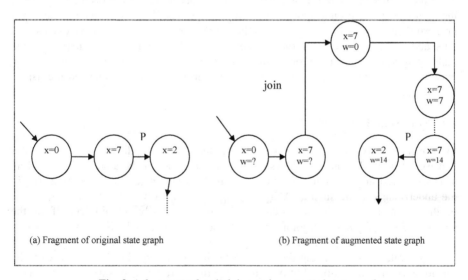

(a) Fragment of original state graph   (b) Fragment of augmented state graph

Fig. 2. A fragment of underlying and augmented state graphs

that would require a cross-product in the augmented state graph. In the augmented fragment, w appears in the states corresponding to those of the underlying system, but no assertion of the underlying system could have referred to it, since it was not defined there.

The influence of applying aspects from each category to an underlying system can now be considered in terms of the state graphs of the original and augmented systems. However, first the limits of this approach are described.

4 Properties Not Inherently Preserved

There are two types of properties that are not analyzed in the continuation: those not in the temporal logic defined earlier over the state space of the underlying or the augmented system, and next-state properties. Both of these have properties that are not maintained, no matter which category of aspect is considered, and a more specialized analysis is needed which is different from the type of semantic reasoning used here.

4.1 Real-Time Properties

If an aspect or underlying system already explicitly contains clock variables, explicitly incremented in code, the framework here can relate to them. However, usually this is not the case, and real-time properties that relate to the elapsed time expected between two events are not expressible in the classes of temporal logic defined in Sect. 2, without special external variables. Time can be introduced either using special time or clock variables that automatically are increased with time values not explicitly in the code, or by extending temporal logic with additional operators. Thus the claims below that automatically extend properties of the original system to the augmented one do not apply to real-time properties. This is fortunate, since such properties can be influenced by aspects that have joinpoints between those events, and thus add the computation of the advice code to the previous computation of the underlying system. Clearly, some real-time properties true of the underlying system may not be true of the augmented one, no matter how loosely connected the aspect functionality is to that of the original system.

4.2 Next-State Properties

Moreover, for any category of aspect, assertions about immediately following states that were true in the underlying system may not be true for the augmented one if an aspect can add advice (that generates new intermediate states). An assertion true in the underlying system, such as $AG(p => Xq)$ (meaning, whenever p is true, q is true in the immediately following state), will not necessarily remain true if in the augmented system an aspect joinpoint can be added immediately after a state where p is true.

In general, assertions using the "next-state" temporal modality X are known to be sensitive to refinements or additions, and have therefore been considered problematic [21]. In fact, in order to achieve greater abstraction and robustness under refinements, it has been suggested that a temporal logic should not be able to "detect stuttering" (i.e., repetitions of states). Lamport and others have shown that a temporal logic without X or the corresponding "immediately previous" operator cannot distinguish among sequences of states that only differ in the number of repetitions of states that appear. We thus have the following simple lemma:

Lemma 1: Any property of the underlying system relating a state and its immediate successor or predecessor state (a "next-state property") is not automatically preserved in an augmented system when any aspect code can be applied at a joinpoint including the earlier state of the pair related.

This claim is straightforward because new intermediate states are always generated by the advice code.   □

5 Spectative Aspects

A spectative aspect can change the values of variables local to the aspect, but does not change either the value of any variable or the flow of method calls of the underlying system. New fields and methods can be added to existing classes of the underlying system, or new classes can be added, but these will not affect either the potential or actual actions of the original system. Each computation path of the augmented system has sections of original computation interleaved with sections of new aspect computation. The result is always equivalent to temporarily suspending the underlying system, recording some information about it, computing new values not influencing the underlying system in any way, and then continuing as before. More precisely we have:

Definition: An aspect is **spectative** if the projection of the augmented state graph onto the state variables of the underlying system is identical to the underlying state graph, except that the projection contains additional repetitions of states connected by edges that correspond to aspect operations.

The repetitions of states in the projection represent the advice segments, which can affect variables local to the aspect, but not those of the underlying system. In Fig. 2b, the projection of the augmented system fragment onto x is identical to the original fragment in Fig. 2a, except for repetitions of the $x=7$ state. Note that the projection of the augmented state graph could have several subpaths with repeated states branching from the state before a joinpoint state and reconnecting at the joinpoint state. This could be due to reading input values or branching in the aspect code. However, the set of traces (i.e., maximal sequences of states) of the projection is identical to the set in the original system except for repetitions of states, and the branching structure of the original is also maintained.

Such a situation might be difficult to detect directly on the state graphs that represent the semantics, and which, of course, are usually not generated in practice. However, detecting that an aspect is spectative is possible on the code level in most aspect languages, using standard type checking and data-flow techniques. For spectative aspects the local fields of the aspect are the only ones computed by that aspect, and no assignments are made by aspect code to fields or to parameters that can be bound to fields, variables, or parameters of the basic system. Care must be taken in defining what is "local." A class and objects or fields declared within the aspect and only accessed there are clearly local. In addition, even if a class is declared globally, but objects are instantiated and the class methods are used only within the aspect, that class is *effectively local* to the aspect. Moreover, parameters of system methods that print values are also considered local to the aspect, because printing a value has no effect on other values printed. This means that assertions about what is *not* printed may be changed in the augmented system (although positive assertions about values printed in the original program are maintained, as will be shown). The aspect code cannot "redirect" the flow of execution, and simply adds to the previous system without skipping any of its computation. Moreover, the aspect code must be "wait-free", i.e., progress of its execution is not dependent on a condition being achieved in the underlying system.

This situation is easiest to detect if all bindings between fields or variables of the aspect and the basic system are made through parameters of the aspect. On the other hand, when arbitrary binding is possible, for example, by using the same name in both code segments, then only when a specific binding has been made can the augmented system be analyzed to determine which elements are bound and whether the aspect is spectative. In either case, dataflow techniques such as the *uses* and the *defined-use* pairs of standard code optimization can be employed to determine whether there is any influence of fields in an aspect on those of the basic system (the other direction is, of course, not a problem). The possibility of analyzing just the aspect is one argument in favor of clearly identifying parameters for weaving, rather than allowing free bindings that force global analysis. The generic *detection procedure* to identify a spectative aspect is:

1. Identify which variables (including parameter names) of the aspect code are bound to variables in the underlying system (either by identifying (actual, formal) parameter pairs from an aspect instance using its declaration, or by identifying the same name in the aspect code and the underlying code, if that is sufficient to bind the variables). The set C denotes the aspect variables bound to an underlying system variable.
2. Check that no variable of C is assigned a value by the aspect (appears on the left-hand side of an assignment in advice of the aspect, or is an actual parameter that is assigned a value in an internal method call of the advice code).
3. Check that each aspect code segment (advice) terminates. Although generally an undecidable problem, syntactic special cases often hold, such as identifying straight-line code (a basic block, in dataflow terms), or loop-free segments.
4. Check that the aspect code does not disable independent underlying operations and is wait-free.
5. Check that the code of the underlying system is resumed at each joinpoint identified and the enabling conditions for the underlying operations have not been affected. Thus there cannot be exceptions thrown in the aspect code that lead to abnormal termination or do not resume the underlying execution at the joinpoint from which it was interrupted, and *around* advice without a *proceed* is not allowed.

First, we show that if the generic syntactic checks are made successfully, then the aspect is spectative. An aspect can be spectative if bound with *before, after,* or *around* including a *proceed*. Here we treat only the *before* case, since the others are similar. Recall that here, as in all subsequent lemmas until Sect. 8, an augmented system is treated where a single aspect is woven to an underlying system.

Lemma 2: If the detection procedure above has been applied successfully to an aspect and underlying code, the aspect is spectative.

Proof: From steps 1 and 2 it follows that the advice does not change the variables of the underlying system. Thus in the projection of the augmented system to the variables of the underlying one, each transition corresponding to operations of the advice code leaves the values of those variables unchanged. From step 3 it follows that the subsequences corresponding to aspect operations are finite. From step 4 it follows that the enabledness of transitions from objects independent of the joinpoint in the underlying system is not affected by the aspect operations. Finally, from step 5 it follows that after the last state resulting from an advice code operation, the location in the code of the program counter is at the operation that identified the joinpoint. Since the values of the variables of the underlying program are also unchanged, that operation will have the same effect as in the underlying system, so the reconnection arrow is to the same state as previously (see Fig. 2). It thus follows that the projection of the augmented graph satisfies the conditions in the definition of a spectative aspect.   □

```
public aspect ScoringAspect {
        // Inter-type declarations
        private int        RationalExam.correct    = 0;
        private int        RationalExam.wrong      = 0;
        // Pointcuts
        pointcut checkingAnswer(RationalExam exam) :
                call(void RationalExam.checkAnswer(Rational, Rational))
                && target(exam) ;
        pointcut doingExam(RationalExam exam) :
                call (void RationalExam.doExam()) && target(exam);

        // Advice
        after(RationalExam exam) returning (boolean ok):
                checkingAnswer(exam) {
                if (ok)
                        exam.correct++;
                else
                        exam.wrong++;
        }
        after(RationalExam exam) : doingExam(exam) {
        System.out.println("You answered " + exam.correct +" correct answers");
        System.out.println("You answered " + exam.wrong +" wrong answers");
        }
}
```

Fig. 3. Aspect for computing scores

Consider the aspect given in Fig. 3. This aspect counts the correct and incorrect answers given to questions about fractions in locally declared fields *correct* and *wrong*. This aspect satisfies all of the conditions above, since it uses the parameters bound to the Exam object, but only changes the local fields, or prints values, and the advice code does not wait for any condition to hold. This aspect is therefore spectative. Note that even though the termination requirement in item 3 is undecidable in general, in this example there are no loops, and only simple system methods, so the termination is trivial.

As another example, an aspect that treats the display of a shape manipulation program is often used as a case study for modularization using aspects, as opposed to a version without aspects that scatters the display updates in the object code. The aspect simply gathers information on the shapes, including joinpoints that occur as shapes are changed or moved, and displays them using classes that are effectively local to the aspect. Since all of the display updating is now done in the aspect using the effectively local display class, the aspect is spectative relative to the underlying system performing shape manipulations. Even if the display object is used by other parts of the system, if an aspect only locally introduces and maintains a new field in the display, it is spectative.

As will be discussed in Sect. 9, in practical analysis systems for identifying spectative aspects, aliasing, inheritance, and polymorphism can significantly complicate the analysis. Dataflow and type-safety techniques such as those used in static analysis are always conservative, in that if successful, the spectative nature of the aspect is guaranteed. If the analysis does not establish that the aspect is spectative, but has not revealed a clear violation of the semantic definition, perhaps only a deeper semantic analysis is needed.

Now a key lemma about spectative aspects can be stated and proven, in terms of the classes of properties defined earlier and the underlying and augmented state graphs.

Lemma 3: If an aspect is spectative, all safety, liveness, and existence properties of the underlying system that are not next-state properties and involve assertions only about variables, fields, and methods of the underlying system will not be influenced by the aspect, and will also hold in the augmented system. Moreover, every such property true of the augmented system was already true of the underlying one.

Proof: By the definition of a spectative aspect, in terms of the variables of the underlying system, the projections to those variables of the new states due to the advice code of a spectative aspect are identical to the state before the joinpoint transition. The subsequences corresponding to states and transitions of the advice are finite and reconnect back to the state in the underlying program after the operation that activated the joinpoint transition (since a *before* advice is being considered). Because the assertions have no next-state properties, they are insensitive to repetitions of states, and thus any such linear or existence assertion true of the underlying system and involving only its variables is also true of the projection of the augmented graph. Since only variables in the projection appear in the assertions, they also hold in the augmented state graph itself.

No new properties involving only the variables of the underlying system can be added by the augmented one because, again, the projection of the state graph of the augmented system to the variables of the underlying one differs from the original underlying state graph only in the number of finite repetitions of states that already exist, and such differences cannot be distinguished without including a next-state property (i.e., a temporal formula with an X or the corresponding "previous" temporal operator).   □

In the example, the underlying system could have invariant properties such as G(denominator>0) (i.e., in every state, the denominator is greater than 0). This will automatically hold for the augmented system with ScoringAspect, because it is spectative. A liveness property such as G(at(setNumerator) => F(at(setDenominator)) (i.e., setNumerator is always eventually followed by setDenominator) will also be automatically extended to the augmented system, if it was already true of the underlying system without the aspect.

However, it should be noted that implicitly scoped visibility properties such as "the value of a field is not visible outside the class" can be violated by spectative aspects, even when the properties were previously true of the underlying system. The problem is that the assertion of "not visible outside the class" when applied to the augmented system involves both the original variables, fields, and methods and new ones added by the aspect, and thus is different from the original assertion. Therefore Lemma 3 does not guarantee that such a property will be preserved in the augmented system. For example, within the aspect code, the value of a (hidden) field X of the underlying system could be "made visible" by examining another field Y (added by the aspect) that is given the value of X, or by adding public methods, both possible in a spectative aspect.

New properties of the augmented system that *do* involve both variables of the aspect and those of the underlying system are also easier to verify if the aspect is spectative:

Lemma 4: Invariant properties true of the variables of a spectative aspect, or connecting the aspect and underlying variables, can be established for the augmented system by separately analyzing the aspect variables not bound to variables of the underlying system in the aspect code and the other variables in the underlying code.

Proof: By the definition of a spectative aspect, variables of the underlying system and variables of the aspect bound to those of the underlying system are only changed in the underlying system. Moreover, variables of the aspect not bound to those of the underlying system are clearly changed only by the aspect advice code.

If variables of both the aspect and the underlying system are in the assertion, it is sufficient to consider separately whether the underlying variables and the aspect variables bound to them (which are only changed in the underlying system) maintain the invariant, and whether the "local" aspect variables (changed only in the aspect code) also maintain the invariant.   □

Lemma 4 can allow the decomposition of the verification task for the augmented system to two smaller problems, especially if model-checking abstraction techniques are used. For the visibility property mentioned earlier, for spectative aspects it is sufficient to check only the aspect code in order to extend the property to the augmented system. Liveness properties added by the aspect, on the other hand, are closely connected to the liveness properties of the underlying system, because aspect advice is only executed when joinpoints of the underlying system are reached. Thus, in general, to establish new liveness properties involving the aspect, the augmented system as a whole must be considered. A simple exception is liveness properties involving only the aspect code segments, such as an assertion that each advice segment that is initiated will properly terminate without throwing exceptions.

6 Regulative Aspects

Regulative aspects can affect the flow of control of the underlying system by restricting operations, delaying some operations, or preventing the continuation of a computation.

Definition: An aspect is **regulative** if the projection of the augmented state graph on the variables of the underlying system is identical to the state graph of the underlying system, except that some states are repeated (with new edges from aspect operations) and some edges are removed. States are ignored that become disconnected (unreachable) from the augmented state graph with entrance points (external method calls).

Note that, as for spectative aspects, a repeated state and added edge can branch off from an existing state. In a regulative aspect, that branch might lead to the repeated state, but with no continuation from there because edges have been removed. For example, in a regulative variant of Fig. 2b, there could be an additional edge from the $(x=7, w=0)$ state after the join, to an identical state, but with no continuation edge. This would correspond to a branch in the aspect code that prevents the continuation. For regulative aspects, each trace of the projection is either a prefix of or the same as a trace in the original, except for repetitions of states. As before, the branching structure of the original is maintained, except for removed edges.

In terms of code, regulative aspects prevent, restrict, or delay some of the actions that were possible in the underlying system. However, they cannot simply skip some steps in a transaction of the underlying program while continuing to other steps. Then a weakly invasive aspect (see Sect. 7) is needed. In a simple case, a regulative aspect might make fields or methods private that were previously publicly available. Then an external message activating the method would be denied in the augmented system, while an internal one would continue to execute as before. If requirements arise to restrict access to method calls that were originally unrestricted, a regulative aspect might add a parameter with a password or authorization key, along with aspect code that continues with the original method only if the password is authorized. When the restrictions are only to external method calls, as in the password authorization example above, the aspect belongs to the special category of an **externally regulative** aspect.

In general, regulative aspects enforce additional checks before allowing the activation of methods or actions that were not restricted in the underlying system. Thus, an aspect might terminate a system if overflow of an integer variable occurs, preventing continuations that were previously possible when overflow was ignored. In Fig. 4 an aspect is given that restricts initiating an exam (by the method doExam, called only externally) to children over the age of 7. Note that the (age < MIN_AGE) test corresponds to a branch that terminates with no continuation, while the negation continues the original computation. The projection to the variables of the original system has a trace with repetitions of the initial state that has no continuation, and another one that is as in the original system, with repeated states. Thus it satisfies the conditions for a restrictive aspect.

Other examples include synchronization or scheduling aspects, such as one that enforces mutual exclusion among methods in different objects that were independent and could overlap without the aspect. In this case some actions are delayed until new synchronization or mutual exclusion conditions are satisfied An aspect that enforces mutual exclusion among instances of exams when they wish to print out summaries on the same printer (so the printer will be used exclusively by one or the other) is regulative in that one of the summaries is delayed until the other completes. The edges leading to states where the two printing tasks overlap are removed.

To detect that an aspect is regulative, we proceed as for a spectative aspect as far as determining that variables are independent of assignments in the underlying system, but are more liberal about the reconnection properties of the advice code and waiting for conditions during the advice. The generic detection procedure for a regulative aspect is:

1. Determine the set C of variables in the aspect that are bound to variables of the underlying system.
2. Check that no variable of C is assigned a value by the aspect.
3. The aspect code may contain wait conditions and restrict execution of previously independent operations of the underlying system, but each advice should be shown to terminate if the wait conditions hold.
4. Check whether one of the following reconnection conditions hold:
   - resume computation of the underlying system at the joinpoint
   - throw an exception that terminates the execution or directly terminate the execution of the entire system or of the present transaction

The possibility of preventing external calls to methods of the underlying system (e.g., by adding parameters and checks on them or making methods or fields private) is included in the above, as it is viewed as terminating a transaction before it can even begin.

Lemma 5: If the detection procedure above succeeds, the aspect is regulative.

Proof: For rules 1 and 2, the reasoning is as for spectative aspects. The liberal termination policy in rule 3 means that the sections of the graph resulting from aspect advice operations should be finite, but might deadlock or terminate, corresponding to removing edges to the continuation. The reconnection conditions ensure that no code of the underlying system is skipped unless the system terminates or at least completes its reaction to the most recent input (in a transaction view). Together these guarantee that the projection of the augmented state graph satisfies the conditions in the definition of a regulative aspect, and only removes edges or adds repetitions of states, including possible branching to repeated states with no continuation.   □

```
public aspect AgeRestrictionAspect {
        private static final int MIN_AGE    = 7;
        // Pointcuts
        pointcut doingExam(RationalExam exam) :
                call (void RationalExam.doExam()) && target(exam);
        // Advice
        void around(RationalExam exam) : doingExam(exam) {
                System.out.print("Hello, how old are you? ");
                int age = Integer.parseInt(getInput());
                if (age < MIN_AGE) {
                        System.out.println("You're too young for fractions");
                        return; //returns without doing the exam
                }
                proceed(exam); //proceeds with the exam when old enough
        }
}
```

Fig. 4. An aspect restricting method activation

In principle, the syntactic conditions above are too strong, and regulative aspects could be allowed to change some variables bound to those of the underlying system, but only under conditions that are hard to check statically. The elements of C that are given values by the aspects may be bound only to variables of the underlying system that are exclusively used in conditional statements, and the aspect assignments must lead to strengthening the condition under which a method is activated. That is, the aspect leads to choosing a method in fewer cases than previously (and never to choosing one more often). Some of the static analysis or type systems for aspects discussed in Sect. 9 also identify special cases of regulative aspects.

Lemma 6: If an aspect is regulative, all safety properties of the underlying system that are not next-state properties and involve assertions only about variables, fields, and methods of the underlying system will not be influenced by the aspect, and will also hold in the augmented system. Liveness and existence properties are not automatically preserved.

Proof: In terms of the state graph of an augmented system with a regulative aspect, relative to the state graph for the underlying system, the projection described for spectative aspects applies, except that some edges are removed. In particular, some potential entrance points (external method calls) are restricted or closed compared to the graph of the underlying system, and some arrows are simply removed, but no new ones are added except between repetitions of states in the original graph. Note that if an operation of the original computation were simply skipped, an arrow would be added from the state before the removed operation to the state now reached by doing a step in the continuation, which is forbidden for a regulative aspect. However, it is possible for the aspect advice to delay some actions by waiting for a global condition involving underlying variables, as in the mutual exclusion example. The other actions that are meanwhile executed could have occurred by chance before the delayed one, so only some interleavings are eliminated, and no new traces are added relative to the underlying system, except for repetitions. The remaining computations maintain the partial order among operations that are not independent.

That is, in the semantic view, the state graph of a regulative aspect prunes edges from the computation graph of the underlying system (along with adding transitions and state only involving aspect variables, as for spectative aspects). The projection of the augmented graph onto the variables of the underlying system is an edge-pruned version of the original underlying computation graph, along with repeated states. Any safety property true of the original graph has the form AGp where p only relates to the history. Since the history of each state in the projection of the augmented system is identical to the history in the original system except for repetitions of states that already appear, and the assertion has no next-state operators, it will be true of the states in the augmented system if it was true of the states in the original one.

Liveness or existence properties need not be preserved by regulative aspects, since states previously reached may be inaccessible both in the augmented system and in the pruned graph with repeated states that is the projection of the augmented system. Thus a computation that existed in the underlying system may be interrupted in the augmented one, and a state that eventually occurred in the original may not appear in the pruned version.   □

Recall that for spectative aspects, no new properties involving only the variables of the underlying system can be added in the augmented one. However, for regulative aspects, besides maintaining safety properties already true, there can be new safety properties even involving only the variables of the underlying system.

Lemma 7: An augmented system with a regulative aspect can have additional safety properties involving only the variables, fields, and methods of the underlying system that were not true in the underlying system.

Proof: As seen above, in an augmented system with a regulative aspect some system states of the original system can be unreachable. Thus, for example, new invariants may hold for all reachable states of the augmented system even if they did not hold for some states of the underlying one, because the problematic states become unreachable in the augmented system. In fact, one of the reasons for weaving a regulative aspect into an underlying system is to eliminate problematic states (that violate desired invariants) by making them unreachable in the state graph of the augmented system.   □

In Fig. 5a, a fragment of an original state graph with state variables X and Y shows independent operations a and b, perhaps activated from different objects. The operation a increments X by one, while b does the same for Y. In the augmented version, a state component of the aspect, S, is added, to restrict which operations are allowed, yielding the augmented state graph in Fig. 5b. This fragment satisfies the conditions for a regulative aspect, because in the projection of Fig. 5b to X and Y, the first state of the original is repeated, and the edge labeled b is removed, making the state $(X=1, Y=1)$ unreachable, so it can be removed. In the augmented version, the invariant $G(X > Y)$ is true, while in the original it is not.

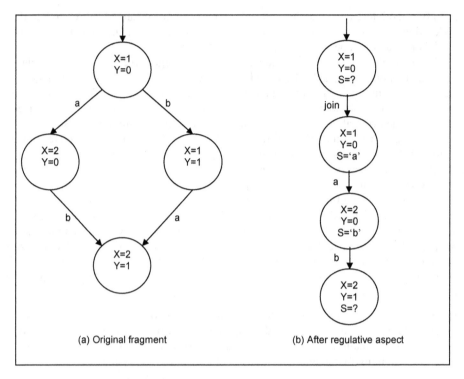

Fig. 5. State graph fragments for a regulative aspect

For an example of a regulative aspect that adds a mutual exclusion property by introducing a local mutex object, the invariant $G(\sim(in(crit1) \wedge in(crit2)))$ (meaning, in every state, we are not both in critical section 1 and in critical section 2 at the same time) becomes true in the augmented system, even though it did not hold in the original system. States where it did not hold in the original system have been eliminated from the state graph of the augmented one by preventing the transitions that lead to a violation.

Lemma 8: If a regulative aspect only restricts external method calls from outside the original system and is thus externally regulative, then existential properties may not be preserved, but all safety and liveness properties preserved by a spectative aspect are also preserved for a resultant augmented program with such a regulative aspect.

Proof: In this case, only potential computations are limited, but all safety and liveness properties within the system (about the state graph of the original or augmented system) are maintained. Since the environment cannot be forced to actually make a particular method call even in the original system, there could not have been a liveness property that guaranteed its occurrence.   □

For example, the aspect restricting initialization of an exam on fractions is externally regulative. Thus it does not influence any of the internal safety or liveness properties, but does mean that there will not be any computations where the age of the user is declared to be under 7.

7 Invasive Aspects and Partial Analysis

7.1 Weakly Invasive Aspects

Invasive aspects do change the values of variables in the underlying system. Thus, in principle, they could completely invalidate any property that held previously in the underlying system. Nevertheless, in many situations invasive aspects change the underlying system in restricted ways suitable for detection and exploitation. The basic question about an invasive aspect is how it reconnects to the computation from the underlying system. This will influence the extent to which the aspect influences the continuation of the computation. Even for a *before* aspect, although the code of the underlying system continues executing after the advice, the advice may have created a new state that did not exist in the underlying system. Thus in the augmented system even the code from the underlying system can continue to create an entirely new subgraph whose properties are unknown. In this situation it seems difficult to avoid having to consider the entire augmented system at once. An interesting special case can help alleviate the difficulty.

Definition: An aspect is **weakly invasive** if in the state graph of the augmented system, transitions that correspond to operations from the underlying system begin in states that already existed in the state graph of the underlying system (perhaps for different inputs from those in the augmented system).

It follows that advice transitions end in states that were in the original state graph, at least whenever an underlying operation can then be executed. Although it can be difficult to identify when an aspect is weakly invasive only using static analysis, there are special cases where this is possible. Otherwise, the user can simply declare that the aspect is weakly invasive, for cases where this is obvious. For example, an aspect may identify conditions (joinpoints) at which it is necessary to *reset* the underlying variables to some fixed values that also occur in the underlying system without the aspect. In a transaction control system, an aspect can be used to record values and later *rollback* the computation to the earlier state with the recorded values when a transaction cannot be completed. In an aspect to impose a discount policy for prices, the prices are changed, but the continuation is equivalent to one in which the price was originally set to the value now obtained through the discount policy. All of these can be identified as weakly invasive aspects.

In Fig. 6, an aspect that changes the values chosen for the arithmetic operations on fractions to reduced fractions is outlined. The partially specified pointcut identifies where new values are given to a fraction, and a method to reduce them is then activated before continuing. (Details of the method *reduce* which performs the reduction, and thus changes the value of the fraction, are not shown.) This aspect is weakly invasive because the original choice of values might already be reduced, so the state reached is a possible state of the original system.

```
public aspect ReductionAspect {
    // Pointcut
    pointcut rationalChanging(Rational r) :
        (call (void Rational.set*(int)) || ...) && target(r);

    // Advice
    after(Rational r) returning : rationalChanging(r) { reduce(r); }
```

Fig. 6. An aspect to reduce fractions

Lemma 9: If an aspect is weakly invasive, then an invariant true for the underlying system can be proven to hold for the augmented system by assuming it true at the beginning of each aspect advice, and showing it true for each state generated during the execution of the advice.

Proof: By induction on the joinpoints reached in any computation of the augmented system. To base the induction, the invariant is true in all states until the first joinpoint is reached, since only states of the underlying computation are reached. For the general case, assume the invariant is true until a joinpoint is reached. If the invariant then also holds for all states generated by the advice code until the computation reconnects to a state that was in the underlying one, then it will continue to hold until the next joinpoint because it is true in all states of the underlying state graph.   □

The implications of this lemma are that to extend an invariant to an augmented system for a weakly invasive aspect, the original system does not have to be rechecked, and the entire augmented system does not have to be considered at once. It is sufficient to reason only about the much smaller state graphs that correspond to the advice of the aspect. Since the lemma holds for global invariants, it clearly also holds for class invariants, invariants at a location, and partial correctness assertions, since all these can be expressed as a global invariant.

In the weakly invasive ReductionAspect, above, if an invariant G(denominator>0) was true of the original system, then to extend it to the augmented system it is sufficient to show that it is maintained by the *reduce* method.

Note that general safety properties do *not* have to be extended to augmented systems with weakly invasive aspects, even when the property holds within the aspect state graph, because the history of how a state is reached can be different in the underlying and in the augmented system. For example, a safety property "a state satisfying P is always preceded by a state in the history satisfying Q" could be true for the underlying system, and could hold for the state graph of the aspect itself, and yet not be true in the augmented system. This could be because the reconnection is to a predecessor of a state satisfying P, and yet Q is not true anywhere in the new history including the aspect. Moreover, liveness and existence properties are also not similarly extended to the augmented system with weakly invasive aspects, and there does not seem to be such a clean separation of reasoning, because states from the underlying system can be skipped or made unreachable in the augmented system.

7.2 Identifying Independence for Invasive Aspects

Another direction for simplifying reasoning for invasive aspects considers the degree of invasiveness. In other words, the aspect usually will only affect some of the variables in the underlying system, and identifying independent parts can allow simplifications similar to those for spectative and regulative aspects. A variable x of the underlying system is *independent* of an aspect if no variable that is assigned values in the aspect code is bound to x and all variables used in the computation of x or that influence conditionals that control basic blocks with assignments to variables that influence x, are also independent of the aspect. As previously, standard dataflow techniques from optimizations in compilers can be used to detect independence in many cases.

Lemma 10: An invariant property of the underlying system that does not include a next-state property and only includes variables *independent* of an aspect is maintained in an augmented program with that aspect woven into the underlying program.

Proof: Due to the definition of "independent", even an invasive aspect does not influence any of the computation that affects the values of the independent variables in the invariant property, and does not add any new computation affecting those variables. This includes not influencing the control flow of assignments to the variables in the invariant. An invariant only relates those values within each state. Thus the invariant property is also true in the augmented system.   □

Note that general safety properties could be affected because of changes in the history. Stronger notions of independence could be defined to treat such cases, but may be difficult to establish through syntactic analysis.

7.3 Verifying Inductive Invariants for Invasive Aspects

When an invariant of the underlying system involves variables that are changed by the aspect, or the invariant includes variables from both the aspect and the underlying system, a simplified verification is nevertheless possible for a restricted class of invariant properties. Consider extending an invariant that was true of an underlying system when the aspect applied is (strongly) invasive, i.e., changes the values of variables in the underlying system, redirects control, and need not resume executing the code of the underlying system where it was suspended. If the invariant is what is known as "inductive", it can be shown to also be an invariant of the augmented system by only checking the advice, even without analyzing in what situations the aspect code will be applied and without rechecking the code of the original system.

An invariant I is *inductive* if $\{I\}$ s $\{I\}$ can be shown directly for each individual step s, without any knowledge of the state before the step s except that it satisfies I. In some sense, it means that the assertion is "self-contained", and by assuming just itself, a proof can be constructed to show that it is reestablished after each step. Note that even states that do not occur in the system but for which I is true are sufficient preconditions to guarantee I after s is executed.

In this situation, to establish that I is also an invariant of the augmented system, it is sufficient to check that each aspect action t also satisfies the same assertion {I} t {I}. For example, consider a situation where x>y>0 is an invariant of a system, and an aspect has changes of the form:

$$<complex> \rightarrow double (x,y),$$

where <complex> is a complex condition for applicability, and double(x,y) doubles the values of x and of y. Then we easily have

$$\{x>y>0\} double(x,y) \{x>y>0\},$$

extending the invariant to the augmented system, even though only the aspect code was newly analyzed, and when it is applied was ignored.

Assume that the invariant G(denominator>0) was inductive for the fractions system, i.e., it was provable for each step of the original system only assuming itself. Then even if the *reduce* method in the above example could introduce negative fractions that were not treated in the original system, only the aspect advice must be newly checked. Note that the aspect now is strongly invasive, since states not in the original system are generated at the end of the advice, and the exact effect of applying code of the basic system to these new states is unknown. Still, the new resultant states will satisfy the invariant. On the other hand, if the invariant was not inductive, in the original proof the fact that the fractions were nonnegative may have been true before some step and used to help establish the invariant after the step. In that case a new proof is needed for the entire augmented system now that the aspect introduces new states.

To summarize this discussion:

Lemma 11: If an invariant has been shown to be inductive, and proven for an underlying system by only using the invariant itself as an assumption (i.e., with assertions {I} s {I} in Hoare logic notation, for each statement s of the original system), then the invariant can be extended to hold for an augmented system with an invasive aspect, by proving {I} t {I} for each statement t only of the aspect code, without reconsidering the original system.

Proof: Since I is already known to be an invariant of the original system, it is true of the augmented system whenever the aspect is first applied, even without analyzing the joinpoints. By induction, it is easy to see that I will hold whenever some t action is taken from the code of the aspect, and it is proven that if I holds, then it will again hold after t, for any state. Thus, I is an invariant of the augmented system, even without rechecking the original code.   □

8   Interference Among Aspects

So far, the relation has been considered between an underlying system and an augmented system with a single aspect added to the underlying one. However, most augmented systems have multiple aspects applied to them, and the issue of whether these aspects interfere with each other is of obvious concern. Several compositions of aspects are possible, as described in [27]. In some cases, there is a clear ordering among the aspects to be applied. In effect, a later aspect is actually applied to the augmented system obtained after applying an earlier aspect. In this case the joinpoints of the later aspect may include events generated by the earlier one. The treatment in earlier sections, of a single aspect woven to an underlying system, may be used iteratively. That is, once the properties of an augmented system with one aspect have been established, possibly using the lemmas above, it can be considered as an underlying system relative to another aspect. However, the syntactic analysis to determine possible interactions becomes more complicated. Program slicing for aspects, as seen in the following section, can be used to determine the category of aspect relative to an underlying system that itself has aspects.

In other situations, several aspects are to be applied independently only to the underlying system. In this case we clearly do not want any direct binding of variables, objects, methods, or parameters local to one aspect to those elements of another aspect. This also can be enforced syntactically, and checked. Still, when pointcuts of several aspects define the same joinpoints, and parameters of more than one aspect are bound to the same underlying variable, indirect (usually unintended) connections can occur. From the property preservation claims seen earlier, we have:

Lemma 12: If there are no direct bindings among aspects, spectative aspects can be applied in any order without influencing safety, liveness, or existence properties of the result. Spectative aspects should be applied before restrictive or invasive ones, and will not influence their safety, liveness, or existence properties.

Proof: An augmented system with a spectative aspect resumes from the state of the joinpoint after executing advice, since only new variables of the aspect are changed. Moreover, the assumptions of an aspect specification about the underlying program and joinpoints to which that aspect may be applied only relate to variables of the underlying program and local variables of that aspect. Therefore, the assumptions of any aspect B will not be influenced by applying a spectative aspect A first, even at joinpoints where both are activated. Since the aspect is presumed correct when woven over any underlying system satisfying its assumptions, it remains correct relative to its specification when a spectative aspect is applied previously.   □

For multiple regulative or invasive aspects, their order of application changes the semantics (i.e., the resultant computation graphs of the augmented systems may be different for different orderings). As previously, a finer analysis of partial independence can be made to determine allowable orderings.

9 Related Aspect Categories and Static Analysis Tools

Additional categories of aspects have been defined in several works. Although in [6] a tool was not developed, that work defines an *observer* aspect (roughly similar to a spectative one). It also points out difficulties of aliasing that can complicate syntactic static analysis of code to determine whether an aspect is an observer and suggests a development methodology using observers. In [17], an aspect is defined to be *harmful* if it invalidates any desired properties of the system to which it is applied. As seen in the lemmas, one way to exploit the categories in this paper is to help determine whether desirable properties true of the underlying system are still true in the augmented one. Clearly, the categories here can help in automatically detecting whether there is any danger of harmful aspects, once the specification properties are identified as belonging to the appropriate classes of temporal logic properties. Then a system can be unaware of, or *oblivious* [11, 12] to, the particular aspects to be applied to it, but its specification can nevertheless restrict new aspects to those that do not violate key properties, so that the system specification can influence which aspects are woven. The obliviousness of the system is thus slightly restricted.

Several works have concentrated on automatic identification of aspect categories either based on static code analysis for aspects using dataflow, or with transformation rules that allow deriving only aspects of a desired type. The code analysis system for a simplified aspect language seen in [26] is intended primarily for code optimization, but the information gathered can also be (and has been) used by the authors to identify spectative aspects. Similarly, in [29] an extensive interference analysis is made for real Java and AspectJ-like programs, emphasizing the complications introduced by inheritance and multiple instances. Again, the result is the effective syntactic identification of spectators/observers and nonoverlap among aspects (which is there called *interference-freedom*).

In [25] finer distinctions are defined, but the basic categories resemble those already described. That work concentrates on determining the relations between an aspect and a method of the underlying system. If they are *orthogonal*, the two access disjoint fields, if they are *independent* neither writes to a field that the other may read or write (but both may read the same field), in an *observation* relation the advice may read fields that the methods may write, *actuation* means that the advice may write to a field that the method may read, but they are otherwise independent, and *interference* means that both may write to the same field. If the aspect code segments can also be shown to always terminate and not redirect control, the first three correspond to spectative aspects. Otherwise, if basic code is not skipped, they are regulative. The later two categories are invasive, but could be further analyzed to identify special cases of weakly invasive aspects. The tool described in [25] uses standard dataflow techniques for AspectJ over Java, and numerous sample programs have been analyzed.

There is also considerable work [1, 2, 33] on extending well-known programming slicing techniques based on dataflow to aspects. These are used to identify the extent of influence of an aspect on the underlying system, and to identify potential conflicts among aspects. In effect, any potential interactions or conflicts are identified. Such techniques can also be used to reduce the size of the model that must be analyzed when model-checking techniques are to be applied. In [2] an implemented slicing system for AspectJ is presented to identify the influence of each aspect. Similar ideas to detect interference has been undertaken for Composition Filters with the Compose* analysis system [23].

Although the systems above do not explicitly deal with families of properties, they are usually demonstrated on spectative aspects as tests. However, many of them either ignore or simply assume termination of the aspect code (some assume straight-line code). Generally, the code of the basic system is resumed from the joinpoint after the aspect advice, and thus the aspects are shown regulative. Lemma 6 is therefore applicable, which means that safety properties are necessarily extended to the augmented system if they held in the original, but liveness might not be preserved.

Correctness-preserving transformation systems guaranteeing that only aspects of a particular type are generated are another approach to establishing aspect categories. An abstract transformational theory is presented in [10] to prevent interference among aspects (discussed in Sect. 8), emphasizing pointcut conflicts for event-based aspects. In [8] a type system and transformation rules are presented to guarantee *harmless advice*. This is defined as advice that does not change the final values produced by the original system, if the augmented system still terminates normally. In the terms here, partial correctness properties are preserved. Since the rules are informally described in their papers as guaranteeing regulative aspects, it is likely that their results can be extended to general safety properties, again using Lemma 6.

In [19] *aspect-aware interfaces* are suggested as a weakening of obliviousness, on the code level. The aspects activated in a module are explicitly identified in these interfaces so that the effects of method activations can be more easily understood for modularity and analysis purposes. Although the construct is orthogonal to the semantically defined categories in this paper, it can help in the syntactic identification of aspect categories by making the connections among aspects and objects more explicit and isolating the effect of advice to parts of the underlying system. In [30] and [13] *crosscut programming interfaces* are introduced to help modularize and decouple aspects from the implementation details of the underlying system when defining pointcuts. These also provide a convenient mechanism for specifying aspects through preconditions and postconditions, supporting the assume–guarantee specifications suggested in Sect. 2.

In [20] aspect advice represented directly as a state transition graph is model-checked to extend properties proven true for the original system to the augmented one. They assume that the advice reconnects to the state transition graph of the original system at the joinpoint. However, they do not identify parts of the statespace local to the aspect. If the changes made by the advice are to parts of the state not used in the original system, the aspect would be spectative, and the model check is extraneous, since all relevant properties are maintained. If the original state variables *are* changed, they must be changed back to the original values before ending the advice, by assumption. In that case, their aspect is weakly invasive, and Lemma 9 applies, justifying a model check of only the aspect state graph, as they also show.

10 Summary

The categories of aspects, the procedures for their identification, and the semantic influence of aspects from each category on classes of properties provide the basis for a code-analysis module for aspects. The distinction between the semantic definitions of the categories and restrictions sometimes needed in order to syntactically determine to which category an aspect belongs can be seen by considering whether the aspects can contain "call-backs" to methods of classes already declared in the original system, beyond a *proceed* statement. The absence of such method calls can be easily determined by static analysis, and may help in determining that the aspect is, for example, spectative. However, there is no real semantic problem with such calls. As seen in Sect. 6, a class declared in the original system may have objects effectively local to the aspect. Moreover, even for objects defined and used in the original system, methods that only return values can be activated by spectative aspects, to obtain information not explicitly in the pointcut definition. Only methods that change values in the original object, or change the conditions under which method calls in the original program may be activated are forbidden. Similar considerations hold for regulative and weakly invasive aspects.

The goal of full specification and verification of aspect-oriented systems is still important. But even when specifications of aspects are difficult to express for nonfunctional concerns, and a full verification may be difficult, identifying categories of aspects through syntactic analysis is a valuable exercise. A significant improvement in code reliability and quality can be obtained at a relatively low cost, especially when specifications of the underlying system and the aspects are available, or at least the classes of properties needed to express desired features are understood. Proper language design for aspects, with local variables and parameterization, can help extend the static analysis of only the aspect code, either for classes of properties and for every possible weaving, or by reanalyzing only the aspect for each weaving. Even for invasive aspects, partial syntactic analysis can be useful and can ease the task of establishing the properties of the augmented system.

As the level of interference of the aspect increases, from spectative, to regulative, to weakly invasive, to strongly invasive, the classes of properties which are automatically extended or have modular proofs become successively smaller. Thus, for spectative aspects all safety, liveness, and existence properties without next-state properties are maintained, while for regulative ones, just safety properties are automatically maintained. For weakly invasive aspects, safety properties are not maintained, but any invariants of the underlying system can be extended to the augmented one by only checking the advice. Finally, for strongly invasive aspects, only the restricted class of inductive invariants can be modularly extended to the augmented system.

As already noted, syntactic checks to determine the category of aspect use dataflow techniques also seen in code optimizations, and therefore should be incorporated into the compilation and optimization of aspect languages. In addition to the analysis systems already developed, detection of the new categories of externally regulatory and weakly invasive aspects seems valuable, since they both are practically widespread, and significantly easier reasoning about properties is possible for augmented systems with aspects in these categories.

A tool for static analysis to determine aspect categories could connect to further analysis, testing, or verification tools (e.g., [16] or [20]) by determining the easiest verification techniques to extend properties from the underlying system, establish new properties, or further analyze the system when a conservative analysis indicates possible interferences that may not occur in practice.

Acknowledgments

I would like to thank the referees of this paper for their valuable and constructive comments. I also acknowledge support from AOSD-Europe, a Network of Excellence in the FP6 IST of the European Union.

References

[1] D. Balzarott and M. Monga. Using program slicing to analyze aspect-oriented composition. In: *Foundations of Aspect Languages (FOAL) Workshop Associated with AOSD*, 2004

[2] D. Balzarotti, A.C. D'Ursi, L. Cavallaro, and M. Monga. Slicing AspectJ woven code. In: *Foundations of Aspect Languages (FOAL) Workshop Associated with AOSD*, 2005

[3] G. Bruns, R. Jagadeesan, A. Jeffrey, and J. Riely. μabc: A minimal aspect calculus. In: *CONCUR 2004, LNCS vol. 3170*, Springer, Berlin Heidelberg New York, 2004

[4] E.M. Clarke and E.A. Emerson. Design and synthesis of synchronization skeletons using branching-time temporal logic. In: *Workshop on Logics of Programs, LNCS vol. 131*, Springer, Berlin Heidelberg New York, pp. 52–71, 1981

[5] E.M. Clarke, O. Grumberg, and D. Peled. *Model Checking,* MIT Press, Cambridge, MA, 1999

[6] C. Clifton and G. Leavens. Observers and assistants: a proposal for modular aspect-oriented reasoning (also, modified as Spectators and assistants: enabling modular aspect-oriented reasoning). In: *Foundations of Aspect Languages (FOAL) Workshop 2002*, Iowa State TR02-10, 2002

[7] D. Dams, R. Gerth, and O. Grumberg. Abstract interpretation of reactive systems. *ACM Transactions on Programming Languages and Systems*, 19(2):253–291, 1997

[8] D. Dantas and D. Walker. Harmless advice. In: *POPL: 33rd ACM Symposium on Principles of Programming Languages*, 2006

[9] B. Devereux. Compositional reasoning about aspects using alternating-time logic. In: *Foundations of Aspect Languages (FOAL) Workshop Associated with AOSD*, 2003

[10] R. Douence, P. Fradet, and M. Sudholt. Trace-based aspects. In: M. Aksit, S. Clarke, T. Elrad, and R. Filman, (eds.) *Aspect-Oriented Software Development*, Addison-Wesley, 2004

[11] R.E. Filman and D.P. Friedman. Aspect-oriented programming is quantification and obliviousness. In: *OOPSLA: Workshop on Advanced separation of Concerns*, 2000

[12] R.E. Filman. What is AOP, Revisited. In: *Workshop on Advanced Separation of Concerns, 15th ECOOP*, 2001

[13] W. Griswald, K. Sullivan, Y. Song, M. Shonle, N. Tewari, Y. Cai, and H. Rajan. Modular software design with crosscutting interfaces. *IEEE Software,* 23:51–60, 2006

[14] J. Hatcliff and M. Dwyer. Using the Bandera tool set to model check properties of concurrent Java software. In: *CONCUR2001, LNCS vol. 2154*, Springer, pp. 39–58, 2001

[15] R. Jagadeesan, A. Jeffrey, and J. Riely. A calculus of untyped aspect-oriented programs. In: *ECOOP 2003, LNCS vol. 2743*, Springer, pp. 54–73, 2003

[16] S. Katz and M. Sihman. Aspect validation using model checking. In: *Symposium on Verification in honor of Zohar Manna, LNCS vol. 2772*, Springer, pp. 389–411, 2003

[17] S. Katz. Diagnosis of harmful aspects using regression verification. In: *Foundations of Aspect Languages (FOAL) Workshop Associated with AOSD*, 2004

[18] G. Kiczales et al. An overview of AspectJ. *16th ECOOP*, 2001

[19] G. Kiczales and M. Mezini. Aspect-oriented programming and modular reasoning. In: *Intl. Conference on Software Engineering (ICSE)*, pp. 49–58, 2005

[20] S. Krishnamurthi, K. Fisler, and M. Greenberg. Verifying aspect advice modularly. In: *Foundations of Software Engineering (FSE) Conference*, pp. 137–146, 2004

[21] L. Lamport. What good is temporal logic?. In: *IFIP 9th World Congress*, pp. 657–668, 1983

[22] Z. Manna and A. Pnueli. The temporal logic of reactive and concurrent systems—specification, Springer, Berlin Heidelberg New York, 1991

[23] I. Nagy, L. Bergmans, and M. Aksit. Declarative aspect composition. In: *SE Properties of Languages and Aspect Technologies (SPLAT) Workshop of AOSD04,* 2004

[24] H. Ossher and P. Tarr. Multi-dimensional separation of concerns and the Hyperspace approach. In: M. Aksit (ed.) *Software Architectures and Component Technology,* Kluwer Academic, Dordrecht, 2001

[25] M. Rinard, A. Salcianu, and S. Bugrara. A classification system and analysis for aspect-oriented programs. In: *Foundations of Software Engineering (FSE) Conference,* 2004

[26] D. Sereni and O. de Moor. Static analysis of aspects. *Aspect-Oriented Software Development (AOSD),* pp. 30–39, 2003

[27] M. Sihman and S. Katz. Superimposition and aspect-oriented programming. *The Computer Journal,* 46:529–541, 2003

[28] H.B. Sipma. A formal model for cross-cutting modular transition systems, In: *Foundations of Aspect Languages (FOAL) Workshop associated with AOSD,* 2003

[29] M. Storzer and J. Krinke. Interference analysis for AspectJ. In: *Foundations of Aspect Languages (FOAL) Workshop,* 2003

[30] K. Sullivan, W.G. Griswold, Y. Song, Y. Cai, M. Shonle, N. Tewari, and H. Rajan. Information hiding interfaces for aspect-oriented design. In: *European Software Engineering Conference/Foundations of Software Engineering (ESEC/FSE),* pp. 166–175, 2005

[31] D. Walker, S. Zdancewic, and J. Ligatti. A theory of aspects. In: *ICFP'03,* ACM, NewYork, pp. 127–139, 2003

[32] M. Wand, G. Kiczales, and C. Dutchyn. A semantics for advice and dynamic join points in aspect-oriented programming. *Transactions on Programming Languages and Systems (TOPLAS),* 26(5):890–910, 2004

[33] J. Zhao. Slicing aspect-oriented software. *IEEE International Workshop on Programming Comprehension,* pp. 251–260, 2002

An Overview of CaesarJ

Ivica Aracic, Vaidas Gasiunas, Mira Mezini, and Klaus Ostermann

Darmstadt University of Technology, D-64283 Darmstadt, Germany
{aracic, gasiunas, mezini, ostermann}@informatik.tu-darmstadt.de

Abstract. CaesarJ is an aspect-oriented language which unifies aspects, classes and packages in a single powerful construct that helps to solve a set of different problems of both aspect-oriented and component-oriented programming. The paper gradually introduces the concepts of the language and illustrates them by showing how they can be used for noninvasive component refinement and integration, as well as for development of well modularized flexible aspects. In this way we demonstrate that the combination of aspect-oriented constructs for joinpoint interception with advanced modularization techniques like virtual classes and propagating mixin composition can open the path towards large-scale aspect components.

1 Introduction

Aspect-oriented programming is mostly perceived as a technology for localizing crosscutting concerns by means of a mechanism to intercept execution at relevant events in order to trigger aspect-specific functionality. More recently [1, 27, 44], more attention has been given to other software engineering properties attributed to good modularization such as robustness against changes, well-defined interfaces and information hiding, or reusability.

CAESARJ[1] is an aspect-oriented language with strong support for reusability. It combines the aspect-oriented constructs, pointcut and advice, with advanced object-oriented modularization mechanisms. From an aspect-oriented point of view, this combination of features is particularly well-suited to make large-scale aspects reusable—one can say it enables aspect components. From a component-oriented view, on the other hand, CAESARJ addresses the problem of integrating independent components into an application without modifying the component to be integrated or the application.

In this paper, we will give an overview of CAESARJ's features. Previous publications have focused on one of the viewpoints in isolation when presenting CAESARJ features. In [37], the language features that are relevant to component integration have been discussed, while the focus in [38] has been on features for improving the modularity and reusability of aspect code. This paper unifies the two viewpoints mentioned above and is the first comprehensive overview of CAESARJ. In particular, we will show how enabling reusable large-scale aspect components and supporting noninvasive integration of independently developed

---

[1] CaesarJ can be downloaded from caesarj.org.

A. Rashid and M. Aksit (Eds.): Transactions on AOSD I, LNCS 3880, pp. 135–173, 2006.
© Springer-Verlag Berlin Heidelberg 2006

components are actually facets of the same problem, which can be addressed by the same set of language features. By doing so, the paper also contributes an in-depth presentation of CAESARJ features that have not or have only sparsely been discussed in previous works in their interplay with the rest of the language.

The structure of the paper is as follows. In the next section, we illustrate the problem we want to address with a concrete example and give a rough overview of how a solution to this problem in CAESARJ would look. In Sect. 3, we introduce the main module construct of CAESARJ—a generalized notion of classes that unifies them with the notion of packages (in terms of sets of collaborating classes) and aspects—and demonstrate how it can be used to capture, extend and compose large-scale software components. In Sect. 4, we show how CAESARJ addresses the crosscutting integration problem by providing means for reconciling independently modularized parts of a system. In Sect. 5, we introduce the notion of *dynamic aspect deployment*, a flexible mechanism that enables control over the scope in which an aspect component is active. The implementation of CAESARJ as an extension of Java [2] that produces JVM-compatible bytecode is outlined in Sect. 6. Related and future work is described in Sects. 7 and 8, respectively.

2   Problems Addressed by CAESARJ in a Nutshell

This section briefly surveys the limitations of mainstream object-oriented (OO) programming that CAESARJ addresses, so as to establish the frame within which to understand the in-depth technical discussion in the following sections. It does so by an example that will subsequently be used throughout the paper.

2.1   Large-Scale Units of Modularity Beyond Individual Classes

A significant body of research has raised the concern that classes are too small a unit of modularity [15, 36, 43, 48, 50]. We think that any large-scale piece of functionality involves a *group* of related classes; hence, abstraction, late-binding and subtype polymorphism should be supported at the level of groups of interrelated classes. Different terminology has been used in the literature to denote such groups of interrelated classes, such as collaborations [22, 32, 36, 43, 53], layers [43, 48], teams [22] and families [14]. In this paper, the notion of a group of interrelated classes corresponds to that of a *class family* [14]. Hence, this term will be used.

To illustrate the need for carrying over the notions of abstraction, late binding and subtype polymorphism to the level of class families, consider the class diagram in Fig. 1. It shows the structure of a software for displaying hierarchical data structures (see the screenshot in Fig. 2). As indicated by Fig. 2, the data model assumed by the display component is one of a composite structure, where nodes are randomly labeled childA, childB, etc. The implemented layout is one in which boxes displaying nodes in the hierarchy have a fixed size, independent of the length of the displayed text; connections between nodes are shown as straight lines between the middle points of the boxes.

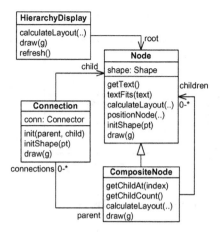

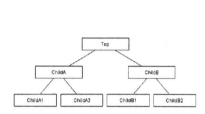

Fig. 1. Hierarchy display class diagram

Fig. 2. Hierarchy display

Now consider some simple variations of this display functionality. One is to enable boxes capable of adjusting their size to the displayed content (screenshot in Fig. 3). Another variation would be to have right-angled connections (screenshot in Fig. 4); yet another would use colors to encode the hierarchical levels. Each of these variations makes sense in isolation and in combination with others; it is reasonable to require that in scenarios where variability is important, e.g., in product line development, all of them coexist. This calls for an incremental style of programming and flexible composition mechanisms.

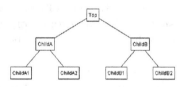

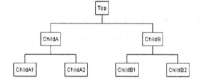

Fig. 3. Hierarchy display adjusted nodes

Fig. 4. Hierarchy display plus right-angled connections

We can incrementally define different variations of the node and connection abstractions by subclassing `Node` and `Connection`. However, in addition we need to make sure that any reference to `Node` and/or `Connection` is (re)bound to the respective new definition. For this, we have to redefine all classes that refer to `Node` and/or `Connection` either by calling their constructor or by being a subclass of them. For constructor calls, we need to redefine all methods where instances of `Node`, respectively `Connection`, are created.[2] For subclasses of the refined classes the problem is even harder—most object-oriented languages provide no obvious solution.

---

[2] Some design patterns can help with this in dynamic languages like Smalltalk.

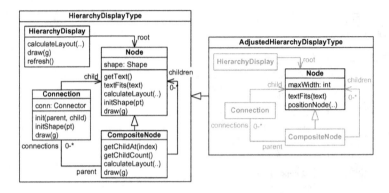

Fig. 5. Hierarchy display extension with virtual classes

This problem is well-known [24]. To cope with it, CAESARJ supports *virtual classes*, a concept that stems from the programming languages Beta [35] and has been refined and generalized in more recent work [12, 16]. Just like a virtual method, a virtual class is also an abstraction that has different meanings depending on the dynamic context of use. Virtual classes are defined as inner classes of an enclosing family class; just like methods and fields, they are also members of instances of their enclosing family class, called *family objects*. Hence, at any time during the execution their meaning is relative to the dynamic type of the family object.

With family classes, we can group sets of collaborating classes into a new unit (which is again a class). Figure 5 shows that the classes of the hierarchy display component are now members (*virtual classes*) of an enclosing class `Hierarchy-DisplayType`. The name `HierarchyDisplayType` suggests that an instance of this family class represents a particular configuration of hierarchy display, by being a repository for the inner classes.

Subclasses of a family class can refine inherited inner classes. Figure 5 shows how `AdjustedHierarchyDisplayType` extends `HierarchyDisplayType` with text-fitting functionality; it contains only a refinement (a so-called *further-binding*) of the virtual class `Node`.[3] In such a further-binding, we can override inherited methods, add new methods or new states, as well as add additional superinterfaces and superclasses (the latter leads to multiple inheritance, which will be explained later).

There is a significant difference between a further-binding and a conventional subclass of `Node`: All references to the type `Node` in the other virtual classes are automatically rebound to the refined `Node` class, when they are referred to during the execution of an object of type `AdjustedHierarchyDisplayType`. This is indicated by the gray shadows of the other virtual classes in Fig. 5. For example, in the context of an instance of `AdjustedHierarchyDisplayType`, a `CompositeNode`

---

[3] One could similarly refine `Connection` in a subclass `AngularHierarchyDisplayType` to extend `HierarchyDisplayType` with angular connections.

is a subclass of the refined `Node` class. Similarly, instance creation expressions are also late bound.

A related problem addressed by CAESARJ is how to compose different variations of some basic functionality. In mainstream object-oriented languages, a subclass is defined to a particular superclass. This lack of abstraction over the implementation of the superclass hinders reusability: The variation defined by the subclass cannot be reused with other superclasses. For illustration, consider that it makes sense to compose different variants of hierarchy displays, e.g., `AdjustedHierarchyDisplayType` and `AngularHierarchyDisplayType`, to have a layout strategy with both, adjusted nodes and angular connections, (see screenshot in Fig. 4). However, such a composition is not possible if both subclasses are defined to a concrete implementation of `HierarchyDisplayType`.

To solve this problem, CAESARJ shares with gbeta [12] a mixin-based class composition mechanism [13]: (a) classes (simple or families) are mixins, i.e., their superclass can be exchanged [9], and (b) mixin composition of family classes automatically propagates into their inner classes. By being mixins defined to a common supertype, modules that implement the display layout strategy with adjustable nodes and with angular connections can be composed with each other; superclasses in the inheritance hierarchy are replaced according to specific composition rules. Mixin composition propagation ensures that the composition structure is propagated from families to their inner classes. Unambiguity of the composition is ensured by the composition order and a linearization algorithm to be discussed in Sect. 3.2.

2.2   Crosscutting Composition Mechanisms

The composition mechanism outlined so far is hierarchical: In order to compose different modules in a nontrivial way, they must have common ancestors because only those inner class definitions are merged that are further-bindings of a common class definition. In our example, all variations inherit the structure of `HierarchyDisplayType`. It is this shared structure that makes them composable with each other; the composition of differently structured class families is still possible, but not very useful, because it would not compose any inner classes.

In many cases, however, one would like to compose independent (family) classes that do not have a hierarchical relationship, and hence no common ancestor, in a meaningful way. For illustration, consider the class diagram in Fig. 6, which shows part of a software system for automating the administration of companies. Assume that we are involved in implementing a GUI, that is capable of displaying the company structure. Given the two components we already have, `HierarchyDisplayType` (or any of its variations) and `Company`, it is desirable to "simply" compose them. The composition cannot, however, be performed automatically by mixin composition, because the operands of the composition are not in a hierarchical relationship as the variations of the hierarchy display functionality.

There are two issues involved in integrating hierarchy display and company components. On the one hand, the generic visualization functionality of the dis-

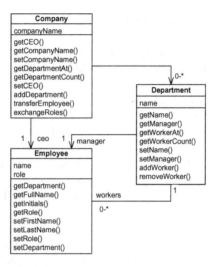

Fig. 6. Company data model

play component must be customized to the specifics of the company administration structure. On the other hand, the functionality of the company component must be tuned in such a way that changes to the company state, e.g., moving of employees from one department to another, are signaled to the display component so that the latter can refresh itself.

Let us quickly discuss why this is a problem in conventional OO languages. One could use the adapter pattern [17] for customizing the hierarchy display functionality to the company structure and the observer pattern [17] for the display refresh aspect of the composition, as outlined in Figs. 7 and 8, respectively. However, the resulting composition exhibits crosscutting structure.

First, the adaptation of the generic display functionality to the structure of the company software requires a lot of infrastructural logic: hash tables to maintain adapter identity [24] and ubiquitous type casts in the adapter code. Second, the adaptation logic cuts across various display variations. Adapters are implemented in subclasses of concrete implementations of the types Node and CompositeNode, e.g., those encoding the standard layout; hence, they only work with that specific implementation. The adaptation logic must be duplicated for all variations of the display implementation.[4] Third, the observation logic for refreshing the display cuts across the modular structure of the company component. Notification logic is not explicit and is mixed within data model operations. Besides, the composition is not incremental: Adding observation support requires changing existing code. The lack of means for explicit expression of the crosscutting structure of the display refreshing aspect results in a lot of infrastructural code for observer registration and event dispatch.

---

[4] A part of the adaptation code can be made reusable in a language that supports multiple inheritance.

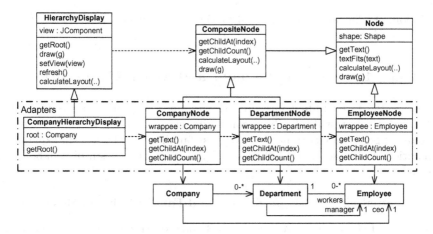

Fig. 7. Integrating components with adapters

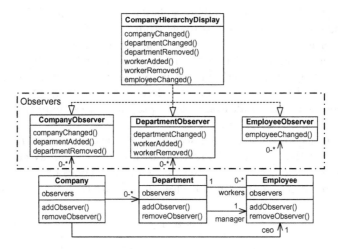

Fig. 8. Integrating components with observers

To cope with the outlined problems, CAESARJ provides two dedicated mechanisms for expressing crosscutting compositions. First, an AspectJ-like pointcut-advice mechanism [26] is available for expressing modifications of existing behavior incrementally. Second, CAESARJ provides a mechanism for automatic management of associations between company objects and their adapters to roles in the hierarchy display concept world. The integration logic is expressed in so-called binding classes.

Similar to the hierarchical variations, bindings are also expressed in family classes as variations on the display functionality, i.e., they rely on the concepts of virtual classes and propagating mixin composition. This has a twofold effect: (a) Type casts present in adapters are no longer needed, and (b) a binding of the hierarchy display can be reused (composed) with any hierarchy display variation. Details on bindings as well as the variability enabled by CAESARJ will be discussed in Sect. 4.

3   Class Families, Refinement and Mixin Composition

In this section, we will first introduce the notion of virtual classes as realized in CAESARJ, then we will talk about composing class hierarchies and how the type system supports polymorphic usage of class families. Finally we will explain the semantics of abstract virtual classes and introduce the notion of collaboration interfaces.

3.1   Virtual Classes, Type System and Family Polymorphism

With virtual classes, we can group sets of collaborating classes into a new unit (which is again a class), and subclasses of such a unit can refine inherited inner classes.

To understand the effect of making a class a virtual member of another class, consider another version of the example from Fig. 5. Figure 9 shows an alternative design for the hierarchy display component: The state and methods of the virtual class `HierarchyDisplay` from Fig. 5 are moved to the top level. These two designs differ from each other in an important way: The `Node`, `CompositeNode` and `Connection` classes are members of individual `HierarchyDisplay` instances in Fig. 9, whereas in Fig. 5 all `HierarchyDisplay` instances share the same `Node`, `CompositeNode` and `Connection` classes.

That is, in Fig. 5 different instances of `HierarchyDisplay` could share or exchange parts of the displayed data, whereas in Fig. 9 the family class acts as a unit of *confinement*: The type system prevents that nodes or connections that stem from different families (in this case the hierarchy display instance is the

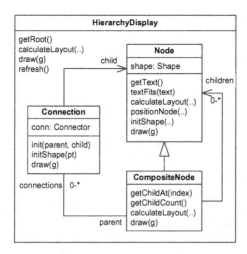

Fig. 9. Alternative design of hierarchy display with confined types

```
 1  cclass HierarchyDisplay {
 2      cclass Node { ... }
 3      cclass CompositeNode extends Node { ...
 4          calculateLayout() { ...
 5              Connection c = new Connection(); ... }
 6      }
 7      cclass Connection { ...
 8          void initShape(Point pt) { ... }
 9      }
10      Node root; ...
11  }
12  cclass AdjustedHierarchyDisplay extends HierarchyDisplay {
13      cclass Node { ...
14          int maxwidth;
15      }
16      void foo(Node n) {... n.maxwidth ... }
17  }
18  cclass AngularHierarchyDisplay extends HierarchyDisplay {
19      cclass Connection { ...
20          void initShape(Point pt) { ... }
21      }
22  }
```

Listing 1. Code for HierarchyDisplay

family) will ever be mixed. This is also the reason why the name of the family class in Fig. 5 is `HierarchyDisplayType`: An instance of it represents a particular configuration or type of hierarchy displays, whereby multiple instances of `HierarchyDisplay` might be instances of the same hierarchy display type.

Choosing between these two design alternatives is an important design decision to be made on a case-by-case basis. Such design considerations are out of the scope of this paper; the distinction between the two alternatives was done with the sole purpose to highlight the effect of making a class a virtual member of another class. In the remainder of the paper we will use the design from Fig. 9 in our examples. Listing 1 shows source code that corresponds to the design in Fig. 9 as well as two extensions, `AdjustedHierarchyDisplay` and `AngularHierarchyDisplay`, of the base component. The keyword `cclass` is used instead of `class` in order to differentiate pure Java classes from (virtual) CAESARJ classes.

Since all virtual classes depend on their family, all types that refer to virtual classes are implicitly (or explicitly) annotated with a path to their owner family object. For example, the type `Connection` in line 5 of List. 1 implicitly means `HierarchyDisplay.this.Connection`,[5] because the actual definition of this type depends on the owner family object. Similarly, the superclass declaration in line 3 should be read as `extends HierarchyDisplay.this.Node`, meaning that the actual superclass definition depends on the family object. The effect of late-bound types is also illustrated in line 16: A type cast is not necessary to access the `maxwidth` property, because it is known that all nodes of an `AdjustedHierarchyDisplay` have this property.

If virtual classes are used as types outside their family classes, the implicit scoping must be replaced by an explicit specification of the owner family object.

---

[5] In Java, as well as in CAESARJ, the owner object is referenced by qualifying this with its class name.

```
1  hd.Node findChild(final HierachyDisplay hd, hd.CompositeNode n, String text) {
2      for (int i = 0; i < n.getChildCount(); i++)
3          hd.Node m = n.getChildAt(i);
4          if (m.getText().equals(text)) return m;
5      }
6      return null;
7  }
8  ...
9  final HierachyDisplay hda = new AdjustedHierarchyDisplay();
10 hda.CompositeNode cna = ...;
11 final HierachyDisplay hdb = new AngularHierarchyDisplay();
12 hdb.CompositeNode cnb = ...;
13 hda.Node n1 = findChild(hda, cna, someString); // ok
14 hdb.Node n2 = findChild(hdb, cnb, someString); // ok
15 hda.Node n3 = findChild(hdb, cnb, someString); // static error
```

Listing 2. Illustration of path-dependent types and family polymorphism

This is illustrated in List. 2, which shows a method defined in some class outside HierarchyDisplay as well as some code that uses this method. The type declaration hd.CompositeNode in the signature of the method findChild means that only instances of CompositeNode that belong to the family hd may be passed as the second parameter to the method. Similarly, the return type hd.Node means that the returned node instance belongs to the family hd.

Hence, the calls in line 13 and 14 are correct, whereas the call in line 15 causes a static type error, because the variable n3 belongs to the family hda rather than hdb. In general, the type checker makes sure that families are never mixed, i.e., an object o1 can only be compatible to an object o2, if o1 and o2 belong to the same family.

Listing 2 also illustrates the concept of *family polymorphism* [14]: The find-Child method can be used polymorphically with different families (in the example hda and hdb). The type checker for these kinds of dependent types is highly nontrivial but not in the focus of this work. A full formalization of the core constructs of virtual classes as used in CAESARJ (operational semantics, type system and a soundness proof) can be found in [16].

3.2   Composing Class Hierarchies

As illustrated in List. 3, CAESARJ classes can be composed with the operator &. The class AdjustedAngularHierarchyDisplay composes AdjustedHierarchyDisplay and AngularHierarchyDisplay. The composition operator realizes a variant of multiple inheritance that linearizes the superclasses, thereby avoiding ambiguities w.r.t. method dispatch and w.r.t. sharing or duplicating of inherited state. The composition uses a variant of *C3 linearization* [3,13], which produces a unique and predictable linearization of the inheritance graph. In the case of AdjustedAngularHierarchyDisplay, the linear order of superclasses produced by the linearization algorithm is [HD,AngHD,AdjHD,AdjAngHD], whereby HD is an abbreviation for HierarchyDisplay, Ang is an abbreviation of angular, Adj is an abbreviation of Adjusted and the last mixin is the most specific one.

The order of the mixin operands of the operator & is important in determining the order of the mixins in the linearized chain. The operator & is not

```
1  cclass AdjustedAngularHierarchyDisplay extends
2             AdjustedHierarchyDisplay & AngularHierarchyDisplay {}
```

Listing 3. Composing variants of hierarchy display

commutative, and the operand on the left-hand side is more specific than the one on the right-hand side. The leftmost mixin is the most specific one. The same linearization algorithm is also used if a further-binding of a class declares additional superclasses.

In the context of virtual classes, this composition operator propagates the composition into inner classes. This means that all inner classes of the composed classes that are further-bindings of a common class are automatically composed via linearization, whereby the linearization of the enclosing family class determines the linearization of the inner classes. This composition works recursively with arbitrary levels of nesting. In our example, this means that `AdjustedAngularHierarchyDisplay` combines further-bindings of both `Adjusted-HierarchyDisplay` and `AngularHierarchyDisplay`. Since the inner classes of a class can represent an entire class hierarchy, the `&` operator can effectively be used to extend and compose class hierarchies.

A definition of how mixins are linearized and composed is given in Fig. 10.[6] Therein, p denotes a mixin by the static path $C_1...C_n$, C_i class names, that denotes the lexical position of the class body corresponding to p. For example, the mixin for the class definition in line 3 of List. 1 is `HD.CompositeNode`. The notation $\bar{p}$ denotes a *list* of mixins $p_1, ..., p_{|\bar{p}|}$, e.g., $\bar{p} = $ `[HD,AdjHD,AdjAngHD]`, and $\bar{\bar{p}}$ denotes a list of mixin lists. The $[... \mid ...]$ notation is used to denote *list comprehensions* as, e.g., in Haskell or Python.[7]

Given a class C and the mixin list of the enclosing family $\bar{p}$, the *Assemble* function computes the mixin list that determines the definition of C relative to $\bar{p}$. For illustration, we will simulate the evaluation of *Assemble*(`[HD,AdjHD]`, CompositeNode), which calculates the mixin list of `CompositeNode` in the context of `AdjustedHierarchyDisplay`, resulting in `[HD.Node,AdjHD.Node,HD.CompositeNode]`. To do so, *Assemble* first calls *Defs* to collect all the definitions of `CompositeNode` (our C) located in any of the class bodies specified by `[HD,AdjHD]` (our $\bar{p}$).[8] The result is `HD.CompositeNode`, because there is only one definition of `CompositeNode` and no further-binding.

The complete mixin list for a class C must also include the mixins of all its ancestors. For this purpose, *Assemble* applies *Expand* over the list of mixins returned by *Defs* and linearizes the result. For each p in this list, *Expand* computes the mixin list for each superclass of p, again relative to the enclosing mixin list $\bar{p}$. For this purpose, *Expand* recursively applies *Assemble* over the list of all superclasses, linearizes the result and adds the mixin p at the end. The recursion is well defined because it recurses only on the superclasses and the superclass rela-

---

[6] These definitions are part of the aforementioned formalization of virtual classes [16].

[7] For example, $[2n \mid n \leftarrow 1...5, n > 3]$ is the list $[8, 10]$.

[8] The function *ClassDef*, which is not defined here, simply looks up a class in the program.

$Assemble(\overline{p}, C) = Linearize([Expand(\overline{p}, p) \mid p \leftarrow Defs(\overline{p}, C)])$

$Defs(\overline{p}, C) = [p.C \mid p \leftarrow \overline{p}, ClassDef(p.C) \neq \perp]$

$Expand(\overline{p}, p) = Linearize([Assemble(\overline{p}, C') \mid C' \leftarrow C_1...C_n]) p$
  where $ClassDef(p) = $ **cclass** C **extends** $C_1 \& ...\& C_n$ **{ ... }**

$Linearize(nil_{\overline{p}}) = nil_p$
$Linearize(\overline{\overline{p}} \; \overline{p}) = Lin2(Linearize(\overline{\overline{p}}), \overline{p})$
$Lin2(nil_p, nil_p) \quad = nil_p$
$Lin2(\overline{p} \; p, \overline{p}' \; p) \quad = Lin2(\overline{p}, \overline{p}') \; p$
$Lin2(\overline{p}, \overline{p}' \; p') \quad = Lin2(\overline{p}, \overline{p}') \; p'$ if $p' \notin \overline{p}$
$Lin2(\overline{p} \; p, \overline{p}') \quad = Lin2(\overline{p}, \overline{p}') \; p$ if $p \notin \overline{p}'$
$Lin2(\overline{p} \; p'\overline{p}'' p, \overline{p}' p') = Lin2(\overline{p} \; \overline{p}'' p, \overline{p}') \; p'$
                    (Note: use first case that matches)

Fig. 10. Mixin computation for class C given mixin list $\overline{p}$ of enclosing family class

tion has no cycles in a well-formed program (we stop when we reach a top-level object, which has a trivial mixin list).

For our setting of p = HD.CompositeNode, and $\overline{p}$ = [HD,AdjHD], $Expand$ will be applied to HD.Node, the only superclass of HD.CompositeNode, which will cause $Assemble$([HD,AdjHD], Node) to be recursively called, resulting in [HD.Node,AdjHD.Node]. Since Node does not have any further superclases, this is the end of the recursion. The mixin HDComposite is added to [HD.Node,AdjHD.Node] yielding the overall result: $Assemble$([HD,AdjHD], CompositeNode) = [HD.Node,AdjHD.Node,HD.CompositeNode].

Linearization is a technique for topological sorting of an inheritance graph, so that method calls can be dispatched along the calculated order. The function $Linearize$ in the lower part of Fig. 10 linearizes a list of mixin lists, i.e., it produces a single mixin list that contains the same mixins as those in the operands, in an order which is controlled by the operands. $Linearize$ is defined in terms of a binary linearization function, $Lin2$. This function is an extension of the C3 linearization algorithm [3, 13]. The linearization algorithm has been designed so that the ordering of mixins in a virtual class can be controlled by the programmer of a subclass, in a similar spirit as when the programmer of a subclass can decide to override a method in any mainstream OO programming language, see [3,13].

3.3   Abstract Classes and Collaboration Interfaces

The benefits of polymorphism can be maximized by using abstract family classes. A separate interface concept is not necessary because we do not have the single inheritance bottleneck. For example, we can use an abstract family class IHierarchyDisplay to define the public interface of the HierarchyDisplay component, as shown in List. 4. The abstract family class exposes the public methods of the component as well as the classes that should be visible to the clients, e.g., the abstraction in List. 4 does not expose the Connection class.

```
1  abstract public cclass IHierarchyDisplay {
2    abstract public Node getRoot(); /* data model */
3    abstract public void calculateLayout(); /* visualization */
4    abstract public void draw(Graphics g); /* visualization */
5    abstract public void refresh(); /* visualization */
6    ...
7    abstract public cclass Node {
8      abstract public String getText(); /* data model */
9      abstract public boolean textFits(String text); /* visualization */
10   }
11   abstract public cclass CompositeNode extends Node {
12     abstract public Node getChildAt(int i); /* data model */
13     abstract public int getChildCount(); /* data model */
14     abstract public void calculateLayout(); /* visualization */
15   }
16 }
17 public cclass HierarchyDisplay extends IHierarchyDisplay { ... }
```

Listing 4. Collaboration interface of hierarchy display

```
1  final public IHierarchyDisplay hier = new HierarchyDisplay();
2  hier.CompositeNode node = hier.new CompositeNode(); /* error */
3  final public IHierarchyDisplay2 hier2 = new HierarchyDisplay2();
4  hier2.CompositeNode node = hier.new CompositeNode(); /* ok */
```

Listing 5. Polymorphic instantiation of classes of an abstract family class

Declaring a class as abstract means that it cannot be instantiated. According to this rule, we cannot create instances of the class IHierarchyDisplay. The virtual classes Node and CompositeNode are declared as abstract too. This means that they cannot be instantiated polymorphically through a family variable with type IHierarchyDisplay; so the line 2 in List. 5 will generate a compiler error.

In a similar way, we can allow polymorphic instantiation of virtual classes by declaring them as concrete. For example, List. 6 shows an alternative interface to the hierarchy display component, which declares its virtual classes Node and CompositeNode as concrete even though they contain abstract methods. The intent of such a design is to allow their polymorphic instantiation as shown in line 4 of List. 5. Here, the instantiation is requested through the abstract interface, but the class that is actually instantiated is CompositeNode of HierarchyDisplay2, which belongs to a concrete family class and must implement all the inherited abstract methods.

Abstract classes are also allowed within concrete classes. For example, in an alternative design of HierarchyDisplay component, there could be a new class LeafNode to represent leaf nodes, while Node would serve only as an abstraction to define the common interface for all types of nodes. In such case, declaring Node as abstract would prevent its instantiation.

If we do not know whether a virtual class will be concrete in concrete subfamilies, it is better to declare it as abstract, because we can override an abstract class with a concrete one, but not the other way around. Overriding a concrete class with an abstract one is not allowed because it would break the soundness of polymorphic instantiation.

In Java, a class containing an abstract method must be declared as abstract. In CAESARJ this rule is weakened: *A method can be abstract when at least one*

```
 1 | abstract public cclass IHierarchyDisplay2 {
 2 |     ...
 3 |     public cclass Node {
 4 |         abstract public String getText();  ...
 5 |     }
 6 |     public cclass CompositeNode extends Node {
 7 |         abstract public Node getChildAt(int i); ...
 8 |     }
 9 | }
10 | cclass HierarchyDisplay2 extends IHierarchyDisplay2 { }
```

Listing 6. Alternative interface to the hierarchy display

```
 1 | abstract public cclass MutableHierarchyModel extends IHierarchyDisplay {
 2 |     protected Node root;
 3 |     public void getRoot() { return root; }
 4 |     ...
 5 |     public cclass Node {
 6 |         protected String text;
 7 |         public String getText() {
 8 |             return fitsText(text) ? text : text.substring(0, 1);
 9 |         } ...
10 |     }
11 |     public cclass CompositeNode {
12 |         protected List children = new LinkedList();
13 |         public Node getChildAt(i) { return (Node)children.get(i); }
14 |         public int getChildCount() { ... }
15 |         ...
16 |     }
17 | }
```

Listing 7. Hierarchy display data model as a separate module

of its enclosing classes is abstract. This rule is sufficient to ensure that abstract methods will never be called, because it excludes the possibility of direct instances of the class declaring the method. According to this rule, it is legitimate to have concrete classes with abstract methods inside an abstract family class, which is the case in List. 6. It is also possible to have abstract classes with abstract methods inside a concrete class.

Abstract classes used as interfaces enable a more fine-grained separation of the different concerns of our hierarchy display. One of these concerns that we might want to separate is how the data to be displayed are represented. Our previous implementation stored the data model directly in corresponding fields. The comments in List. 4 now identify a set of methods that are the interface to the data model. With inheritance and class composition we can now separate the display logic from the data model.

Listing 7 shows a sample implementation of the data model. The corresponding family class is abstract because it is only an implementation of the data model; hence, the part of the IHierarchyDisplay interface responsible for the visualization is missing. On the other hand, List. 8 shows a version of HierarchyDisplay that does not define the data model, hence, it is abstract as well. Note that the code in List. 8 uses the methods responsible for the data model without defining them. In an appropriate composition, such as in List. 9, both facets of a hierarchy display are composed. Since the composition is complete, it does not need to be abstract and can be used directly.

```
1  abstract public cclass HierarchyDisplay extends IHierarchyDisplay {
2      protected Component view = null;
3      public void calculateLayout()
4         getRoot().calculateLayout();
5         refresh ();
6      }
7      public void draw(Graphics g) { ... }
8      public void refresh() {  ... }
9      ...
10     abstract public cclass Node {
11        protected TextShape shape = new Rectangle();
12        public void draw(Graphics g) { shape.setText(getText()); shape.draw(g);  }
13        public boolean textFits(String text) { ... }
14        ...
15     }
16     abstract public cclass CompositeNode {
17        protected List connections = new LinkedList();
18        public void draw(Graphics g) {
19           super.draw(g);
20           for (int i1 = 0; i1 < getChildCount(); i1++) getChildAt(i1).draw(g); ...
21        }
22        public void calculateLayout() { ... }
23        ...
24     }
25     public cclass Connection { ... }
26  }
```

Listing 8. HierarchyDisplay without data model implementation

```
1  public cclass MutableHierarchyDisplay
2      extends HierarchyDisplay & MutableHierarchyModel { }
```

Listing 9. Reconstructing the mutable hierarchy display component

There are two important aspects in the design embodied in Lists. 4, 8 and 9: (a) the partition of the interface methods into different facets, as indicated by the comments in List. 4, and (b) the design rule that subclasses of the interface responsible for one facet implement only those methods belonging to this facet (whereby any method declared in the interface can be called). In such a design, the interface in List. 4 controls the collaboration between different facets of its implementation, hence, we call such interfaces *collaboration interfaces*.

It is tempting to turn this design pattern into a language feature, so that conformance to a particular interface facet is checked by the compiler. In previous publications [37, 38] we actually proposed to divide the methods of such a *collaboration interface* into two generic fixed facets: *expected* and *provided*. In the implementation of CAESARJ, we dropped this mechanism because it is not general enough. In general, there can be many different facets of an interface, not just two. We are currently working on a new interface concept that allows more freedom in this regard while still retaining static checking of classes with respect to the facets they are responsible for.

4   Crosscutting Integration

In this section, we will introduce CAESARJ features for supporting crosscutting composition.

4.1 Bindings

The implementations of hierarchy display facets that are presented in List. 7 and List. 8 are self-consistent and completely encapsulated behind the collaboration interface. Alternatively, facets can be implemented as adapters of already existing classes. In our example, we might want to display the company model from Fig. 6 with our hierarchy display. The company model can indeed be seen as a data model for our hierarchy display, except that it does not fit to its internal modular structure. Hence, in the following we will implement the data model facet of the hierarchy display as an adapter to the company model, which allows us to view the company model as a data model for the hierarchy display.

A family class that implements a component facet by adapting external classes is called *binding*. Concrete family classes are produced by combining bindings with the families implementing the component functionality to be integrated. Figure 11 shows how the family class CompanyHierarchyDisplay for visualizing the company organizational hierarchy is defined as a combination of the implementation of the visualization facet of the IHierarchyDisplay interface implemented in HierarchyDisplay and the data model facet of IHierarchyDisplay defined as its binding to the company model CompanyHierarchyBinding.

Bindings map between types from two domains by means of *wrapper* classes—dynamic extensions of other classes, called *wrappees*. A wrapper can introduce new state and operations, as well as adapt the wrappee to required interfaces. The wrapper–wrappee relationship is established by the keyword wraps. A wrapper can access its wrappee by means of the special identifier wrappee.

To map the display and the company domains of our example, we have to bind hierarchy display nodes to company model objects. One wrapper class is needed for each type of display node. Top nodes are bound to company objects, nodes at the second level of the display hierarchy to department objects, and bottom nodes to employees. In List. 10, WorkerNode is a wrapper for Employee. It adapts Employee to the data model facet of Node by implementing getText,

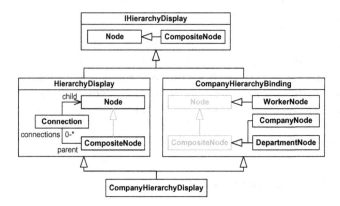

Fig. 11. Integration of hierarchy display into company model

```
1  abstract public cclass CompanyHierarchyBinding extends IHierarchyDisplay {
2      protected Company _company = null;
3      public Node getRoot() { return CompanyNode(_company); }
4      ...
5      public cclass WorkerNode extends Node wraps Employee {
6          public String getText() {
7              return textFits(wrappee.getFullName()) ?
8                      wrappee.getFullName() : wrappee.getInitials();
9          }
10     }
11     public cclass DepartmentNode extends CompositeNode wraps Department {
12         public String getText() { ... }
13         public Node getChildAt(int i) {
14             return WorkerNode(wrappee.getWorkerAt(i));
15         }
16         public int getChildCount() { return wrappee.getWorkerCount(); }
17     }
18     public cclass CompanyNode extends CompositeNode wraps Company {
19         public Node getChildAt(int i) {
20             return DepartmentNode(wrappee.getWorkerAt(i));
21         }
22         ...
23     }
24     pointcut departmChildrenChange() : execution(* Department.addWorker(..)) ||
25         execution(* Department.removeWorker(..));
26     pointcut companyChildrenChange() : execution(* Company.addDepartment(..)) ||
27         execution(* Company.removeDepartment(..));
28     pointcut displayChange() : execution(* company.*.set*Name(..)) ||
29         departmChildrenChange() || companyChildrenChange();
30     after(Department d) : departmChildrenChange() && this(d) {
31         DepartmentNode(d).calculateLayout();
32     }
33     after(Company c) : companyChildrenChange() && this(c) {
34         CompanyNode(c).calculateLayout();
35     }
36     after() : displayChange() && !cflowbelow(displayChange()) { refresh(); }
37 }
```

Listing 10. Company hierarchy binding

the only method related to the data model in `Node`, using methods of `Employee`. Wrappers for `Company` and `Department` turn these classes into composite nodes in the display world: They inherit from `CompositeNode` and implement its data model-related methods for retrieval of text and children.

Wrappers are created by *wrapper constructors*, which take as parameters the objects to be wrapped and return the corresponding wrapper objects. For example, a `DepartmentNode` should return the nodes representing the workers at that department as its children. Its method `getChildAt(i)` in List. 10 retrieves the ith employee of the department and wraps it into a `WorkerNode` object. A wrapper constructor differs from a conventional instantiation: Given a certain wrappee object, o, only the first call of a wrapper constructor with o as a parameter creates a new wrapper for o; consecutive calls will always return the same wrapper instance.

Such "wrapper recycling" ensures that there is only one wrapper for one wrappee per binding and, hence, enables *stateful wrappers*. Attaching additional state to wrapped objects is important: A component to be integrated has its own state which cannot be inferred from wrappee's state. For example, the position of a node and its graphical attributes cannot be inferred from the data model and must be stored in node objects.

```
1  public cclass CompanyHierarchyDisplay
2      extends HierarchyDisplay & CompanyHierarchyBinding { }
```

Listing 11. Component for company hierarchy display

However, an object can have multiple wrappers of the same type within different family instances. The wrapper constructor call `WorkerNode(..)` in List. 10 is, in fact, an abbreviation for `this.WorkerNode(..)`. Wrappers are also virtual classes—their meaning is relative to an enclosing family. Wrapper constructors are also available outside the family class by explicitly qualifying their calls with a reference to a family instance.

Mapping between the abstractions in their respective domains is not enough for full integration: The components often need to adapt their behavior within the composition. In our example, organizational changes, e.g., transfer of employees from one department to another, affects the layout of the hierarchy display and should cause the layout of certain branches in the hierarchy to be recalculated. In CAESARJ, such behavioral integrations are expressed within a binding by means of pointcuts and advice. CAESARJ supports AspectJ-like pointcuts and advice. In the following discussion, we assume that the reader is familiar with the crosscutting mechanisms in AspectJ [26] and the advantages of observing with pointcuts [20, 27].

In our example, the binding in List. 10 uses pointcuts to observe relevant changes. Pointcuts `departmChildrenChange` and `companyChildrenChange` observe `DepartmentNode`, respectively `CompanyNode`, children changes. The pointcut `displayChange` observes any kind of change that affects the company hierarchy display.[9] Display update is done in advice (List. 10) using methods of the collaboration interface (List. 4). Top-level methods, such as `refresh`, can be called directly, the methods of the nodes, e.g., `calculateLayout`, are called on the corresponding wrapper object.

As already mentioned, the company hierarchy display component is constructed by applying mixin composition to the implementation of its visualization facet and its company binding (List. 11). Figure 12 depicts the implicit class diagram inside `CompanyHierarchyDisplay`, which is the result of merging the inherited classes and their relationships. It contains both the wrapper classes from the binding as well as the `Connection` class from the family `HierarchyDisplay`, which implements the visualization facet. The classes `Node` and `CompositeNode` of `HierarchyDisplay` become the superclasses of the wrapper classes in the context of `CompanyHierarchyDisplay`. Thus, the resulting wrapper classes inherit both the functionality related to the data model and to the visualization.

Of course, bindings do not necessarily need to be coded to collaboration interfaces. If the code of a binding is not reusable, it can be defined as a simple subclass of the family type that we want to adapt in a specific context.

---

[9] It reuses the pointcuts for children changes and quantifies over all methods that affect names of the data model objects. We use the `cflowbelow` pointcut to ensure that the display is refreshed only once after a sequence of changes that constitutes a logical transaction.

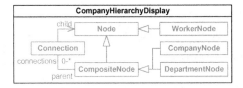

Fig. 12. Class diagram of the virtual classes within CompanyHierarchyDisplay

For example, `CompanyHierarchyDisplay` could also be implemented as subclass of `HierarchyDisplay`. Then the binding would be a concrete family class and could be instantiated directly.

4.2   Dynamic Wrapper Selection

This section considers the issue of defining wrappers in the presence of inheritance hierarchies. For example, the class `Employee` may have various subclasses, e.g., `InternalEmployee` and `ExternalEmployee` to distinguish between internal employees of the company and the employees subcontracted from other companies. We may want this difference to be reflected in the display of the organizational structure. The question is how to define wrappers for subclasses of already wrapped classes.

In CAESARJ, wrappers for classes in a hierarchy chain build a hierarchy of related wrappers that share the same name but are distinguished by the type of the objects they wrap, i.e., they have different `wraps` clauses. All these wrappers share the same constructor, which decides which specific wrapper type to create by the dynamic type of the wrappee object passed as a parameter. The general rule of wrapper selection is that the most specific wrapper is selected for the given object. In this way, a wrapper for an object can be retrieved polymorphically.

For illustration, consider the `WorkerNode` wrapper for `ExternalEmployee` in List. 12. It refines the implementation of `getText` so that the display text includes the name of the external company. For an instance of `ExternalEmployee`, the version of `WorkerNode` that wraps `ExternalEmployee` will be used, whereas for an instance of `InternalEmployee`, the `WorkerNode` wrapping `Employee` will be used, because there is no more specific wrapper declared for `InternalEmployee`. The wrapper is retrieved polymorphically in the `getChildAt` method of `Department-Node` (List. 12).

Polymorphic usage of wrappers imposes certain typing constraints. The `WorkerNode` wrapper constructor in the method `getChildAt` in List. 12 may return an instance of type `this.WorkerNode`, where the `WorkerNode` is the wrapper class for `Employee` or an instance of `WorkerNode` wrapper for `ExternalEmployee`. To allow the polymorphic usage of wrappers, `WorkerNode` for `ExternalEmployee` must be a subtype of `WorkerNode` for `Employee`. In CAESARJ, this is ensured by implicit inheritance between such wrapper classes, which is why we do not need to declare explicitly `WorkerNode` for `ExternalEmployee` as a subclass of `Node`. The general rule is that subtype relationship between wrappee classes implies inheritance between corresponding wrapper classes. As a consequence, wrappers with the same name

```
1  abstract public cclass CompanyHierarchyBinding extends IHierarchyDisplay {
2      ...
3      public cclass DepartmentNode extends CompositeNode wraps Department {
4          public Node getChildAt(int i) {
5              return WorkerNode(wrappee.getWorkerAt(i));
6          } ...
7      }
8      public cclass WorkerNode extends Node wraps Employee {
9          public String getText() { ...   }
10     }
11     public cclass WorkerNode wraps ExternalEmployee {
12         public String getText() {
13             return super.getText() + "(" + wrappee.getCompanyName() + ")";
14         }
15     }
16 }
```

Listing 12. Wrapper hierarchy for different types of employees

build inheritance hierarchies, which reflect the inheritance hierarchies of their wrappees.

Dynamic wrapper selection can be ambiguous in the case of multiple inheritance relationships between wrappees. This can occur when wrapping Java interfaces or CAESARJ classes. Consider the case of two wrappers for types A and B, where both A and B are supertypes of a given wrappee class W. If B is subtype of A, B's wrapper will be selected for W. The ambiguous situation occurs when A and B are not comparable. The ambiguity can be resolved by declaring a wrapper for a supertype of W that is a subtype both of A and of B.

The problem is, however, that detection of such ambiguities cannot be done in a modular way and requires a global analysis of the type system of an application. An analogous problem has been raised in the context of the implementation of external methods in Multijava [10]; the problem is addressed there by disallowing dynamic dispatch on interface types. External methods on interfaces are allowed in Relaxed Multijava [40], but the ambiguities are detected only at class load time. In the current implementation of CAESARJ, ambiguities of dynamic wrapper selection are detected at run time.

We plan to generalize the dynamic wrapper selection to multiple wrappees (such that there is, e.g., a unique wrapper for a *pair* of wrappees). At the time of writing this paper, the best strategy for dealing with ambiguities and with the inheritance relationships between wrappers (see the next section) has not yet been fully worked out; hence, this is part of our future work. Note that multiple wrappees can still be used if the programmer defines a usual constructor and takes care of the wrapper management manually.

So far, we have discussed the case of defining wrappers for classes that have an inheritance relationship but are adapted to the same abstraction. In List. 12, both Employee and its subclass ExternalEmployee are adapted to Node. In the general case, given two abstractions A1 and A2 pertaining to one concern, where A2 is a subtype of A1, it might be necessary to adopt them to two different abstractions pertaining to another concern B1 and B2, where B2 is a subtype of B1.

```
 1   abstract public cclass GUIHierarchyBinding extends IHierarchyDisplay {
 2       protected Component rootComp = null;
 3       public Node getRoot() { return ComponentNode(rootComp); }
 4
 5       public cclass ComponentNode extends Node wraps Component {
 6           public String getText() {
 7               String name = wrappee.getClass().getName();
 8               return name.substring(name.lastIndexOf('.') + 1);
 9           }
10       }
11       public cclass ComponentNode extends CompositeNode wraps Container {
12           public Node getChildAt(int i1) {
13               return ComponentNode(wrappee.getComponent(i1));
14           }
15           public int getChildCount() { return wrappee.getComponentCount(); }
16       }
17   }
```

Listing 13. Binding for containment hierarchy of GUI elements

Consider for illustration the binding of IHierarchyDisplay to the containment hierarchy of GUI elements in a typical Java application in List. 13. In the standard Java library, Component is the supertype of all GUI elements, and Container is the supertype of GUI elements containing other elements. In order to display a GUI hierarchy, we have to bind Node to Component and CompositeNode to Container. Further, since Container is subtype of Component, their wrappers must belong to the same hierarchy.

So we have a situation where wrappers of the same hierarchy must implement different interfaces of the collaboration interface. This is possible in CAESARJ, because each wrapper in the hierarchy can introduce new inheritance relationships. For example, in List. 13 the ComponentNode wrapper for Container inherits from CompositeNode besides its implicit inheritance from the wrapper ComponentNode for Component.

4.3   CAESARJ **Bindings Versus AspectJ Intertype Declarations**

Bindings share pointcut and advice declarations with AspectJ's aspects, but they are based on a different static crosscutting model. CAESARJ aspects use wrappers instead of intertype declarations to add new functionality to existing objects. Bindings support reuse by the techniques of coding to interfaces, virtual types and mixin composition. AspectJ's reuse mechanisms, on the other hand, are limited to abstract aspects and aspect inheritance. In this section, we will discuss the implications of these differences.

Polymorphic aspectual extensions. Wrappers and dynamic wrapper selection allow to define functionality outside a base class (a.k.a open classes [10]), while retaining subtype polymorphism. Wrapper classes define functionality that is polymorphic with respect to both base object types (wrappees) and aspect types.

Consider for illustration List. 10. The method calculateLayout belongs to aspect functionality. It is polymorphic with respect to hierarchy node types (each node type has its own draw method, which is called by calculateLayout). In its control flow, calculateLayout eventually calls methods pertaining to data

management, such as, e.g., `getChildAt` or `getText`. The latter are defined relative
to different base types in List. 10, i.e., they are polymorphic w.r.t. base types.
Each company object has its specific way to access children or to display a text
label. Futhermore, this specific way is also relative to a particular aspect. That
is, it is not only possible to define different ways of accessing children for different
company objects within the same aspect; the latter can also be different from
aspect to aspect.

As discussed in [38], polymorphic behavior in the extent described above is
not possible with intertype declarations. One can only achieve polymorphism
w.r.t base types by invasively adding state and methods to base classes directly,
however, at the cost of losing independent extensibility and polymorphism with
respect to aspect types [38, 49].

Late-bound operations outside the base model is also the motivation of the
visitor design pattern [17]. Both late-bound wrappers and visitors activate their
functionality dynamically. Nevertheless, differently from wrappers, visitors require preplanned preparations in the data model and manual implementation of
the dispatch code. Furthermore, wrappers give more flexibility for default handling of certain variants of the data model. In List. 12, e.g., we specify default
display behavior for all types of `Employee` and handle only `ExternalEmployee` in a
specific way. Finally, a visitor implements the late-binding of a single operation
and, therefore, does not support interactions between multiple operations.

Wrappers also allow one to associate arbitrary aspect-specific state with base
objects; the state can either be defined in the wrapper or inherited from the
component class the wrapper binds. As shown in List. 10, wrapper constructors provide a convenient way to navigate from a base (application) object to
the corresponding aspect (component) wrapper. An alternative to wrapper constructors in AspectJ would be manual implementation of similar mechanisms
for each specific case in the aspect code. Other solutions require modification
of application classes to contain links to the corresponding wrapper objects. A
more detailed discussion of the problems with managing aspect specific state
extensions can also be found in [38].

Abstraction and Reuse. Collaboration interfaces support reuse of the same
functionality in different contexts. In Sects. 4.1 and 4.2 we discussed two reuse
scenarios for `HierarchyDisplay`: one with the organizational hierarchy of a company and another with the containment hierarchy of GUI elements. Bindings are
also reusable, as long as they are defined to the collaboration interface. We can
provide other implementations of hierarchy display for the same collaboration
interface. In Sect. 3, we have defined different extensions to `HierarchyDisplay`,
which are also alternative implementations of the visualization facet of the same
collaboration interface. They can all be reused with our bindings to both the
company and GUI structure.

By mixin composition, any display implementation is composable with any
binding, as shown in Fig. 13. This is not an accident, but instead is a consequence
of proper abstraction. The collaboration interface sets an explicit contract for
the composition. It ensures that methods used by the display implementation

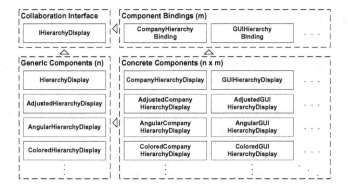

Fig. 13. Composing variations of display implementations and bindings

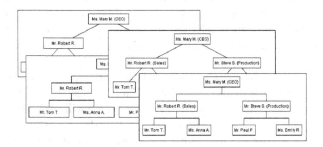

Fig. 14. Company hierarchy display variations

have the same signature as those implemented by the binding, and the other way around. The collaboration interface also unifies the names of the shared classes, making them automatically composable. Any deviation from this contract would be detected by the compiler. The rules for abstract classes help to check correctness of the composition, too. The compiler can ensure that only concrete classes are instantiated and that concrete classes in concrete collaborations are fully implemented.

Once the variability basis (meaningful variations of the display functionality) is set up, CAESARJ developers can easily support different strategies for displaying the company structure, as illustratively shown in Fig. 14, with no additional overhead. The decision as to which strategy to use in a concrete situation can be made statically or even dynamically. Here the CAESARJ's deployment mechanism, which will be discussed in the next section, comes into play.

As also discussed in [38], the same degree of reuse and variability is not possible with abstract aspects and intertype declarations of AspectJ. First, the linear inheritance hierarchy is not sufficient for multidimensional reuse, i.e., either the bindings would inherit from concrete display implementations, or the other way around. Second, the intertype declarations of an abstract aspect cannot be reused in multiple concrete aspects that provide alternative implementations of the introduced operations.

5   Dynamic Aspect Control

We can increase applicability of aspects by enabling flexible control over their activation time and scope. One way to achieve this is to encode the activation logic directly in the aspect. But, this tightly couples the aspect to specific parts of the application and limits its reusability in other contexts. A better solution is to provide control mechanisms over aspects from outside. In this section, we review features of CAESARJ that enable dynamic control over aspects and their scope of activity.

5.1   Explicit Instantiation, Local and Thread-Based Deployment

In CAESARJ an aspect is simply a class containing pointcuts and advice. Like conventional objects, aspects in CAESARJ can be instantiated at any point of the program execution using the keyword `new`. There can be multiple instances of an aspect type with independent state, life cycle and scope of deployment. Like any other objects, aspects can be referenced, passed as parameters and used polymorphically.

Instantiation does not automatically activate an aspect; the latter must be *deployed* in order to activate its pointcuts and advice. Aspects can be deployed on different dynamic scopes. For simplicity, we will first consider the simplest deployment method, called *local deployment*. By means of `deploy`, respectively `undeploy`, statements, aspects are deployed, respectively undeployed, on all joinpoints occurring in the local virtual machine process, as illustrated in List. 14 (lines 9 and 15).

Let us illustrate the usefulness of explicit aspect instantiation for the design of the company hierarchy display. The component `CompanyHierarchyDisplay` (List. 11) is an aspect, because it inherits pointcuts and advice from its binding (List. 10). On the other hand, `CompanyHierarchyDisplay` has all the properties of a conventional class. It can be instantiated whenever the application needs to display the company hierarchy. It can be instantiated once more, if the user opens one more view. Furthermore, the decision which concrete variation of the aspect to instantiate may depend on run-time conditions, e.g., user preferences can specify which of the hierarchy display variations should be used.

In List. 14, `CompanyHierarchyDisplay` is created in a class that handles the menu action to open a hierarchical view of a company. After instantiation we can initialize it with additional data and pass it as a parameter to a view object, which uses its visualization functionality. Once initialized, the aspect is deployed and starts observing changes in the company model.[10]

An aspect is garbage-collected when it is not referenced anymore and is not deployed. It would be incorrect to garbage-collect deployed aspects, because even if they are not explicitly referenced, they are still reachable through joinpoint interception and provide a meaningful functionality just by reacting to certain

---

[10] We could also deploy the aspect in its constructor, i.e., automatically at creation time; the solution in List. 14 is however safer, because the observation begins only after completing initialization, which establishes necessary application invariants.

```
1  public class ShowCompanyHierarchyAction implements ActionListener {
2      List companyList; Frame mainWindow;
3      ...
4      public void actionPerformed(ActionEvent e) {
5          CompanyHierarchyDisplay hier = new CompanyHierarchyDisplay();
6          hier.setCompany(selectCompanyFromList(companyList));
7          HierarchyView view = createNewView(mainWindow);
8          view.setHierarchy(hier);
9          deploy hier;
10     }
11 }
12 public class HierarchyView extends JComponent {
13     IHierarchyDisplay hierarchy;
14     ...
15     public void close() { undeploy hierarchy; }
16 }
```

Listing 14. Life cycle of company hierarchy display component

```
1  deployed public cclass CompanyDisplayLogging {
2      void around() : execution(* draw(..)) && this(CompanyHierarchyDisplay) {
3          CompanyLogger logger = new CompanyLogger();
4          deploy (logger) { proceed(); }
5      }
6  }
```

Listing 15. Thread-based deployment

application events. Aspects can be undeployed explicitly from outside or implicitly as a reaction to some joinpoint. For example, `CompanyHierarchyDisplay` can be undeployed by its client view when the view is closed (List. 14).

By deploying and undeploying aspects at certain points of program execution we control their scope of application. In List. 14, we deploy `CompanyHierarchyDisplay` when its owner view is created, and undeploy it when the view is destroyed. In this way we limit the scope of the aspect application to the lifetime of the corresponding view. We can also restrict the scope of the applicability of the aspect to individual control flows. A similar level of flexibility of aspect control is hard to achieve with static aspect activation as in AspectJ.

The scoping enabled by local deployment is limited only by time of activation. This may not be sufficient in a multithreaded environment, where we might want to limit the scope of aspects to a single thread. For this purpose, CAESARJ provides *thread-based deployment*, expressed by the **deploy** block. For illustration, consider how the aspect in List. 15 is deployed on the scope of the control flow inside the block and does not have any influence on concurrent executions.

Thread-based deployment works well for crosscutting of inherently synchronous processes, such as calculations or workflows. However, in event-driven, data-centric environments, we may want to observe updates and events independently of the thread that causes them; in this case, local deployment is more suitable.

5.2 Static Deployment

When an aspect needs to be active all the time, it can be deployed statically. There are two ways to express static deployment. One can declare an aspect class

```
1  deployed public cclass CompanyLogger {
2      pointcut logMethods() : execution(* company.*.*(..)) || execution(company.*.new(..));
3      before() : traceMethods() {
4          System.out.println(thisJoinPointStaticPart.toString());
5      }
6  }
```

Listing 16. Singleton aspect to trace company model

```
1  public cclass CompanyLogger extends AbstractLogger { ... }
2  public cclass Application {
3      deployed final private static CompanyLogger compLogger = new CompanyLogger();
4      ...
5  }
```

Listing 17. Static deployment outside the aspect

as statically deployed by adding the `deployed` modifier to its declaration. This means that a single instance of the class must be created and deployed at load time. This is useful for implementing singleton aspects. Listing 16 demonstrates a singleton aspect `CompanyLogger`, which traces all operations on the company model to the console window.

By declaring the aspect class as statically deployed, we couple its definition with the decision that it will not be used dynamically. The decision can be postponed by expressing it outside the aspect: the `deployed` keyword can also be applied to static fields, declared as `final`. This causes the instance referenced by the field to be automatically deployed at the load time of the enclosing class. Listing 17 shows the alternative way to create a statically deployed instance of `CompanyLogger`.

Static deployment is mainly a matter of convenience. It allows us to express a special case of dynamic deployment in a more compact way.

5.3   Remote Deployment

Distributed applications open one more dimension for scoping. Process boundaries should not be an obstacle for aspect-oriented interaction techniques. Just as distributed OO applications need to call methods on remote objects, distributed aspect-oriented applications need to intercept remote joinpoints.

In a distributed environment, the company model—instances of `Company`, `Department`, `Employee`—would most probably reside on a server; the display functionality—the `CompanyHierarchyDisplay` together with dependent instances of `Node` and `CompositeNode`—would be on the client. Observation with pointcuts would have to cross the process boundaries: advice would be executed in the context of the hierarchy display component on the client as a reaction to joinpoints of the company model on the server.

Interception of remote joinpoints is enabled by *remote deployment*, which allows one to deploy aspects on the scope of remote processes. Remote aspect deployment must be enabled on the server process by calling a special API method `activateAspectDeployment` on an instance of `CaesarHost` initialized with the RMI address identifying the server (List. 18). This creates and publishes an

```
1  public class CompanyServer {
2    public static void main(String[] args) {
3        ...
4      CaesarHost host = new CaesarHost("rmi://myserver.net/MyServer/");
5      host.activateAspectDeployment();
6        ...
7    }
8  }
```

Listing 18. Server process hosting company model

```
1  public class ShowCompanyHierarchyAction implements ActionListener {
2    CaesarHost host = new CaesarHost("rmi://myserver.net/MyServer/");
3        ...
4    public void actionPerformed(ActionEvent e) {
5      try {
6        CompanyHierarchyDisplay hier = new CompanyHierarchyDisplay();
7        hier.setCompany((Company)host.resolve("Company"));
8        HierarchyView view = createNewView(mainWindow);
9        view.setHierarchy(hier);
10       host.deployAspect(hier);
11     }
12     catch (CaesarRemoteException e) { System.out.println(e.getMessage()); }
13   }
14 }
```

Listing 19. Initializing display of remote company model

object that accepts aspect deployment requests on the process where `activate-AspectDeployment` is called.

On the client side, aspects can be deployed on the remote process by constructing an instance of `CaesarHost` with the same RMI address and using its `deployAspect` and `undeployAspect` methods. Listing 19 shows a modified version of List. 14, which initializes the hierarchy display of a remote company object. We just have to change the way the `Company` object is retrieved and replace local deployment of display component with remote deployment.

Remote aspect deployment is built on top of the Java RMI infrastructure that deals with such issues as remote calls, marshaling of method arguments and management of remote references. Additionally, we provide a tool that generates stubs for CAESARJ classes that must be executed for each CAESARJ class that is used or deployed remotely.

5.4   Deployment on a Distributed Control Flow

In Sect. 5.1, we argued that the aspects observing processes need to be deployed on single threads. In List. 15, the aspect `CompanyLogger` was deployed inside the execution of the method `draw` of the company display component to monitor how the display uses the data model. Such a solution fails in a distributed environment, where the display component is working on the client side, but the data model is located on the server.

On the other hand, the remote deployment described in Sect. 5.3 enables observation of the data model activity on the server process, but it does not distinguish between requests from different clients. So, if we deploy `CompanyLogger` using the remote deployment method, it will monitor all the activity on the

```
1 deployed public cclass CompanyDisplayLogging {
2     void around() : execution(* draw(..)) && this(CompanyHierarchyDisplay) {
3         CompanyLogger logger = new CompanyLogger();
4         RemoteDeployment.deployOnControlFlow(logger);
5         proceed();
6         RemoteDeployment.undeployFromControlFlow(logger);
7     }
8 }
```

Listing 20. Deployment on distributed control flow

data model during its deployment period. However, we need to intercept only the joinpoints on the server side that are in the control flow of the draw method including the synchronous remote calls.

The necessary filtering is provided by another deployment method supported in CAESARJ, *deployment on a distributed control flow*. This deployment method is expressed by API calls, as shown in List. 20. The aspect affects the synchronous control flow, which the current thread is part of. The synchronous control flow may involve multiple threads from different processes, which interact through synchronous calls. In this way, we can filter the joinpoints of company model methods, which were requested by the draw functionality.

6   Implementation

In this section, we discuss the implementation of CAESARJ on top of the Java Virtual Machine (JVM) by presenting the steps performed by the CAESARJ compiler.

6.1   Implementation of Virtual Classes

By explicitly redefining virtual classes in a subfamily, we potentially also introduce implicit (inherited) types and relations. Let us consider List. 1 for illustration. Although the virtual type CompositeNode is not explicitly declared in AdjustedHierarchyDisplay, there is an *implicit* virtual type AdjustedHierarchy-Display.CompositeNode (dashed rectangles in Fig. 15). Furthermore, there are a number of implicit relations, namely the relations inherited from the super-family and the subtype relations between different refinements of a virtual class (dashed inheritance arrows in Fig. 15).

In CAESARJ, all available virtual types are generated at compile time as Java classes. Hence, the first step in the compilation process is the calculation of the

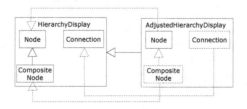

Fig. 15. Implicit types and relations

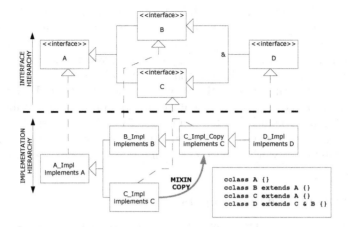

Fig. 16. Separated interface and implementation hierarchies

type graph by extending the explicit (in source code) declared structure with the information about the implicit types and relations. For example, all boxes and relations in Fig. 15 (explicit and implicit ones) constitute the type graph of List. 1. Note that the `cclass` interface hierarchy directly reflects the structure of the type graph.

Next, for each CAESARJ type contained in the type graph, the compiler generates a corresponding mixin list with the algorithm already discussed in Sec. 3.2. Finally, the generated mixin lists are transformed to Java language constructs. This is achieved as follows. For each `cclass` declaration, the CAESARJ compiler generates a Java interface, called the *cclass interface* in the following discussion, and a Java class, called the *cclass implementation* below. This results in an *interface* and an *implementation hierarchy*. For example, Fig. 16 shows separated implementation and inheritance hierarchies for the set of classes defined in the framed listing. The interfaces have the same name as the `cclass` declarations in the source code. A _Impl-suffix is appended to the names of implementation classes.

To construct the implementation hierarchy, every `cclass` is conceptually viewed as a mixin whose superclass parameter is restricted to the declared parent or a subclass of it. The `cclass` implementations are gained from a composition of an ordered mixin list. For example, the mixin list of `B_Impl` is `[A, B]`.

Given the set of mixin lists for a set of CAESARJ classes, the compiler constructs the single inheritance implementation hierarchy using plain Java classes. Nodes in the resulting inheritance hierarchy are `cclass` implementations; each path in it, starting with the root node, corresponds to a mixin list. Sometimes, mixins need to be duplicated and the declared parent of a mixin has to be changed. For example, the mixin list of `D_Impl` is `[A, B, C, D]`. That is, the super of `C`, which is `A` by default, needs to be replaced with `B`.

To generate the corresponding path in the implementation hierarchy, the compiler generates a new Java class by cloning the bytecode of the original mixin, then it replaces in the cloned bytecode all occurrences of the old superclass references with the new one. In our example, C_Impl_Copy is the clone of C_Impl, having the references to the old superclass replaced by B_Impl.

The interface hierarchy hides the implementation hierarchy. It contains the public methods of the cclass implementations and represents their subtype relations. For example, the interface D is a subtype of B and C. Since the implementation class always implements the corresponding cclass interface, we can preserve type compatibility by working with cclass interfaces, e.g., we can assign D_Impl to B and C.

6.2   Implementation of Wrappers

Wrapper recycling is managed by family objects via a map from wrappees to wrappers for each hierarchy of wrappers with the same name. When a wrapper constructor is called, a wrapper is retrieved from a hash table using the wrappee as a key. If the wrapper for given wrappee is not available, a new most-specific wrapper for given wrappee is created and registered in the hash table.

Wrapper classes are translated to virtual classes that are identified by the pairs of wrapper and wrappee names, as shown in Figs. 17 and 18. The example shows that wrappers can be overridden in the subfamily by declaring a new wrapper with the same name and for the same wrappee class. The inheritance relationships between the translated wrappers are generated according the subtype relationships of their wrappee classes. In the next compilation steps,

```
1  class N extends M { }
2  class O extends N { }
3  class P extends O { }
4
5  cclass CollabA {
6      cclass A wraps M { ... }
7      cclass A extends B wraps O { ... }
8      cclass B { ... }
9  }
10 cclass CollabB extends CollabA {
11     cclass A wraps M { ... }
12     cclass A wraps P { ... }
13 }
```

```
1  cclass CollabA {
2      cclass A_M { ... }
3      cclass A_O extends B & A_M { ... }
4      cclass B { ... }
5      public A_M newAforM(M x) {
6          if (x instanceof O) {
7              return newAforO((O)x);
8          }
9          return new A_M(x);
10     }
11     public A_O newAforO(O x) {
12         return new A_O(x);
13     }
14 }
15 cclass CollabB extends CollabA {
16     cclass A_M { ... }
17     cclass A_P extends A_O { ... }
18     public A_O newAforO(O x) {
19         if (x instanceof P) {
20             return newAforP((P)x);
21         }
22         return new A_O(x);
23     }
24     public A_P newAforP(P x) {
25         return new A_P(x);
26     }
27 }
```

Fig. 17. Code with wrapper classes   **Fig. 18.** Generated code

wrappers are treated in the same way as described in Sect. 6.1 for the simple virtual classes.

Figure 18 also shows methods generated for the creation of the most specific wrapper for the given wrappee. Such methods are generated for each wrapper class. Each method checks if the direct subclasses of the wrapper class can be applied for the given wrappee: If yes, the selection is delegated to the more specific method; if not, the current wrapper class is instantiated. Note that the instantiation is polymorphic, which ensures that the most-specific versions of the wrappers will be instantiated. The selection methods must be overridden when the set of the direct subclasses of the wrapper is changed, e.g., newAforO is overridden in List. 18, because a new subclass of A_O was defined.

Another important implementation issue is the life cycle management of wrappers. The life cycle of a wrapper is coupled to the life cycle of two objects, the family and the wrappee. In the current implementation, families use a standard Java hash map to implement the mapping from wrappees to wrappers. This means that entries in the map are garbage-collected only when the corresponding family object is garbage-collected. A better solution would be to release a mapping as soon as neither the wrappee nor the wrapper are reachable. Weak references sound like a solution at first glance, but it turned out that the support for weak references as currently implemented in the JVM is not sufficient to implement this strategy.

6.3   Implementation of Dynamic and Remote Deployment

In this section, we sketch the implementation of aspect deployment in CAESARJ. The aspect deployment framework builds upon static aspects. Each crosscutting class is split into two classes: an *implementation class* and a *registry class*. The implementation class encapsulates the behavior of the aspect objects, while the registry class manages their deployment. Pieces of advice, declared in the aspect, are translated to methods in the implementation class, while the pointcuts are copied to the registry class.

The registry is a singleton aspect, which is statically woven using the AspectJ weaver [26]. The methods of the registry can be seen as statically woven hooks, which are responsible to dispatch calls to the corresponding methods of the deployed instances of the implementation class. The singleton registry instance maintains a container of the deployed instances of the implementation class, as shown in Fig. 19.

Aspect containers in Fig. 19 decide on the deployed objects that must be called at a certain joinpoint. Different deployment methods use different types of containers. The container for local deployment notifies all objects it manages. The thread-based deployment strategy, on the other hand, uses a map-based container that notifies only the objects that are deployed on the current thread. Simultaneous use of multiple deployment strategies is supported by using a composite container, which aggregates the aspect containers of multiple deployment methods. The relationship between the implementation and the registry classes is not one to one. The compiler analyzes inheritance relationships between as-

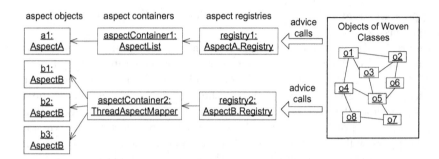

Fig. 19. Sample run-time configuration with dynamically deployed aspects

pect classes, which may involve mixin composition, and generates shared registry classes for aspects with identical crosscutting behavior.

The implementation of dynamic deployment has been carried out with care about performance. The weaver inserts advice calls only at joinpoints that are referenced by the aspects in the application. If no aspect is deployed at a joinpoint, the dispatch logic causes one redundant static method call and one field check for the null value. When aspects are deployed, there is only one additional virtual method call as compared to AspectJ. The reader interested in a more details on aspect registries is referred to [18].

Remote Deployment. Remote aspect deployment in CAESARJ uses Java RMI, which generates stub classes for transparent communication with remote objects. Stubs must also be generated for aspects that are remotely deployed. When an aspect object is deployed remotely, a stub is created for this object on the remote process. The stub intercepts joinpoints on the remote process and marshals the advice calls to the real aspect object. The stubs are generated by a specialized RMI compiler for CAESARJ classes. Classes, which are used or deployed remotely, must be prepared by this tool. Differently from standard Java RMI, the CAESARJ RMI compiler does not require specially prepared remote interfaces. The stub can be generated for any CAESARJ class.

Deployment on Distributed Control Flow. Each synchronous control flow is represented by a single thread in each involved process; therefore, the aspects deployed on the control flow are actually deployed on these threads. During remote call the client process must send the aspects deployed within the current thread, and the remote process must again deploy the received aspects on the thread that serves the client request.

To send aspects to another process, the marshaling of remote method calls has been modified. Normally the stub of a remote object marshals the reference to the object, the name of the called method and the arguments. In the modified version, the stub additionally sends the references to the aspects, which are deployed on the current control flow. The remote process unpacks the received references to the aspects and deploys them on the corresponding thread.

7   Related Work

We have divided work similar to the paper itself into three different groups: hierarchical composition crosscutting composition and dynamic aspect control.

7.1   Hierarchical Composition

Virtual classes were originally introduced in Beta [34] and were further developed in gbeta [12], which supplemented them with mixin composition and family polymorphism. CAESARJ provides a solid implementation of these concepts on the JVM and combines them with language features for crosscutting composition.

Jx [42] supports a kind of nested inheritance. A major difference is that Jx considers inner classes not as properties of the enclosing object, but as properties of the surrounding class. Applicability of Jx is limited to linear refinements, because it does not provide any composition mechanisms for family classes. A similar linear refinement of classes is also supported in Keris [54], but as an extension technique for static modules rather than for instantiable family classes.

AHEAD [4] is the newest technology based on ideas of GenVoca [5] and Mixin Layers [48]. AHEAD supports modularization of application features in large-scale units called layers, which are sets of files describing fragments of different artifacts of the application including fragments of Java classes. The layers are composed using a mixin composition technique that is similar to the one of CAESARJ. The provided implementation is based on source-to-source transformation. Layers lack subtyping and abstraction capability. In CAESARJ, abstractions play an important role for ensuring validity of individual family classes and their composition. In AHEAD reliable composition of layers is assured by additional specifications. Differently from CAESARJ family classes, layers cannot be instantiated and used polymorphically.

Virtual classes are composed along two dimensions: At first the mixins of the same virtual class are composed, and then such a mixin list is composed with analogous mixin lists of its superclasses. Traits [6] also support the composition of the classes along two dimensions: composing the traits inside a class and then along the inheritance hierarchy. Composition of traits inside a class is an orthogonal dimension w.r.t. both the composition dimensions of virtual classes. Traits in combination with virtual classes would mean that virtual classes could be extended with new traits in their further bindings.

7.2   Crosscutting Composition

Hölzle analyzed the problem of integrating independent components in OO languages [24]. Our work addresses many problems identified by Hölzle. CAESARJ is also related to Hyper/J [51] and the notion of multidimensional separation of concerns (MDSOC) [52]. In order to avoid the "tyranny of the dominant decomposition" CAESARJ is not limited to hierarchical refinement and composition techniques, but supports the development the of multiple independent hierarchies and their crosscutting composition by means of bindings.

However, on the technical level CAESARJ is very different from Hyper/J. In Hyper/J, one can define an independent component in a hyperslice. A hyperslice is integrated into an existing application by means of composition rules, specified in a hypermodule. Hyperslices are independent of their context of use, because they are declaratively complete, i.e., they declare as abstract methods everything that they need, but cannot implement themselves. This is different from the CAESARJ approach of shared abstractions in form of a collaboration interface, which facilitates reliable composition and makes the composition code itself reusable. The composition mechanisms in Hyper/J are class-based and cannot be applied in a dynamic way like CAESARJ bindings. Furthermore, Hyper/J's sublanguage for mapping specifications from different hyperslices is fairly complex and not well integrated into the common OO framework.

Integration of multiabstraction of components was addressed by the predecessor technologies of CAESARJ: Adaptive Plug and Play Components (APPCs) [36], Aspectual Components (AC) [31] and Pluggable Composite Adapters (PCA) [39]. Due to a lack of necessary abstraction capabilities, connectors and adapters in APPC, AC, and PCA models are bound to a fixed implementation of an aspect and cannot be reused. CAESARJ also extends these technologies with mechanisms for layered refinement and composition.

The idea of collaboration-based design and composition with bindings is also implemented in ObjectTeams [22]. The notion of a team is analogous to our family classes, and the roles inside teams have similar semantics as virtual classes. This enables linear refinement of teams and separation of generic team implementation from its concrete binding to application classes. However, similarly to APPC, AC and PCA, ObjectTeams does not support collaboration interfaces and reuse of bindings. Besides, the crosscutting capabilities supported in the form of call-ins are significantly less expressive than the pointcuts supported by CAESARJ.

Framed Aspects [33], Sally [19] and LogicAJ [28] provide a form of genericity for AspectJ-like aspects. In this way an aspect is more reusable, because it can be bound to various application classes by specifying different generic parameters. In CAESARJ, we assume that bindings to different classes are different and may require totally different adaptation code. Nevertheless, CAESARJ can benefit from generic pointcuts for better reuse of similar bindings.

7.3 Dynamic Aspect Control

Method Call Interception (MCI) [29] offers dynamically deployed joinpoint interception on the basis of source code instrumentation. Their idea to use central registry to control execution of explicitly instantiated and deployed advice objects is similar to our local dynamic deployment mechanism outlined in List. 14. In comparison to the implementation of MCI [30], CAESARJ provides additional optimizations by creating a specialized registry for each type of aspect and weaves it only at the joinpoints, referenced by the pointcuts of the aspect.

CAESARJ and most other dynamic aspect activation approaches, such as EAOP [11], JAC [45], PROSE [46], JBoss AOP [25] and AspectWerkz [8], require one or another form of pre-run-time class preparation for weaving. The classes are either prepared at compile time, at class load time or during just-in-time compilation. There are two possibilities for pre-run-time class preparation: either to insert hooks at all joinpoints of a loaded class or to limit to a fixed set of known joinpoints. While the first option causes significant performance overhead, the second option (also used in CAESARJ) assumes initial knowledge about aspects that will be activated.

Dynamic aspect deployment can be more efficiently implemented on the systems supporting real run-time weaving, such as Steamloom [7] and AspectS [23]. Steamloom is particularly well-suited for the needs of aspect deployment in CAE-SARJ, because it supports thread local aspects as well as aspect deployment on individual objects.

Remote pointcuts introduced in DJcutter [41] allow definition of aspects which refer to joinpoints on remote processes. All aspects run on a special aspect server and intercept joinpoints in all or some of the registered hosts. CAESARJ extends applicability of remote joinpoints, by combining them with dynamic aspect deployment. This enables dynamic selection of servers as well as connecting and disconnecting from the server at any point of program execution. Besides, dynamic deployment postpones the decision about local or remote usage of an aspect until run time.

The idea of unifying aspects and classes, i.e., support for stateful aspects and their explicit instantiation, has also recently been implemented in the Eos-U language [47]. In Eos-U, the advice overriding problem is solved by completely replacing advice with methods. A similar effect can be achieved in CAESARJ by inserting method calls on self in the advice bodies.

8 Summary and Future Work

In this paper we gave an overview of the CAESARJ programming language. We demonstrated that advanced OO techniques for multiclass components and interaction based on joinpoint interception are complementary technologies, which can be used together to solve important software design problems.

In Sect. 3, we showed that by treating collaborations as classes, we can apply OO techniques on a larger scale. Virtual classes and propagating mixin composition provide a means for abstraction, refinement and polymorphism of multiclass components, but they are not sufficient for integration of independently developed components with different modular structure. The problem of crosscutting integration of structure and behavior can be solved by the mechanisms for joinpoint interception and dynamic object extensions in form of wrappers. The unification of aspects and collaborations facilitates development of reusable well-modularized aspects, as was explained in Sect. 4. Finally, Sect. 5 demonstrated that treating an aspect as a class enables its free instantiation and flexible control over its scope of application.

The current implementation of the CaesarJ compiler covers all the features presented in this paper except the dynamic wrapper selection, which is part of our ongoing work. The existing implementation is stable and is already used in case studies of our industrial partners. We also provide an integrated development environment for the language in the form of an Eclipse plug-in, which, among other features, includes views for visualization of CAESARJ virtual classes and crosscutting structure. The compiler, the Eclipse plug-in, the language reference as well as other documentation are available from `caesarj.org`.

There are several areas of ongoing and future work. We are investigating ways to provide better support for CAESARJ language features on the virtual machine level. So far, we have been building support for shadow search, weaving and dynamic aspect deployment into the aspect-oriented virtual machine Steamloom [21]. However, CAESARJ is not built on top of Steamloom so far. We believe that implementing CAESARJ compiler on top of Steamloom could significantly improve the implementation, but JVM compatibility would have to be sacrificed.

Also, we plan to add support for the virtual classes directly at the virtual machine level. This will significantly facilitate the implementation of the compiler and will avoid a lot of code duplication generated right now by the compiler to simulate the virtual class semantic on top of standard Java classes. Another path in our future research will be concerned with bringing into CAESARJ a more powerful pointcut language such as the one supported by the prototype language presented in [44].

Yet other threads of future work will be concerned with the module system of CAESARJ. One interesting issue to consider is to support a more flexible bundling of classes into families. Right now, related virtual classes have to be defined within a module. This might be too restrictive. We would like to be able to bundle classes that are defined independently into families. This imposes hard challenges on static typing, which need to be considered carefully. Another issue to investigate is the relation between CAESARJ modules, generic components and crosscutting bindings to genericity. We believe that CAESARJ modules, equipped with some extensions such as so-called *final bindings*, are able to simulate generics properly, but this needs to be investigated more in the future.

Acknowledgments

This work is partly supported by TOPPrax Project sponsored by the German Ministry of Education and Science (BMBF) and the European Network of Excellence on Aspect-Oriented Software Development (AOSD-Europe) sponsored by the EU FP6.

References

[1] J. Aldrich. Open modules: Modular reasoning in aspect-oriented programming. In: *Workshop on Foundations of Aspect-Oriented Languages (FOAL) at AOSD'04*, 2004

[2] K. Arnold and J. Gosling. *The Java Programming Language*. Addison-Wesley, Reading, MA, 1996

[3] K. Barrett, B. Cassels, P. Haahr, D.A. Moon, K. Playford, and P.T. Withington. A monotonic superclass linearization for Dylan. In: *Proceedings of the 11th ACM SIGPLAN Conference on Object-Oriented Programming, Systems, Languages, and Applications*, ACM, pp. 69–82, 1996

[4] D. Batory, J.N. Sarvela, and A. Rauschmayer. Scaling step-wise refinement. In: *ICSE '03: Proceedings of the 25th International Conference on Software Engineering*, IEEE Computer Society, pp. 187–197, 2003

[5] D. Batory, V. Singhal, J. Thomas, S. Dasari, B. Geraci, and M. Sirkin. The GenVoca model of software-system generators. *IEEE Softw.*, 11(5):89–94, 1994

[6] A.P. Black and N. Scharli. Traits: Tools and methodology. In: *ICSE '04: Proceedings of the 26th International Conference on Software Engineering*, IEEE Computer Society, pp. 676–686, 2004

[7] C. Bockisch, M. Haupt, M. Mezini, and K. Ostermann. Virtual machine support for dynamic join points. In: *AOSD '04: Proceedings of the 3rd International Conference on Aspect-Oriented Software Development*, ACM, New York, pp. 83–92, 2004

[8] J. Boner. Aspectwerkz. http://aspectwerkz.codehaus.org/index.html. 2004

[9] G. Bracha and W. Cook. Mixin-based inheritance. In: *OOPSLA/ECOOP '90: Proceedings of the European Conference on Object-Oriented Programming Systems, Languages, and Applications*, ACM, New York, pp. 303–311, 1990

[10] C. Clifton, G.T. Leavens, C. Chambers, and T. Millstein. Multijava: Modular open classes and symmetric multiple dispatch for java. *SIGPLAN Not.*, 35(10):130–145, 2000

[11] R. Douence and M. Südholt. A model and a tool for event-based aspect-oriented programming. *Technical Report 02/11/INFO*, Ecole des Mines de Nantes, 2002

[12] E. Ernst. *gbeta—A Language With Virtual Attributes, Block Structure, and Propagating, Dynamic Inheritance.* PhD thesis, Department of Computer Science, University of Aarhus, Denmark, 1999

[13] E. Ernst. Propagating class and method combination. In: *ECOOP '99: Proceedings of the 13th European Conference on Object-Oriented Programming*, Springer, pp. 67–91, 1999

[14] E. Ernst. Family polymorphism. In: *ECOOP '01: Proceedings of the 15th European Conference on Object-Oriented Programming*, Springer, pp. 303–326, 2001

[15] E. Ernst. Higher-order hierarchies. In: L. Cardelli (ed.) *Proceedings ECOOP 2003*, *LNCS vol. 2743*, Springer, pp. 303–329, 2003

[16] E. Ernst, K. Ostermann, and W. Cook. A virtual class calculus. In: *POPL'06: 33rd ACM Symposium on Principles of Programming Languages*, ACM SIGPLAN-SIGACT, to appear, 2006

[17] E. Gamma, R. Helm, R. Johnson, and J. Vlissides. *Design Patterns*. Addison-Wesley, Reading, MA, 1995

[18] J. Hallpap. Towards Caesar: Dynamic deployment and aspectual polymorphism. Master's thesis, Department of Computer Science, Darmstadt University of Technology, 2003. http://www.st.informatik.tu-darmstadt.de/database/theses/thesis/DiplomaThesis.pdf?id=15

[19] S. Hanenberg and R. Unland. Parametric introductions. In: *AOSD '03: Proceedings of the 2nd International Conference on Aspect-Oriented Software Development*, ACM, New York, pp. 80–89, 2003

[20] J. Hannemann and G. Kiczales. Design pattern implementation in Java and AspectJ. In: *OOPSLA '02: Proceedings of the 17th ACM SIGPLAN Conference on Object-Oriented Programming, Systems, Languages, and Applications*, ACM, New York, pp. 161–173, 2002

[21] M. Haupt, M. Mezini, C. Bockisch, T. Dinkelaker, M. Eichberg, and M. Krebs. An execution layer for aspect-oriented programming languages. In: *VEE '05: Proceedings of the 1st ACM/USENIX International Conference on Virtual Execution Environments*, ACM, New York, pp. 142–152, 2005

[22] S. Herrmann. Object teams: Improving modularity for crosscutting collaborations. In: *NODe '02: Revised Papers from the International Conference NetObjectDays on Objects, Components, Architectures, Services, and Applications for a Networked World*, Springer, pp. 248–264, 2003

[23] R. Hirschfeld. AspectS – aspect-oriented programming with squeak. In: *NODe '02: Revised Papers from the International Conference NetObjectDays on Objects, Components, Architectures, Services, and Applications for a Networked World*, Springer, pp. 216–232, 2003

[24] U. Hölzle. Integrating independently-developed components in object-oriented languages. In: *ECOOP '93: Proceedings of the 7th European Conference on Object-Oriented Programming*, Springer, pp. 36–56, 1993

[25] JBoss Inc. JBoss aop beta3. http://www.jboss.org. 2004

[26] G. Kiczales, E. Hilsdale, J. Hugunin, M. Kersten, J. Palm, and W. G. Griswold. An overview of AspectJ. In: *ECOOP '01: Proceedings of the 15th European Conference on Object-Oriented Programming*, Springer, pp. 327–353, 2001

[27] G. Kiczales and M. Mezini. Aspect-oriented programming and modular reasoning. In: *ICSE '05: Proceedings of the 27th International Conference on Software Engineering*, ACM, New York, pp. 49–58, 2005

[28] G. Kniesel, T. Rho, and S. Hanenberg. Evolvable pattern implementations need generic aspects. In: *RAM-SE*, Fakultät für Informatik, Universität Magdeburg, Germany, pp. 111–126, 2004

[29] R. Lämmel. A semantical approach to method-call interception. In: *AOSD '02: Proceedings of the 1st International Conference on Aspect-Oriented Software Development*, ACM, New York, pp. 41–55, 2002

[30] R. Lämmel and C. Stenzel. Semantics-Directed Implementation of Method-Call Interception. *IEE Proceedings Software*, 151(2):109–128, 2004

[31] K. Lieberherr, D. Lorenz, and M. Mezini. Programming with aspectual components. *Technical Report NU-CCS-99-01*, Northeastern University, Boston, MA, 1999

[32] K. Lieberherr, D. Lorenz, and J. Ovlinger. Aspectual collaborations – combining modules and aspects. *Journal of British Computer Society*, 46(5):542–565, 2003

[33] N. Loughran and A. Rashid. Framed aspects: Supporting variability and configurability for AOP. In: J. Bosch and C. Krueger (eds.) *International Conference on Software Reuse, Madrid, Spain, LNCS vol. 3107*, Springer, pp. 127–140, 2004

[34] O.L. Madsen and B. Møller-Pedersen. Virtual classes: A powerful mechanism in object-oriented programming. In: *OOPSLA '89: Conference Proceedings on Object-Oriented Programming Systems, Languages and Applications*, ACM, New York, pp. 397–406, 1989

[35] O.L. Madsen, B. Møller-Pedersen, and K. Nygaard. *Object Oriented Programming in the Beta Programming Language*. Addison-Wesley, Reading, MA, 1993

[36] M. Mezini and K. Lieberherr. Adaptive plug-and-play components for evolutionary software development. In: *OOPSLA '98: Proceedings of the 13th ACM SIGPLAN Conference on Object-Oriented Programming, Systems, Languages, and Applications*, ACM, New York, pp. 97–116, 1998

[37] M. Mezini and K. Ostermann. Integrating independent components with on-demand remodularization. In: *OOPSLA '02: Proceedings of the 17th ACM SIGPLAN Conference on Object-Oriented Programming, Systems, Languages, and Applications*, ACM, New York, pp. 52–67, 2002

[38] M. Mezini and K. Ostermann. Conquering aspects with Caesar. In: *AOSD '03: Proceedings of the 2nd International Conference on Aspect-Oriented Software Development*, ACM, New York, pp. 90–99, 2003

[39] M. Mezini, L. Seiter, and K. Lieberherr. Component integration with pluggable composite adapters. In: M. Aksit (ed.) *Software Architectures and Component Technology: The State of the Art in Research and Practice*, Kluwer, 2000

[40] T. Millstein, M. Reay, and C. Chambers. Relaxed multijava: Balancing extensibility and modular typechecking. *SIGPLAN Not.*, 38(11):224–240, 2003

[41] M. Nishizawa, S. Chiba, and M. Tatsubori. Remote pointcut: A language construct for distributed aop. In: *AOSD '04: Proceedings of the 3rd International Conference on Aspect-Oriented Software Development*, ACM, New York, pp. 7–15, 2004

[42] N. Nystrom, S. Chong, and A.C. Myers. Scalable extensibility via nested inheritance. *SIGPLAN Not.*, 39(10):99–115, 2004

[43] K. Ostermann. Dynamically composable collaborations with delegation layers. In: *ECOOP '02: Proceedings of the 16th European Conference on Object-Oriented Programming*, Springer, pp. 89–110, 2002

[44] K. Ostermann, M. Mezini, and C. Bockisch. Expressive pointcuts for increased modularity. In: *ECOOP'05: European Conference on Object-Oriented Programming*, LNCS vol. 2586, Springer, pp. 214–240, 2005

[45] R. Pawlak, L. Seinturier, L. Duchien, and G. Florin. JAC: A flexible solution for aspect-oriented programming in Java. In: *Proceedings REFLECTION '01, LNCS vol. 2192*, pp. 1–24, 2001

[46] A. Popovici, T. Gross, and G. Alonso. Dynamic weaving for aspect-oriented programming. In: *AOSD '02: Proceedings of the 1st International Conference on Aspect-Oriented Software Development*, ACM, New York, pp. 141–147, 2002

[47] H. Rajan and K.J. Sullivan. Classpects: Unifying aspect- and object-oriented language design. In: *ICSE '05: Proceedings of the 27th International Conference on Software Engineering*, ACM, New York, pp. 59–68, 2005

[48] Y. Smaragdakis and D.S. Batory. Implementing layered designs with mixin layers. In: *ECCOP '98: Proceedings of the 12th European Conference on Object-Oriented Programming*, Springer, pp. 550–570, 1998

[49] C. Szyperski. Independently extensible systems – software engineering potential and challenges. In: *Proceedings 19th Australian Computer Science Conference*, Australian Computer Science Communications, Melbourne, 1996

[50] C. Szyperski. *Component Software – Beyond Object-Oriented Programming*. Addison-Wesley, New York, 1998

[51] P. Tarr and H. Ossher. Hyper/J user and installation manual, 1999. http://www.research.ibm.com/hyperspace

[52] P. Tarr, H. Ossher, W. Harrison, and S.M. Sutton. N degrees of separation: Multi-dimensional separation of concerns. In: *ICSE '99: Proceedings International Conference on Software Engineering*, ACM, pp. 107–119, 1999

[53] M. VanHilst and D. Notkin. Using role components in implement collaboration-based designs. In: *OOPSLA '96: Proceedings of the 11th ACM SIGPLAN Conference on Object-Oriented Programming, Systems, Languages, and Applications*, ACM, New York, pp. 359–369, 1996

[54] M. Zenger. Evolving software with extensible modules. In: *International Workshop on Unanticipated Software Evolution, LNCS vol. 2548*, Springer, pp. 92–106, 2002

An Expressive Aspect Language for System Applications with Arachne

Rémi Douence[1],[*], Thomas Fritz[2],[**], Nicolas Loriant[1], Jean-Marc Menaud[1], Marc Ségura-Devillechaise[1], and Mario Südholt[1],[*]

[1] OBASCO project,
École des Mines de Nantes - INRIA, LINA,
4, rue Alfred Kastler,
44307 Nantes Cedex 3, France
{douence, nloriant, jmenaud, msegura, sudholt}@emn.fr
[2] Gruppe PST,
Institut für Informatik,
Ludwig-Maximilians-Universität München,
Oettingenstraße 67,
80538 München, Germany
fritz@informatik.uni-muenchen.de

Abstract. Security, networking and prefetching are typical examples of concerns which crosscut system-level C applications. While a careful design can help to address these concerns, they frequently become an issue at runtime, especially if avoiding server downtime is important. Vulnerabilities caused by buffer overflows and double-free bugs are frequently discovered after deployment, thus opening critical breaches in running applications. Performance issues also often arise at run time: in the case of Web caches, e.g., a prefetching strategy may be required to increase performance. Aspect-oriented programming is an appealing solution to solve these issues. However, none of the current dynamic aspect systems is expressive and efficient enough to support them properly in the context of C applications. Arachne is a new aspect system specifically designed to address these issues. Its aspect language allows aspects to be expressed concisely using a sequence construct for quantification over function calls and accesses through variable aliases. Arachne enables aspects to be woven "on the fly" in running legacy applications. We show how these abilities can be used to prevent security breaches, to modularize the replacement of network protocols by more efficient ones, and to introduce prefetching in Web caches. We present two formal semantics for Arachne: one which defines in abstract terms the main properties of the sequence construct, and a second one which enables reasoning about the actual implementation. Following a detailed presentation of Arachne's implementation, we give performance evaluations showing that Arachne is fast enough to extend high-performance applications, such as the Squid Web cache.

[*] This work has been supported by AOSD-Europe (http://www.aosd-europe.net).
[**] Part of this work was done during the author's stay at École des Mines de Nantes.

A. Rashid and M. Aksit (Eds.): Transactions on AOSD I, LNCS 3880, pp. 174–213, 2006.
© Springer-Verlag Berlin Heidelberg 2006

1   Introduction

Real-world applications are typically made of a number of different concerns. System-level C applications are no exception: security considerations, network concerns, caching and prefetching concerns are usually scattered in the entire program code. Furthermore, there is a strong need to isolate and manipulate these concerns at run time, especially in server environments whose downtime must be minimal. Security breaches such as double-free bugs and buffer overflows might be discovered after server deployment. Hardware resources might turn out to be undersized calling, for instance, for use of more appropriate network protocols or for the inclusion of prefetching strategies within Web caches. The Web cache Squid [1] is a typical illustration of this situation. First, we have found that several such concerns are scattered over large portions of the code of Squid. Second, such a Web cache should not be stopped in order to avoid performance loss by keeping caches filled continuously. Similarly, a buffer overflow should be fixed without incurring server downtime.

Potentially aspect-oriented programming (AOP) [2] should allow one to properly modularize and manipulate crosscutting concerns such as those we have identified for the Squid Web cache. Furthermore, Squid is designed to be as efficient as possible and therefore exploits any suitable operating system and hardware particularity. Its code base is therefore difficult to understand and manipulate, thus hinting at the use of specialized aspect systems instead of traditional means for modularization. However, these concerns exhibit three characteristics which make difficult the application of basic aspect technology. First, any of these concerns expose intricate relationships between execution points: network protocols, e.g., are most concisely expressed in terms of sequences of execution points, not individual ones. Second, as motivated above, the concerns need to be manipulated "on the fly" once the application is running. A dynamic aspect weaver is therefore needed. Finally, their lack of modularization at design time typically results from performance considerations. Use of aspect-oriented (AO) techniques in this context must only degrade efficiency to a very small extent.

To our knowledge, none of the current aspect systems for C is suitable for the modularization of such concerns. In particular, no existing aspect systems meets the three requirements introduced above, e.g., dynamic weavers often trade efficiency for expressivity. This paper summarizes our attempt to treat such concerns as aspects using the Arachne system. The core to our solution is a new expressive aspect language providing a sequence construct which allows us to quantify over function call events and access to local aliases of global variables. A main contribution of this paper is to show how sequences allow us to facilitate nontrivial evolution tasks of legacy systems software. Technically, we show how they support the proper modularization of the four concerns introduced above. Its implementation is based on binary code rewriting techniques and allows aspects to be woven dynamically in running C applications (which uses implementation techniques quite different from load-time or dynamic weaving in, e.g., Java-based aspect systems).

The paper is structured as follows. Section 2 presents the motivating concerns we identified within Squid. Section 3 shows how to modularize these concerns as aspects and presents the Arachne aspect language. The language is defined in Sect. 3, where two formal semantics for this language are presented: an abstract one defining the main properties of the language and an implementation-level one that allows us to reason about the code executed by the Arachne tool. Section 5 describes Arachne's implementation. Section 6 assesses the performance of our implementation. In Sect. 7, we discuss related work, and we conclude in Sect. 8.

2   Motivation

Legacy C applications involve multiple crosscutting concerns. Many of them remain challenging, both in terms of expressiveness required to handle them properly in an AO language and in terms of constraints posed on the weaver. In this section we discuss four such concerns in C applications: memory management problems caused by double-free bugs, buffer overflows, switching network protocols and Web cache prefetching. The security threats posed by double-free bugs and buffer overflows are typically scattered over the entire application. Since guarding all buffers against overflows or monitoring memory manipulations might considerably decrease performance, administrators are often left with no other option than accepting the trade-offs between security and performance chosen at design time of an application. Likewise, switching network protocols is a real problem for administrators facing bandwidth problems. Prefetching is another well-known crosscutting concern that traditionally require similar trade-offs [3, 4]. Since prefetching aims at increasing performance, prefetching aspects make only sense with an efficient weaver. Yet, it is still difficult to modularize these four concerns in today's AO languages. In this section, we first describe the contexts in which the different concerns arise before giving evidence of their crosscutting nature and finally motivating the lack of appropriate means of expression in current AO languages.

2.1   Double-Free Bugs

Unix systems introduced the `brk` system call, allowing programs to dynamically resize the heap. Later on, the standard C library has provided the `malloc` interface that acts as a layer between applications and the system. It allocates large chunks of memory through `brk` and fragments these chunks for the application, thus providing a more efficient and finer-grained interface for dynamic memory manipulation.

For performance reasons the GNU C library performs no sanity check on use of the `malloc` interface: freeing a nonallocated memory chunk leads to an implementation-dependant behavior, most frequently a segmentation fault. This has widely been exploited by hackers to build denial of service attacks [5]. In order to deal both with performance and fragmentation issues, the GNU C library implementation stores information such as the list of free chunks, the chunk size and other management information within the heap itself. If an application tries to free a nonallocated memory chunk, hackers can exploit the GNU C memory layout to take control of the application by corrupting its memory [6]. To protect against these so-called double-free bugs (which occur frequently because of erroneously freeing a memory location twice), a safe implementation of the malloc interface, which can be selected at load time, is provided by the GNU C library. Nevertheless, this safe implementation turns out to be very inefficient and is rarely if ever used. Hence, administrators discovering that an application contains a double-free bug cannot ensure security without deploying a bug-free version of the application. This requires the application to be stopped at the cost of potentially trashing the work in progress.

Despite the fact that Squid implements its own heap manipulation API,[1] it has recently been proven to be vulnerable to double-free bugs [7]. In Squid, memory allocation is a crosscutting concern: 71% of the .c files, which constitute its source code, contain direct references to the heap manipulation API.

In order to ensure continuous servicing without hurting performance, sanity checks on double-free calls should be limited to untrusted code (i.e., external libraries) or to periods when the environment is known to be hostile. Adding sanity checks to memory manipulation code may affect an entire application source code as dynamic memory allocation is highly common in string and buffer manipulations. In this case, an AO system is likely to permit users to improve on the lengthy and error-prone process of manually adding sanity checks. Furthermore, it should be helpful to address the security versus performance trade-off.

2.2   Buffer Overflows

In C, the size of an array is fixed at allocation time. According to ISO and ANSI standards [8], an invalid array access, i.e., an access out of the bounds of the array, does not result in an immediate error but leads to an implementation-dependent behavior. These vulnerabilities are increasingly exploited by computer worms such as CodeRed [9, 10], Slammer [11, 12] and Blaster [13, 14], and cause billions of dollars worth of damage [15]. Today, about 50% of vulnerabilities reported by CERT [16] arise from buffer overflows, and buffer-overflow attacks present the most common security attacks on software systems [17, 18].

A typical buffer-overflow attack tries to modify the memory by injecting code and altering the control flow so that the attacker gains control of the machine [19]. The most common buffer-overflow attack, the so-called stack smashing, overwrites the return address of a function on the stack with an address pointing to previously inserted malicious code (Fig. 1). This overwriting of the return address is possible as the program does not check if input exceeds the bounds of the buffer, and thus the attacker can overwrite code adjacent to the buffer. Once the function returns, the control is handed to the malicious code, and the attacker may get control over the machine [20]. A simple echo server in C containing such a buffer-overflow vulnerability is shown in Fig. 2. The code lacks

---

[1] Squid can also be configured to use its own heap manipulation routines on top of GNU malloc.

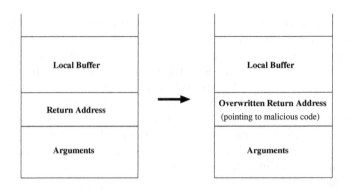

Fig. 1. Buffer-overflow attack overwriting the return address of a function

```
void echo() {
  char* in = malloc(255);
  gets(in);              /*read user input*/
  printf("%is\n",in);    /*display it*/
  free(in);
}
```

Fig. 2. Echo server in C with buffer-overflow vulnerability

a test whether the user input exceeds the size of the array, and an attacker could easily exploit this vulnerability as described.

Therefore, it is crucial to ensure every access to a buffer to be in its bounds. But bound-checking is error-prone and easily forgotten, and it is infeasible to detect all buffer-overflow vulnerabilities by statically analyzing code [20]. Several buffer overflow detectors have thus been proposed. Some of these approaches do not protect against all attacks, like StackGuard [21]. This approach is based on placing a dummy value between the stack data and the return address and then checking whether it has been altered or not. Thus, it just detects attacks overwriting everything along the stack. Bound-checkers, on the other hand, detect all buffer-overflow attacks as they check all buffer accesses. But approaches like Cyclone [22] or CCured [23], which are based on bound-checking, imply changes to the code. Cyclone is a "safe dialect of C" [22]. To prevent safety violations, the approach requires a subset of the C language to be used, e.g., by restricting pointer arithmetic, and the corresponding compiler performs static analysis and inserts run-time checks. CCured is a program transformation system that statically analyzes the program by classifying pointers and, depending on the classification, also adds run-time checks. Compilers have also been proposed that enforce proper array access by bound-checking [15, 24][2] without requiring code changes. But even the most efficient of these compilers, CRED [15], incur an overhead of up to 130%. Moreover, most frequently used C compilers, like the gcc compiler, do not support bound-checking.

---

[2] http://sourceforge.net/projects/boundschecking/

Also, with respect to performance, most approaches are too generic. They check every buffer access, even if the environment is not hostile and there is no vulnerability. However, as bound-checking is expensive, it should only run on buffer-overflow vulnerabilities [25].

Nowadays, administrators discovering a buffer-overflow vulnerability in a running application are mostly left with no other option than stopping the application and restarting a bug-free version, as done in Squid [26]. However, this technique does not conserve the continuous service property required by applications like the Squid Web cache. Furthermore, by stopping the application, the administrator has no means to know whether and how the vulnerability has been exploited, and thus this technique entails an important loss of information.

Bound-checking code tends to crosscut the entire application. In Squid, bound-checking code can be found in any of the 104 .c files of its source code. Of the 57,635 lines composing these .c files, at least 485 relate to bound-checking.

This problem fails to be handled properly in current aspect languages since they lack the ability to trigger advices upon access made through the alias of a variable. Furthermore, many AO systems offer only static weaving capabilities, preventing the administrator from choosing the trade-off between security and performance that suits his needs.

2.3   TCP to UDP Protocol

The Hypertext Transfer Protocol (HTTP) [27] is the primary method of the World Wide Web to transfer information over the Internet. The most frequently used communication protocol underlying HTTP is the Transmission Control Protocol (TCP) [28]. TCP is a connection-oriented protocol ensuring reliable communication by explicitly setting up and tearing down connections. While TCP is used as the underlying transport protocol of HTTP, it is not well-suited for short-lived connections exchanging only little data. However, short interactions comprise a significant amount of Web traffic. According to a study conducted on the soccer World Cup Web site of 1998 [29], the average request size is about 4 KB, and there are results that 40% of the Web traffic can even fit into a single datagram of 1500 bytes, making up the size of a maximum transfer unit (MTU) of Ethernet [30]. Thus, the cost of a Web interaction is dominated by data exchanged for control purposes of the TCP connection rather than the actual requested data. Furthermore, HTTP 1.1 has introduced persistent connections, allowing a client to retrieve multiple pages from the same server through the same TCP connection. However, the number of simultaneous TCP connections is limited by operating systems, and thus servers have a strong incentive to close HTTP connections as soon as possible.

Therefore, as also supported in [30, 31, 32], it seems beneficial to use the User Datagram Protocol (UDP) [33]. UDP incurs much less overhead for connection establishment than TCP as the underlying transport protocol of HTTP for short-lived connections and thereby reduces the overhead induced by TCP.

In spite of the corresponding potential performance gains, the existence of a large number of legacy Web applications and the corresponding adaptation costs

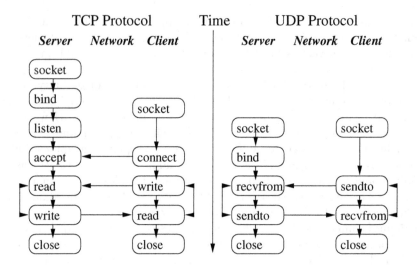

Fig. 3. Typical usage of the TCP and UDP APIs

have hindered widespread adoption of this solution. In particular, a complete redesign of legacy applications is typically not reasonable. Besides the corresponding development costs, deployment of the modified applications is problematic. Existing approaches to application deployment require stopping the legacy Web application to switch the protocol. This, however, does not satisfy the continuous servicing property inherent in such applications and, for example, in the case of an e-commerce Web server, causes a direct loss of money. Therefore, one may swap the application between different machines to avoid shutting down the service, but this requires redundant servers, which are often not affordable for small companies. For wide acceptance, a HTTP dialect using UDP as transport protocol should thus be deployable on demand at run time.

In addition, replacing TCP by UDP is relatively difficult in an application. The choice of a transport protocol is usually based on standards believed to be everlasting and is made at an early design stage. Hence, no particular effort is made to localize this design decision in a single piece of code. For example, despite a modularization effort, the TCP API provided by the operating system is used directly in 7 of the 104 .c source files of the Squid Web cache.

As shown in Fig. 3, the TCP API is built around a set of C functions to be invoked sequentially by the application [34]. In a properly written program, TCP functions are first used to establish the connection (typically with socket, connect, bind and listen), exchange data through the connection (typically with read and write) and then close it (typically close). Similarly, UDP applications first direct the operating system to dedicate the appropriate resources to exchange data (typically with socket and bind), then exchange data through these resources (typically with sendto and recvfrom) before releasing them (typically with close). Hence, the problem is not only difficult because TCP-related function invocations are scattered but also because the relative order of each invocation is important in order to map it onto the appropriate UDP function. Furthermore, there can be several connections at the same time, i.e., several clients that connect with one server, and each connection can be in a different state.

2.4   From Fetching to Prefetching

Operations like retrieving a file on a local disk or over the Web can be sped up if the underlying software anticipates user requests and fetches documents in advance of explicit requests. Such prefetching schemes differ from one another by how they predict future user requests. These "oracles" actually prevent a clean encapsulation of prefetching in a single module communicating with the rest of the application through well-defined interfaces since predictions are based on information meant to be private to other modules. In addition, it is obvious that there is no universally perfect oracle [35]. A statically linked prefetching module is therefore inappropriate; instead, prefetching modules along with the necessary oracles should be loaded and unloaded on the fly. Because of their crosscutting nature, prefetching modules including such oracles are better written with aspects, as motivated by Coady et al. for file prefetching in the FreeBSD OS [3] and our previous work considering the Squid Web cache [4].

Despite potential performance improvements, prefetching also increases resource consumption (e.g., network prefetching consumes local storage and bandwidth). When the need for such resources is too high, prefetching computation competes for them against regular user requests and slows down their treatment instead of speeding it up. In such cases, prefetching should therefore be temporarily disabled. Squid, for instance, essentially manages file descriptors, a resource only available in a limited quantity. A file descriptor is used by the underlying operating system and applications to describe a network connection or a file on the disk. Squid's file descriptor management is based on a global variable that tracks the number of file descriptors currently in use. By comparing its value with the maximum number of file descriptors allowed by the operating system, it is possible to evaluate whether prefetching should be disabled or activated.

Using current AO technology, enabling/disabling of prefetching depending on the number of open file descriptors would be handled within advice by explicitly managing a corresponding state and triggering the corresponding actions. This is bad practice because it impedes both readability and maintainability. A mechanism is needed within the aspect language to restrict advice execution at times where resource usage is too high.

3   An Expressive Aspect Language for System Programming in C

While AOP is an obvious choice to tackle the crosscutting concerns introduced above, none of the existing AO systems provides explicit support for some of their essential elements, in particular, references to aliases which are local to a function, and joinpoint sequences for protocols.

In this section we introduce a new aspect language for system programming in C that allows such crosscutting concerns to be expressed concisely. In order to make this point, we first revisit the examples by concisely "aspectizing" them using our language. (Note that our aspect language is expressive in the sense that it enables the concise definition of certain types of aspects, especially compared to other tools for system-level manipulations, but it is not necessarily more expressive than existing approaches in a language-theoretic sense.) We then define the joinpoint model underlying our language precisely, followed by the definition of its syntax and informal semantics. Its formal semantics is the subject of the following section.

3.1   Example Crosscutting Concerns Revisited

We now revisit the concerns discussed in Sect. 2 in order to show our language in action and to give evidence that it allows such concerns to be concisely modularized. Our motivating examples are reordered following increasing complexity of the language constructs involved.

Double-Free Bugs. The aspect shown in Fig. 4 detects double-free bugs. It uses two sets, `addMalloc` and `addFree`, which are initially empty to collect addresses that have been allocated and freed as exemplified by the first advice. The second advice checks whether these sets are consistent when `free(buffer)` is to be called. First, when the current address has already been freed previously, the advice terminates the execution of the application. Second, when `buffer` does not belong to `addMalloc`, either the aspect has been dynamically woven *after* the corresponding call to `malloc` that returned `buffer` and this call to `free(buffer)`

```
void * checkMalloc(size_t size) {
        void * buffer = malloc(size);
        addMalloc = addMalloc ∪ {buffer};
        addFree  = addFree \ {buffer};
        return buffer;
}

void checkFree(void * buffer) {
        if (buffer ∈ addFree) exit(error);
        else if (buffer ∉ addMalloc) warning();

        free(buffer);
        addFree  = addFree ∪ {buffer};
        addMalloc = addMalloc \ {buffer};
}

call(void * malloc(size_t)) && args(size) then checkMalloc(size);

call(void free(void*)) && args(buffer) then checkFree(buffer);
```

Fig. 4. An aspect for detecting double-free bugs

is correct, or the aspect has been dynamically woven *after* the previous call to free(buffer) and the current call is a bug. These two cases cannot be distinguished, so the advice only prints a warning. The memory is freed, and the two sets of addresses are maintained. Note that, if the user does not care about warnings, the aspect can be simplified by suppressing the set addMalloc.

TCP to UDP Protocol. The aspect shown in Fig. 5 translates transport protocols from TCP to UDP. A protocol defines a sequence of function calls, so the top-level operator of this aspect is seq. The sequence aspect syntactically consists of a list of pairs of pointcut and advice, with the pairs being separated by ";". In the example, the TCP protocol starts with a call to socket() with three arguments that are bound to family, type and protocol and compared to constants (AF_INET, SOCK_STREAM and 0) in the if-expression. When such a call is matched for which the comparisons in the if-expression also evaluates to true, the second parameter is replaced by SOCK_DGRAM as required by the UDP protocol. The result of this transformed call, the file descriptor, is bound to fd by return(fd). Then the next call to connect() is matched for which the same file descriptor has to be the first parameter (achieved by binding it to fd1 and comparing it to fd in an if-expression). In this case, the values of the other parameters are bound to arguments address and length, and the original call is replaced by returnZero(), which simulates a successful connection establishment by returning zero and doing nothing else. Indeed, there is no connect step in the UDP protocol. After that, calls to read() and write() (using the "or" on aspects: ||) on the same file descriptor fd are translated to UDP recvfrom() and sendto(), respectively. Note that sequences of such access are potentially repeatedly translated (due to use of the repetition operator "*"). Finally, a call to close() on the same file descriptor fd terminates the TCP protocol as well as

```
seq( call(int socket(int, int, int)) && args(family, type, protocol)
        && if((family == AF_INET) && (type == SOCK_STREAM)
            && (protocol == 0))
        && return(fd)
        then socket(AF_INET, SOCK_DGRAM, 0);

    call(int connect(int, struct socketaddr*, socklen_t))
        && args(fd1, address, length)  && if(fd1 == fd)
        then returnZero();    // where int returnZero() { return 0; }

    ( call(size_t read(int, void*, size_t))  && args(fd2, readBuffer, readLength)
        && if(fd2 == fd)
        then recvfrom(fd, readBuffer, readLength, 0, address, length);
    || call(size_t write(int, void*, size_t))
            && args(fd3, writeBuffer, writeLength)  && if(fd3 == fd)
            then sendto(fd, writeBuffer, writeLength, 0, address, length); ) *

    call(int close(int)) && args(fd4) && if(fd4 == fd) ; )
```

Fig. 5. An aspect for switching transport protocols, from TCP to UDP

seq(call(void ∗ malloc(size_t))
      && args(allocatedSize) && return(buffer) ;

   write(buffer) && size(writtenSize)
      && if(writtenSize > allocatedSize)
      then *reportOverflow*(); ∗

   call(void free(void∗)) && args(b1) && if(b1 == buffer) ;)

Fig. 6. An aspect for detecting buffer overflow

require *Number_Of_Fd* as *int∗*;
require *Squid_MaxFd* as *int∗*;

controlflow(call(void clientSendMoreData(void∗, char∗, size_t)),
             call(HttpReply ∗ clientBuildReply(clientHttpRequest∗, char∗, size_t))
             && args(request, buffer, bufferSize))
   then startPrefetching(request, buffer, bufferSize);
&&   until(writeGlobal(int ∗ Number_Of_Fd)   &&   if(($*Number_Of_Fd$ ∗
$100/(*Squid_MaxFd) \geq 75$) ;)

controlflow(call(void clientSendMoreData(void∗, char∗, size_t)),
             call(void comm_write_mbuf(int, MemBuf, void∗, void∗))
             && args(fd, mb, handler, handlerData) && if(! isPrefetch(handler)))
   then parseHyperlinks(fd, mb, handler, handlerData);

call(void clientWriteComplete(int, char∗, size_t, int, void∗))
   && args(fd, buf, size, error, data) && if(! isPrefetch(handler))
   then retrieveHyperlinks(fd, buf, size, error, data);

Fig. 7. An aspect for prefetching

the UDP protocol and thus is not modified (i.e., there is no **then** clause). This last step is required to free the variables used in the sequence (here, fd, address and length). Indeed, this aspect can use numerous (instances of these) variables when it deals with interleaved sequences, as each call to socket() creates a new instance of the sequence.

Buffer Overflows. The aspect shown in Fig. 6 detects buffer overflows. The corresponding sequence starts when the function malloc() returns the buffer address that is then bound to the buffer. Then, each time this address is accessed (through a global variable or a local alias) the size of the data to be written is compared with the size of the initially allocated memory. If the former exceeds the latter, an overflow is indicated. The sequence ends when the memory is deallocated using free().

From Fetching to Prefetching. The aspect in Fig. 7 introduces prefetching in a Web cache. The first **controlflow** phrase initializes prefetching when an

HTTP response is built (clientBuildReply()) within the control flow of a client request (clientSendMoreData()). The until clause stops prefetching when the number of connection becomes too large, a situation where prefetching would effectively degrade performance. The second controlflow phrase analyzes hyperlinks in a page being transmitted (i.e., when comm_write_mbuf() is called within the control flow of clientSendMoreData()). Finally, the last call phrase prefetches hyperlinks analyzed by the second aspect. It does so by replacing the method call to clientWriteComplete() with retrieveHyperlinks(). Finally, note that the two require clauses at the top of the aspect declare the types of the global variables of the base program used in the aspects.

3.2   Joinpoints

A joinpoint model defines the points in the execution of the base program to which pointcuts may refer. In our case, joinpoints are defined by JP in the grammar shown in Fig. 8. A joinpoint is either:

- A call of a function $\mathtt{callJP}(v_1\ funId(\overrightarrow{v_2}))$ with function name $funId$, return value v_1 and a vector of arguments $\overrightarrow{v_2}$.
- A read access that comes in two variants: $\mathtt{readGlobalJP}(varId, v)$ denotes reading a global variable with name $varId$ holding the value v; $\mathtt{readJP}(@, v)$ denotes reading a global variable or a local alias with address @ holding the value v.
- Write access, which also comes in two variants: $\mathtt{writeGlobalJP}(varId, v, size)$ denotes assignment to a global variable with name $varId$ of the value v of size $size$. $\mathtt{writeJP}(@, v, size)$ denotes assignment to a global variable or a local alias with address @ of the value v of size $size$.
- A cflow expression $\mathtt{controlflowJP}(\overrightarrow{funId},\ c)$, where $\overrightarrow{funId} = [funId_1, ..,$ $funId_n]$ is a stack of function names, and c (either a function call or an

$$
\begin{array}{lll}
JP & ::= & \mathtt{callJP}(\mathrm{val}\ \mathrm{funId}(\overrightarrow{\mathrm{val}})) \\
& | & \mathtt{readGlobalJP}(\mathrm{varId}, \mathrm{val}) \\
& | & \mathtt{readJP}(@, \mathrm{val}) \\
& | & \mathtt{writeGlobalJP}(\mathrm{varId}, \mathrm{val}, \mathrm{size}) \\
& | & \mathtt{writeJP}(@, \mathrm{val}, \mathrm{size}) \\
& | & \mathtt{controlflowJP}(\overrightarrow{\mathrm{funId}}, \mathrm{cfEnd}) \\
& | & \mathtt{controlflowstarJP}(\overrightarrow{\mathrm{funId}}, \mathrm{cfEnd}) \\
\\
cfEnd & ::= & \mathtt{callJP}(\mathrm{val}\ \mathrm{funId}(\overrightarrow{\mathrm{val}})) \\
& | & \mathtt{readGlobalJP}(\mathrm{varId}, \mathrm{val}) \\
& | & \mathtt{writeGlobalJP}(\mathrm{varId}, \mathrm{val}, \mathrm{size}) \\
\\
val & ::= & 0\ |\ 1\ |\ 2\ |\ ... \qquad // \mathtt{int} \\
& | & @0\ |\ @1\ |\ @2\ |\ ... \quad // \mathtt{int*} \\
& | & ...\quad // \mathtt{values\ of\ other\ C\ types}
\end{array}
$$

Fig. 8. Joinpoint model

access to a global variable) occurs within the body of function $funId_n$. Such a joinpoint requires a call to $funId_{i+1}$ within the body of $funId_i$.

- A cflow expression $\texttt{controlflowstarJP}(\overrightarrow{funId}, \text{ c})$, where $\overrightarrow{funId} = [funId_1, .., funId_n]$ is a *partial* stack of function names, and c (either a function call or an access to a global variable) occurs within the *control flow* of function $funId_n$. Such a joinpoint requires a call to $funId_{i+1}$ within the control flow of (i.e., not necessarily in the body of) $funId_i$. Therefore, in contrast to the preceding cflow expression, no direct nesting is required, but the functions and the final execution point c may be nested at arbitrary depth within the preceding function.

Two features of this joinpoint model may be surprising at first sight: distinction of accesses to aliases from those to global variables and explicit representation of control flow expressions. Both are motivated by our quest for efficiency and are grounded in strong implementation constraints in the context of dynamic weaving of binary C code: An access to a local alias is several magnitudes slower than that to a global variable, and matching of control flow joinpoints can be done using an atomic test on the implementation level.

3.3   Pointcuts

We now present a pointcut language (Fig. 9) that provides constructs to match individual joinpoints.

Primitive pointcuts are defined by *PPrim* and comprise three basic pointcuts: matching calls, global variable accesses and control flow joinpoints. Primitive pointcuts can also be combined using a logical "or", noted $||$.

A call pointcut *PCall* selects all call joinpoints $\texttt{callJP}(\text{val funId}(\overrightarrow{val}))$, i.e., all calls to a function matching the signature *type* $funId(\overrightarrow{type})$, where the arguments of the function can be bound to pointcut variables using argument binder $\texttt{args}(\overrightarrow{pattern})$ and the return value can be bound to a pointcut variable using a return clause $\texttt{return}(\text{ pattern })$. The two constructs $\texttt{args}(\overrightarrow{pattern})$ and $\texttt{return}(\text{ pattern })$ can also provide pattern matching by using values (or already bound pointcut variables) in *pattern*. Pointcuts can also depend on a Boolean condition using the $\texttt{if}$-constructor.

A global access pointcut *PAccGlobal* selects either all read joinpoints, i.e., $\texttt{readGlobalJP}(\text{varId}, \text{val})$, or all write joinpoints $\texttt{writeGlobalJP}(\text{varId}, \text{val}, \text{size})$ on the global base program variable *varId*. In these cases, the read or written value can be bound to a variable using $\texttt{value}(\text{pattern})$. In addition, the size of the written value can be bound with $\texttt{size}(\text{varName})$. Pattern matching can also be used for variable access.

A control flow pointcut *PCf*, which is of the form $\texttt{controlflow}(\text{ } PCallSig_1, ..., PCallSig_n, PCfEnd)$, matches $\texttt{controlflowJP}(\text{funId}_1, ..., \text{funId}_n, \text{cfEnd})$ joinpoints, where the function identifier in $PCallSig_i$ is $funId_i$. Similarly, a control flow pointcut may match a global variable access for a given stack configuration. The pointcuts of the form $\texttt{controlflowstar}(...)$ select calls or global variable accesses in a stack context, allowing for calls that are not directly nested within one another.

$$
\begin{array}{lll}
PPrim & ::= & PCall \\
& | & PAccGlobal \\
& | & PCf \\
& | & PPrim \parallel PPrim \\
\\
PCall & ::= & PCallSig \; [\; \&\& \; \textbf{args}(\; \overrightarrow{pattern} \;) \;] \; [\; \&\& \; \textbf{return}(\; pattern \;) \;] \\
& & [\; \&\& \; PIf \;] \\
PCallSig & ::= & \textbf{call}(\; type \; funId(\overrightarrow{type}) \;) \\
\\
PIf & ::= & \textbf{if}(\; expr \;) \; [\; \&\& \; PIf \;] \\
\\
PAccGlobal & ::= & \textbf{readGlobal}(\; type \; varId \;) \; [\; \&\& \; \textbf{value}(\; pattern \;) \;] \; [\; \&\& \; PIf \;] \\
& | & \textbf{writeGlobal}(\; type \; varId \;) \; [\; \&\& \; \textbf{value}(\; pattern \;) \;] \\
& & [\; \&\& \; \textbf{size}(\; pattern \;) \;] \; [\; \&\& \; PIf \;] \\
\\
PCf & ::= & \textbf{controlflow}(\; PCallSigList, \; PCfEnd \;) \\
& | & \textbf{controlflowstar}(\; PCallSigList, \; PCfEnd \;) \\
PCallSigList & ::= & PCallSig \; [\; , \; PCallSigList \;] \\
PCfEnd & ::= & PCall \; | \; PAccGlobal \\
\\
PAcc & ::= & \textbf{read}(\; var \;) \; [\; \&\& \; PIf \;] \\
& | & \textbf{write}(\; var \;) \; [\; \&\& \; \textbf{size}(\; pattern \;) \;] \; [\; \&\& \; PIf \;] \\
\\
pattern & ::= & var \; | \; val \\
\end{array}
$$

Fig. 9. Pointcut language

Finally, $PAcc$, an access pointcut for a global variable or all of its local aliases, matches all joinpoints of the form `readJP` or `writeJP`.

3.4 Aspect Language

The aspect language we propose is defined in Fig. 10. Aspects Asp are either primitive aspects $AspPrim$, or sequences of primitive aspects $AspSeq$.

Both primitive and sequence aspects can be combined with requirement statements. A requirement statement is needed for each function or global variable of the base program used in the aspect. Similar to the declaration of a function before its first use in a C file, e.g., in a header file, a function or global variable with identifier Id has to be specified in a requirement statement **require** Id **as** $Type$; before it can be used in an aspect.

A primitive aspect $AspPrim$ combines a primitive pointcut with an advice that will be applied to all joinpoints selected by the pointcut. An advice ($Advice$) is a C function call that replaces a joinpoint in the base program execution (similarly to **around** in AspectJ). It must have the same return type as the joinpoint it replaces, that is, the type of the global variable in case of a read access, **void** for a write access and the return type of the function for a call. When the advice is empty (no **then** clause), the original joinpoint is executed. The original joinpoint can be skipped by calling an empty C function.

$$
\begin{array}{lll}
Asp & ::= & RequireStmt\ Asp \\
& | & AspPrim\ [\ \&\&\ \textbf{until}(\ AspPrim\ )\ ] \\
& | & AspeSeq\ [\ \&\&\ \textbf{until}(\ AspPrim\ )\ ] \\
\\
RequireStmt & ::= & \textbf{require}\ Id\ \textbf{as}\ Type\ ; \\
\\
AspPrim & ::= & PPrim\ Advice \\
\\
AspSeq & ::= & \textbf{seq}(\ AspPrim \\
& & \qquad AspSeqElts \\
& & \qquad AspSeqElt\ ) \\
\\
AspSeqElts & ::= & AspSeqElt\ \ [AspSeqElts] \\
& | & AspSeqElt\ *\ \ [AspSeqElts] \\
\\
AspSeqElt & ::= & AspPrim \\
& | & PAcc\ Advice \\
& | & (AspSeqElt\ ||\ AspSeqElt) \\
\\
Advice & ::= & \ \ ; \\
& | & \textbf{then}\ funId(\overrightarrow{pattern})\ ; \\
\\
pattern & ::= & var \\
& | & value \\
\end{array}
$$

Fig. 10. Aspect language

A sequence aspect is composed of a sequence of primitive aspects. A sequence instance is created when the pointcut of the first primitive aspect matches. The following primitive aspects in the sequence are activated as soon as the corresponding pointcut matches (i.e., a primitive aspect has priority over its predecessor if both match). All but the first and last primitive aspects can be repeated zero or multiple times by using the operator "*". Branching, i.e., a logical "or" between two primitive aspects in a sequence, is supported by the operator ||. Different sequence instances are (conceptually) matched in parallel.

A primitive or a sequence aspect a can be used in combination with an expression $\textbf{until}(a_1)$, to restrict its scope. In this case, once a joinpoint has been matched by a, the execution of a proceeds as previously described until a_1 matches.

To conclude the presentation of our language, note that it does not include some features, such as named pointcuts as arguments to controlflows, and conjunctive terms, which are not necessary for the examples we considered but which could easily be added. (As an aside, note that such extensions of the pointcut language may affect the computability of advanced algorithmic problems, such as whether a pointcut matches some part of any base program [36].)

4   Formal Semantics for Expressive Aspects

In the previous sections, we have given an informal semantics of our aspect language. We now illustrate how the aspect language can be formally defined by means of two different semantics:

- A semantics translating our aspects language into an extension of the language used in the formal framework of [37]. This semantics abstracts from most implementation details but allows a clear and succinct definition of the main properties of our sequence construct.
- A semantics providing a translation scheme into the actual C implementation used in the Arachne tool. This semantics has been harnessed to establish correctness arguments about and and thus guide the implementation of our tool.

4.1   An Abstract Formal Semantics

Douence et al. [37, 38] have introduced a generic framework for AOP supporting stateful crosscuts, i.e., pointcuts with explicit state. Without relying on any specific programming language, they have applied this framework to the formal definition of aspects and for certain kinds of reasoning techniques over aspects. In the case of our aspect language, their language must be extended in order to deal with halting aspects, an unbounded number of sequential aspects executed in parallel and arbitrary joinpoint predicates. The grammar of our extended version, our tiny aspect language, is defined in Fig. 11. In this language, aspect expressions A consist of parallel combinations of aspects. C is a joinpoint predicate (similar to our pointcut language) expressed as a conjunction of a term pattern and possibly an expression from the constraint logic programming language $\text{CLP}(\mathcal{R})$ [39].

An aspect A' is either:

- A parallel composition of two aspects $A_1 \parallel A_2$.
- A recursive definition.
- A sequence formed using the prefix operation $C \triangleright I;\ X$, where X is an aspect, a recursion variable, or a halting aspect STOP, and I a piece of code (i.e., an advice).

$$
\begin{aligned}
A\ ::=&\ A' \\
&|\ A \parallel A \qquad\quad ;\ \textit{parallelism} \\[6pt]
A'\ ::=&\ \mu a.A' \qquad\qquad ;\ \textit{recursive definition } (a \in \mathcal{R}ec) \\
&|\ C \triangleright I;\ A \qquad ;\ \textit{prefixing} \\
&|\ C \triangleright I;\ a \qquad ;\ \textit{end of sequence } (a \in \mathcal{R}ec) \\
&|\ C \triangleright I;\ \text{STOP} \ ;\ \textit{halting aspect} \\
&|\ A' \ \square \ A' \qquad\quad ;\ \textit{choice}
\end{aligned}
$$

Fig. 11. Tiny aspect language

– A choice construction $A_1 \,\square\, A_2$ (A_1, A_2 must not be parallel expressions) which chooses the first aspect that matches a joinpoint (the other is thrown away). If both match the same joinpoint, A_1 is chosen.

One can think of a stateful aspect A (as well as A') as a kind of transition system. Thereby, an aspect is always in a certain state in its execution, e.g., at rule $C \triangleright I$ (which is the head of a sequence of rules, which in turn is possibly part of a more complex expression), and waiting on a joinpoint to match C. If a joinpoint matching C occurs, the aspect executes I and advances to the next state, i.e., the next rule in the sequence.

Protocol Translation. The semantics of the protocol translation aspect (from TCP to UDP) is given in Fig. 12. A sequence can have several instances. This is translated into the language A by the expression $a_1 \,||\, ...$, which starts a new sequence a_1 once the first joinpoint has been matched and continues to match the rest of the sequence in progress. The repetition operator "$*$" is translated into recursion on the variable a_2. The branching operator $||$ of the source language is translated into the choice operator $\square$ of A. Finally, the last primitive aspect of the sequence occurs as the first aspect of a choice to get priority over the joinpoints *read* and *write* because of the repetition marked by "$*$". Note that we use joinpoint patterns with variables, where an overbar marks the first occurrence of a variable (i.e., its definition in opposition to a use) and subsequent variable occurrences without overbar mark variable uses (e.g., to use the value of the file descriptor *fd* in argument positions).

Buffer Overflow Detection. The semantics of the aspect for detecting buffer-overflows is given in Fig. 13. This definition reports overflows after memory for a buffer has been allocated until a joinpoint matches the `free` crosscut, in which case the sequence instance corresponding to the freed buffer will be stopped.

These examples demonstrate that this style of semantics clearly exhibits the advantages stated in the beginning by concisely defining three important properties of our sequence aspect:

1. A sequence can have several instances, as for each joinpoint matching the pointcut of the first primitive aspect, a new sequence instance is created. The parallel operator $a_1 \,||\, ...$ in the translation of the sequence aspect

$$\mu a_1.\ \texttt{callJP}(\overline{\text{fd}}\ socket(\text{AF\_INET}, \text{SOCK\_STREAM}, 0)) \triangleright$$
$$socket(AF\_INET, SOCK\_DGRAM, 0);$$
$$a_1\ ||\ (\ \texttt{callJP}(\overline{\text{var}_1}\ connect(\text{fd}, \overline{\text{address}}, \overline{\text{length}})) \triangleright \text{returnZero}();$$
$$\mu a_2.\ \texttt{callJP}(\overline{\text{var}_2}\ close(\text{fd})) \triangleright close(\text{fd});\ \text{STOP}$$
$$\square\ \texttt{callJP}(\overline{\text{var}_3}\ read(\text{fd}, \overline{\text{readBuffer}}, \overline{\text{readLength}})) \triangleright$$
$$recvfrom(fd, readBuffer, readLength, 0, address, length); a_2$$
$$\square\ \texttt{callJP}(\overline{\text{var}_4}\ write(\text{fd}, \overline{\text{writeBuffer}}, \overline{\text{writeLength}})) \triangleright$$
$$recvfrom(fd, writeBuffer, writeLength, 0, address, length); a_2$$

Fig. 12. Definition of the protocol translation using the tiny aspect language

$\mu a_1.$ $\mathtt{callJP}(\overline{\mathtt{buffer}\ \mathtt{malloc}(\overline{\mathtt{allocatedSize}})}) \triangleright \mathtt{malloc}(\mathtt{allocatedSize});$
$\quad a_1 \parallel \mu a_2.$ $\mathtt{callJP}(\overline{\mathtt{var_1}}\ \mathtt{free}(\mathtt{buffer})) \triangleright \mathtt{free}(\mathtt{buffer});\ \mathrm{STOP}$
$\qquad\qquad \Box\ \mathtt{writeJP}(\mathtt{buffer}, \overline{\mathtt{var_2}}, \overline{\mathtt{writtenSize}})$
$\qquad\qquad\qquad \&\&\ (writtenSize > allocatedSize) \triangleright reportOverflow()\ ;\ a_2$

Fig. 13. Definition of the buffer overflow aspect using the tiny aspect language

expresses this property. Once the first joinpoint has been matched, a new sequence a_1 is started and the rest of the sequence in progress continues to match in parallel.

2. The last step in a sequence aspect determines the finalization of sequence instances. When a joinpoint matches the pointcut of the last sequence element and a sequence instance is in a state waiting for such a joinpoint, i.e., the instance has already passed all previous steps of the sequence, the advice of the last step is executed and then the instance is terminated. In A', the finalization is expressed by STOP, which terminates the corresponding sequence.

3. The star operator $*$ attached to a sequence step, besides expressing repetition, causes the following step to have priority over its predecessor. The choice operator $\Box$ and the order of arguments of the choice in the translation ensure this property.

Note that formal definitions such as that of the protocol translation aspect and the buffer overflow detection aspect precisely define several important issues, which are somewhat implicit in the sequence aspect construct. In particular, they define when new instances of the sequence aspect are created: A new sequence instance is created once the first step in the sequence is matched, i.e., sequences are implicitly in scope of a repetition. The abstract semantics could be used, e.g., to formally prove that two instances match when a joinpoint matches the first as well as another step of a sequence. Furthermore, they disambiguate potentially nondeterministic situations, e.g., when two pointcuts of consecutive primitive aspects in the sequence match at the same time. Finally, this style of semantics clearly abstracts from implementation details, e.g., how the sequence state is represented in the implementation.

4.2 An Implementation-Level Semantics

Due to its abstractness, the semantics presented in the previous section illustrates certain properties of Arachne's aspect language very clearly, e.g., when new sequence instances are created. However, it abstracts from many details that are relevant, in particular, to judge the correctness of the Arachne tool: most important the above semantics abstracts from the generated C code, the C run-time environment and the concrete weaving process. In order to support a detailed understanding of the Arachne tool we have therefore developed an implementation-level formal semantics, which we present in this section.

This implementation-level semantics — in the remainder of this section the term "semantics" always refers to the implementation-level semantics — is formulated as a denotational semantics [40] whose valuation functions define transformations from aspects into the corresponding C code executed by the Arachne tool. Technically, the valuation functions map syntactic categories of our language to a list of code generation functions. The *code generation functions* define code that handles the initialization of aspects, the dynamic conditions that are used to check whether a joinpoint actually matches the pointcut of an aspect as well as calls to the advice.

In addition, the generated code contains symbolic references to rewriting sites, i.e., places in the base program that have to be rewritten. The exact sites to be rewritten are first known at run time, as only then the aspect is woven into the base program. After the aspect code is generated, it will be compiled into a dynamic link library (DLL).[3] At weave time, the aspect DLL will then instruct Arachne to instrument the base program at the appropriate places and once such a site is encountered at run time, the dynamic predicates are tested and the advice function eventually executed.

This semantics therefore helps understanding of the Arachne tool by the following two characteristics:

- code generation functions providing a structured presentation of the executed C code
- a notion of rewriting sites providing an explicit representation of the weaving process

This way it is concrete enough to serve for correctness considerations of our tool, while being abstract enough to enable such considerations compositionally in terms of structural entities.

In this section we first present the denotational semantics in the context of a concrete example aspect and the evaluation of that aspect by means of the semantics. Second, we present a detailed overview of the semantics (a complete account can be found in [41]).

Example: Semantics of a Control Flow-Based Aspect. In order to illustrate the semantics and provide some information about the complexity in using the semantics (which cannot be completely avoided since it enables, in fine, derivation of the executed C code), we first discuss a concrete transformation. The following example shows an aspect that executes an advice `action(x)` when the function `h` is called within a control flow path on which functions `f` and `g` have already been called (see Listing 1 for the aspect definition).

Figure 14 presents three steps resulting from the application of the valuation functions of the semantics to the preceding aspect definition:

(a) The initial transformation step introduces initialization code and calls the valuation function corresponding to the aspect at hand (here **AP**).

---

[3] A library that is linked to a process/application at run time rather than at compile time and can be shared between several processes (called "shared object libraries" under Unix).

```
A⟦controlflow(call(int f(int)),call(long g(short)),
            call(float h(double))&&args(x))
        then action(x);⟧
```

= (step a)
  ```
  createAspectInitialization(1);
  createAspectCompletionGuard();
  AP⟦controlflow(call(int f(int)),call(long g(short)),
              call(float h(double))&&args(x))
          then action(x);⟧(1)
  ```

  . . .

= (step b)
  ```
  createAspectInitialization(1);
  createAspectCompletionGuard();
  defineAF_ACTION(1,1, action(x) );
  defineMacro(NUMBER_OF_JPS,1,1);
  defineJPMacro(1,1);
  let (c,d) = PCSL⟦call(int f(int)),call(long g(short))⟧("",0)
      in defineCF_BEGIN(1,0,c,d);
          defineCF_END_FC(1,0);
  PC⟦call(float h(double))&&args(x))⟧(1,0)
  createPrimitiveAspect(1);
  ```

  . . .

= (step c)
  ```
  createAspectInitialization(1);
  createAspectCompletionGuard();
  defineAF_ACTION(1,1, action(x) );
  defineMacro(NUMBER_OF_JPS,1,1);
  defineJPMacro(1,1);
  defineCF_BEGIN(1,0,""f","g"",2);
  defineCF_END_FC(1,0);
  defineORIGINAL_FC(1,"float","h","double","x");
  createEntryPointFunctionFC(1,0,"float","h","double","x",
                                          "double x");
  createJoinPointFunCall(1,0,"h");
  createPrimitiveAspect(1);
  ```

Fig. 14. Example: Transformation of an control flow-based aspect (excerpt)

```
controlflow(call(int f(int)),call(long g(short)),
            call(float h(double)) && args(x)) then action(x);
```

Listing 1. Aspect using a control flow pointcut

(b) An intermediate step which enables matching of the call to **h** (via the point-cut valuation function **PC**) after the call sequence **f;g** has been matched (valuation function **PCSL**)).

(c) The final step represents the complete aspect code. This definition is given in terms of functions manipulating macro definitions (which, in turn, correspond to "real" C macros). The use of macro manipulation functions allows the semantics to be expressed quite concisely while still completely defining the executing code. The final step makes explicit, e.g., that pointcut matching is specialized w.r.t. the concrete number of joinpoints (through the use of NUMBER_OF_JPS), which governs how many concrete joinpoint macros can be instantiated (via defineJPMacro).

Listing 2 shows the executed code, i.e., once all the macro definitions and manipulations resulting from the final step of the transformation shown in Fig. 14 have been resolved.

This code (which is actually executed code, not some pseudocode) that will be generated by the compiler consists of initialization code, the advice and entrypoint of the aspect, a file guard and an aspect structure.

When the compiled aspect DLL is loaded, the initialization code (lines 1–4) triggers the automatic initialization of the aspect. Thereby the aspect is added to the active aspects and Arachne's kernel instruments all sites in the base program affected by the aspect structure (lines 32–54), which in the example are all function calls to **h**. Once the base: program executes a site rewritten for the aspect, the guard (lines 6–10) of the aspect, which indicates the progress of the weaving process, is checked to see whether it is true or false. In case all affected sites have been rewritten, the guard is set to true and the corresponding entrypoint function (lines 12–30) is invoked. In the entrypoint function the dynamic part of the pointcut is checked, to see whether the joinpoint really matches. In our example, the stack is checked for the functions **f** and **g** that are specified in the **controlflow** pointcut. If the dynamic predicate of the pointcut holds for the joinpoint, the advice/action (line 24) is executed; otherwise the original function is executed (lines 27–28).

The aspect structure (lines 32–54) consists of an array of joinpoints affected by the aspect (lines 35–48). Each joinpoint in the array specifies an entrypoint function (line 42), has a type and, in case of a function call or a global read or write access, additionally specifies a function identifier or a variable identifier, respectively. In the example, the only joinpoint of the array is a function call joinpoint, and thus the function identifier is specified (line 43). The **AllocatorAPI** provides an interface for the dynamic allocation and deallocation of structures, and each structure required for an aspect thus has a pointer to it (lines 8, 15, 34, 37, 41).

Overview of the Implementation-Level Semantics. Figure 15 shows a typical excerpt of the semantics itself. Valuation functions typically map syntactic entities to lists of code generation functions (see the signature of the valuation function **A**). They may, however, also depend on context information, e.g., the

```
    static Aspect * __aspect_1__; static void initAspect_1()
2   __attribute__ ((constructor)); static void initAspect_1() {
        AspectsInFile->api->add(AspectsInFile,__aspect_1__)
4   }

6   static Guard * __fileGuard__ = & (Guard) {
        (GuardAPI*) & __guardAPI__,
8       (AllocatorAPI*) & __transparentAllocatorAPI__,
        false
10  };

12  float entryPointOfJoinPoint_1_0(double x) {
        static CFlow * cflow = & (CFlow) {
14              (CFlowAPI*) & __CFLowAPI__,
                (AllocatorAPI*) & __transparentAllocatorAPI__,
16              (char* []) {"f","g"},
                UNKNOWN_EIP_2_FUNCTION_ADDRESS
18          };
        static boolean init = false;
20      if(!init) {
            defaultLoader->api->loadJoinpoint(defaultLoader,cflow);
22      }
        if(CHECK_STACK(cflow->functions,cflowFunctions,2,1,1)){
24          return action(x);
        }
26      else{
          return ((float (*) (double))
28         (defaultAspectLoader->api->getSymbolsByName("h")))(x);
        }
30  }

32  static Aspect* __aspect_1__ = & (Aspect) {
        (AspectAPI*) & __AspectAPI__,
34      (AllocatorAPI*) & __transparentAllocatorAPI__,
        & (ArrayOfJoinpoint) {
36          (ArrayOfJoinpointAPI*) & __ArrayOfJoinpointAPI__,
            (AllocatorAPI*) & __transparentAllocatorAPI__,
38          (Joinpoint*) {
                Joinpoint) &(void*[]) {
40                  (JoinpointAPI*) &__FunctionCallJoinpointAPI__,
                    (AllocatorAPI*) &__transparentAllocatorAPI__,
42                  (void*) entryPointOfJoinPoint_1_0,
                    "h"
44              };
            },
46          1,
            1
48      },
        UNKNOWN_SOURCE,
50      UNKNOWN_PATH,
        UNKNOWN_LINE,
52      TO_STRING("hand␣generated"),
        __fileGuard__
54  }
```

Listing 2. Example: Generated code for a control flow aspect (Listing 1)

A: Aspect $\longmapsto$ $CG*$

A⟦AspSeq⟧ =
                createAspectInitialization(1);
                createAspectCompletionGuard();
                AS⟦AspSeq⟧(1)

PCF: ControlFlowPointcut $\longmapsto$($INT \times INT$) $\longmapsto$$CG*$

PCF⟦controlflow(PCallSigList,PCall)⟧(n,m) =
                let (l,d) = **PCSL**⟦PCallSigList⟧("",0)
                       in defineCF_BEGIN(n,m,l,d);
                       defineCF_END_FC(n,m);
                PC⟦PCall⟧(n,m)

PCSL: FunctionCallSignature* $\longmapsto$($STRING \times INT$) $\longmapsto$($STRING \times INT$)

PCSL⟦call(Type FunId(TypeList))⟧(s,i) =
                (concat(s,concat("\"",concat(**S**⟦FunId⟧ ,"\"")))),i+1)

PCSL⟦call(Type FunId(TypeList)),PCallSigList⟧(s,i) =
                PCSL⟦PCallSigList⟧(concat(concat(s,","),
                                concat("\"",concat(**S**⟦FunId⟧ ,"\"")))),i+1)

Fig. 15. Valuation function of implementation-level semantics (excerpt)

function identifiers (e.g., the string arguments in the signature of function **PCF**) and position arguments in a sequence of a list of code generation functions (see the signatures of functions **PCF** and **PCSL**). The valuation function **A** defines how aspects are transformed by introducing aspect intialization code and then calling the valuation function of the current aspect construct (sequences, in the excerpt). The valuation function **PCF** defines that control-flow pointcuts are translated by first generating test code (by means of **PCSL**) for the sequence of calls in whose flow the final call has to occur, setting the macros CF_BEGIN, CF_END_FC which allow to test such a context and, finally, generating test code for the final call (using **PC**).

5   Dynamic Weaving with Arachne

Arachne is built around two tools (Fig. 16), an aspect compiler and a run-time weaver. The aspect compiler translates the aspect source code into a compiled library that, at weaving time, directs the weaver to place the hooks in the base program. The hooking mechanisms used in Arachne are based on improved techniques originally developed for μDyner [4]. These techniques allow users to rewrite the binary code of executable files on the fly, i.e., without pausing the

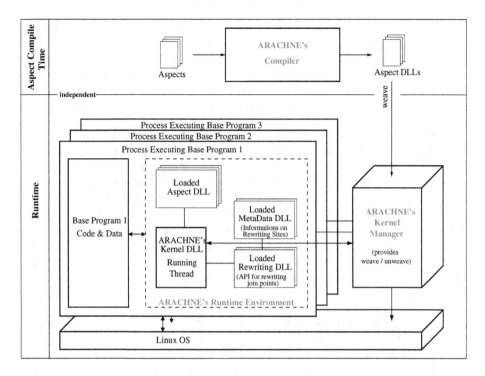

Fig. 16. Arachne's architecture

base program, as long as these files conform to the mapping defined by the Unix standard [42] between the C language and x86 assembly language. Arachne's implementation is structured as an open framework that allows one to experiment with new kinds of joinpoints and pointcut constructs. Another important difference between Arachne and μDyner is that μDyner requires a compile time preparation of the base program, whereas Arachne does not. Hence Arachne is totally transparent for the base program while μDyner is not.

5.1   The Arachne Open Architecture

The Arachne open architecture is structured around three main entities: the aspect compiler, the instrumentation kernel and the different rewriting strategies. The aspect compiler translates the aspect source code into C before compiling it. Weaving is accomplished through a command line tool **weave** that acts as a front end for the instrumentation kernel. **weave** relays weaving requests to the instrumentation kernel loaded in the address space of the program through Unix sockets. Upon reception of a weaving request, the instrumentation kernel selects the appropriate rewriting strategies referred by the aspects to be woven and instruments the base program accordingly. The rewriting strategy consults the pointcut analysis performed by the aspect compiler to locate the places where the binary code of the base program needs to be rewritten. It finally modifies the binary code to actually tie the aspects to the base program.

With this approach, the Arachne core is independent of a particular aspect, of the aspect language, of the particular processor architecture and of a particular base program. In fact, all dependencies to aspect language implementation are limited to the aspect compiler. All dependencies to the operating system are localized in the instrumentation kernel and, finally, all dependencies to the underlying hardware architecture are modularized in the rewriting strategies.

The Arachne Aspect Compilation Process. The aspect compilation scheme is relatively straightforward: It transforms advices into regular C functions. Pointcuts are rewritten as C code driving hook insertions into the base program at weaving time. There are, however, cases where the sole introduction of hooks is insufficient to determine whether an advice should be executed. In this case, the aspect compiler generates functions that complement the hooks with dynamic tests on the state of the base program. These dynamic tests are called *residues* in AspectJ, and the rewritten instructions within the base program the *shadow* [43]. Once the aspects have been translated into C, the Arachne compiler uses a legacy C compiler to generate a dynamically linked library (DLL) for the compiled aspects.

The Arachne Weaving Process. From a user viewpoint, the Arachne `weave` and `deweave` command line programs the same syntax as μDyner's version. They both take two arguments. The first identifies the process to weave aspects in or deweave aspects from, and the second indicates the aspect DLL. However, Arachne can target potentially any C application running on the machine, while μDyner was limited to applications compiled with it running on the machine. When Arachne's `weave` receives a request to weave an aspect in a process that does not contain the Arachne instrumentation kernel, it loads the kernel in the process address space using standard techniques [44].

The instrumentation kernel is transparent for the base program, since the latter cannot access the resources (memory and sockets essentially) used by the former. Once injected, the kernel creates a thread with the Linux system call: `clone`. This thread handles the different weaving requests. Compared to the POSIX `pthread_create` function, the usage of `clone` allows the instrumentation thread to prevent the base program to access its sockets. The instrumentation kernel allocates memory by using side-effect-free allocation routines (through the Linux `mmap` API). Because the allocation routines are side-effect-free, Arachne's memory is totally invisible to the base program. It is up to the aspect to use Arachne's memory allocation routines or base program-specific allocation functions. This transparency turns out to be crucial in our experiments. Legacy applications such as Squid use dedicated resource management routines and expect any piece of code they run to use these routines. Failures will result in an application crash.

After loading an aspect, the instrumentation kernel rewrites the binary code of the base program. These rewriting strategies are not included in the kernel and must be fetched on demand by each loaded aspect.

5.2 Rewriting Strategies

Rewriting strategies are responsible for transforming the binary code of the base program to effectively tie aspects to the base program at weaving time. These strategies localize Arachne's main dependencies to the underlying hardware architecture. In general, rewriting strategies need to collect information about the base program. This information typically consists of the addresses of the different shadows, their sizes, the symbol (i.e., function or global variable name) they manipulate, their length, etc. In order to keep compiled aspects independent from the base program, this information is gathered on demand at run time. The mapping between a symbol name in the base program source code and its address in memory is inferred from linking information contained in the base program executable. However, because this information can be costly to retrieve, **Arachne** collects and stores it into metainformation DLLs. These DLLs behave as a kind of cache and lessen the problem of collecting the information required to instrument the base program. To implement our aspect language, Arachne provides a set of eight rewriting strategies that might eventually use each other.

Strategies for `call`, `readGlobal` and `writeGlobal`. In Arachne, `call`, `readGlobal` and `writeGlobal` allow an advice to be triggered upon a function call, a read on a global variable or a write, respectively. While the implementation

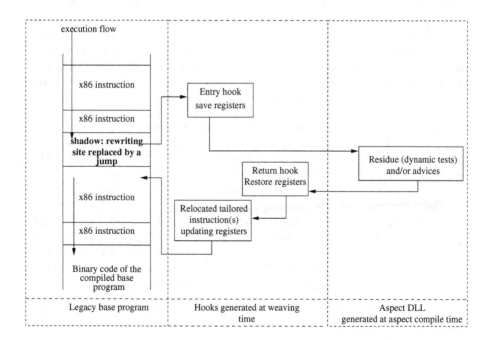

Fig. 17. Generic hook operations

of readGlobal and writeGlobal in Arachne is close to the one in μDyner, Arachne implements the strategy for call by rewriting function invocations found in the base program. μDyner instead rewrites the function body of the callee. On the Intel architecture, function calls benefit from the direct mapping to the x86 call assembly instruction that is used by almost, if not all, compilers. Write and read accesses to global variables are translated into instructions using immediate, hard-coded addresses within the binary code of the base program. By comparing these addresses with linking information contained in the base program executable, Arachne can determine where the global variable is being accessed. Therefore those primitive pointcuts do not involve any dynamic tests. The sole rewriting of the binary base program code is enough to trigger advice and residue[4] executions at all appropriate points.

The size of the x86 call instruction and the size of an x86 jump (jmp) instruction are the same. Since the instruction performing an access to a global variable involves a hard-coded address, x86 instructions that read or write a global variable have at least the size of a x86 jmp instruction. Hence at weaving time, Arachne rewrites them as a jmp instruction to a hook. Hooks are generated on the fly on freshly allocated memory. As shown in Fig. 17, hooks contain a few assembly instructions that save and restore the appropriate registers before and after an advice (or shadow) execution. A generic approach is to have hooks save the whole set of registers, then execute the appropriate residue and/or advice code before restoring the whole set of registers. Finally, the instructions found at the joinpoint shadow are executed to perform the appropriate side effects on the processor registers. This is accomplished by relocating the instructions found at the joinpoint shadow. Relocating the instructions makes the rewriting strategies handling read and write access to global variables independent from the instruction generated by the compiler to perform the access.[5] The limited number of x86 instructions used to invoke a function allows Arachne's rewriting strategy to exploit more efficient, relocation-free hooks.

Strategies for controlflow and controlflowstar. Every time a C function is called, the Linux runtime creates an activation record on the call stack [42]. Like μDyner, Arachne's implementation of the rewriting strategy for controlflow uses the most deeply nested function call (or global read or write access) in the control flow pointcut as shadow. This shadow triggers a residue. This residue uses the activation record's chaining to check whether the remaining function calls of the control flow are on the call stack maintained by the Linux run time. An appropriate usage of hash tables that store the linking information contained in the base program executables can thereby decrease the cost of determining if a specific function is the caller of another to a pointer comparison. Therefore, the residue for a controlflow with n directly nested functions implies exactly

---

[4] Residues (i.e., dynamic tests on the base program state) are required when these primitive pointcuts are combined with conditional pointcuts or when pattern matching is involved.

[5] About 250 x86 instruction mnemonics can directly manipulate a global variable. This corresponds to more than 1000 opcodes.

n pointer comparisons. However, the residue worst-case run time for the indirect control flow operator `controlflowstar` that allows for not directly nested functions is proportional to the base program stack depth.

Strategies for read and write. read and write are new joinpoints not included in μDyner that have been added to the latest version of Arachne. Their implementation relays on a page memory protection as allowed by the Linux operating system interface (i.e., `mprotect`) and the Intel processor specifications [46].[6] A read or write pointcut triggers a residue to relocate the bound variable into a memory page that the base program is not allowed to access and adds a dedicated signal handler. Any attempt made by the base program to access the bound variable identified will then trigger the execution of the previously added signal handler. This handler will then inspect the binary instruction trying to access the protected page to determine whether it was a read or a write access before eventually executing the appropriate advice.

Strategies for seq. Like read and write, seq is a new language feature of Arachne. μDyner offers no equivalent construct. Arachne's rewriting strategy of this operator associates a linked list to every stage inside the sequence except the last one. Each stage in a sequence triggers a residue that updates these linked lists to reflect state transitions of currently matching execution flows. Upon matching of the first pointcut of the first primitive aspect in the seq, a node is allocated and added to the associated linked list. This node contains a structure holding variables shared among the different pointcuts within the sequence. Once a joinpoint matches a pointcut of an primitive aspect denoting a stage in the sequence, Arachne consults every node in the linked list associated with the previous stage and executes the corresponding advice.[7] Arachne eventually updates the node and, in the absence of a *, moves it to the list associated with the currently matched pointcut. If the matching pointcut corresponds to the end of the sequence, structures are not moved into another list but are freed. Our aspect compiler includes an optimization where structures are allocated from a resizable pool, and upon a sequence termination, structures are not freed but returned to the pool.

5.3 Limitations of Arachne

Aggressive optimizations of the base program might prevent Arachne from seamlessly weaving aspects. Two optimizations are not yet supported by Arachne. First, if the compiler inlines a function in another one within the binary code of the base program, the Arachne weaver will fail to properly handle pointcuts referring to that function. Second, control flow pointcuts are based on the chaining

---

[6] Even if this implementation is Linux/x86 specific, it is applicable to arbitrary architectures supporting memory paging.

[7] In case the previous stage pointcut was used with a star *, Arachne examines nodes from linked list associated with the last two previous stages, and so on, until a not-starred primitive aspect in the sequence is reached.

of activation records. On the x86 architecture, in leaf functions, optimizing compilers sometimes do not maintain this chaining to free one register for the rest of the computation. This, however, has not been a problem during our experiments as we used the open-source C compiler `gcc`. Arachne does not require the base program's source code in order to weave aspects, however it relies on linking information embedded within the executable to determine where the program code must be rewritten. Hence the stripping of symbols from executables as well as aggressive optimizations that break the interoperability between compilers and/or debuggers are incompatible with Arachne. In practice, Arachne can be used on applications compiled like Squid with two of the three `gcc` optimization levels.

6   Performance Evaluation

Aspect-oriented solutions will be used if the aspect system's language is expressive enough and if the aspect system overhead is low enough for the task at hand. The purpose of this section is to study Arachne's performance. We first present the speed of each Arachne language construct and compare it to similar C language constructs. Second, we study the overhead of extending Squid with a prefetching policy. Third, we measure the overhead induced by protecting the Washington University's FTP server `wu-ftpd` from a buffer-overflow vulnerability. These two case studies show that even if the cost of some Arachne aspect language constructs might be high compared to C language constructs, this overhead is largely amortized in real applications.

6.1   Evaluation of the Language Constructs

This performance evaluation focuses on studying the cost of each construct of our aspect language. To estimate the cost for each construct of our aspect language, we wrote an aspect using this construct that behaves as an interpreter of the base program. For example, to study the performance of `readGlobal`, we wrote an aspect whose action returns the value of the global variable referred to in the pointcut, i.e., we wrote aspects behaving like the base program. For each of these aspects, we compare the time required to perform the operation matching the pointcut, in case the operation is interpreted by the woven aspect, with the time required to carry out the operation natively (without the woven aspect). For example, to study the performance of `readGlobal`, we first evaluate the time needed to retrieve the global variable value through the code generated by the C compiler `gcc` without any aspect woven and compare this value to the time needed to retrieve the global variable value through the aspect once it has been woven in the base program. We express our measurements as a ratio between these two durations to abstract from the experimentation platform.

   This approach requires the ability to measure short periods of time. For instance, a global variable value is usually retrieved (`readGlobal` in our aspect language) in a single clock tick. Since standard time measurement APIs were not precise enough, our benchmarking infrastructure relies on the `rdtsc` assembly instruction [45]. This instruction returns the number of clock cycles elapsed since power up. The Pentium 4 processor has the ability to dynamically reorder the instructions it executes. To ensure the validity of our measurement, we thus insert `mfence` instructions in the generated code whose execution speed is being measured. An `mfence` forces the preceding instructions to be fully executed before going on. The pipeline mechanism in the Pentium 4 processor entails that the speed of a piece of assembly code depends on the preceding instructions. To avoid such hidden dependencies, we place the operation whose execution time is being measured in a loop. We use `gcc` to unroll the loop at compile time, and we measure the time to execute the complete loop. This measure divided by the number of loop repetitions yields an estimation of the time required to execute the operation. The number of times the loop is executed is chosen after the relative variations of the measures, i.e., we increased the number of repetitions until ten runs yields an average relative variation not exceeding 5%. To check the correctness of our experimental protocol, we measured the time needed to execute a `nop` assembly instruction, which requires one processor cycle according to the Intel specification. The measures of `nop` presented a relative variation of 1.6%.

Table 1 summarizes our experimental results. Using the aspect language to replace a function that returns immediately is only 1.3 times slower than a direct, aspectless call to that empty function. Since the aspect compiler packages advices as regular C functions, and because a `call` pointcut involves no residue, this good result is not surprising. When an access to a global variable is replaced by an advice execution, the hooks generated by the rewriting strategy need to prepare the processor to call the advice function. This increases the time spent in the hooks. A `seq` of three invocations of empty functions is only 3.2 times slower than the direct, aspectless, three successive functions calls. Compared to the pointcuts used to delimit the different stages, the `seq` overhead is limited to a few pointer exchanges between the linked lists holding the bound variable. On Intel x86, global variable accesses benefit from excellent hardware support. In the absence of aspects, a direct global variable read is usually carried out in a single unique cycle. To trigger the advice execution, the Arachne runtime has to save

Table 1. Speed of each language construct used to interpret the base program compared to a native execution

	Execution times (cycles)		
	Arachne	Native	Ratio
`call`	28±2.3%	21±1.9%	1.3
`seq`	201±0.5%	63±1.7%	3.2
`cflow`	228±1.6%	42±1.8%	5.4
`readGlobal`	2762±4.3%	1±0.2%	2762
`read`	9729±4.9%	1±0.6%	9729

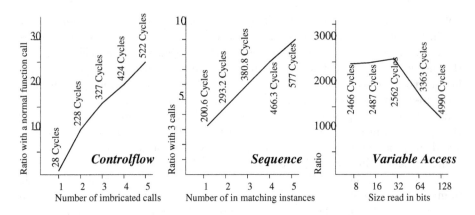

Fig. 18. `controlflow`, `seq` and `readGlobal` performances

and restore the processor state to ensure the execution coherency, as advices are packaged as regular C functions (see also Sect. 5.2). It is therefore not surprising that a global variable `readGlobal` appears as being 2762 times slower than a direct, aspectless global variable read. `read` performance can be accounted in the same way: In the absence of aspect, local variables are accessed in a single unique cycle. The signal mechanism used in the `read` requires that the operating system detects the base program attempt to read into a protected memory page before locating and triggering the signal handler set up by Arachne, as shown in Sect. 5.2. Such switches to and from kernel space remain slow. Using `read` to read a local variable is 9729 times slower than retrieving the local variable value directly, without aspects.

`seq` and `controlflow` can refer to several points in the execution of the base program (i.e., different stages for `seq` and different function invocations for the `controlflow`). The run time of these pointcuts grows linearly with the number of execution points they refer to and with the number of matching instances. Variable access pointcut performance varies depending on the size of the data accessed. Indeed, on IA32 architectures, an access to a variable smaller or equal to 32 bits is performed atomically in one processor cycle, while time to access a variable larger than 32 bits grows linearly with the variable size. Hence, the overhead of an aspect replacing an access to an up to 32-bit variable is constant and beyond amortized corresponding to the variable size. Figure 18 summarizes a few experimental results for `controlflow`, `seq` and `readGlobal` that provide evidence for these performance propositions.

6.2   Case Study on a Real Application

Since executing a base program with aspects can slow it down by a factor ranging between 1.3 and 9729, depending on the aspect construct used, we studied Arachne's performance on a real-world application, the Web cache Squid. We extended Squid with a prefetching policy [46]. As described in Sect. 3.1, we implemented this policy as a set of aspects and made a second implementation of this policy by editing the Squid source code and recompiling it. This section compares the performance of these two implementations using standard Web cache performance indicators: throughput, response time and hit ratio.

A tool which seemingly is appropriate for such a real-world experience is the traces generated during Web cache executions. However, obtaining access traces adequate to study a Web cache performance is difficult. The trace must be long enough to fill the cache. Because of privacy issues, traces are usually not publicly available. Since traces do not include the content of the accessed pages, these pages must be downloaded again. In the meantime, the page contents may have changed and even the URLs may have disappeared.

Instead of traces, we based our evaluation on Web Polygraph [47]. Polygraph is a benchmarking tool developed by the Squid team that features a realistic HTTP and SSL traffic generator and a flexible content simulator.

We filled up the cache and simulated a one-day workload with its two request rate peaks observed in real-life environments [47]. Table 2 shows some results of our simulation. Measures have been made during the two request peaks. All measures, be it the hit time, the miss time, the time needed to deliver a document presenting the cache or not, are very similar, independent of Arachne being used or not. These measures prove that differences are imperceptible between the version of Squid extended by Arachne and the one extended manually (less than 1%). Hence, even if the cost of some of Arachne's aspect language constructs might seem high, they are largely amortized in real applications. To give a typical example observed on our experimental platform: in case of a cache hit, a 3.8-MB page was retrieved in a single second, the time spent in prefetching advices amounted to 1801 μsec, and the time spent within Arachne to execute the hooks and dynamic tests was 0.45 μsec. In a miss case, on the average, a client

Table 2. Performance comparison between manual modification and Arachne, for prefetching policy integration in Squid

	Arachne Top1 Top2	Manual Top1 Top2	Diff (%)
Throughput (request/s)	5.59	5.59	–
	5.58	5.59	
Response time (ms)	1131.42	1146.07	1.2 – –1
	1085.31	1074.55	
Miss response time (ms)	2533.50	2539.52	0.2 – 1.8
	2528.35	2525.34	
Hit response time (ms)	28.96	28.76	–0.6 – 3.8
	30.62	31.84	
Hit ratio	59.76	59.35	–0.6 – 0.7
	61.77	62.22	
Errors	0.51	0.50	–1.9 – 0
	0.34	0.34	

retrieved the same page in 1.3 seconds, 16679 μsec were spent in the advices and 0.67 μsec within Arachne itself.

6.3   A Second Case Study: `wu-ftpd`

We also applied Arachne on the real-world application `wu-ftpd` (Washington University file transfer protocol Daemon), a widely deployed file transfer protocol service. It constitutes the basis for development of several other ftp servers, e.g., BSD ftpd, ProFTPD.

We performed measurements on `wu-ftpd` applying an aspect for the correction of a buffer overflow. We chose a buffer-overflow vulnerability identified in the s/key authentication mechanism discovered in 2004 and referenced by the Common Vulnerabilities and Exposures under the identifier `CVE-2004-0185`.

In order to evaluate `wu-ftpd`'s performance, we used `dkftpbench` [48], a benchmarking tool for FTP servers. `dkftpbench` permits users to stress ftp servers by faking client connections using automata. Each fake client authenticates to the server, retrieves a particular file and disconnects. `dkftpbench` constantly creates new automata and then permits users to measure instant/average/maximum numbers of simultaneous users. We recorded our measurements between two machines: one for `dkftpbench` and one for `wu-ftpd` over a 100-Mb/s ethernet. `wu-ftpd` was running on a Pentium 4, 3.3 GHz, with 512-MB RAM. Each file to be retrieved was 5-MB long, and network bandwidth dedicated to each client was set so that the network was never subject to congestion.

We measured the maximum number of users simultaneously served by `wu-ftpd` when running unprotected and protected with our aspect. Results show no significant difference between the two versions, which allow for 1008 and 1012 simultaneous users, respectively. This demonstrates that even if our aspect constructs might seem to consume an important amount of local resources, they are clearly reasonably applicable in real-world situations by permitting users to protect applications against attacks without impacting performance significantly.

Nevertheless, performance penalties could be significant. Indeed, frequent use of the `read` construct could greatly slow down program execution. Such a situation would arise, for example, when every single buffer in an application should be protected from overflowing. However, one of the main characteristics of our approach is that it supports the selective modification of system-level applications using aspects. Furthermore, those situations seem to be quite unlikely anyway: for all applications we have encountered, `read/write` and `readGlobal/writeGlobal` pointcuts have been marginal compared to `call` pointcuts.

7   Related Work

Aspect-oriented research currently focuses on object-oriented languages. Apart from μDyner and Arachne, there are few *aspect weavers for C* (or even C-like languages). AspectC [3] and AspectC++ [49] are two noteworthy exceptions.

They both rely on source-code transformation and solely weave aspects at compile time. DAC++ [50] and Toskana [51] are dynamic weavers for C++ and C. DAC++ is built around a metaobject protocol enabling the run time instrumentation required to weave aspects at run time. Since C++ does not include a standard metaobject protocol, the base program has to be compiled with a dedicated specific compiler. Toskana weaves aspects in a running Linux kernel. It does not allow users to weave aspects in user applications. In addition, the joinpoint model in Toskana is limited to function calls. Hence, none of these weavers is suitable to modularize and dynamically compose the concerns we considered.

There is quite a large body of work now on the notion of *expressive aspect languages*, where "more expressive" typically compares to AspectJ's pointcut and advice models. Our work has been inspired by Event-based AOP [52], which aims at the definition of pointcuts in terms of arbitrary relations between events. Nevertheless, many other approaches to expressive aspect languages exist. For example, data-flow relations [53], logic programming [54], process algebras [55], graphs [56] and temporal logics [57] have all been proposed as a basis for the definition of expressive aspect languages. However, few of these encompass dynamic weaving, and only the latter has been applied to C code under efficiency considerations similar to our setting (but using a static approach to weaving).

Research on explicit sequence pointcuts and aspects is still in its infancy. Sequential aspects were first introduced by Douence et al. with the notion of stateful aspects [37, 38]. They exploited the underlying notion of regular sequence aspects — which are thus of more restricted expressiveness than the sequence aspects considered in this article — to analyze aspect interactions, and a prototype supporting arbitrary relations between joinpoints for Java was implemented [58]. However, this prototype is based on static weaving and does not allow dynamic modification of aspects. Regular sequence aspects have also been integrated in the Java-based JAsCo aspect system [59]. In [60] a specialized language was proposed to define pointcuts as sequences of method calls in Java. A pointcut is associated with a single advice, which is executed at the end of the sequence. This approach does not support advice attached to the middle of a sequence. Moreover, this Java-based tool supports static source-code-only weaving.

Another class of techniques relevant to our work is dynamic binary code instrumentation, which has already been widely studied. These techniques were used in the first computers [61]. In these techniques, difficulty issues range from the complexity to rewrite binary code to the lack of a well-defined relationship between source code and the compiler-generated binary code. Pin [62] and Dyninst [63] enable programmers to modify any binary instruction belonging to an executable. Based on a just-in-time translation, Pin is very efficient but is limited to insert code before or after a binary instruction of the base program. This prevents Pin from serving as a back end for an aspect system using around-like aspect. Dyninst does not suffer from this limitation; it is designed around the Unix debugging API: `ptrace`. After suspending the base program execution, this

API allows a third-party process to read and write the base program memory. In comparison, Arachne suspends the base program at most once to inject, with `ptrace`, its kernel DLL into the base program process. In addition, instrumentation schemes written with Dyninst are not ensured to be reliable: Dyninst's implementation relocates several adjacent instructions. Since one of the relocated instructions can be a branching instruction target, the instrumentation success depends on the base program considered. In comparison, Arachne's joinpoint model has been devised to avoid these kind of issues by design.

Finally, there are many Java-based approaches to nonstatic code weaving, i.e., *dynamic weaving* and *load-time weaving*. Load-time weaving refers to the process of instrumenting the base program when the execution environment — the Java virtual machine, for instance — transfers it from disk storage to memory-executable structures. To provide aspect deployment at run time they have to prepare, i.e., instrument, the base program at load time and thus can imply a nonnegligible overhead, even in the absence of aspects [64, 65, 66, 67]. Contrary to those approaches, Arachne does not weave aspects at load time but dynamically at run time and does not require any anticipation of aspect weaving at load time. Furthermore, Arachne keeps a clear separation at run time between the base program code and the aspect code, so that aspects can be unwoven without leaving residues in the base program code. Some approaches, most notably JAsCo [68], Steamloom [69], JBoss AOP [70], Spring AOP [71] and AspectWerkz (which is currently under integration with AspectJ) support run-time weaving of aspects for Java. As Java-based approaches they cannot be applied to solve the legacy code problems we consider. Furthermore, they do not provide Arachne's fine-grained weaving (weaving on the level of processor instructions). Finally, since they rely on particularities of the Java platform (such as the debugging interface or Hotswap), the incurred performance overhead is large to very large compared to that of Arachne, and the implementation techniques themselves are not transferable to C.

8 Conclusion and Future Work

Technical issues such as double-free bugs and buffer overflows, networking, and prefetching are typical examples of concerns which crosscut system-level C applications: in many real-world legacy applications such as the Squid Web cache, these concerns are scattered over the entire program source code. Since security breaches and insufficient resources are often discovered after deployment, and because downtime must be avoided in many application contexts, there is a growing need to modularize and manipulate these concerns at runtime.

Security, networking and prefetching are appealing candidates for modularization using aspects. However, basic aspect-oriented techniques are not applicable due to the complex relationships between executions points these aspects are required to account for. We have proposed an aspect language enabling us to specify these relationships involving sequences of execution points as well as for variable aliases. We have shown how to successfully modularize security, networking and prefetching concerns within this aspect language. Furthermore, we have presented two formal semantics for this language that clearly express different properties of the language due to their different abstraction levels.

The Arachne tool implements this language. It can weave and deweave aspects dynamically in running legacy C applications like Squid or the wu-ftpd ftp server. We have provided detailed evidence that the performance of these two applications, including modifications by Arachne aspects, competes with (optimal) manual source code modifications.

As future work, we intend to investigate how unexpected interactions between aspects can be detected at compile time and at weaving time. Unexpected interactions can occur when two aspects refer to the same joinpoint or by sharing variables. Detecting these interactions would greatly ease the development of large aspects libraries. Another lead for future work is to exploit the better modularization of system-level functionalities by Arachne aspects for the testing of such functionalities. We also plan to integrate debugging information support to Arachne. Because this is the missing link between source and binary code, that information should permit users to overcome aggressive optimizations performed by compilers.

References

[1] Wessels D. Squid: *The Definitive Guide.* O'Reilly, 2004
[2] Kiczales G., Lamping J., Menhdhekar A., Maeda C., Lopes C., Loingtier J.M., Irwin J. Aspect-oriented programming. In: Akşit, M., Matsuoka, S. (eds.) *Proceedings European Conference on Object-Oriented Programming, LNCS vol. 1241,* Springer, Jyväskylä, Finland, pp. 220–242, 1997
[3] Coady Y., Kiczales G., Feeley M., and Smolyn G. Using AspectC to improve the modularity of path-specific customization in operating system code. In: Gruhn, V. (ed.) *Proceedings of the Joint 8th European Software Engeneering Conference and 9th ACM SIGSOFT Symposium on the Foundation of Software Engineering (ESEC/FSE-01).* Volume 26, 5 of SOFTWARE ENGINEERING NOTES, ACM, New York, pp. 88–98, 2001
[4] Ségura-Devillechaise M., Menaud J.M., Muller G., and Lawall J. Web cache prefetching as an aspect: Towards a dynamic-weaving based solution. In: *Proceedings of the 2nd International Conference on Aspect-Oriented Software Development,* ACM, pp. 110–119, 2003
[5] Arce I., Levy E. An analysis of the slapper worm. *IEEE Security and Privacy* 1:82–87, 2003
[6] Solar Designer: JPEG COM Marker Processing Vulnerability in Netscape Browsers. http://www.openwall.com/advisories/OW002-netscape-jpeg/ (1997)
[7] Ubuntu: Squid Proxy Cache Double Memory Free Vulnerability. http://www.security.nnov.ru/Idocument338.html (2005)
[8] American National Standards Institute: ANSI/ISO/IEC 9899-1999: *Programming Languages — C.* American National Standards Institute, New York, 1999
[9] CERT Coordination Center: CERT Advisory CA-2001-13 Buffer Overflow in IIS Indexing Service DLL. http://www.cert.org/advisories/CA-2001-13.html (2001)
[10] CERT Coordination Center: "Code Red" Worm Exploiting Buffer Overflow in IIS Indexing Service DLL (CERT Incident Note IN-2001-10). http://www.cert.org/incident_notes/IN-2001-08.html (2001)

[11] US-CERT (United States Computer Emergency Readiness Team): Microsoft SQL Server 2000 contains stack buffer overflow in SQL Server Resolution Service (Vulnerability Note VU#484891). http://www.kb.cert.org/vuls/id/484891 (2002)

[12] CERT Coordination Center: CERT Advisory CA-2003-04 MS-SQL Server Worm. http://www.cert.org/advisories/CA-2003-04.html (2003)

[13] US-CERT (United States Computer Emergency Readiness Team): Microsoft Windows RPC vulnerable to buffer overflow (Vulnerability Note VU#568148). http://www.kb.cert.org/vuls/id/568148 (2003)

[14] CERT Coordination Center: CERT Advisory CA-2003-20 W32/Blaster worm. http://www.cert.org/advisories/CA-2003-20.html (2003)

[15] Ruwase O. and Lam M.S. A practical dynamic buffer overflow detector. In: *Proceedings of the 11th Annual Network and Distributed System Security Symposium*, Internet Society, San Diego, CA, 2004

[16] CERT Coordination Center: CERT/CC advisories. http://www.cert.org/advisories/ (1988)

[17] Wagner D., Foster J.S., Brewer E.A., and Aiken A. A first step towards automated detection of buffer overrun vulnerabilities. In: *Network and Distributed System Security Symposium*, Internet Society, San Diego, CA, pp. 3–17, 2000

[18] Cowan C., Wagle P., Pu, C., Beattie S., and Walpole J. Buffer overflows: Attacks and defenses for the vulnerability of the decade. In: *DARPA Information Survivability Conference and Exposition (DISCEX)*. Vol. 2, Hilton Head Island, SC, USA, 119–129, IEEE 2000

[19] Wilander J. and Kamkar M. A comparison of publicly available tools for dynamic buffer overflow prevention. In: *Proceedings of the 10th Network and Distributed System Security Symposium*, Internet Society, San Diego, CA, pp. 149–162, 2003

[20] Larochelle D. and Evans D. Statically detecting likely buffer overflow vulnerabilities. In: *Proceedings of the 10th USENIX Security Symposium*, USENIX, Washington, DC, pp. 177–190, 2001

[21] Cowan C., Pu C., Maier D., Walpole J., Bakke P., Beattie S., Grier A., Wagle P., Zhang Q., and Hinton H. StackGuard: Automatic adaptive detection and prevention of buffer-overflow attacks. In: *Proc. 7th USENIX Security Conference*, USENIX, San Antonio, TX, pp. 63–78, 1998

[22] Jim T., Morrisett G., Grossman D., Hicks M., Cheney J., and WangY. Cyclone: A safe dialect of C. In: *Proceedings of the USENIX Annual Technical Conference*, USENIX, Monterey, CA, pp. 275–288, 2002

[23] Condit J., Harren M., McPeak S., Necula G.C., and Weimer W. CCured in the real world. In: *PLDI '03: Proceedings of the ACM SIGPLAN 2003 Conference on Programming Language Design and Implementation*, ACM, San Diego, CA, pp. 232–244, 2003

[24] Jones R. and Kelly P. Backwards-compatible bounds checking for arrays and pointers in C programs. In: Kamkar, M. (ed.) *Proceedings of the Third International Workshop on Automatic Debugging*. Vol. 2, Linköping, Sweden, Linköping Electronic Articles in Computer and Information Science, pp. 13–26, 1997

[25] Keromytis A.D. "Patch on demand" saves even more time? *IEEE Computer*, 37:94–96, 2004

[26] US-CERT (United States Computer Emergency Readiness Team): Squid Proxy Server contains buffer overflow in parsing of the authentication portion of FTP URLs (Vulnerability Note VU#613459). http://www.kb.cert.org/vuls/id/613459 (2002)

[27] Berners-Lee T., Fielding R., Frystyk H. RFC 1945: Hypertext Transfer Protocol — HTTP/1.0 (1996) Status: INFORMATIONAL.

[28] Postel J. Transmission Control Protocol. RFC 793. http://www.rfc-editor.org/rfc/rfc793.txt (1981)

[29] Arlitt M., Jin T. A workload characterization study of the 1998 world cup web site. *IEEE Network*, 14:30–37, 2000

[30] Cidon I., Gupta A., Rom R., Schuba C. Hybrid TCP-UDP transport for web traffic. *Technical Report 99-71*, Sun Microsystems Laboratories, Palo Alto, CA, 1999

[31] Rabinovich M. and Wang H. DHTTP: An efficient and cache-friendly transfer protocol for web traffic. In: *IEEE INFOCOM*, pp. 1597–1606, 2001

[32] Chen H. and Mohapatra P. CATP: A context-aware transportation protocol for HTTP. In: *International Workshop on New Advances in Web Servers and Proxy Technologies Held with ICDCS*, Providence, RI, USA, pp. 922–927, 2003

[33] Postel J. User datagram protocol. RFC 768. http://www.rfc.net/rfc768.html (1980)

[34] Comer D., Stevens D. Internetworking with TCP/IP, Volume III — Client-Server Programming and Applications for the BSD Socket Version. Volume III. Prentice Hall, 1993

[35] Issarny V., Banâtre M., Charpiot B., Menaud J.M. Quality of service and electronic newspaper: The Etel solution. *LNCS vol. 1752*, pp. 472–496, 2000

[36] Lieberherr K.J., Palm J., Sundaram R. Expressiveness and complexity of crosscut languages. *Technical Report NU-CCIS-04-10*, Northeastern University, 2004

[37] Douence R., Fradet P. and Südholt M. A framework for the detection and resolution of aspect interactions. In: *GPCE'02: Proceedings of the ACM SIGPLAN/SIGSOFT Conference on Generative Programming and Component Engineering*, *LNCS vol. 2487*, Springer, Pittsburgh, PA, USA, pp. 173–188, 2002

[38] Douence R., Fradet P., and Südholt M. Composition, reuse and interaction analysis of stateful aspects. In: *AOSD'04: Proc. of 3rd International Conference on Aspect-Oriented Software Development*, ACM, Lancaster, UK, pp. 141–150, 2004

[39] Jaffar, J., Michaylov, S., Stuckey, P.J., Yap, R.H.C. The clp(r) language and system. *ACM Trans. Program. Lang. Syst.*, 14:339–395,1992

[40] Schmidt D.A. Denotational semantics - A methodology for language development. Allyn and Bacon, http://www.cis.ksu.edu/~schmidt/text/densem.html (1986)

[41] Fritz T. An expressive aspect language with arachne. *Master's thesis*, Ludwig-Maiximilians-Universität München, 2005

[42] System Unix U.S.L.: System V application binary interface intel 386 architecture processor supplement. Prentice Hall Trade, 1994

[43] Hilsdale E. and Hugunin J. Advice weaving in AspectJ. In: *Proceedings of the 3rd International Conference on Aspect-Oriented Software Development*, ACM, pp. 26–35, 2004

[44] Clowes S. Injectso: Modifying and spying on running processes under linux. In: *Black Hat Briefings*, 2001

[45] Intel Corportation: IA-32 Intel Architecture software developer's manual. *Intel Corportation*, 2001

[46] Chinen K.I. and Yamaguchi S. An interactive prefetching proxy server for improvement of WWW latency. In: *INET'97: Seventh Annual Conference of the Internet Society*, Internet Society, Kuala Lumpur, Malaysia, 1997

[47] Rousskov A., Wessels D. High-performance benchmarking with Web Polygraph. *Software Practice and Experience*, 34:187–211, 2004

[48] Kegel, D. dkftpbench. http://www.kegel.com/dkftpbench/ (2000)

[49] Spinczyk O., Gal A., and Schröder-Preikschat W. AspectC++: An aspect-oriented extension to the C++ programming language. In: *Proceedings of the Fortieth International Conference on Tools Pacific*, Australian Computer Society, Sydney, Australia, pp. 53–60, 2002

[50] Almajali S. and Elrad T. Coupling availability and efficiency for aspect-oriented runtime weaving systems. In: *DAW'05: Proceeding of the 2nd Dynamic Aspects Workshop at AOSD*, Chicago, IL, pp. 47–56, 2005

[51] Engel M. and Freisleben, B. Supporting autonomic computing functionality via dynamic operating system kernel aspects. In: *AOSD '05: Proceedings of the 4th International Conference on Aspect-Oriented Software Development*, ACM, New York, pp. 51–62, 2005

[52] Douence R., Motelet O., and Südholt M. A formal definition of crosscuts. In: Yonezawa, A., Matsuoka, S. (eds.) *Proceedings of the 3rd International Conference on Metalevel Architectures and Separation of Crosscutting Concerns, LNCS vol. 2192*, Kyoto, Japan, Springer, Berlin Heidelberg New York, pp. 170–186, 2001

[53] Masuhara H. and Kawauchi K. Dataflow pointcut in aspect-oriented programming. In: Ohori, A. (ed.) *APLAS'03: First Asian Symposium on Programming Languages and Systems, LNCS vol. 2895*, Beijing, China, Springer, Berlin Heidelberg New York, pp. 105–121, 2003

[54] de Volder K. Aspect-oriented logic meta programming. In: Cointe, P. (ed.) *Meta-Level Architectures and Reflection, 2nd International Conference on Reflection, LNCS vol. 1616*, Saint Malo, France, Springer, Berlin Heidelberg New York, pp. 250–272, 1999

[55] Andrews J.H. Process-algebraic foundations of aspect-oriented programming. In: Yonezawa, A., Matsuoka, S. (eds.) *Proceedings of the 3rd International Conference on Metalevel Architectures and Separation of Crosscutting Concerns, LNCS vol. 2192*, Kyoto, Japan, Springer, Berlin Heidelberg New York, pp. 187–209, 2001

[56] Aßmann U. and Ludwig A. Aspect weaving with graph rewriting. In: Czarnecki, K., Eisenecker, U.W. (eds.) *GCSE: Generative Component-Based Software Engineering*, Erfurt, Germany, pp. 24–36, 1999

[57] Åberg R.A., Lawall J.L., Südholt M., Muller G., and Meur A.F.L. On the automatic evolution of an OS kernel using temporal logic and AOP. In: *ASE 2003: Proceedings of the 18th IEEE International Conference on Automated Software Engineering*, IEEE Computer Society, Montreal, Canada, pp. 196–204, 2003

[58] Douence R., Südholt M. A model and a tool for event-based aspect-oriented programming (eaop). *Technical Report 02/11/INFO*, École des mines de Nantes (2002) French version published in Proc. of LMO'03, Hermes Sciences,

[59] Vanderperren W., Suvee D., Cibran M.A., and De Fraine B. Stateful aspects in JAsCo. In: *SC'05: Proc. of the 4th Int. Workshop on Software Composition, LNCS vol. 3628*, Springer, Berlin Heidelberg New York, 2005

[60] Allan C., Avgustinov P., Christensen A.S., et al. Adding trace matching with free variables to AspectJ. In: Gabriel, R.P. (ed.) *OOPSLA'05: ACM Conference on Object-Oriented Programming, Systems and Languages*, ACM, 2005

[61] Aspray W. John von Neumann's contributions to computing and computer science. *Annals of the History of Computing*, 11:189–195, 1989

[62] Luk C.K., Cohn R., Muth R., Patil H., Klauser A., Lowney G., Wallace S., Reddi V.J., and Hazelwood K. Pin: Building customized program analysis tools with dynamic instrumentation. In: *PLDI: Proceedings of the ACM SIGPLAN 2005 Conference on Programming Language Design and Implementation*, ACM, Chicago, IL, pp. 190–200, 2005

[63] Hollingsworth J.K., Miller B.P., Goncalves M.J.R., Naim O., Xu, Z., and Zheng L. MDL: A language and compiler for dynamic program instrumentation. In: *PACT: Proceedings of the 6th Conference on Parallel Architectures and Compilation Techniques*, IEEE Computer Society, San Francisco, CA, USA, pp. 201–213, 1997

[64] Chiba S. Load-time structural reflection in Java. In: *ECOOP 2000: Sophia Antipolis and Cannes, LNCS vol. 1850*, France, Springer, Berlin Heidelberg New York, pp. 313–336, 2000

[65] Pawlak R., Seinturier L., Duchien L., and Florin G. JAC: A flexible solution for aspect-oriented programming in Java. In: *Proceedings of Reflection'01. LNCS vol. 2192*, Springer, Berlin Heidelberg New York, pp. 1–24, 2001

[66] Popovici A., Alonso G., and Gross T.R. Just-in-time aspects: Efficient dynamic weaving for Java. In: *AOSD: Proceedings of the 2nd International Conference on Aspect-Oriented Software Development*, ACM, pp. 100–109, 2003

[67] Chiba S. and Nakagawa K. Josh: An open AspectJ-like language. In: Murphy, G.C., Lieberherr, K.J. (eds.) *AOSD: Proceedings of the Third International Conference on Aspect-Oriented Software Development*, ACM, pp. 102–111, 2004

[68] Suvée D., Vanderperren W., and Jonckers V. JasCo: An aspect-oriented approach tailored for component-based software development. In: Press, A. (ed.) *AOSD'03: Proc. of 2nd International Conference on Aspect-Oriented Software Development*, pp. 21–29, 2003

[69] Bockisch C., Haupt M., Mezini M., and Ostermann K. Virtual machine support for dynamic join points. In: *AOSD '04: Proceedings of the 3rd International Conference on Aspect-Oriented Software Development*, ACM, New York, pp. 83–92, 2004

[70] JBoss Inc: JBoss AOP. http://jboss.com/products/aop. (2005)

[71] Spring Framework: Spring AOP. http://www.springframework.org/. (2005)

Towards a Catalogue of Refactorings
and Code Smells for AspectJ

Miguel P. Monteiro[1] and João M. Fernandes[2]

[1] Escola Superior de Tecnologia, Instituto Politécnico de Castelo Branco,
Avenida do Empresário, 6000-767, Castelo Branco, Portugal
mmonteiro@di.uminho.pt
[2] Departamento de Informática, Universidade do Minho, Campus de Gualtar,
4710-057 Braga, Portugal
jmf@di.uminho.pt

Abstract. In this paper, we contribute to the characterisation of a programming style specific to aspect-oriented programming. For this purpose, we present a collection of refactorings for aspect-oriented source code, comprising refactorings to enable extraction to aspects of crosscutting concerns from object-oriented legacy code, the subsequent tidying up of the extracted aspects and factoring out of common code from similar aspects to superaspects. The second group of refactorings is documented in detail. In addition, we propose some new aspect-oriented code smells, including one smell that is specific to aspect modules. We also propose a reinterpretation of some of the traditional object-oriented code smells in the light of aspect-orientation, to detect the presence of crosscutting concerns.

1 Introduction

Refactoring [10, 13, 31] and aspect-oriented programming (AOP) [23] are two techniques that contribute to dealing with the problems of continuous evolution of software. Refactoring processes enable the improvement of the internal structure of source code without changing a system's external behaviour, thus facilitating its evolution in line with changes in environments and requirements. AOP enables the modularisation of *crosscutting concerns* (CCCs), thus diminishing the potential impact of changes to the code related to a given concern on code not related to that concern.

AOP's steady progress from a "bleeding edge" research field to mainstream technology [33] brings forward the problem of how to deal with large number of object-oriented (OO) legacy code bases. Experience with refactoring of OO software in the latest half-decade suggests that refactoring techniques have the potential to bring the concepts and mechanisms of aspect-orientation to existing OO frameworks and applications.

1.1 Some Challenges of Refactoring Aspect-Oriented Systems

We believe there are three main hurdles that should be addressed so that refactoring techniques can be effectively used in AOP software. The first hurdle is the present

A. Rashid and M. Aksit (Eds.): Transactions on AOSD I, LNCS 3880, pp. 214–258, 2006.
© Springer-Verlag Berlin Heidelberg 2006

lack of a fully developed idea of "good" AOP style. This is an important issue, for a clear notion of style is a fundamental prerequisite for the use of refactoring. Notions of good style enable programmers to see where they are heading when refactoring their code. For instance, Fowler et al. [10] advocated a specific notion of style for OO code through a catalogue of 22 *code smells*, compounded by a catalogue of 72 refactorings through which those smells can be removed from existing code. These catalogues proved very useful in bringing the concepts of refactoring and good OO style to a wider audience and in providing programmers with guidelines on when to refactor and how best to refactor. Refactoring and notions of good style are key concepts of *extreme programming* [1], which regards a system's source code as primarily a communication mechanism between people, rather than computers.

A second hurdle – both a cause and a consequence of the first – is the present lack of an AOP equivalent of such catalogues. Our work is based on the assumption that AOP would equally benefit from AOP-specific catalogues of smells and refactorings, helping programmers to detect situations in the source code that could be improved with aspects, as well as guiding them through the transformation processes.

A third hurdle is the absence of tool support for AOP constructs and mechanisms in integrated development environments (IDEs). The catalogues presented by Fowler et al. [10] provided a basis on which developers could rely to build tool support for OO refactoring; similar catalogues for AOP are likely to bring similar benefits to tool developers. Tool developers will not be able to provide adequate support to refactoring operations unless they first have a clear idea of AOP style, and consequently of which specific refactorings are worthy of their development efforts.

1.2   On the Need for an AOP-Specific Notion of Style

The notion of style in a programming language expresses the coding practices that yield code that is easier to maintain and evolve. Whenever a programming language provides alternative ways to achieve some result, the way that causes the least problems to present and future programmers should be considered the one in the best style. Throughout the various stages of development of programming languages, many ideas of style appeared due to the advent of new, superior mechanisms. We mention three examples:

1.   Dijkstra's famous dictum that the "Go-to statement [should be] considered harmful" [7] stemmed from the availability of control structures, namely loops.
2.   Fowler et al. [10] considered the use of the "switch" statement a code smell, due to the availability of polymorphism and dynamic binding.
3.   Orleans suggested in [32] that the "if" statement be considered harmful in the context of languages using elaborate forms of predicate dispatch.

All these considerations suggest that the appropriate notion of style for a given language strongly depends on what can be achieved with that language. In this light, the suitable style of AspectJ [22, 26] cannot be the same as for Java. AspectJ enables programmers to perform compositions that are impossible with Java and to avoid negative qualities such as code scattering and code tangling. This suggests that many of traditional OO solutions resulting in those negative qualities should now be considered bad style. This includes OO implementations of many design patterns [16].

The compositional power itself of AspectJ can be cause for problems. AspectJ offers multiple ways to achieve various effects and compositions. For instance, implementation of mixins [2] can be achieved both through marker interfaces and through inner static aspects placed within interfaces. Likewise, nonsingleton aspect associations provide alternatives to solutions obtained with default singleton aspects. AspectJ programmers are sometimes faced with so many choices that it becomes hard to decide on the design most appropriate to a particular situation. There is a need to further study the consequences and implications of each solution in order to make choices clear. We believe that catalogues of code smells and refactorings [10] are an effective way to present this knowledge to programmers.

1.3 Contributions

In this paper, we expand the existing refactoring space for AOP and thus contribute to the characterisation of an AOP style. We present a collection of refactorings for AOP source code. The refactorings were developed to be performed manually, and for this reason we describe them with a style similar to that of [10]. We complement the refactorings with descriptions of AOP code smells [10], which the refactorings are supposed to remove. In addition, we review the traditional OO code smells in the light of AOP and propose a reinterpretation of a few traditional OO smells as indicators of the presence of CCCs.

The subject language we use is AspectJ [22, 26] whose backward compatibility with Java opens the way for refactoring existing Java applications by introducing AOP constructs. The task of assessing the extent to which our results can be applied to different aspect-oriented languages is left to future work.

This paper is a revised and extended version of a paper presented at AOSD 2005 [30]. The main additional contribution relative to the other paper is the detailed documentation of a group of refactorings. This paper also provides more information on how refactorings and code smells were derived and updated and revised sections on related and future work.

1.4 Issues Not Addressed

Our focus in this paper is on creating a catalogue of refactorings that can enable the development of tool support rather than on the implementation of the support. We analyze the effect of our refactorings qualitatively because our focus is on understanding the breadth of refactorings needed to transform OO code into well-styled AO code, rather than on a formal description of each refactoring, which is left as future work [3]. To further clarify the context of this paper, we next mention several related subjects that we do not cover.

No tool support. Developing tools that automate standard transformations of source code is related to the subject covered in this paper, but it is not the same. Even when provided with appropriate refactoring tools, developers still need to have a proper notion of style to decide when code should be refactored and to be able to choose the specific refactoring appropriate for each situation. It is this knowledge that we aim to expand. Nevertheless, we believe this paper can be helpful to developers of tool support for aspect-oriented refactorings by suggesting refactorings that may be worthy of their development efforts. Therefore, this paper indirectly contributes to the development of future tools.

No metrics. We do not attempt to formally measure and quantify the benefits in code of the proposed refactorings. Work on metrics for the complexity of aspect-oriented source code can be found in [12, 38, 39].

No formalism. We do not attempt to provide a formal, mathematical basis for the refactorings. Cole and Borba worked in this field, and in [3] they state their interest in extending their work to cover our refactorings.

1.5 Outline

The rest of this paper is structured as follows. In Sect. 2, we describe the approach we took to develop the collection of refactorings. In Sect. 3, we present an overview of the refactorings, which are documented in Sect. 4. In Sect. 5, we review some of the traditional smells in the light of AOP and propose three novel such smells. In Sect. 6, we present a code example illustrating the presence of some smells and results of applying the refactorings that remove those smells. In Sect. 7, we survey related work, and in Sect. 8 we consider future directions. In Sect. 9, we summarise the paper.

2 The Approach

We took the approach of performing refactoring experiments on code bases, as a vehicle for gaining the necessary insights. The selected case studies were code bases in Java and/or AspectJ with the appropriate structural characteristics. We approached Java code as bad-style or "smelly" AspectJ code, and looked for the kinds of refactorings that would be effective in removing the smells. The selected case studies were systems likely to include CCCs or code bases that promised to yield interesting insights.

The first experiment comprised the extraction of a CCC from a workflow framework to an aspect, yielding refactorings *extract feature into aspect, extract fragment into advice, move field from class to intertype, move method from class to intertype* (Table 1), as well as experience that was invaluable for the subsequent case study. Despite yielding some positive results, we do not consider the extraction we undertook to be a good example of the use of AspectJ. The extraction we undertook was really an attempt to decompose the system according to *use cases* [19] or *features* [20] (for the purposes of this paper we regard the two concepts as equivalent). The extracted aspect is a monolithic module that uses the mechanisms of AspectJ to compose its internal elements to the appropriate points of the primary system. Though the extracted aspect as a whole is crosscutting, each intertype declaration has a single target type and each pointcut captures a single joinpoint. We concluded that the feature we extracted does not comprise a good example of the sort of CCC that AspectJ can advantageously modularise. AspectJ is appropriate for cases with many duplicated fragments that can be replaced by one or a few pointcuts plus advice acting on the captured joinpoints, thus yielding significant savings in lines of code. Since the extracted CCC is an instance of Interpreter, we compared its code with the AspectJ implementation of Interpreter proposed by Hannemann and Kiczales [16]. Unlike several of the examples from the collection from [16], the implementation of Interpreter comprises a single *concrete* aspect (i.e., it does not extend a reusable abstract aspect). Hannemann and Kiczales placed a few comments at the beginning of the aspect source file, remarking in the end that Interpreter "does not lend itself nicely to aspectification". The aspect we extracted is simply a more complex instance with similar problems. For more information regarding the relevant characteristics of the framework, the extraction experiment and the results derived from it, the reader is referred to [28] and [27].

The second case study was the collection of implementations (version 1.1) in both Java and AspectJ of the 23 Gang-of-Four (GoF) design patterns [11], presented by Hannemann and Kiczales [16]. The 23 GoF patterns illustrate a variety of design and structural issues that would be hard to find in a single code base (except in very large and complex systems). The GoF patterns effectively comprise a microcosm of many possible systems. They provided us with a rich source of insights, without the need to analyse large code bases or learn domain-specific concepts. The implementations presented by Hannemann and Kiczales [16] can be counted among the currently available examples of good AOP style and design, presenting a clear picture of the desirable internal structure of aspects. Many of the findings presented in this paper stem from our study of these examples, compounded with studies of Java implementations of the same patterns by other authors [5, 8] which further enriched the patterns' potential as providers of insights.

Our approach to the GoF implementations was to pinpoint the refactorings that would be needed to transform the Java implementations into the AspectJ implementations. This comprised an iterative process, in which each Java code example was subject to multiple refactoring sessions aiming to yield the corresponding AspectJ version. The experience gained from each session was used to refine and enrich the descriptions of the code transformations being used. The descriptions of the refactorings presented in this paper emerged gradually through this process. Care was taken to only develop descriptions of generally applicable transformations, i.e., refactorings that can be applied to multiple, unrelated cases. During this process, various refactoring candidates were discarded because they turned out to be too case-specific.

In the subsequent phase, we tested and refined the refactorings thus obtained on the implementations of other, structurally similar patterns, or in different Java implementations of the same patterns [5, 8]. The code examples presented at the end of each description found in this paper originate from those test sessions, as well as the refactoring process described in detail in [29].[1] The latter also serves as a first validation effort.

---

[1] [29] is complemented with an eclipse project containing 33 complete code snapshots, available at www.di.uminho.pt/~jmf/PUBLI/papers/ObserverExample.zip.

Throughout our work on the mechanics of the refactorings, we took care to choose the safest path. As the refactorings are intended to be performed manually, it is important that each refactoring step be small, in order to ensure an easy backtracking and to maximise safety. In a few cases, this led us to decompose the refactoring under study into several smaller steps.

After the experiments were carried out and the refactoring descriptions were stable, we analysed the results in order to characterise the smells that the refactorings were supposed to remove. The novel smells presented in Sects. 5.2 – 5.4 are distillations of these ideas. In addition, we analysed existing, traditional OO smells [10, 21, 37,] to assess whether some of these smells could also be used as indicative of the presence of CCCs (see Sect. 5.1).

The refactorings described in this paper are to some extent specific to the characteristics of the languages used – Java and AspectJ. Our approach has the limitation that insights obtained to derive refactorings and code smells directly depend on the characteristics of the code bases used as case studies, and are only as good as the insights obtained from them. If a given characteristic or mechanism is not used in the subject code base, the experiments are not likely to yield insights related to that characteristic or mechanism. For instance, none of the code bases we used includes elaborate uses of exceptions. For this reason, our work did not yield any refactorings related to exceptions or exception handling. Further work on more case studies is needed to overcome these limitations. We elaborate on this subject in Sect. 8.

All refactorings presented in this paper were applied in at least one code example, with the exception of most of the simple *push down* refactorings from Table 3, which were derived for completeness. *push down advice* is used in the refactoring process described in [29].

3   Overview of the Refactorings

This section presents an overview of the refactorings. All descriptions use a format and level of detail similar to the one used by Fowler et al. [10] (Kerievsky took the same approach in [21]). The format includes (1) name, (2) typical situation, (3) recommended action, (4) motivation stating the situations when applying the refactoring is desirable, (5) a detailed mechanics section and (6) code examples. Tables 1–3 present the refactorings, mentioning the first three elements of the format. Section 4 presents complete descriptions of the refactorings from Table 2. Complete descriptions of refactorings from Tables 1–3 can also be found in [27].

The mechanics do not attempt to cover all possible situations that can potentially arise in source code. For instance, they do not account for uses of reflection. Likewise, they do not deal with the *fragile pointcut problem* [24], which is caused by the fact that almost all refactorings can potentially break existing aspects, particularly pointcuts (in [28, 29] we call it the *fragile base code problem*). We believe human programmers will be able to thoroughly deal with this problem only when provided with a new generation of tools, specifically designed to account for the presence of aspects.

Table 1. Refactorings for extraction of crosscutting concerns

Name of the refactoring	Typical situation	Recommended action
Change abstract class to interface	An abstract class prevents subclasses from inheriting from another class	Turn the abstract class into an interface and change its relationship with subclasses from inheritance to implementation
Extract feature into aspect	Code related to a feature is scattered across multiple methods and classes, tangled with unrelated code	Extract to an aspect all implementation elements related to the feature
Extract fragment into advice	Part of a method is related to a concern whose code is being moved to an aspect	Create a pointcut capturing the appropriate joinpoint and context and move the code fragment to an advice based on the pointcut
Extract inner class to stand-alone	An inner class relates to a concern being extracted into an aspect	Eliminate dependencies from the enclosing class and turn the inner class into a stand-alone class
Inline class within aspect	A small stand-alone class is used only within an aspect	Move the class to within the aspect
Inline interface within aspect	One or several interfaces are used only by an aspect	Move the interfaces to within the aspect
Move field from class to intertype	A field relates to a concern other than the primary concern of its owner class	Move the field from the class to the aspect as an intertype declaration
Move method from class to intertype	A method belongs to a concern other than the primary concern of its owner class	Move the method into the aspect that encapsulates the secondary concern as an intertype declaration
Replace implements with declare parents	Classes implement an interface related to a secondary concern. Class code implementing the interface is used only when the secondary concern is included in the system build	Replace the implements in the class with a equivalent declare parents in the aspect
Split abstract class into aspect and interface	Classes are prevented from using inheritance because they inherit from an abstract class defining several concrete members	Move all concrete members from the abstract class to an aspect. You can then turn the abstract class into an interface

Table 2. Refactorings for restructuring the internals of aspects

Name of the refactoring	Typical situation	Recommended action
Extend marker interface with signature	An inner interface models a role used within the aspect. You would like the aspect to call a method specific to a type that implements the interface but that is not declared by it	Add an intertype abstract declaration of the case-specific method signature to the interface
Generalise target type with marker interface	An aspect refers to case-specific concrete types, preventing it from being reusable	Replace the references to specific types with a marker interface and make the specific types implement the marker interface
Introduce aspect protection	You would like an intertype member to be visible within the declaring aspect and all its subaspects, but not outside the aspect inheritance chain	Declare the intertype member as public and place a declare error preventing its use outside the aspect inheritance chain
Replace intertype field with aspect map	An aspect statically introduces additional state to a set of classes, when a more dynamic or flexible link between state and targets would be desirable.	Replace the intertype declarations with a structure owned by the aspect that performs a map between the target objects and the additional state
Replace intertype method with aspect method	An aspect introduces additional methods to a class or interface, when a more dynamic and flexible composition would be desirable	Replace the intertype method with an aspect method that gets the target object as an extra parameter
Tidy up internal aspect structure	The internal structure of an aspect resulting from the extraction of a crosscutting concern is sub-optimal	Tidy up the internal structure of the aspect by removing duplicated intertype declarations and dependencies on case-specific target types

However, we also believe it is possible to keep this problem under control, provided adequate practices are followed, including programming AspectJ's constructs with a prudent and appropriate style, such as that proposed by Laddad [25]. This is particularly important with pointcuts, which should be made in a style stressing intent rather than a specific case (e.g., expressions using wildcards). This way, pointcuts can express a general policy and may be robust enough to not be affected by minor modifications in the target code, such as the removal or addition of a new class or method. Another good practice is to place the aspects close to the code they affect whenever

Table 3. Refactorings to deal with generalisation

Name of the refactoring	Typical situation	Recommended action
Extract superaspect	Two or more aspects contain similar code and functionality	Move the common features to a superaspect
Pull up advice	All subaspects use the same advice acting on a pointcut declared in the superaspect	Move the advice to the superaspect
Pull up declare parents	All subaspects use the same declare parents	Move the declare parents to the superaspect
Pull up intertype declaration	An intertype declaration would be best placed in the superaspect	Move the intertype declaration to the superaspect
Pull up marker interface	All subaspects use a marker interface to model the same role	Move the marker interfaces to the superaspect
Pull up pointcut	All subaspects declare identical pointcuts	Move the pointcuts to the superaspect
Push down advice	A piece of advice is used by only some subaspects, or each subaspect requires different advice code	Move the advice to the subaspects that use it
Push down declare parents	A declare parents in a superaspect is not relevant for all subaspects	Move the declare parents to the subaspects where it is relevant
Push down intertype declaration	An intertype declaration would be best placed in a subaspect	Move the intertype declaration to the subaspect where it is relevant
Push down marker interface	A marker interface declared within a superaspect models a role used only in some subaspects	Move the marker interface to those subaspects
Push down pointcut	A pointcut in the superaspect is not used by some subaspects	Move the pointcut to the subaspects that use the pointcut

possible, to increase the likelihood that all team members be aware of the aspects potentially affected by refactorings. This often entails placing the aspect in the same package, or even within the same source file as the target class (as inner or peer aspects).

All refactorings from Tables 1–3 assume AspectJ as the subject language. However, the refactorings from Table 1 are a special case in that the starting points of all refactorings from that group are in plain Java. This is not a specifically intended restriction, it just follows that all refactorings deal with extractions of the various elements of a CCC. CCCs are expected to reside in plain Java bases but not in AspectJ code, and therefore the existence of aspects in the code base is not taken into account in the mechanics. Actually, the code bases targeted by the refactorings from Table 1 can include aspects (namely a Java base that is undergoing the extraction of multiple aspects). However, we assume that already existing aspects do not interfere with the constructs manipulated during the extraction process.

The traditional OO refactorings can be used in AspectJ code as well. We did not detect any refactoring from [10] targeting an OO construct that could not be applied to the same construct within aspects. For instance, in the mechanics of *Extend Marker Interface with Signature* we prescribe the use of *Extract Method* ([10], p. 110) inside aspects.

3.1 Grouping the Refactorings

The collection is structured in groups of refactorings with similar purposes, as is done in [10]. The adopted grouping also reflects a strategy likely to be followed in many refactoring processes. This establishes that prior to anything else, all elements related to a CCC should be moved to a single module (following *extract feature into aspect*[2]). Only afterwards should we start improving the underlying structure of the resulting aspects (following *tidy up internal aspect structure*), because such tasks are considerably easier to perform after the associated implementation is modularised. In case duplication is detected among different but related aspects, we extract the commonalities to a (possibly reusable) superaspect (using *extract superaspect*). This strategy leads to the following grouping: (1) extraction of CCCs, (2) improvement of the internal structure of an aspect and (3) generalisation of aspects. The sequence of code transformations described in [29] also fits naturally with this grouping.

The three refactorings mentioned above are composite refactorings that provide the entry points to someone approaching the catalogue. Rather than prescribe specific actions on the source code, as is the case of those documented in [10], they provide a framework for the other refactorings from the same group, specifying the situations when they should be used and when they should not. They are also useful in providing a broader view of a refactoring process.

3.2 Refactorings for Extracting Features to Aspects

We expect the refactorings from this group (Table 1) to comprise the starting point for the majority of refactoring processes targeting OO legacy code. *Extract feature into aspect* pinpoints procedures for extracting scattered elements of a CCC into a single module [28]. We suggest using *move field from class to intertype* to move state to the aspect. Behaviour can be moved using *move method from class to intertype* and *extract fragment into advice*. Moving an inner class to an aspect is done in two stages: first using *extract inner class to stand-alone*, to obtain a stand-alone class from the inner class, and next using *inline class within aspect* to turn the resulting class into an

---

[2] In the context of these refactorings, we use the term "feature" to mean a CCC of the kind that can be effectively modularised by an AOP language such as AspectJ.

inner class within the aspect. We did not see a justification for defining a refactoring equivalent to *extract inner class to stand-alone* for interfaces, as interfaces are not generally used within classes. Interfaces are inlined into aspects using *inline interface within aspect*, after which they can be turned into marker interfaces. To complete the modularisation of the code related to the interface, we propose *replace implements with declare parents* for inlining the "implements" clause of implementing classes.

Split abstract class into aspect and interface enables the extraction of definitions from an abstract class to an aspect, opening the way to using *change abstract class to interface* to turn the abstract class into an interface. This way, subclasses of the abstract class become free to inherit from some other class. Together, the pair effectively extracts a mixin [2] from the original abstract class. The pair was derived from the analysis on the group of the GoF patterns that Hannemann and Kiczales related to multiple inheritance (Sect. 4.2.4 of [16]) and can be used to transform the Java implementations of those patterns into the corresponding AspectJ implementations.

3.3 Restructuring the Internals of Aspects

The refactorings from this group (Table 2) deal with the task of improving the internal structure of an aspect after all elements from a CCC were moved into it, using the refactorings presented in Sect. 3.2 (Table 1). *Tidy up internal aspect structure* provides the general framework for improving the internal structure of extracted aspects. The mechanics prescribe at the start the use of *generalise target type with marker interface*, which entails replacing references to case-specific types with marker interfaces representing the roles played by the participants. *Generalise target type with marker interface* removes the duplication caused by multiple intertype declarations of the same member. In straightforward cases, it is enough to attain (un)pluggability.

When using *generalise target type with marker interface* we may sometimes find that a single call to a case-specific method prevents a code fragment from being reusable. For such cases, *extend marker interface with signature* separates the generically applicable code from case-specific code, by extending marker interface with the method's signature.

Replace intertype field with aspect map and *replace intertype method with aspect method* prescribe how to replace intertype state and behaviour with a mapping structure providing the same functionality in a more dynamic way, and amenable to being controlled by client objects. These two refactorings can also deal with hurdles that arise when we try to move duplicated intertype declarations along aspect hierarchies (Sect. 3.4).

The motivation for *introduce aspect protection* stems from the impossibility of using the protected access in intertype members. This refactoring prescribes how to preserve this access through declare error clauses.

Split abstract class into aspect and interface and *change abstract class to interface* deal with the extraction of inner classes to aspects. The former removes dependencies of the inner class on the enclosing class and turns into a stand-alone class. The latter inlines the class within the aspect.

3.4 Dealing with Generalisation

The refactorings from this group (Table 3) deal with the extraction of common code to superaspects, with *extract superaspect* providing the general framework. All the remaining refactorings in this group deal with moving members up and down the inheritance hierarchies of aspects. New refactorings for moving traditional OO members such as fields and methods were not created, as the issues and mechanics are similar to those documented in [10]. In [29] we show how the reusable aspect presented in [16] can be extracted from similar aspects.

Pull up intertype declaration and *push down intertype declaration* have a very restricted scope of applicability, only to simple cases not involving duplication. They are almost antirefactorings – one motivation for including them in the collection is to better document some issues and warn against attempts to treat intertype declarations as if they were like other members. The hurdles arise because duplicated intertype declarations of fields cannot generally be moved between superaspects and subaspects: such movements change the number of instances of intertype fields and their relation to aspect instances. It is important to keep in mind that (1) the visibility scopes of multiple intertype declarations of the same member cannot overlap and that (2) target objects (i.e., instances of classes affected by the intertype declaration) have one separate instance of the intertype member for *each* subaspect. If duplicated intertype declarations are factored out to a single declaration in a superaspect, target objects will have just *one* instance of the introduced member. In most cases, dealing with duplicated intertype declarations entails the prior replacement of the introduced fields with some mapping logic that maintains the association between target objects and the additional state and behaviour (using *replace intertype field with aspect map* and *replace intertype method with aspect method*).

The remaining refactorings from this group deal with pulling up and pushing down aspect-specific constructs, including pointcuts, advice and declare parents clauses. Inner interfaces are also covered due to their widespread use as marker interfaces.

3.5 Refactorings for Plain Java

Two pairs of refactorings presented in the previous sections were initially conceived as single refactorings but were later split into the present pairs because this way seemed to have a more appropriate granularity:

- *extract inner class to stand-alone* and *inline interface within aspect* (Sect. 3.2)
- *split abstract class into aspect and interface* and *change abstract class to interface* (Sect. 3.3)

In both cases, one of the resulting refactorings deals only with plain Java constructs: *extract inner class to stand-alone* and *change abstract class to interface*, though this was not specifically intended. We believe the motivation for these particular plain Java refactorings arises only or mostly in the context of aspects. For these reasons they are included in their respective groups.

4   Refactorings for Tidying Up Extracted Aspects

This section documents the refactorings from Table 2. Complete descriptions of all refactorings from Tables 1–3 can be found in [27].

4.1   Extend Marker Interface with Signature

Typical situation. An inner interface models a role used within the aspect. You would like the aspect to call a method specific to a type that implements the interface but that is not declared by it.

Recommended action. Add an intertype abstract declaration of the case-specific method signature to the interface.

Motivation. Sometimes you would like to temporarily resolve a dependence on a case-specific part because that would enable you to do some tidying up of the aspect's internals, after which you would be in a better position to deal with the dependence. *Extend marker interface with signature* can be used as a stopgap in such situations to temporarily resolve dependences to a type-specific method. One case in which this situation arises often is during the use of *generalise target type with marker interface.*

   An alternative solution to these problems would be to resort to downcasts. However, downcasts create dependencies to the target type of the cast: the specific type will need to be included in the aspect's "import" section, the type's binary file will have to be available when performing a build, etc. *Extend marker interface with signature* can be preferable in some situations because it avoids such dependencies. The dependence it creates is restricted to a method signature only, not to specific types. For these reasons, this refactoring is worth using in simple cases.

Preconditions. The signature must be public in order to be acceptable to the compiler. In addition, this solution is feasible only if all the types made to implement the marker interface export the signature.

Mechanics.

- If the method is not public, change it to public.
- Create in the aspect an intertype abstract declaration of the method's signature targeting the marker interface that will be used in place of the specific type.
- Compile and test.

Example. The ExampleAspect aspect uses the Role marker interface. Some instructions using Role resort to a downcast to specific type SpecificType, to resolve the call to the doSomething method, which is specific to this type. By using *extend marker interface with signature,* we eliminate this dependence to SpecificType. Provided this is the only use of SpecificType within ExampleAspect, the import clause itself can be removed, as shown below.

```
import ...SpecificType;

public aspect ExampleAspect {
    private interface Role { }
    ... action(Role obj) {
        //...
        ((SpecificType)obj).doSomething()
```

⬇

```
import ...SpecificType;

public aspect ExampleAspect {
    private interface Role { }
    public abstract void Role.doSomething();
    //...
    obj.doSomething()
```

4.2 Generalise Target Type with Marker Interface

Typical situation. An aspect refers to case-specific concrete types, preventing it from being reusable.

Recommended action. Replace the references to specific types with a marker interface and make the specific types implement the marker interface.

Motivation. This refactoring contributes to reduce the coupling between an aspect and its target code bases. It can also be used to expose and eliminate much duplication that could not be eliminated if the code kept referring to specific types. It can also be useful when we want to apply *extract superaspect* to aspects providing similar functionality, because it contributes to rationalise its internal structures.

Several situations can prevent *extract superaspect* from being applied to a set of similar aspects. The aspects can contain code specific to concrete classes in the midst of generally applicable code. If a general marker interface could be used instead of the specific types, use *generalise target type with marker interface*. The resulting marker interfaces may be candidates for pulling up to a superaspect.

Mechanics.

- Create a marker interface representing the role played by the target classes. Create the "declare parents" to associate the concrete classes to the role.
- Replace the references to the class with references to the marker interface. In cases when the aspect introduces the same field or method to more than one class, remove the duplication by replacing the various introductions with a single introduction to the interface.
- Sometimes the replacement cannot be made in method bodies because parts of the code depend on elements specific to a concrete class. In such cases, consider using *extract method* ([10], p. 110) to separate the parts covered by the role interface from the parts specific to particular classes. This may be an indication that in the future the aspect should be split into a generally applicable abstract superaspect and one or several specific concrete subaspects, using *extract superaspect*.

- Compile and test.
- When all method introductions refer to the interface, it is possible to remove the declarations of operations (methods) within the interface (if the interface is a inner interface, nested within the aspect, the related operations are defined within the aspect anyway, so removing the declarations from the interface will result in simpler code). If, however, the interface is kept stand-alone, leave the declarations in place. This way the code will be easier to understand.

Example: Simple Replacements. In the following example, GUIColleague is an interface representing a role. The aspect Mediator assigns the GUIColleague role to the Button class, but some parts of the code still specifically refer to Button instead of GUIColleague. We want to make all code to depend only on the interface (see below).

```
public aspect Mediator {
    declare parents: Button implements GUIColleague;
    declare parents: Label implements GUIMediator;
    GUIMediator Button._mediator;
    public void Button.setMediator(GUIMediator mediator) {
        this._mediator = mediator;
    }
    pointcut buttonClicked(Button button):
        execution(public void clicked()) && this(button);
    after(Button button): buttonClicked(button) {
        button._mediator.colleagueChanged(button);
    }
    //...
}
```

⬇

```
public aspect Mediator {
    declare parents: Button implements GUIColleague;
    declare parents: Label implements GUIMediator;
    GUIMediator GUIColleague._mediator;
    public void GUIColleague.setMediator(GUIMediator mediator) {
        this._mediator = mediator;
    }
    pointcut buttonClicked(GUIColleague button):
        execution(public void clicked()) && this(button);
    after(GUIColleague button): buttonClicked(button) {
        button._mediator.colleagueChanged(button);
    }
    //...
}
```

Naturally, the names of some variables (such as button) should now be renamed to reflect their more general context.

Example: Eliminating Duplication. This example is based on the Observer pattern ([11], p. 293). The ObservingOpen aspect encapsulates an observing relationship that was extracted from the participant classes. ObservingOpen introduces some fields and methods into several classes playing the Observer role (in this case Bee and Hummingbird). The classes are the only differing things among the introductions. By applying *generalise target type with marker interface*, we create the Subject marker interface and remove the duplication.

```
public aspect ObservingOpen ... {
   //...
   private OpenObserver Hummingbird.openObsrv =
     new OpenObserver(this);
   private OpenObserver Bee.openObsrv = new OpenObserver(this);

   public java.util.Observer Bee.openObserver() {
     return openObsrv;
   }
   public java.util.Observer Hummingbird.openObserver() {
     return openObsrv;
   }
}
```

↓

```
public aspect ObservingOpen ... {
   //...
   private interface Subject { }
   declare parents: (Bee || Hummingbird) implements Subject;
   private OpenObserver Subject.openObsrv = new OpenOb-
server(this);

   public java.util.Observer Subject.openObserver() {
     return openObsrv;
   }
}
```

4.3 Introduce Aspect Protection

Typical situation. You would like an intertype member to be visible in an aspect and all its subaspects, but not outside the aspect inheritance chain.

Recommended action. Declare the intertype member as public and place a "declare error" preventing its use outside the aspect inheritance chain.

Motivation. AspectJ does not allow the protected access on intertype members, so whenever we would like to extend its access to subaspects we must classify the member as public. In some cases, it is desirable to have some form of access protection preventing the use of the member outside aspect code. The "declare error" mechanism enables us to emulate that protection.

Mechanics.

- Add a "declare warning" in the aspect enclosing the intertype member, specifying the intended restriction on its use.
- Compile and test.
- For each warning generated by the compiler, perform the refactorings necessary to move the use of the member to the authorised modules of the system.
- When there are no more warnings, change the "declare warning" to "declare error".

Example: Protecting an Intertype Field. Consider an abstract superaspect General-Policy declaring intertype the field _sensitiveData. We want to restrict use of the field to aspect and its subaspects.

```
abstract aspect GeneralPolicy {
   protected interface Participant {}
   public Data Participant._sensitiveData;
   //...
}
```

```
aspect ConcretePolicy extends GeneralPolicy {
   //code using Participant._sensitiveData
}
```

We can add in the superaspect the following "declare warning":

```
abstract aspect GeneralPolicy {
   protected interface Participant {}
   public Data Participant._sensitiveData;
   declare warning:
     (set(public Data Participant+._sensitiveData) ||
     get(public Data Participant+._sensitiveData))
     && !within(GeneralPolicy+):
     "field _sensitiveData is aspect protected. Not visible
here.";
   //...
}
```

Next, we deal with all points in the system, giving rise to warnings. After all warnings are gone, we change the "declare warning" to "declare error".

Example: Protecting an Intertype Method. Suppose the same abstract aspect as in the previous example also includes method processSensitiveData, which we also would like to protect:

```
abstract aspect GeneralPolicy {
   protected interface Participant {}
   public Data Participant._sensitiveData;
   public void processSensitiveData() {
      //code using Participant._sensitiveData
   }
   //...
}
```

We create the following "declare warning":

```
abstract aspect GeneralPolicy {
   protected interface Participant {}
   public Data Participant._sensitiveData;
   public void processSensitiveData() {
      //code using caspule._sensitiveData
   }
   declare warning:
     call(void processSensitiveData())
     && !within(GeneralPolicy+):
     "method processSensitiveData is aspect protected. Not visible
here.";
   //...
}
```

Likewise, the "declare warning" should be changed to "declare error" when all the warnings are gone.

Example: Protecting Intertype Method from Access Outside Inheritance Class and Aspect Inheritance Chains. What if we want to allow the access to a member in the host class, in addition to the aspect and their descendents? In the above example all that is needed is one more within to the above "declare error":

```
declare error:
   call(void processSensitiveData())
   && !within(Participant+)
   && !within(GeneralPolicy+):
   "Call to processSensitiveData() outside Participant and General
Policy chains.";
```

4.4 Replace Intertype Field with Aspect Map

Typical situation. An aspect statically introduces additional state to a set of classes, when a more dynamic or flexible link between state and targets would be desirable.

Recommended action. Replace the intertype declarations with a structure owned by the aspect that performs a map between the target objects and the additional state.

Motivation. An intertype declaration is a static mechanism. It affects all instances of the target class, throughout their entire life cycles. For some problems, this is exactly right, but for others something more flexible would be preferable. In some cases only a subset of all instances of a class needs the extra state and behaviour, or they need it only in a specific phase of their life cycles. Sometimes the same instance simultaneously needs multiple instances of the extra state and behaviour. Sometimes the application only knows at run time which instances need the extra state and behaviour. Intertype declarations do not provide the necessary flexibility in these cases.

An intertype declaration is itself a kind of mapping, usually from a class to a field or method. However, we cannot control the moments when it applies, when it ceases to apply, and the precise set of objects to which it applies. Whenever this kind of flexibility is required and the existing solution relies on introductions, use *replace intertype field with aspect map* to replace the introductions with a suitable mapping.

This refactoring is also useful in a different situation. Sometimes we have several aspects performing similar actions on similar data, and these include intertype declarations. Such duplication should be removed by pulling the common parts to a superaspect. Here arises another problem. Target objects have separate instances of the additional state for each subaspect, but if the code is pulled up to the superaspect, there will be a single instance of the introduced state common to all subaspects. A similar problem would arise if we tried to replace an instance field with a static field. Such pulls will almost certainly not be behaviour-preserving. In most cases, an intertype declaration cannot be pulled up to a superaspect as is. The pulls usually require the prior replacement of intertype state with aspect state.

As it happens, the kind of replacements that solve the first problem can solve the second problem as well. Unlike with intertype declarations, there is a separate instance of the state declared in the superaspect in each active subaspect. In most cases, solving the problem merely entails selecting a suitable structure to replace the intertype fields, and update the associated logic accordingly.

To ease the replacement of the original intertype state with the new mapping structure, you should first isolate it behind a small layer within the aspect, to protect the rest of the aspect code from being exposed to it. In the simplest case, all that has to be done is to ensure that the aspect is provided with accessor methods encapsulating the intertype fields. Only those methods will need to be changed when the structure is replaced. In the case of preparing intertype declarations to be pulled up, *replace intertype field with aspect map* must be applied to each of subaspects in turn. Next, use *pull up field* ([10], p. 320) and *pull up method* ([10], p. 322) to pull the state and its associated logic to the common superaspect.

Preconditions. Ensure that the fields in the various aspects do indeed provide equivalent interfaces and functionality.

Mechanics.

- Use *encapsulate field* ([10], p. 206) on the introduced field. Unlike traditional accessor methods, create aspect methods, receiving the target object as argument.
- Add to the aspect a mapping structure capable of supporting the equivalent mapping functionality. Add accessors similar to the ones created in the previous step, retrieving the introduced fields from the mapping structure. Ideally, these map-based accessors should have the same signatures and names as those created in the previous step. Add any additional management methods (i.e., for insertion, removal, etc.) that may also be required.
- If the aspect has intertype methods using the intertype field, use *replace intertype method with aspect method* to create aspect versions of those methods, based on the new mapping structure.
- Compile and test.
- Replace each call to the accessors created in the first step with the map-based accessors. Compile and test when all replacements are done.
- Remove the accessor methods created in the first step. Compile and test.
- Remove the intertype field and related code. Compile and test.

Example: Replacing an Intertype Field with an Aspect Map. The following example presents fragments of an aspect implementing an instance of the Mediator pattern ([11], p. 273), adapted from a Java implementation by Cooper [5]. In this example, there is a mediator object (of type Mediator) acting as the hub of communication between various colleagues. The colleagues are instances of ClearButton and Move Button, both subclasses of javax.swing.JButton, and KidList, which is a subclass of javax.swing.JScrollPane, implementing a listener interface from the javax.swing.event API. This example declares the Colleague role as a marker interface and assigns it to the three colleague participant types. The aspect indirectly introduces in each colleague a reference to the mediator, by way of the marker interface.

This implementation is unsuitable because it introduces the additional state and behaviour to all instances of the participant classes, independently of whether all of them need it or not. By replacing this implementation with one based on a map, we eliminate this inflexibility.

```
public aspect Mediating ...
    private interface Colleague {}
    private Mediator Colleague.mediator;

    declare parents:
      (ClearButton || MoveButton || KidList) implements Colleague;

    pointcut clearButtonExecute(ClearButton clearButton): ...
    after(ClearButton clearButton):clearButtonExecute(clearButton){
      clearButton.mediator.clear();
    }

    pointcut moveButtonExecute(MoveButton moveButton): ...
    after(MoveButton moveButton): moveButtonExecute(moveButton) {
      moveButton.mediator.move();
    }

    pointcut kidListChanged(KidList kidList): ...
    after(KidList kidList) returning: kidListChanged(kidList) {
      kidList.mediator.select();
    }
```

As a first step, we perform a refactoring similar to *encapsulate field* ([10], p. 206) to produce a temporary getter method for the intertype field. The same getter can be used in all different target types. It cannot be given exactly the same name as the map-based getter, so we add a zero to avoid compiler errors.

```
public aspect Mediating ...
    private Mediator getMediator0(Colleague colleague) {
      return colleague.mediator;
    }
    pointcut ...
    after(ClearButton clearButton):clearButtonExecute(clearButton) {
      getMediator0(clearButton).clear();
    }
    pointcut ...
    after(MoveButton moveButton): moveButtonExecute(moveButton) {
      getMediator0(moveButton).move();
    }
    pointcut ...
    after(KidList kidList) returning: kidListChanged(kidList) {
      getMediator0(kidList).select();
    }
```

Now that all accesses to the intertype field are done through this temporary getter, the intertype nature of the mediator field is effectively encapsulated. Next, we add a suitable data structure to map the target objects to the mediator field. A hash table is a good choice for these cases. The introduced field was private to the aspect, so the getters are private as well. The access mode of the map-based setter can be more problematic. Note that the map-based setter is responsible for associating the target object with the mediator field, using the newly added mapping structure. It does not have a correspondent statement in the original version of the code, but we must find an appropriate point of the program to place it. The access mode of the map-based setter depends on where the field is used in the system: private if it is used only within the aspect, nonprivate otherwise. In this example, we assume a public access.

```
import java.util.WeakHashMap;

public aspect Mediating ...
  WeakHashMap colleague2mediatorMap = new WeakHashMap();

  private Mediator getMediator(Colleague colleague) {
      return (Mediator)colleague2mediatorMap.get(colleague);
  }
  public void setMediator(Colleague colleague, Mediator mediator) {
      colleague2mediatorMap.put(colleague, mediator);
  }
  private Mediator getMediator0(Colleague colleague) {
      return colleague.mediator;
  }
```

We must now decide on the places where to put the calls to the map-based setters. The places where the objects containing the field are created could be used as a basis, though in some cases it may be preferable to place the calls elsewhere. After all, that is precisely one of the advantages of replacing a static mapping with a dynamic one: we have more choices. Outside the aspect, the calls to the final setter should be something like this:

```
Mediating.aspectOf().setMediator(clearButton, mediator);
```

Inside advice within the aspect, the same call can be expressed in a simpler way:

```
setMediator(clearButton, mediator);
```

We insert the calls to the map-based getter and make the calls to the temporary getter refer to the map-based getter. After compiling and testing again, we can delete the original declaration and the temporary getter. Now the aspect's code looks like this:

```
public aspect Mediating ...
  private Mediator Colleague.mediator;
  declare parents: (ClearButton || MoveButton || KidList)
      implements Colleague;

  WeakHashMap colleague2mediatorMap = new WeakHashMap();

  private Mediator getMediator(Colleague colleague) {
      return (Mediator)colleague2mediatorMap.get(colleague);
  }
  public void setMediator(Colleague colleague, Mediator mediator) {
      colleague2mediatorMap.put(colleague, mediator);
  }

  private Mediator getMediator0(Colleague colleague) {
      return colleague.mediator;
```

```
 ┐
    pointcut clearButtonExecute(ClearButton clearButton): ...
    after(ClearButton clearButton): clearButtonExecute(clearButton) {
       getMediator(clearButton).clear();
    }
    pointcut moveButtonExecute(MoveButton moveButton): ...
    after(MoveButton moveButton): moveButtonExecute(moveButton) {
       getMediator(moveButton).move();
    }
    pointcut kidListChanged(KidList kidList): ...
    after(KidList kidList) returning: kidListChanged(kidList) {
       getMediator(kidList).select();
    }
```

Example: Making an Implementation of Observer Amenable for the Extraction of a Superaspect. This second example is an implementation of Observer ([11], p. 293). This implementation was extracted into an aspect from the example by Cooper [5], using *extract feature into aspect*. This example is a bit more complex than the previous one, because it includes intertype methods that use the intertype field. These intertype methods must be replaced using *replace intertype method with aspect method*. We assume the scenario in which the system has other, similar implementations of the pattern and we would like to factor out the common elements by pulling them up to a superaspect. These implementations rely on the introduction of a java.util.Vector field to the subject participant, which is among the elements we would like to pull up, along with its associated logic.

The present implementation does not lend itself to be pulled up to the superaspect, for the same reasons as in the previous example: It was designed assuming there would be only one instance of the pattern for each subject. That is, the vector cannot support multiple observing relationships for the same object. To solve this problem, we will replace the intertype vector with a more suitable hash table owned by the aspect, which will manage the mappings between subjects and the list (i.e., a java.util.Vector object) of its observers. We will use *replace intertype method with aspect method* to replace the original logic using the vector with aspect logic using the hash table.

Cooper's example includes a Watch2LSubject object as subject and two types of observers, which are instances of ListFrameObserver and ColorFrameObserver (both subclasses of javax.swing.JFrame). The Watch2LSubject object includes three radio buttons, one for each of the colours red, green and blue. Whenever a different radio button is selected, the ColorFrameObserver instances change their background colour accordingly, and the ListFrameObserver adds the name of the selected colour to its list.

The refactored aspect uses two inner interfaces (they were inlined to within the Observing aspect during the refactoring process) to represent the roles of subject and observer. It introduces the java.util.Vector field to the objects playing the role of subject, which holds the subject's registered observers. The aspect also introduces two methods to the subjects: addObserver(Observer), which is used to register a new observer for the subject, and notifyObservers(JRadioButton), through which subjects notify all their registered observers of a change in the selected colour. That notification is carried out through the sendNotify method, which is declared in the Observer inner interface. The sendNotify method receives a string representing the new colour as parameter. The aspect also introduces the implementation of sendNotify for each concrete observer type.

```
public aspect Observing ...
    private interface Subject {}
    interface Observer {
        /** notify the Observers that a change has taken place */
        public void sendNotify(String s);
    }
    declare parents: Watch2LSubject implements Subject;
    declare parents: (ListFrameObserver || ColorFrameObserver)
        implements Observer;

    private Vector Subject._observingFramesList = new Vector();

    public void Subject.addObserver(Observer obs) {
        //   adds observer to list in Vector
        _observingFramesList.addElement(obs);
    }
    /* sends text of selected button to all observers */
    private void Subject.notifyObservers(JRadioButton rad) {
        String sColor = rad.getText();
        for (int i = 0; i < _observingFramesList.size(); i++ ) {
            ((Observer) (_observingFramesList.elementAt(i))).
                sendNotify(sColor);
        }
    }

    public void ListFrameObserver.sendNotify(String s) {
        _listData.addElement(s);
    }
    public void ColorFrameObserver.sendNotify(String str) {
        changeColor(str);
    }
```

The aspect also includes a pointcut and corresponding advice to trigger the adequate behaviour when the subject changes the selected colour:

```
pointcut watchStateChange(Watch2LSubject watch,ItemEvent event) :...
after(Watch2LSubject watch, ItemEvent event):
        watchStateChange(watch, event) {
    if(event.getStateChange() == ItemEvent.SELECTED)
        watch.notifyObservers((JRadioButton) event.getSource());
}
```

The mechanics prescribe the use of *Encapsulate Field* ([10], p. 206) on the existing field. In this particular case, we must instead create a new field as the mapping structure (we will create the accessor methods for the structure as soon as there is a need to do so).

```
import java.util.WeakHashMap;
...
public aspect Observing ...
    //...
    WeakHashMap _subject2Observers = new WeakHashMap();
```

Next, we use *replace intertype method with aspect method* to replace the addObserver and notifyObservers intertype methods with aspect versions using the new mapping structure. See the example section of *replace intertype method with aspect method* (Sect. 4.5) for more details of this step.

The new implementation is now in place and working. There was no need to add accessors to the mapping structure, as it is already encapsulated by addObserver and notifyObservers. These two aspect methods comprise a small layer hiding the structure. We can now delete the old implementation, after which the aspect looks like this:

```
public aspect Observing ...
   private interface Subject {}
   interface Observer {
     /** notify the Observers that a change has taken place */
     public void sendNotify(String s);
   }
   declare parents: Watch2LSubject implements Subject;
   declare parents: (ListFrameObserver || ColorFrameObserver)
     implements Observer;

   private Vector Subject._observingFramesList = new Vector();

   public void Subject.addObserver(Observer obs) {
     //   adds observer to list in Vector
     _observingFramesList.addElement(obs);
   }
   /* sends text of selected button to all observers */
   private void Subject.notifyObservers(JRadioButton rad) {
     String sColor = rad.getText();
     for (int i = 0; i < _observingFramesList.size(); i++ ) {
       ((Observer) (_observingFramesList.elementAt(i))).
         sendNotify(sColor);
     }
   }

   WeakHashMap _subject2Observers = new WeakHashMap();

   public void addObserver(Subject subject, Observer observer) {
     Vector observers;
     Object obj = _subject2Observers.get(subject);
     if(obj == null)
       observers = new Vector();
     else observers = (Vector) obj;
     observers.add(observer);
     _subject2Observers.put(subject, observers);
   }
   public void
   notifyObservers(Subject subject, JRadioButton radioButton) {
     String sColor = radioButton.getText();
     Vector observersList =
       (Vector)_subject2Observers.get(subject);
     for (int i = 0; i < observersList.size(); i++ ) {
       ((Observer) (observesList.elementAt(i))).
         sendNotify(sColor);
     }
   }
```

```
    public void ListFrameObserver.sendNotify(String s) {
        _listData.addElement(s);
    }
    /* Observer is notified of change here */
    public void ColorFrameObserver.sendNotify(String str) {
        changeColor(str);
    }

    pointcut watchStateChange(Watch2LSubject watch,ItemEvent event):
        ...
    after(Watch2LSubject watch, ItemEvent event):
        watchStateChange(watch, event) {
        if(event.getStateChange() == ItemEvent.SELECTED)
        notifyObservers(watch, (JRadioButton) event.getSource());
    }
}
```

4.5 Replace Intertype Method with Aspect Method

Typical situation. An aspect introduces additional methods to a class or interface, when a more dynamic and flexible composition would be desirable.

Recommended action. Replace the intertype method with an aspect method that gets the target object as an extra parameter.

Motivation. This refactoring was designed to be a follow-up to *replace intertype field with aspect map*. That refactoring deals with intertype fields and the present refactoring deals with the (intertype) methods that use those fields.

The present refactoring is made possible by the fact that a method introduced to a class can always be replaced by a similar aspect method receiving an instance of the target class as an additional argument, which will use the target object as a key.

```
public class Capsule {
    private int _value;
    public Capsule(int value) {
        _value = value;
    }
public aspect Additional {
    public void Capsule.doSomethingMore() {
        System.out.println("Doing something more with " + this);
    }
        Capsule capsule = new Capsule(7);
        capsule.doSomethingMore();
```

⬇

```
public class Capsule {
    private int _value;
    public Capsule(int value) {
        _value = value;
    }
public aspect Additional {
    public void doSomethingMore(Capsule capsule) {
        System.out.println("Doing something more with " + capsule);
    }
        Capsule capsule = new Capsule(7);
        Additional.aspectOf().doSomethingMore(capsule);
```

Replacements of this kind should not be made in the general case, and that is why we prescribe using this refactoring only in the context of *replace intertype field with aspect map*. This refactoring is equally useful to deal with both situations covered by the other refactoring: (1) replacing intertype declarations with a dynamic mechanism and (2) preparing intertype state duplicated in various aspects to be factored out to a common superaspect. This refactoring transforms existing intertype methods into aspect methods based on the map that was created when applying *replace intertype field with aspect map*.

Mechanics.

- Create in the aspect a copy of the intertype method, with the same name and signature. Insert, in the beginning of the aspect method's parameter list, an additional parameter whose type is the original target of the intertype declaration.
- Replace each reference to "this" with the new parameter. Change all self-calls and references to fields to refer to the new first parameter.
- Compile and test.
- Change the body of the intertype method so that it calls the aspect method, if there are no further dependences preventing you.
- Add a "declare warning" exposing all calls to the intertype method:

```
declare warning:
   (call(<type> <host class>.someMethod(<arguments>))):
   "method <host class>.someMethod() is called here.";
```

- Following the warnings, replace each call to the intertype method with a call to the aspect method. Compile and test after each change.
- When there are no more warnings, delete the "declare warning" and the intertype method (when covering the mechanics of several refactorings from [10], Fowler considers the situation when the existing method is part of the interface and cannot be changed; Fowler recommends that in such cases the old method be left in place and marked as deprecated).
- Compile and test.

Example. This example is part of the second example for *replace intertype field with aspect map*. In it, an aspect introduces the following methods to the Subject marker interface:

```
public void Subject.addObserver(Observer obs) {
   _observingFramesList.addElement(obs);
}
private void Subject.notifyObservers(JRadioButton rad) {
   String sColor = rad.getText();
   for (int i = 0; i < _observingFramesList.size(); i++ ) {
      ((Observer) (_observingFramesList.elementAt(i))).
         sendNotify(sColor);
   }
}
```

As an example of client code, the following subject and observers are created and registered, through calls to the Subject.addObserver method:

```
Watch2LSubject subject = new Watch2LSubject();
//Observing.aspectOf().setSubject(subject);

ColorFrameObserver cframeObs1 = new ColorFrameObserver();
ColorFrameObserver cframeObs2 = new ColorFrameObserver();
ColorFrameObserver cframeObs3 = new ColorFrameObserver();
ListFrameObserver lframeObs = new ListFrameObserver();

subject.addObserver(cframeObs1);
subject.addObserver(cframeObs2);
subject.addObserver(cframeObs3);
subject.addObserver(lframeObs);
```

The aspect itself also includes an advice calling the other method, Subject.notifyObservers:

```
after(Watch2LSubject watch, ItemEvent event):
    watchStateChange(watch, event) {
  if(event.getStateChange() == ItemEvent.SELECTED)
    watch.notifyObservers((JRadioButton) event.getSource());
}
```

This functionality should be replaced by aspect methods based on a hash table owned by the aspect: the aspect field _subject2Observers, which uses subject objects as keys, and vectors of observers as values:

```
WeakHashMap _subject2Observers = new WeakHashMap();
```

As a first step, we create the following two aspect methods, with the same names:

```
public void addObserver(Subject subject, Observer observer) {
  Vector observers;
  Object obj = _subject2Observers.get(subject);
  if(obj == null) observers = new Vector();
  else observers = (Vector) obj;
  observers.add(observer);
  _subject2Observers.put(subject, observers);
}
public void
notifyObservers(Subject subject, JRadioButton radioButton) {
  String sColor = radioButton.getText();
  Vector observersList =
    (Vector)_subject2Observers.get(subject);
  for (int i = 0; i < observersList.size(); i++ ) {
    ((Observer) (observersList.elementAt(i))).
      sendNotify(sColor);
  }
}
```

We cannot replace the body of the intertype methods with calls to the new ones at this point. We must first replace the calls to the addObserver method, which register the observers to their subjects. Otherwise, the tests would fail. We therefore perform the next step as prescribed, adding "declare warning" clauses that will expose all calls to these methods:

```
declare warning: call(void Subject.addObserver(Observer)):
    "Method Subject.addObserver(Observer) is called here.";
declare warning: call(void Subject.notifyObservers(JRadioButton)):
    "Method Subject.notifyObservers(JRadioButton) is called here.";
```

We compile, resulting in a series of warnings locating the calls to the old methods. After replacing each of them with calls to the aspect methods, we compile again. All warnings disappeared, and we test. We remove the "declare warning" clauses. Now the client code calling addObservers looks like this:

```
        Watch2LSubject watch2LFrame = new Watch2LSubject();

        ColorFrameObserver cframeObs1 = new ColorFrameObserver();
        ColorFrameObserver cframeObs2 = new ColorFrameObserver();
        ColorFrameObserver cframeObs3 = new ColorFrameObserver();
        ListFrameObserver lframeObs = new ListFrameObserver();

        subject.addObserver(cframeObs1);
        subject.addObserver(cframeObs2);
        subject.addObserver(cframeObs3);
        subject.addObserver(lframeObs);

        Observing.aspectOf().addObserver(watch2LFrame, cframeObs1);
        Observing.aspectOf().addObserver(watch2LFrame, cframeObs2);
        Observing.aspectOf().addObserver(watch2LFrame, cframeObs3);
        Observing.aspectOf().addObserver(watch2LFrame, lframeObs);
```

The call to notifyObservers now takes the form:

```
    after(Watch2LSubject watch, ItemEvent event):
        watchStateChange(watch, event) {
        if(event.getStateChange() == ItemEvent.SELECTED)
            notifyObservers(watch, (JRadioButton) event.getSource());
    }
```

4.6 Tidy Up Internal Aspect Structure

Typical situation. The internal structure of an aspect resulting from the extraction of a CCC is suboptimal, being based on static compositions and betraying duplication.

Recommended action. Tidy up the internal structure of the aspect by removing duplicated intertype declarations and dependencies on case-specific target types.

Motivation. This refactoring serves as the general framework indicating when to use the remaining refactorings from the same group,[3] and in what situations.

---

[3] Each refactoring from the group is not necessarily referred to *directly*.

AOP adds a new type of situation in which code duplication can arise (i.e., is exposed). Refactoring an object-oriented (OO) code base to aspects entails extracting concerns and features whose very crosscutting nature gives rise to duplication that is hard or impossible to avoid when using traditional OO mechanisms. A typical situation is a system containing repeated implementations of the same functionality scattered in multiple classes. Simply extracting those code snippets into an aspect does not guarantee, by itself, removal of this duplication. It merely moves the duplicated code into aspects. In some cases, the duplication becomes obvious only when it is placed in a single module. Therefore, extracting the crosscutting code is only the first part of the job. Next, duplication within the aspect must be removed and its internal structure improved.

Intertype declarations make it very easy to move members from classes to aspects without impact on client code, and aspects resulting from extractions are likely to use them. However, in some cases, we would like the aspect to introduce the additional state and behaviour on an object-by-object basis, and intertype declarations are not flexible enough to achieve that. This entails the replacement of these introductions with different logic.

Mechanics.

- If the code assigns roles to participant classes, see if the aspect code uses marker interfaces to represent those roles instead of referring directly to case-specific classes. If it is not the case, use *generalise target type with marker interface*.
- If parts of the code make explicit references to specific classes that cannot be generalised, separate the specific parts from the generally applicable ones by using *extract method* ([10], p. 110). You should do this if the aspect contains enough generally applicable logic to be worth extracting to a reusable abstract superaspect.
- Inspect the intertype declarations looking for cases in which the extra state and behaviour is needed only at specific times, or is needed by only a subset of the instances of the target classes, or may be needed in multiple instances simultaneously. In such cases, consider using *replace intertype field with aspect map* to deal with the introduced state, and *replace intertype method with aspect method* to deal with the behaviour based on that state.

Example. The refactoring process described in [29] includes a thorough example of this composite refactoring.

5 Code Smells

Code smells are the way proposed by Beck and Fowler (Chap. 3 of [10]) to diagnose problems in existing code that could be removed through refactorings. Code smells do not aim to provide precise criteria for when refactorings are overdue. Instead, code smells suggest symptoms that *may* be indicative of something wrong in the code. Programmers are required to develop their own sense of style and to decide when a symptom indeed warrants a change. Decisions also depend on the specific aims of the programmer and the specific state and structure of the code on which she is working.

5.1 OO Smells in Light of AOP

We analysed the code smells presented in [10, 21, 37] and propose that some be used as symptoms of the presence of CCCs. This particularly applies to *divergent change* ([10], p. 79) and *shotgun surgery* ([10], p. 80). According to Fowler et al., "*Shotgun surgery* is one change that alters many classes" (i.e., a symptom of code scattering) and "*Divergent change* is one class that suffers many kinds of changes" (i.e., a symptom of code tangling). Wake [37] mentions configuration information, logging and persistence as possible causes to the *shotgun surgery* smell, all of which can be counted among the favourite examples for the use of AOP.

Kerievsky [21] proposes a variant of *shotgun surgery* that he calls *solution sprawl*. Kerievsky states ([21], p. 43) that "you become aware of this smell when adding or updating a system feature causes you to make changes to many different pieces of code". The difference between the two smells is the way they are sensed – "we become aware of *solution sprawl* by observing it, while we detect *shogun surgery* by doing it". Both variants are equally promising as indicators of CCCs.

We think it is useful to extend the above definitions to cover methods as well as classes, to account for class-wide aspects that cut across the methods of a single class. We propose the *extract feature into aspect* refactoring (Table 1 and Sect. 3.2) as a general framework for the modularisation of concerns detected through these smells.

5.2 The *Double Personality* Code Smell

The *double personality* smell can be found in classes that play multiple roles. Ideally, each class should play a single role, meaning that it contains only one, coherent set of responsibilities. This often is not possible in OO frameworks and applications.

Examples of *double personality* can be found in the OO implementations of design patterns [11] that include what Hannemann and Kiczales call *superimposed roles* – roles assigned by the pattern to classes that have functionality and responsibility outside the pattern [16]. Examples are *chain of responsibility* ([11], p. 223), which superimposes the Handler role to some of the participant classes, and *observer* ([11], p. 293), which superimposes the Subject and Observer roles.

One symptom that can help to detect *double personality* in Java source code is implementation of interfaces. Interfaces are a popular way to model roles in Java – e.g., the motivation for *extract interface* ([10], p. 341). When a class implements an interface modelling a role that does not relate to the class's primary concern, the class smells of *double personality*.

When *double personality* is detected in one class, we suggest that developers analyse the code base to see if it applies to just that class. Again, looking to the interfaces may help: if multiple classes implement the interface, this means the secondary concern is crosscutting (it cuts across multiple classes).

If a single class is affected, or if the code of the secondary role is restricted to the implementation of the interface, the solution is to extract the secondary role to a mixin

[2]. There are several ways to do this. Laddad's *extract interface implementation* [25] suggests placing the secondary concern inside an inner aspect enclosed within the interface modelling the superimposed role. If the programmer strives for total obliviousness [9] of the secondary role, she can use *replace implements with declare parents* (Table 1). As an alternative to *extract interface implementation* [25], we propose *split abstract class into aspect and interface* (Table 1), which completely encapsulates the secondary concern into an aspect, including the "implements" clause. When the related code is more complex than a simple implementation of an interface, we suggest using *extract feature into aspect* (Table 1) to move all the related code to an aspect (see also Sect. 3.2).

5.3 Abstract Classes as a Code Smell

The AspectJ composition mechanisms that enable the emulation of mixins [2] also enable the separation of definitions (i.e., implementation code) from declarations in abstract classes, opening the way to turn the classes into interfaces. Hannemann and Kiczales take this approach in implementing five of the GoF design patterns in AspectJ [16]. This separation has the advantage that classes become free to inherit from some other class and interfaces can still be provided with a default implementation. This suggests that abstract classes should be considered a code smell in some situations – e.g., whenever we would like a class to inherit from some other class, but the class already inherits from an abstract class that contains implementation elements. Two of the refactorings presented here (Table 1) remove that smell. *Split abstract class into aspect and interface* can be used to extract the concrete members of an abstract class into an aspect, and resulting pure abstract class can be turned into an interface using *change abstract class to interface*.

5.4 The *Aspect Laziness* Code Smell

The *aspect laziness* smell applies to aspects that do not carry the full weight of their responsibilities and instead pass the burden to classes, in the form of intertype declarations. We detect this smell in aspects that resort to the mechanism of intertype declarations to add state and behaviour to a class when something more dynamic and/or flexible would be desirable. Intertype declarations are static mechanisms that apply to all instances of the target class, throughout their entire life cycle. Its use should be considered a smell in some situations. We detect *aspect laziness* in uses of intertype declarations for solving problems whose requirements have one or several of the following characteristics:

- The additional state and/or behaviour are needed by only a subset of the instances of the target classes.
- The additional state and/or behaviour are needed only during certain specific phases in the execution of the program.
- Instances of the target classes (may) require multiple instances of that state and behaviour simultaneously.

In such cases, intertype declarations are not dynamic or flexible enough. It is preferable for the aspect itself to hold the additional state and behaviour and programmatically associate the additional state to the individual target objects. We propose *replace intertype field with aspect map* and *replace intertype method with aspect method* (Table 2) to replace the existing design with a mapping logic that provides the same functionality more flexibly.

6 Illustrative Example

In this section, we present a code example to illustrate some of the smells and the results of many of the refactorings. The example is based on an implementation of the *Observer* pattern ([11], p. 293) by Eckel [8]. In [29], we describe in detail a refactoring process that starts with Eckel's implementation and ends with the AspectJ implementation proposed by Hannemann and Kiczales [16]. The process uses 17 of the refactorings presented in this paper, shown in Table 4.

Table 4. Refactorings used in the illustrating example

Encapsulate implements with declare parents	*Move field from class to intertype*
Extend marker interface with signature	*Move method from class to intertype*
Extract feature into aspect	*Push down advice*
Extract inner class to stand-alone	*Pull up marker interface*
Extract fragment into advice	*Pull up pointcut*
Extract superaspect	*Replace intertype field with aspect map*
Generalize target type with marker interface	*Replace intertype method with aspect method*
Inline class within aspect	*Tidy up internal aspect structure*
Inline interface within aspect	

The intent of Observer is to "define a one-to-many dependency between objects so that when one object changes state, all its dependents are notified and updated automatically" [11]. The example includes two observers, one of which is class Bee, shown in Fig. 1 with the primary concern shaded (the other observer class, Hummingbird, is similar). Figure 2 shows the class Flower, which plays the role of Subject (shaded code relates to the primary concern). Each of Flower's two operations, open and close the petals, originates one observing relationship.

Eckel's implementation uses the Observer/Observable protocol from Java's standard java.util API, which requires Subject participant to inherit from java.util.Observable. Eckel's design manages to partially isolate the two observing relationships

```
01  public class Bee {
02      private String name;
03      private OpenObserver openObsrv = new OpenObserver();
04      private CloseObserver closeObsrv = new CloseObserver();
05
06      public Bee(String nm) { name = nm; }
07      private class OpenObserver implements Observer {
08          public void update(Observable ob, Object a) {
09              System.out.println("Bee "+name +"'s breakfast time!");
10          }
11      }
12      private class CloseObserver implements Observer{
13          public void update(Observable ob, Object a) {
14              System.out.println("Bee " + name + "'s bed time!");
15          }
16      }
17      public Observer openObserver() {
18          return openObsrv;
19      }
20      public Observer closeObserver() {
21          return closeObsrv;
22      }
23  }
```

Fig. 1. Bee class as observer in the implementation of the observer pattern from [8]

by defining, for each relationship, an inner class inside each participant. Thus, Flower defines two inner classes (Fig. 2, lines 25–37 and 38–50, respectively) that inherit from java.util.Observable. The classes within Flower use two inherited methods: (1) setChanged (used in lines 29 and 42), which marks a subject as having been changed, and (2) notifyObservers, which notifies all its observers if subject was changed. Though notifyObservers is overridden (lines 27–33 and 40–46), its functionality is reused (in lines 30 and 43).

Each observer likewise encloses one inner class implementing java.util.Observer for each observing relationship (Fig. 1, lines 7–11 and 12–16, respectively). As prescribed by the interface, each inner class defines an update method (lines 8–10 and 13–15). All participants in the pattern betray strong doses of *double personality*.

The example shows that OO does not cope well with concerns affecting multiple objects and classes, forcing programmers to produce decentralised designs for CCCs, when they would rather centralise the concern's implementation within some module. Such designs lead to duplicated code in every class playing some role in the concern.

OO programmers trying to cope with code scattering and tangling often resort to interfaces and/or inner classes to ameliorate the effects. These constructs improve both the interface and internal structure of classes: interface types help to better organise the interactions of a class with other classes, and inner classes help to better structure the internals of a class, namely to separate the code related to the class's primary concern from unrelated code. We believe the limitations in the compositions achievable with OO provide one of the motivations to use inner classes and interfaces. Independent authors reached the same conclusion regarding interfaces [35].

```
01  public class Flower {
02      private boolean isOpen;
03      private OpenNotifier oNotify = new OpenNotifier();
04      private CloseNotifier cNotify = new CloseNotifier();
05
06      public Flower() { isOpen = false; }
07      public void open() { // Opens its petals
08          System.out.println("Flower open.");
09          isOpen = true;
10          oNotify.notifyObservers();
11          cNotify.open();
12      }
13      public void close() { // Closes its petals
14          System.out.println("Flower close.");
15          isOpen = false;
16          cNotify.notifyObservers();
17          oNotify.close();
18      }
19      public Observable opening() {
20      return oNotify;
21      }
22      public Observable closing() {
23          return cNotify;
24      }
25      private class OpenNotifier extends Observable {
26          private boolean alreadyOpen = false;
27          public void notifyObservers() {
28              if(isOpen && !alreadyOpen) {
29                  setChanged();
30                  super.notifyObservers();
31                  alreadyOpen = true;
32              }
33          }
34          public void close() {
35              alreadyOpen = false;
36          }
37      }
38      private class CloseNotifier extends Observable {
39          private boolean alreadyClosed = false;
40          public void notifyObservers() {
41              if(!isOpen && !alreadyClosed) {
42                  setChanged();
43                  super.notifyObservers();
44                  alreadyClosed = true;
45              }
46          }
47          public void open() {
48              alreadyClosed = false;
49          }
50      }
51  }
```

Fig. 2. Flower class as subject in the implementation of the observer pattern from [8]

Figure 3 shows the participants from Figs. 1 and 2, after each of the two observing relationships was extracted to its own aspect, using the refactorings from Table 1. During the extraction of both observing relationships [29] the isOpen field (Fig. 3, line 4) was encapsulated, yielding two new methods for the Flower class: isOpen (lines 7–9) and setIsOpen (lines 10–12). The code for the reaction of the observers when they are notified of open and close events was likewise extracted to methods breakfastTime (lines 28–30) and bedtimeSleep (lines 31–33) respectively.

```
01  public class Flower {
02      private boolean _isOpen;
03
04      public Flower() {
05      _isOpen = false;
06      }
07      boolean isOpen() {
08          return _isOpen;
09      }
10      private void setIsOpen(boolean newValue) {
11          _isOpen = newValue;
12      }
13      public void open() { // Opens its petals
14          System.out.println("Flower open.");
15          setIsOpen(true);
16      }
17      public void close() { // Closes its petals
18          System.out.println("Flower close.");
19          setIsOpen(false);
20      }
21  }
22  public class Bee {
23      private String name;
24
25      public Bee(String nm) {
26          name = nm;
27      }
28      public void breakfastTime() {
29          System.out.println("Bee " + name + "'s breakfast time!");
30      }
31      public void bedtimeSleep() {
32          System.out.println( "Bee " + name + "'s bed time!");
33      }
34  }
```

Fig. 3. Code of Flower and Bee after extracting the observing relationships to an aspect

Figure 4 shows part of the aspect related to observing the open operation. The other aspect (not shown), related to the observation of close, is similar. We can see from Figs. 3 and 4 that the code for implementing the Observer pattern is no longer spread across the participant classes. However, the structure of the aspect resulting from the extraction still hardly resembles the one presented in [16], as ideally would be the case. The internal structure of the extracted aspect (Fig. 4) still reflects the original, decentralised design. The aspect betrays *duplicated code* ([10], p. 76), as it introduces identical fields (Fig. 4, lines 9 and 10–11) and methods (lines 16–18 and 19–21) to the two observer participants. The duplication was always present, but now that the code is modularised, it is clearly exposed. After modularisation, the original design is no longer justified and the inner classes comprise a needlessly complicated structure. The

```
01  public aspect ObservingOpen {
02     static class OpenNotifier extends Observable {
03        //...
04     }
05     static class OpenObserver implements Observer {
06        //...
07     }
08     private OpenNotifier Flower.oNotify = new OpenNotifier(this);
09     private OpenObserver Bee.openObsrv = new OpenObserver(this);
10     private OpenObserver
11        Hummingbird.openObsrv = new OpenObserver(this);
12
13     public Observable Flower.opening() {
14        return oNotify;
15     }
16     public Observer Bee.openObserver() {
17        return openObsrv;
18     }
19     public Observer Hummingbird.openObserver() {
20        return openObsrv;
21     }
22     pointcut flowerOpen(Flower flower):
23        execution(void open()) && this(flower);
24     after(Flower flower) returning : flowerOpen(flower) {
25        flower.oNotify.notifyObservers();
26     }
27     pointcut flowerClose(Flower flower):
28        execution(void close()) && this(flower);
29     after(Flower flower): flowerClose(flower) {
30        flower.oNotify.close();
31     }
32  }
```

Fig. 4. Part of the extracted aspect ObservingOpen modularising observations of Flower's open operation

code also betrays *aspect laziness*. In this example, it is desirable to select the individual objects participating in the observing relationships and the moments when these become effective, but the present structure does not enable this.

Hannemann and Kiczales mention four modularity properties [16] for their implementation of the Observer pattern: locality, reusability, composition transparency and (un)pluggability. Just after the extraction, the aspect (Fig. 4) has only the first and last of these properties. Figure 5 shows a refactored aspect whose structure is close to that presented in [16].

The static nature of intertype declarations can lead to the *aspect laziness* smell. At the very least, the extracted aspect will need a tidying up. In some cases, including the present one, it requires a complete redesign. Intertype declarations are one of the reasons why the structure of aspects resulting from extraction processes is often unsuitable. Intertype declarations are usually transparent to client code (to our knowledge, only code using AspectJ's "within" pointcut designator can be affected by extraction refactorings based on intertype declarations) and therefore make it simple to move members from classes to aspects. However, only the source code is modularised: the intertype members still belong to their respective target classes at the binary and runtime levels.

```
public aspect ObservingOpen {
    private interface Subject {}
    private interface Observer {}
    public abstract boolean Subject.isOpen();
    private boolean Subject.alreadyOpen = false;
    public abstract void Observer.breakfastTime();

    private WeakHashMap subject2ObserversMap = new WeakHashMap();
    private List getObservers(Subject subject) {
       List observers = (List)subject2ObserversMap.get(subject);
       if(observers == null) {
          observers = new ArrayList();
          subject2ObserversMap.put(subject, observers);
       }
       return observers;
    }
    public void addObserver(Subject subject, Observer observer){
       List observers = getObservers(subject);
       if(!observers.contains(observer))
          observers.add(observer);
       subject2ObserversMap.put(subject, observers);
    }
    public void removeObserver(Subject subject,Observer observer){
       getObservers(subject).remove(observer);
    }
    public void clearObservers(Subject subject) {
       getObservers(subject).clear();
    }
    private void notifyObservers(Subject subject) {
       if(subject.isOpen() && !subject.alreadyOpen) {
          subject.alreadyOpen = true;
          List observers = getObservers(subject);
          for(ListIterator it=observers.listIterator();
              it.hasNext();) {
             ((Observer)it.next()).breakfastTime();
          }
       }
    }
    pointcut flowerOpen(Subject subject):
       execution(void open()) && this(subject);
    after(Subject subject) returning : flowerOpen(subject) {
       notifyObservers(subject);
    }
    pointcut flowerClose(Subject subject):
       execution(void close()) && this(subject);
    after(Subject subject): flowerClose(subject) {
       subject.alreadyOpen = false;
    }
    declare parents: Flower implements Subject;
    declare parents: (Bee || Hummingbird) implements Observer;
}
```

Fig. 5. Aspect ObservingOpen after being tidied up

The transformations prescribed by *tidy up internal aspect structure* (Table 2 and Sect. 3.3) can transform the ObservingOpen aspect from Fig. 4 to the one shown in Fig. 5. In this example, we use the same implementation as in the reusable aspect for the Observer pattern [16], based on a weak hash map. The abstract declarations of methods isOpen and breakfastTime (Fig. 5) result from using *extend marker interface with signature*, which was needed to separate generically applicable code from case-specific code.

7   Related Work

Deursen et al. [6] give a brief overview of the state of art in the area of aspect mining and refactoring. Though their main concern seems to be tools for the automatic detection of aspects, they also mention several open questions about refactoring to aspects, including "how can existing code smells be used to identify candidate aspects?" and "how can the introduction of aspects be described in terms of a catalogue of new refactorings?" In this paper, we contribute to answering both questions.

Iwamoto and Zhao announced in [18] their intention to build a catalogue of AOP refactorings. They present a catalogue of 24 refactorings, but the information provided about them is limited to the names of the refactorings. The refactorings we describe in this paper and in [27] include a description of the situations where the refactoring applies, mention of preconditions, detailed mechanics and code examples.

Several authors [15, 18, 24, 36, 38] call into attention the *fragile pointcut problem* (not always naming it this way), in some cases illustrating it with some code examples. The authors conclude that existing OO refactorings [10] cannot be applied to code bases with aspects. In [25], Laddad provides a few guidelines to ameliorate the problem, including suggestions on how to design and evolve pointcuts. Laddad prescribes several guidelines to ensure AOP refactorings for concern extraction are applied in a safe way. These involve the creation of a first version of the pointcut, based on a case-by-case enumeration of the interesting joinpoints, followed by its replacement with a semantically more meaningful pointcut, based on wildcards. Laddad also proposes a mechanism based on AspectJ's declare error mechanism to verify whether two different pointcut expressions capture exactly the same set of joinpoints. In addition, Laddad recommends that aspects start being developed with a restricted scope, often affecting the methods of a single class, in order to make it simpler to test their impact on the base code. Only afterwards should the scope of the aspect widen, when its functionality is already tested with the restricted case. Considering that at present there is no adequate tool support for AOP refactorings, and that aspects can potentially impact a large number of joinpoints across an entire system, procedures such as these are essential to any refactoring process targeting nontrivial systems.

Hanenberg et al. [15] propose *aspect-aware* refactorings – refactorings that take into account the presence of aspects and preserve behaviour by updating any pointcuts that may be affected by the transformation – and propose a set of enabling conditions to preserve the observable behaviour. By the author's admission, these conditions must be automatically verified by an aspect-aware tool, as the manual verification is an exhausting task, even in small systems. Hanenberg et al. announce a tool providing a subset of the functionality they deem desirable.

In [14] and [34] Griswold, Sullivan and other authors propose a novel approach based on information-hiding interfaces for CCCs. Their approach entails hiding the implementation details (i.e., joinpoints) of code base behind *crosscut programming interfaces* (XPIs) [14] against which aspects are written. The XPIs prevent direct dependencies of aspects on the code bases they advise and enforce design rules [34] that constrain the base code developers to honour the contract expressed through XPIs. Thus, this approach promises to decouple base code from aspect code in a more symmetric way and to solve the fragile pointcut problem. In [34], the authors discuss a comparative study they undertook of three implementations of a real software system, developed independently of the analysis. The authors refactored the system to both a version that conforms to the rules they propose and the more traditional nonsymmetric AOP approach that relies on obliviousness. The study suggests that the new approach brings benefits relative to the other two. To our knowledge, [14] is the first work attempting to provide clear rules on how to design base code for ease of advising. Though it is not expressed in terms of refactorings and code smells, the approach proposed in [14] and [34] contributes to developing a new style appropriate for AOP.

Hanenberg et al. [15] propose three AOP refactorings – *extract advice, extract introduction* and *separate pointcut*. Their *extract advice* corresponds to our *extract fragment into advice* (Table 1). Our collection of refactorings goes deeper in exploring the refactoring space; in this paper and in [27] we provide more detail and tackle issues such as the tidying up of the internal structure of aspects resulting from extraction processes. We do not subscribe the recommendation, in their *extract advice* refactoring, to use "around" advice in the general case. We think that in cases where either "before" or "after" advice can be used, these should be used in preference to "around", because it makes the scope of the advice easier to perceive at a first look at the code. In addition, the "around" advice is also more powerful than is often needed. In the case of code using it without a strict need for it, we envision refactorings such as *change around advice to before* and *change around advice to after returning*. Their proposed *extract introduction* refactoring corresponds to our *move field from class to intertype* and *move method from class to intertype* (Table 1) refactorings, which provide more detail. *Separate pointcut* relates to evolution of pointcuts and has no correspondence in our collection. This refactoring argues that, just as it is beneficial to organise our systems using small methods with meaningful names, we should do the same with pointcuts. Hanenberg et al. do not elaborate on code smells, but we can infer from *separate pointcut* that anonymous pointcuts should be a code smell.

In [25], Laddad presents a collection of refactorings [25] tailored to practitioners working in industry, particularly developers of J2EE applications. The refactorings vary widely in both level and scope of applicability, including generally applicable refactorings like *extract interface implementation, extract method calls* and *replace override with advice*, but also concern-specific refactorings such as *extract concurrency control* and *extract contract enforcement*. In addition, some refactorings belong to the category of "refactoring to patterns" as presented by Kerievsky [21] – *extract worker object creation* and *replace argument trickle by wormhole*. These two refactorings are based on two of the design patterns presented by Laddad in [26] – *worker object creation* ([26], p. 247) and *wormhole* ([26], p. 256) respectively. The *extract exception handling* refactoring as presented in [25] goes towards a variant implementation of the *exception introduction* pattern ([26], p. 260).

Laddad's refactorings and ours cover different areas of the AOP refactoring space, providing different and complementing contributions to filling that space. Some of

Laddad's refactorings are presented with only a mention of their name and a brief motivating paragraph. We believe the refactorings would benefit if presented in the same format as used by Fowler et al. [10] and Kerievsky [21], and which we use as well [27, 28]. A mechanics section would be particularly beneficial, having proved very useful as a checklist and to lead developers through the safest sequences of steps, in preference to riskier or less convenient ones. The important step-by-step guidelines proposed by Laddad for creating a new aspect and subsequently evolving it are included in the code example illustrating the use of *extract method calls*, but not in several other refactorings to which they also apply (Laddad places some reminders). A mechanics section would make that part process clearer, and would clarify the relations between refactorings. In addition, several refactorings (namely the problem-specific ones) can be decomposed into simpler, lower-level steps, always an important thing with refactoring.

Laddad does not pinpoint the code smells that his refactorings are supposed to remove. We think that the material presented by Laddad has the potential to throw new light on existing OO code smells or to yield new ones. For instance, his *extract method calls* and *replace argument trickle by wormhole* refactorings respectively suggest the *scattered method calls* and *argument trickle* smells. Further research is required to discover latent smells and assess their feasibility and applicability.

Tonella and Ceccato [35] base their work on the assumption that interfaces are often (not always) related to concerns other than the one pertaining to the system's main decomposition. This is an *interface implementation* smell, though the authors do not name it this way. They provide specific guidelines for when an interface implementation is a symptom of a latent aspect and present a tool for mining and extracting aspects based on these criteria, and report on experimental results. These extractions are also covered by the refactorings we present in Table 1 and document in [27]. The authors also point out various issues that can arise in a typical extraction of an interface implementation into an aspect. Our refactorings prescribe procedures to deal with all these issues.

In [17], Hannemann et al. propose that refactoring support for AOP be divided into three categories: aspect-aware OO refactorings (the concept proposed by Hanenberg et al.), aspect-oriented refactorings (i.e., refactorings that specifically target AOP constructs, such as those presented in this paper) and *refactorings of crosscutting concerns*, i.e., refactorings in which the scattered elements comprising a target CCC and their individual transformations are considered together, instead of handling each element separately. The latter category can only be carried out with the support of a suitable tool. The focus of [17] is to present one such tool. Some of Laddad's refactorings [25], such as *extract method calls, extract concurrency control* and *extract contract enforcement*, would be refactorings of CCCs if had some suitable tool support. Such refactorings tend to be concern-specific: these contrasts with ours, which aim to be applicable to multiple concerns, like those documented by Fowler et al. [10].

Like us, Hannemann et al. [17] use the Observer pattern ([11], p. 293) as a basis for an illustrating example. They provide the outline for a refactoring process comprising the extraction from a code base of a general implementation of Observer. The outline is much less detailed than the one we present in [29], which focuses on a specific Java implementation of Observer by Eckel. The outcome of their illustrating refactoring is the AspectJ implementation [16] of Observer, which we also use in Sect. 6 and in [29]. Not surprisingly, there are similarities between some refactorings presented here and various refactorings that Hannemann et al. report using in their work:

- Their *add internal interface* is subsumed by our *generalise target type with marker interface* (Table 2 and Sect. 4.2).
- Their *replace object method with aspect method* is similar to our *replace intertype method with aspect method* (Table 2 and Sect. 4.5).
- Their *replace method call with pointcut and advice* corresponds to our *extract fragment into advice* (Table 1), the code fragment being a method call.
- Their *replace method with intertype method declaration* and *replace field with intertype field declaration* corresponds to ours *move method from class to intertype* and *move field from class to intertype* (Table 1), respectively.

In [3], Cole and Borba propose programming laws from which refactorings for AspectJ can be derived. The authors focus on the use of their laws to derive existing refactorings such as those proposed in [15, 18, 25], and describe two case studies in which the laws were tested, comprising the extraction of concurrency control and distribution, respectively. Many, though not all, of the laws relate to the extraction of CCCs to aspects, and therefore there is some overlap between the refactorings they derive and our own extraction refactorings (Sect. 3.2). However, their focus is on providing proofs that the transformations are behaviour-preserving, while we focus on covering new ground in the refactoring space. Nevertheless, the authors remark that extraction procedure for the second case study is generalisable, because its implementation of distribution is commonly used, and claim that it is possible to derive a concern-specific *extract distribution* refactoring. No details are given, though.

To our knowledge, no work besides ours deals with the potentially bad internal structure of aspects resulting from extraction processes. With the exception of the work by Tonella and Ceccato [35], we do not have knowledge of any other work covering the issue of AOP code smells.

8   Future Work

8.1   Maturing the Refactorings

There is scope for maturing the refactorings presented here. It is important to test the refactorings with more case studies, particularly larger and more complex ones. More complex refactoring experiments may expose problems and situations that should be taken into account in the preconditions and mechanics sections. Refactoring experiment targeting other languages should be performed to assess the validity of the refactorings beyond the Java/AspectJ space.

8.2   Expanding the Refactoring Space

Covering Other Language Characteristics. The refactorings we present here result from the two specific case studies, and do not use every available aspect construct, nor do they explore every possible combination. New research should cover the remaining aspect constructs, as well as the interactions between them and with existing Java constructs. We next mention two subjects.

- *Nonsingleton Aspect Association*: Our work so far concentrated on singleton aspects. In future, we expect to cover other kinds of aspect association in order to obtain a clearer idea of the advantages and disadvantages of nonsingleton aspects, e.g., when should they be preferred and what refactorings should be used to transform singleton aspects.
- *Pointcuts*: At present, refactorings and code smells specifically targeting pointcuts are still a largely unexplored area. AspectJ's pointcut protocol comprises a rich language for quantification [9] and is likely to yield an equally rich pattern language for refactoring pointcut expressions, as well as their interaction with advice. Further research is needed on the adequate use of pointcut designators (e.g., pointcut smells), and how best to evolve pointcut expressions.

Opposite Refactorings. We do not provide opposites for the presented refactorings, preferring to focus on extending the reach of the existing collection of refactorings. However, opposites are important to enable developers to backtrack, whenever they find out they took a wrong turn. In IDEs and refactoring tools, the opposite of a refactorings correspond to the "undo" of that refactoring. In addition, opposites are often useful in their own right (e.g., pull up vs. push down refactorings).

Dealing with Published Interfaces. In this paper, we cover the restructuring of aspect code resulting from the extraction of CCCs, taking advantage of the newfound modularisation. It is also worth studying the impact of such extractions on the remaining code base and what actions would be desirable (e.g., post-extraction refactorings).

Restructuring the Remaining Base Code. In this paper, we cover the restructuring of aspect code resulting from the extraction of CCCs, taking advantage of the newfound modularisation. It is also worth studying the impact of such extractions on the remaining code base and what actions would be desirable (e.g., post-extraction refactorings). The XPI concept proposed by Griswold et al. [14] and associated design rules proposed by Sullivan et al. [34] provide new opportunities to expand and evolve the current refactoring space for AOP.

8.3 Other Code Smells

We believe many AOP smells wait to be discovered. For instance, use of privileged aspects is a candidate: The rationale for avoiding them is the same as for avoiding the use of public data. As Colyer and Clement remark in [4], aspect privilege confers the general privilege to see any private state anywhere, while one often wishes to express privilege with respect to a single class or a restricted set of classes. Presently, this is not possible with AspectJ. Unfortunately, privileged aspect may be unavoidable in cases affecting multiple packages and in which the aspect needs access to nonpublic (e.g., protected and package-protected) data. Refactoring the affected code bases to expose the nonpublic data is one alternative. We need to study use cases of privileged aspects to assess whether common patterns can be found, and pinpoint refactorings that tackle this issue.

9 Summary

In this paper, we argue that collections of refactorings and code smells can be an effective way to express notions of style for AOP source code. We propose AOP-specific code smells, both for detecting CCCs in existing OO code and for improving the structure of extracted aspects – *double personality*, *abstract classes* and *aspect laziness*. We review existing OO code smells in the light of AOP. *Divergent Change* can be a sign of code tangling, and both *shotgun surgery* and *solution sprawl* can be signs of code scattering.

Simply moving the members relating to a CCC does not yield a well-formed aspect. Extracted aspects expose problems caused by crosscutting, including *duplicated code* ([10], p. 76). *Aspect laziness* relates to the static nature of intertype declarations. We can take advantage of the newfound modularity to tidy up the aspect's internal structure with further refactorings.

We present a collection of AOP refactorings, which can remove these smells from source code, comprising the following groups:

- Ten refactorings to remove the smells related to CCCs from existing OO code. Besides covering common members such as fields and methods, these refactorings also deal with inner classes and interfaces. These refactorings are fully documented in [27].
- Six refactorings to remove problems found in extracted aspects, including *duplicated code* and *aspect laziness*. These refactorings are described in detail in this paper.
- Eleven refactorings to deal with the generalisation of aspects, i.e., the extraction of common code to superaspects. These refactorings are fully documented in [27].

We discuss some of the many future directions in the hunt for new AOP refactorings and code smells, taking as a basis the contributions of this paper and related work.

References

[1] Beck K. Extreme programming explained: Embrace change. Addison-Wesley, Reading, MA, USA, 2000

[2] Bracha G. and Cook W. Mixin-based inheritance. In: *ECOOP/OOPSLA1990: Proceedings of Conference on Object-Oriented Programming: Systems, Languages, and Applications and European Conference on Object-Oriented Programming*, ACM, pp. 303–311, 1990

[3] Cole L. and Borba P. Deriving refactorings for AspectJ. In: *AOSD 2005: Proceedings of the 4th International Conference on Aspect-Oriented Software Development*, ACM, pp. 123–134, 2005

[4] Colyer A. and Clement A. Large-scale AOSD for middleware. In: *AOSD 2004: Proceedings of the 3rd International Conference on Aspect-Oriented Software Development*, ACM, pp. 56–65, 2004

[5] Cooper J. Java design patterns: A tutorial. Addison-Wesley, Reading, MA, USA, 2000. Also availabe at www.patterndepot.com/put/8/DesignJava.PDF

[6] Deursen A.v., Marin M., and Moonen L. Aspect mining and refactoring. In: *REFACE03: Workshop on REFactoring: Achievements, Challenges, Effects*, Waterloo, Canada, 2003

[7] Dijkstra E. Go-to statement considered harmful, *Communications of the ACM*, 11(3):147–148, 1968

[8] Eckel B. Thinking in Patterns, revision 0.9. book in progress, 2003. Available at http://www.pythoncriticalmass.com/downloads/TIPatterns-0.9.zip

[9] Filman R.E. and Friedman D.P. Aspect-oriented programming is quantification and obliviousness. In: *Workshop on Advanced Separation of Concerns at OOPSLA 2000*, Minneapolis, 2000

[10] Fowler M. et al. Refactoring – Improving the design of existing code, Addison-Wesley, Reading, MA, USA, 2000.

[11] Gamma E., Helm R., Johnson R., Vlissides J. Design patterns. *Elements of Reusable Object-Oriented Software*. Addison-Wesley, Reading, MA, USA, 1995

[12] Garcia A., Sant'Anna C., Figueiredo E., Kulesza U., Lucena C., and Staa A. Modularizing design patterns with aspects: A quantitative study. In: *AOSD 2005: Proceedings of the 4th International Conference on Aspect-Oriented Software Development*, ACM, pp. 3–14, 2005

[13] Griswold W.G. Program restructuring as an aid to software maintenance. *PhD Thesis*, University of Washington, USA, 1991

[14] Griswold W.G., Sullivan K.J., Song Y., Cai Y., Shonle M., Tewari N., Rajan H. Modular software design with crosscutting interfaces. *IEEE Software, Special Issue on Aspect-Oriented Programming*, pp. 51–60, 2006

[15] Hanenberg S., Oberschulte C., Unland R. Refactoring of aspect-oriented software, net.objectdays 2003, Erfurt, Germany, 2003

[16] Hannemann J. and Kiczales G. Design pattern implementation in Java and AspectJ. In: *OOPSLA 2002: Proceedings of the 17th ACM SIGPLAN Conference on Object-Oriented Programming, Systems, Languages, and Applications*, ACM, pp. 161–173, 2002

[17] Hannemann J., Murphy G., and Kiczales G. Role-based refactoring of crosscutting concerns. In: *AOSD 2005: Proceedings of the 4th International Conference on Aspect-Oriented Software Development*, ACM, pp. 135–146, 2005

[18] Iwamoto M. and Zhao J. Refactoring aspect-oriented programs. In: *4th AOSD Modelling With UML Workshop at UML'2003*, San Francisco, USA, 2003

[19] Jacobson I., Christerson M., Jonsson P., Övergaard G. Object-oriented software engineering: A use case driven approach, Addison-Wesley, Reading, MA, USA, 1992

[20] Kang K.C., Cohen S.G., Hess J.A., Novak W.E., Peterson A. Feature-oriented domain analysis feasibility study, SEI, Technical Report CMU/SEI-90-TR-21, 1990

[21] Kerievsky J. Refactoring to patterns. Addison-Wesley, Reading, MA, USA, 2004

[22] Kiczales G., Hilsdale E., Hugunin J., Kersten M., Palm J., and Griswold W.G. An overview of AspectJ. In: *ECOOP 2001: Proceedings of the 15th European Conference on Object-Oriented Programming, LNCS vol. 2072*, Springer, pp. 327–353, 2001

[23] Kiczales G., Lamping J., Mendhekar A., Maeda C., Lopes C., Loingtier J., and Irwin J. Aspect-oriented programming. In: *ECOOP'97: Proceedings of the 11th European Conference on Object-Oriented Programming, LNCS vol. 1241*, Springer, pp. 220–242, 1997

[24] Koppen C. and Störzer M. PCDiff: Attacking the fragile pointcut problem. In: *EIWAS 2004: Interactive Workshop on Aspects in Software*, Berlin, Germany, 2004

[25] Laddad R. Aspect-oriented refactoring, parts 1 and 2. The Server Side, 2003. www. theserverside.com/

[26] Laddad R. AspectJ in action – practical aspect-oriented programming, Manning, Greenwich, CT, USA, 2003

[27] Monteiro M.P. Refactorings to evolve object-oriented systems with aspect-oriented concepts. *Ph.D. Thesis*, Universidade do Minho, Portugal, 2005

[28] Monteiro M.P. and Fernandes J.M. Object-to-aspect refactorings for feature extraction. In: *AOSD 2004: Industry Track Paper at the 3rd International Conference on Aspect-Oriented Software Development*, Lancaster, UK, 2004

[29] Monteiro M.P. and Fernandes J.M. Refactoring a java code base to AspectJ – An illustrative example. In: *ICSM 2005: Proceedings of the IEEE International Conference on Software Maintenance 2005,* Budapest, Hungary, 2005

[30] Monteiro M.P. and Fernandes J.M. Towards a catalogue of aspect-oriented refactorings. In: *AOSD 2005: Proceedings of the 4th International Conference on Aspect-Oriented Software Development,* ACM, pp. 111–122, 2005

[31] Opdyke W.F. Refactoring object-oriented frameworks. *Ph.D. Thesis*, University of Illinois at Urbana-Champaign, USA, 1992

[32] Orleans D. Separating behavioral concerns with predicate dispatch, or, if statement considered harmful. In: *Workshop on Advanced Separation of Concerns in Object-Oriented Systems at OOPSLA 2001*, Tampa Bay, USA, 2001

[33] Sabbah D. Aspects – From promise to reality. In: *AOSD 2004: Proceedings of the 3rd International Conference on Aspect-Oriented Software Development*, ACM, pp. 1–2, 2004

[34] Sullivan K.J., Griswold W.G., Song Y., Cai Y., Shonle M., Tewari N., and Rajan H. Information hiding interfaces for aspect-oriented design. In: *ESEC/FSE 2005: Proceedings of the Joint 10th European Software Engineering Conference and 13th ACM SIGSOFT Symposium on the Foundations of Software Engineering,* ACM, pp. 166–175, 2005

[35] Tonella P. and Ceccato M. Migrating interface implementation to aspects. In: *ICSM'04: Proceedings of 20th IEEE International Conference on Software Maintenance,* IEEE Computer Society, Chicago, USA, pp. 220–229, 2004

[36] Tourwé T., Brichau J., and Gybels K. On the existence of the AOSD-Evolution paradox. In: *Workshop on Software-Engineering Properties of Languages for Aspect Technologies at AOSD 2003*, Boston, USA, 2003

[37] Wake W. Refactoring workbook, Addison-Wesley, Reading, MA, USA, 2004

[38] Zhang C. and Jacobsen H.-A. Quantifying aspects in middleware platforms. In: *AOSD 2003: Proceedings of the 2nd International Conference on Aspect-Oriented Software Development,* ACM, Boston, USA, pp. 130–139, 2003

[39] Zhao J. Towards a metrics suite for aspect-oriented software. *Technical-Report*, SE-2002-136-25, Information Processing Society of Japan (IPSJ), 2002

Design and Implementation of an Aspect Instantiation Mechanism

Kouhei Sakurai[1], Hidehiko Masuhara[2], Naoyasu Ubayashi[3],
Saeko Matuura[1], and Seiichi Komiya[1]

[1] Shibaura Institute of Technology
sakurai@komiya.ise.shibaura-it.ac.jp,
matsuura@se.shibaura-it.ac.jp,
skomiya@sic.shibaura-it.ac.jp
[2] University of Tokyo
masuhara@acm.org
[3] Kyushu Institute of Technology
ubayashi@acm.org

Abstract. This paper describes the design and implementation of *association aspects*, which are a linguistic mechanism for the AspectJ language that concisely associates aspect instances to object groups by extending the per-object aspects in AspectJ. This mechanism allows an aspect instance to be associated to a group of objects, and by providing a new pointcut primitive to specify aspect instances as execution context of advice. With association aspects, we can straightforwardly implement crosscutting concerns that have stateful behavior related to a particular group of objects. The new pointcut primitive can more flexibly specify aspect instances when compared against previous implicit mechanisms. We implemented a compiler for association aspects by modifying the AspectJ compiler, which reduces the size of data structures for keeping associations. Our benchmark tests confirm that the overheads of association aspects are reasonably small when compared against functionally equivalent aspects in pure AspectJ that manually manage associations. The expressiveness of association aspects is demonstrated through development of an integrated development environment with and without association aspects.

1 Introduction

In aspect-oriented programming (AOP), an aspect is the unit of modular definitions of crosscutting concerns. Aspects may be provided as a different module system from existing ones (e.g., in AspectJ [1]), or may be defined by using an existing module system (e.g., in Hyper/J [2]). In both cases, an aspect serves as the encapsulation of state and behavior, which are represented by instance variables and advice declarations, respectively, in AspectJ-like languages.

AspectJ-like languages run an advice body *in the context of* an aspect instance, in a similar sense that object-oriented languages run a method body in the context of an object. A problem is how to determine an aspect instance as

A. Rashid and M. Aksit (Eds.): Transactions on AOSD I, LNCS 3880, pp. 259–292, 2006.
© Springer-Verlag Berlin Heidelberg 2006

the context of an advice execution, since aspect instances are not usually obvious during the program execution. AspectJ, for example, offers a few mechanisms[1] to this problem:

- *Singleton* aspects create only one aspect instance for each aspect declaration. This type of aspect is useful to implement concerns that have systemwide behaviors.
- *Per-object* aspects *associate* a unique aspect instance for each object. When an operation in terms of an object triggers an advice execution, the system automatically looks up the aspect instance associated to the object, and uses the instance as the execution context. This type of aspect is useful to implement concerns that have a unique state for each object.

Those mechanisms are useful to certain kinds of crosscutting concerns, but Sullivan et al. pointed out that they do not straightforwardly support *behavioral relationships*, which are the concerns that integrate the behaviors of collections of objects by extending or modifying their respective behaviors [3]. With the above mechanisms, such behavioral relationships are usually implemented by creating a singleton aspect with a table for associating the states unique to object groups. The resulting implementations have to have not only the code for the core behavior but also the code for managing association in a single aspect definition.

Subsequently, Rajan and Sullivan proposed instance-level advising by aspect instances as a solution, as demonstrated in their AOP language Eos [4]. In Eos, the programmer dynamically creates an aspect instance to represent behavioral relationships. Each aspect can be associated to the objects in its representing relation. When a method is called during program execution, the advice body is executed in the context of each aspect instance that is associated to the target of the call. As a result, the mechanism can cleanly implement such behavioral relationships. However, the mechanism can still be improved with respect to the following problems: (1) It is not flexible in the selection of aspect instances as it always selects with respect to the target object, and (2) it requires additional language constructs in order to distinguish associated objects of the compatible types.

This paper proposes an alternative mechanism called *association aspects*, which also allows us to associate an aspect instance to a group of objects. The mechanism addresses the above-mentioned problems by providing a new pointcut primitive that can more flexibly select aspect instances upon advice execution, and can distinguish associated objects without introducing other language constructs. The mechanism is implemented by modifying an AspectJ compiler(ajc [5]). Our benchmark tests showed that the association aspects can be implemented with acceptable amounts of overhead in comparison to the singleton or per-object aspects that manually manage tables.

The rest of the paper is organized as follows. Section 2 presents an example of behavioral relationships. Section 3 explains the design of association aspects, our

---

[1] There are also mechanisms based on the control flow, but they are not directly relevant to the topic of the paper.

proposed mechanism. Section 4 describes how association aspects are compiled into native Java programs. Section 5 gives the result of our benchmark tests to compare the efficiency of association aspects with respect to the programs in pure AspectJ. Section 6 shows an application program written with association aspects for comparing expressiveness against pure AspectJ. Section 7 compares association aspects to similar approaches. Section 8 concludes the paper.

2 Motivating Example

This section presents an example system to motivate the need for association aspects. Section 2.1 presents a system integration that becomes a crosscutting concern in object-oriented programming, and starts with prerequisites and requirements of the example system. Section 2.2 presents an object-oriented implementation of the system integration using a design pattern. Section 2.3 then shows that AspectJ implements the concern in an awkward manner. Section 2.4 analyzes the conditions when such problems happen. The problem presented in this section was first pointed out by Sullivan et al. [3].

2.1 System Integration

Integration of independently developed systems often raises crosscutting concerns; it often requires modifications on many descriptions of participating systems [3, 6, 7]. For example, assume that one builds an integrated development environment (IDE) by integrating a text editor and a compiler [6, 7]. Without AOP, descriptions for the integration concern have to appear in several places in both subsystems; e.g., a "save" method not only writes to a file, but also needs to invoke the compiler. We will revisit this example in Sect. 6.

For concreteness, we consider integration of Bit objects, which was originally introduced by Sullivan et al. [3]. A Bit object has a Boolean instance variable and methods for setting, clearing, and getting the value of the variable:

```
class Bit {
    boolean value = false;
    void set()   { value = true; }
    void clear() { value = false; }
    boolean get() { return value; }
}
```

The integration concern is to synchronize the states of particular Bit pairs, which are represented by relations. A relation consists of a type (either equality or trigger) and a pair of Bit objects. The relations are created dynamically during program execution.

Figure 1 shows three Bit objects (illustrated as ovals) connected by two equality relations (illustrated as diamonds). An equality relation propagates set and get calls on the left-hand side to the right-hand side, and vice versa. Therefore, when set is called on b_2, the top equality relation calls set on b_1, which in turn

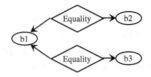

Fig. 1. Integration of Bits

makes the bottom equality relation to call `set` on b_3. Note that the relations must not cause an infinite loop; i.e., the call on b_1 by the top equality relation should not be propagated back to b_2.

We require the following properties for implementing the equality (and other) relations for comprehensiveness, maintainability, and extensibility:

Nonintrusiveness. The implementation does not require modification of the definition of `Bit`.

Variability. Not only equality, but also other kinds of relations are supported simultaneously. For example, a trigger relation, which merely propagates calls on the left-hand side to the right-hand side should also be used.

Simplicity. When the programmer uses relations, he/she need not consider the implementation details of the relations.

2.2 A Solution in Java with Observer Pattern

Figure 2 shows an implementation of the `Bit` integration system in Java with the Observer pattern. The Observer pattern is one of the Gang-of-Four (GoF) design patterns [8] that define a dependency relationship between one to many objects. When the monitored object changes its state, it notifies the depending objects.

In order to implement the `Bit` integration system, we let `Bit` objects play the `Subject` role and define `Equality` objects to represent describing equality relationships, and let `Equality` play the `Observer` role so that they can propagate operations on `Bit` objects.

An `Equality` relation establishes an association by calling the `attach` method on two `Bit` objects. Propagation of the set and clear operations are achieved by inserting a call to the `change` method at the end of these methods. When the `change` is called, it calls the `update` method of the `Equality` object associated to the `Bit` object. The `update` method determines the opponent `Bit` object of the relation, determines whether it should call `set` or `clear` method by sensing the state of the changed object, and then calls the method on the opponent. The instance variable `busy` of `Equality` is an algorithmic state for avoiding cyclic calls of `update` on the same object.

With respect to the required properties presented in the last section, the implementation is intrusive because we have to modify the `Bit` class. The modifications are not only at the end of each propagated operation, but also in the inheritance hierarchy. This suggests that we cannot apply the implementation to a class in the middle of an inheritance hierarchy. The implementation is also

```
interface Observer {
  void update(Subject s);
}


class Subject {
  List observers =
    new LinkedList();
  void attach(Observer o) {
    observers.add(o);
  }
  void detach(Observer o) {
    observers.remove(o);
  }
  void change() {
    for (Iterator iter
        = observers.iterator();
      iter.hasNext();) {
      Observer o
        = (Observer) iter.next();
      o.update(this);
    } }
}
```

```
class Equality implements Observer {
  Bit l, r;
  boolean busy;
  Equality(Bit l, Bit r) {
    this.l = l; this.r = r;
    l.attach(this); r.attach(this);
  }
  public void update(Subject s) {
    Bit b = (s == l) ? r : l;
    if (!busy) {          //to avoid
      busy = true;        //infinite loop
      if (((Bit) s).get())
          b.set(); else b.clear();
      busy = false;
  }}
}

class Bit extends Subject {
  boolean value = false;
  void set()   {value=true;  change();}
  void clear() {value=false; change();}
  boolean get() {return value;}
}
```

Fig. 2. Bit integration system with observer pattern

less variable. When we introduce a different kind of relation that is to propagate a different set of operations, the pattern forces every relation to receive notifications of all kinds of state changes, even if the changes are not relevant to a specific relation.

2.3   A Solution in AspectJ

It is possible to define aspects in AspectJ that implement the above relations. Figure 3 shows a possible definition of the equality relation in AspectJ.[2] In order to represent the state of each relation, the aspect defines an innerclass called Relation, which has references to the related Bit objects and a busy flag. The aspect adds a list of Relations to each Bit object, so that the advice can find Relations from a Bit object.

Two advice declarations capture set and clear calls, respectively, to any Bit object. The bodies of advice obtain a relations list from a target object. For each Relation in the list, it checks the flag and invokes the same method when the advice is not recursively executed for the same Relation.

The static method associate creates a relation. When the method is called with two Bit objects, it creates a Relation object and registers it into each

---

[2] The definition is written by the authors who follow the outline originally presented by Sullivan et al. in [3].

```
aspect Equality {
  static class Relation {              after(Bit b): call(void Bit.set())
    Bit left, right;                                  && target(b) {
    boolean busy = false;                for (Iterator iter
    Bit getOpp(Bit b) {                        = left.relations.iterator();
      return b==left? right:left;           iter.hasNext(); ) {
  } }                                       Relation r
  private List Bit.relations                  = (Relation) iter.next();
           = new LinkedList();            if (!r.busy) {     //to avoid
                                            r.busy = true;   //infinite loop
  static void associate(                    r.getOpp(b).set();
          Bit left, Bit right) {            r.busy = false;
    Relation r = new Relation();        } }
    r.left = left;                      }
    r.right = right;                    //advice for the clear
    left.relations.add(r);             //method goes here
    right.relations.add(r);            //...
  }                                    }
```

Fig. 3. An implementation of Equality relation in AspectJ

of the `relations` lists in the given `Bit` objects. The integrated system of `Bits` specified in Fig. 1 can be constructed by executing the following code fragment:

```
Bit b1 = new Bit(), b2 = new Bit(), b3 = new Bit();
Equality.associate(b1,b2); //connect b1 and b2
Equality.associate(b1,b3); //connect b1 and b3
```

2.4 Problems of AspectJ Solution

The AspectJ solution is better than the pure Java solution, but it still has problems. Here, we analyze the AspectJ implementation with respect to the required properties in Sect. 2.1:

Nonintrusiveness. The `Equality` aspect is not intrusive as its pointcut and advice captures calls to `Bit` objects without modifying the class declaration of `Bit`.

Variability. AspectJ allows the programmer to define relations other than `Equality` without major interference. However, such a relation cannot share the implementation with `Equality` as those different relations manage the relations among objects in different ways.

Simplicity. The solution is not simple enough as it has to declare a separate inner class for representing relations, and each advice body has to have an iteration to find all the relevant relations. The latter point would be significant when there are more advice declarations for more complicated relationships. At the design level, an equality relation is an entity that encapsulates the state (related objects and a busy flag) and the behavior (detection and propagation of method calls). It would be straightforward if a relation is modeled by an instance at the programming level. However, the AspectJ solution models the relation as an aspect declaration (for the behavior) and an instance of an inner class (for the state).

To summarize, aspect instantiation mechanisms in AspectJ are not sufficient to straightforwardly implement concerns that affect a group of objects and have stateful behavior. As it is a natural idea to encapsulate the state and behavior in an aspect instance, a mechanism that enables us to create aspect instances on a per-object-group basis is useful.

In other words, the *singleton* aspects in AspectJ are not suitable because they can create no more than one instance. As a result, the implementation would have to allocate the states in different objects, and manage a table to keep those objects.

The *per-object* aspects in AspectJ, namely `pertarget` and `perthis` aspects, are not suitable either. This is because only one per-object aspect instance is allowed to exist for each object. In order to represent relations between objects, more than one aspect instance exists for one object.

Although one may think standard protocols or APIs for managing relations could solve problems of simplicity and variability, they actually help little for achieving both. If we designed the protocols or APIs variable enough to support various usages of relations, the resulting aspects would be no longer simple as the protocols and APIs would require a number of descriptions such as iterators, unsafe type casting, subclassing, and so forth.

We do not believe that this problem is unique to large-scale system integrations. Rather, similar problems could be observed in smaller-scale systems. For example, in the AspectJ implementation of the GoF design patterns [8] by Hannemann and Kiczales [9], 6 out of 23 patterns manage the relations and their states by using tables.

3   Association Aspects

3.1   Overview

We propose an extension to the AspectJ's aspect instantiation mechanism, called *association aspects*, that allows the programmer to associate an aspect instance to a tuple of objects. Association aspects are designed to straightforwardly model crosscutting concerns like behavioral relations, which coordinate behavior among a particular group of objects. Two basic functions support the association aspects: (1) a function to associate an aspect instance to tuples of objects, and (2) a function to select aspect instances based on the association at advice execution.

Figure 4 shows the `Bit` integration example rewritten with the association aspects. The `perobjects` modifier on the first line declares that its instance is to be associated to a pair of `Bit` objects. The following statements builds the integrated `Bit`s in Fig. 1:

```
aspect Equality perobjects(Bit, Bit) {
  Bit left, right;
  Equality(Bit l, Bit r) {
    associate(l, r);        //establishes association
    left = l; right = r;
  }
  after(Bit l) :
    call(void Bit.set()) && target(l) && associated(l,*){
    propagateSet(right);    //when left is called, call set on right
  }
  after(Bit r) :
    call(void Bit.set()) && target(r) && associated(*,r){
    propagateSet(left);     //when right is called, call set on left
  }
  boolean busy = false;     //indicates if the relation is active
  void propagateSet(Bit opp) {
    if (!busy) {            //call set on opp
      busy = true;          //unless it already has propagated
      opp.set();
      busy = false;
  } }
  // advice decls. for clear method go here
}
```

Fig. 4. Equality relation with association aspects

```
Bit b1 = new Bit(), b2 = new Bit(), b3 = new Bit();
Equality a1 = new Equality(b1,b2);
Equality a2 = new Equality(b1,b3);
```

The new expressions create Equality aspect instances. The constructor of Equality associates the created instance to the given Bit objects.

The associated pointcuts in the advice declarations specify what aspect instances shall be used as the execution context of the advice bodies. The combination of pointcuts target(l) && associated(l,*) selects aspect instances that are associated to the current target object. The selected aspect instances serve as execution context of advice; i.e., the body of advice runs with accesses to the instance variables of the selected aspect instances. For example, when a program evaluates b2.set(), aspect instance a1 is selected by the second advice, and executes the advice body. The advice checks busy flag in a1, and calls set on left, which is bound to b1 in a1. We hereafter refer to the process that selects aspect instances and runs advice body in the context of selected instances as *advice dispatching to aspect instances*.

3.2   Properties of Association Aspects

Association aspects satisfy the three properties that are presented in Sect. 2.1.

Nonintrusiveness. Equality in Fig. 4 is as nonintrusive as the one in AspectJ.

Variability. By combining associated pointcuts with AspectJ's abstraction mechanism such as abstract aspect and pointcut overriding, association aspects are variable. As we will see in Sect. 3.4, `associated` pointcuts are powerful enough to describe both symmetric and asymmetric relations. For the `Bit` integration, it therefore is possible to define an aspect that has an abstract pointcut and subaspects with concrete pointcuts to specify either symmetric or asymmetric relation.

Simplicity. `Equality` in Fig. 4 is simpler than the one in Fig. 3 because association aspects hide the implementation details of relations, which are explicit in Fig. 3 (e.g., the field `Bit.relations` and the use of iterator in the after advice). Moreover, composition of associated pointcuts with free variables, which will be explained in Sect. 3.4, avoids the duplication of advice declarations.

The following sections explain the association and advice dispatching mechanisms in greater detail.

3.3   Creating and Associating Aspect Instances

Association aspects are declared with `perobjects` modifiers. They are defined by the following syntax:

$$\texttt{aspect } A \texttt{ perobjects}(T,\ldots) \texttt{ \{ } mdecl \ldots \texttt{ \}}$$

where A is the name of the aspect, T is the type of objects to be associated, and $mdecl$ is the member declaration including constructor, method, variable, advice, etc.

An association aspect can be instantiated by executing a `new` $A(\ldots)$ expression in a similar manner to object instantiation. Creation of a new aspect instance also invokes a constructor for initialization. A newly created aspect instance is not associated to any objects.

The `perobjects`$(T_1, T_2, \ldots, T_n)$ modifier automatically defines an `associate` method in A. It takes n objects of type $T_1, \ldots, T_n$, and associates the aspect instance to the given objects $o_1, \ldots, o_n$. The modifier also defines a `void` A`.delete()` method, which revokes association.

In contrast to per-object aspects in AspectJ, creation and association of association aspects are explicit. This is due to the typical usage of association aspects, in which they represent explicit artifacts such as the `Equality` relations in the `Bit` integration example. When association aspects are required for objects in certain joinpoints, it is possible to make those operations nonintrusive by defining advice, as we will see in Sect. 3.5.

3.4   Dispatching to Aspect Instances

Semantically, dispatching advice to aspect instances is realized by trying to execute the same advice in the context of *all* aspect instances, and only the instances that satisfy the pointcut *actually* run the body. In order to select associated aspect instances, we provide the `associated` pointcut primitive.

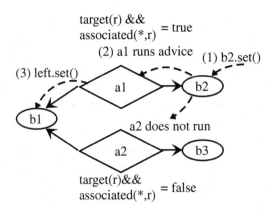

Fig. 5. Advice dispatching to associated aspects

Figure 5 illustrates the semantics in terms of the example presented at the beginning of the section. The evaluation of **b2.set()** creates a call joinpoint (1). We focus here on the execution of the second advice declaration. Each aspect instance tests the pointcut. Since the pointcut is satisfied only when an aspect instance is associated to **b2** as the second parameter, **a1** is the only aspect instance to run the advice (2). The advice body propagates the call by accessing the **left** instance variable stored in the execution context, **a1** (3).

Aspect instances are ordered in undetermined order to test and execute an advice declaration. For around advice, the following four steps are executed. First, an aspect instance is randomly selected from all aspect instances. Second, the selected aspect instance tests and executes the advice declaration. Third, when the aspect instance executes a **proceed** form, or the aspect instance does not match the advice declaration, a next aspect instance is selected and repeats from the second step. When the aspect instance does not execute a **proceed** form, it continues the execution without running the joinpoint. Fourth, when there are no more aspect instances at the first step or the last part of the third step, it continues the joinpoint.

An **associated** pointcut determines how an aspect instance is associated to objects. In an aspect declared with **perobjects** $(T_1, \ldots, T_n)$, the pointcut is written as **associated** $(v_1, \ldots, v_n)$, where v_i is either

- a variable that is bound by another pointcut (e.g., by **target** (v_i))
- an asterisk (*****) as a wild card, or a free variable

An additional restriction is that an **associated** pointcut has at least one bound variable in its parameter.

The pointcut **associated** $(v_1, \ldots, v_n)$ is evaluated to true for an aspect instance that is associated to $\langle o_1, \ldots, o_n \rangle$, if, for any $1 \leq i \leq n$, v_i is either an asterisk or a free variable, or a variable bound to o_i. The asterisks and free variables allow more than one aspect instance to match the same joinpoint.

Note that the pointcut distinguishes parameter positions. This is useful to define directed relations that capture different events on the different sides of the relations.

Binding to Associated Objects. The `associated` pointcut can bind variables to associated objects when free variables are written instead of wild cards. For example, the following declaration, which is slightly modified from the first advice declaration in Fig. 4, has a free variable `r` instead of the wild card:

```
after(Bit l, Bit r) : call(void Bit.set())
  && target(l) && associated(l,r) {
  propagateSet(r);
}
```

The modified advice has the same behavior as the original one except that it binds r to each associated object at the second parameter position when it executes the body.

The binding feature can give shorter definitions to symmetric association aspects, which equally treat their associated objects. For example, the following single advice declaration can be substituted for the first two advice declarations in Fig. 4:

```
after(Bit b,Bit o): call(void Bit.set()) && target(b)
  && (associated(b,o) || associated(o,b)) {
  propagateSet(o);
}
```

This is because the combination of `associated` pointcuts by an disjunctive operator identify aspect instances that are associated to the target object regardless of parameter position, and then the binding feature binds o to the associated object that is not the target.

3.5   Static Advice

Association aspects can declare *static* advice, which provides similar semantics to the advice declarations in singleton aspects. When an advice declaration has a `static` modifier, pointcut matching and execution is performed exactly once, regardless of the number of existing aspect instances. Obviously, a static advice declaration may not use an `associated` pointcut. The execution context of static advice is the aspect-class; the advice body can only access static (or class) variables.

The static advice declarations are typically useful for bootstrapping. In order to create a new aspect instance by using the advice mechanism, a static advice declaration should be used because there are no aspect instances at the beginning. For example, the advice in the following code creates an `Equality` instance when `callSomeMethod()` happens:

```
aspect Equality perobjects(Bit, Bit) {
  static after(Bit l, Bit r) : callSomeMethod() && args(l,r) {
    new Equality(l,r); //creates an aspect instance
  }
  ...
}
```

3.6   Idioms to Find Aspect Instances

It is sometimes necessary to check if there is any aspect instance associated to a particular tuple of objects, or to do something on all aspect instances associated to a particular object (e.g., deleting all aspect instances associated to an object). Those operations can be realized by means of advice declarations with associated pointcuts. We therefore do not provide specific primitives for such purposes.

An example is to prevent creating no more than one Equality aspect instance for the same pair of objects. The next advice does the job:

```
aspect Equality perobjects(Bit,Bit) {
  ...
  Equality around(Bit l, Bit r) :
      call(Equality.new(Bit,Bit)) && args(l,r)
      && (associated(l,r) || associated(r,l)) {
    return this;
} }
```

When a program executes new Equality(b,b') and there is an aspect instance a associated to $\langle b, b' \rangle$ or $\langle b', b \rangle$, the above advice returns a instead of creating a new one. When there is no such an aspect instance, a new Equality instance will be created because the advice does not run at all.

Enumerating all aspect instances associated to a particular object can be realized by an empty static method with an advice declaration. For example, execution of Equality.showAll(b) in Fig. 6 displays all aspect instances that are associated to b.

```
aspect Equality perobjects(Bit,Bit) {
  ...
  static void showAll(Bit b) { }    // empty body
  after(Bit b) :
      call(void Equality.showAll(Bit)) && args(Bit b)
      && (associated(b,*) || associated(*,b)) {
    System.out.println(this);   //this is bound to
} }                             //associated instance
```

Fig. 6. An idiom to enumerate aspect instances

4   Implementation

The mechanisms for association aspects are implemented[3] by modifying the
AspectJ compiler (`ajc`) version 1.2.0. Similar to the original compiler, it takes
class and aspect declarations as inputs, and generates Java bytecode as compiled
code. We first review how the original AspectJ compiler generates compiled code.
We then show how the extended compiler generates code for association aspects.
For readability, we present compiled code at the Java source-code level.

4.1   Compilation of Regular AspectJ Programs

The AspectJ compiler translates an aspect declaration into a class, and an advice body into a method of the class, respectively [10]. Advice is executed by the
inserted method calls into locations where the pointcut of the advice statically
matches. Dynamic conditions in the pointcut (e.g., `cflow` and `if`) are translated into conditional statements inserted at the beginning of translated advice.
Masuhara et al. gave a semantic model of the translation by using partial evaluation of an interpreter [11].

Consider the following (nonassociation) aspect definition, which counts invocations of a method on a per-target-object basis:

```
aspect Counter pertarget(callSet()) {
    pointcut callSet() : call(void Bit.set());
    int count = 0;
    after() returning() : callSet() {
        count++;
} }
```

Compilation of `Counter` aspect with `Bit` class yields the code shown in Fig. 7.[4]
A statement `b.set();` where `b` is of type `Bit` is translated into the following
statements:

```
b._bind();          //create&associate if not yet
b.set();
b._aspect._abody0();//advice dispatching
```

The `Counter` aspect is translated into a class. The variable `count` becomes
an instance variable, and the after advice becomes a method. The `Bit` class has
an instance variable `_aspect`, which keeps an aspect instance (i.e., a `Counter`
object) associated to the `Bit` object. The `_bind` method creates an associated
`Counter` instance for a `Bit` object if it is not yet created.

The translated call to `set` method is surrounded by a call to `_bind` and a
call to run the advice body. The latter call is realized by invoking an instance

---

[3] The implementation is available at `http://www.komiya.ise.shibaura-it.ac.jp/~sakurai/`.

[4] Note that the code is drastically simplified from what the actual compiler generates.
For readability, we inlined method calls and renamed compiler-generated methods
and fields, and removed unimportant access modifiers.

```
class Bit {                //translated
  Counter _aspect;         //associated aspect instance
  boolean value;           //original instance variable
  public synchronized void _bind() {
    if (_aspect == null) _aspect = new Counter();
  }
  //definitions of set, clear and get methods
  //...
}

class Counter {                      //translated
  int count = 0;                     //instance variable
  public final void _abody0() {//body of the after
    count++;                         //advice
} }
```

Fig. 7. Code compiled by AspectJ

method of `Counter` class. As a result, the body of the advice is executed in the context of an associated aspect instance.

4.2 Overview of Compilation of Association Aspects

Compilation of Bit Integration Example. Association aspects are compiled into Java classes in a similar manner to other aspects, except for association and advice dispatching. We first show how the `Bit` class and the `Equality` aspect in Fig. 4 are compiled.

The translated `Bit` class[5] has a field `_aspects1` to keep a map from `Bit` to `Equality`, and a field `_aspects2` to keep a list of `Equality`. The fields are of different types because of optimizations reasons, which will be explained in Sect. 4.3.

```
class Bit {// translated
  Map<Bit, Equality> _aspects1 = new HashMap();
  List<Equality>     _aspects2 = new ArrayList();
  ...
}
```

These two collections are used for processing pointcuts `associated(b,*)` and `associated(*,b)`, respectively. They preserve the following invariants: when an aspect instance a associated to $\langle b_1, b_2 \rangle$, b_1._aspects1.get$(b_2) = a$ and b_2._aspects2.contains$(a) =$ true.

Note that those fields are not symmetric even though the `Equality` aspect definition treats the first and second `Bit` objects equally. This is because our compiler minimizes the collection types to reduce memory overheads. The detailed compilation strategy is described in the next section.

---

[5] We use Java 1.5 notation for collection types. Map<T_1, T_2> denotes the type of map objects from T_1 to T_2. List<T> denotes the type of lists of T. The syntax for(T v : e) s is a shorthand for looping s for each v of type T in iterator e.

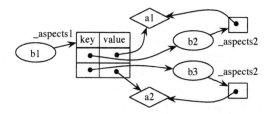

Fig. 8. Implementation of association with maps

Figure 8 shows how the implementation represents the associations of the integrated Bits in Fig. 1.

Advice dispatching is translated into a loop over all key-value pairs in a map or into a loop over a list. A statement b.set(); is translated into the following code for dispatching the two advice declarations:

```
b.set();                            //original call
for(Bit v: b._aspects1.keys()) {    //for the first
  Equality a=b._aspects1.get(v);    //after-advice
  a._abody0(b);
}
for(Equality a: b._aspects2) {      //for the second
  a._abody1(b);                     //after-advice
}
```

The two for-loops correspond to the two advice declarations. Since the first advice has the associated(1,*) pointcut, where 1 is the target of the call, it processes all the aspect instances a in the _aspects1 map of the target object, and runs the body of the advice by invoking the instance method of a. The code for the second advice corresponds to the associated(*,r) pointcut, where r is the target of the call and processes all the aspect instances a in the _aspects2 list of the target object, and runs the body of the advice by invoking the instance method of a.

When all parameters to the associated pointcut are bound, advice dispatching is translated into simple lookup in the map. For example, the parameters to the associated pointcut in the following advice are both bound by args:

```
after(Bit l, Bit r) : call(Equality.new(Bit,Bit))
    && args(l,r) && associated(l,r) {
  System.out.println("duplicated!");
}
```

Then the translation of an expression new Equality(b1,b2) yields the next statements subsequent to the original expression:

```
Equality a = b1._aspects1.get(b2); //for the third
if (a != null) a._abody2(b1,b2);   //after advice
```

4.3   Compilation Process

The general compilation process is slightly more complicated because we allow aspects to be associated with arbitrary numbers of (i.e., even more than two) objects, and to use wild cards at any parameter positions in associated pointcuts. Note that free variables are regarded as wild cards.

The compilation takes place in the following steps:

1. For each aspect declaration with a `perobjects` modifier, it enumerates a set of *parameter combinations* that serve as keys for dispatching advice execution.
2. It computes a set of *sequences of parameter indices*. Each sequence represents a type of data structure that records associations for specific `associated` pointcuts.
3. Based on the set of sequences, it installs fields into the associated types for recording associations, and generates methods for registering associations.
4. Finally, for each joinpoint shadow that matches an `associated` pointcut, it inserts a code fragment for dispatching advice.

Below, we assume aspect A is declared with `perobjects`$(T_1, T_2, \cdots, T_n)$ and advice declarations with `associated` pointcuts. We write the ith occurrence of `associated` pointcut as $p_i = $ `associated`$(v_{i1}, v_{i2}, \ldots, v_{in})$, where v_{ij} is either a bound variable or a wild card. Free variables are regarded as wild cards.

We define a *parameter combination* of an `associated` pointcut as a set of indices of bound variables in the pointcut. The parameter combination of p_i is written as τ_i. When $p_i = $ `associated`$(v1, v2, *)$, $\tau_i = \{1, 2\}$.

For each `associated` pointcut, the compiler uses a *sequence of indices* σ_i to determine the type of the data structure for recording associations, and to generate a code fragment to dispatch advice execution. We write $|\sigma_i|$ as the length of the sequence, and $\sigma_i(j)$ as the jth index in σ_i for $1 \leq j \leq |\sigma_i|$. The sequence σ_i contains all indices in τ_i at the first $|\tau_i|$ positions; i.e., $\forall k \in \tau_i, \exists j$ such that $j \leq |\tau_i|$ and $\sigma_i(j) = k$.

Given a sequence σ_i, we use a map of type $T_{\sigma_i(1)} \to T_{\sigma_i(2)} \to \cdots \to T_{\sigma_i(|\sigma_i|)} \to A$ for recording associations. When objects $o_1, o_2, \ldots, o_{|\sigma_i|}$ of type $T_{\sigma_i(1)}, T_{\sigma_i(2)}, \ldots, T_{\sigma_i(|\sigma_i|)}$ are given, the dispatching procedure is to apply $o_1, o_2, \ldots, o_{|\sigma_i|}$ to the map, in order to obtain a reference to the associated aspect instance. Usually, there are several possibilities to choose a set of σ_is for the given aspect. We will discuss this issue after presenting how associations are managed based on τ_is.

Managing Associations. In order to maintain an association between objects and an aspect instance, the compiler actually installs fields into type declarations of associated objects, and generates an `associated` method in the aspect declaration by following the rules in Fig. 9.

Given a sequence of indices σ_i for pointcut p_i, the compiler first installs a field `_aspects`$_i$ of type U_{i1} (defined in Fig. 9) into class $T_{\sigma_i(1)}$. The associate method, shown in Fig. 9, consists of the statements *install$_i$*, which installs an aspect

$$U_{ij} = \begin{cases} \texttt{Map<}T_{\sigma_i(j+1)}, U_{ij+1}\texttt{>} & j < |\sigma_i| \\ A & j = |\sigma_i| = n \\ \texttt{List<}A\texttt{>} & j = |\sigma_i| < n \end{cases}$$

```
void associate(T₁ v₁,T₂ v₂,...,Tₙ vₙ) {
    install₁
    install₂
      ⋮
}
```

$$install_i = \begin{cases} U_{i1}\texttt{m}_{i1} \ \texttt{=} \ \texttt{v}_{\sigma_i(1)}\texttt{.\_aspects}_i; \\ U_{i2}\texttt{m}_{i2} \ \texttt{=} \ \texttt{getOrCreate}_{i2}(\texttt{m}_{i1},\texttt{v}_{\sigma_i(2)}); \\ U_{i3}\texttt{m}_{i3} \ \texttt{=} \ \texttt{getOrCreate}_{i3}(\texttt{m}_{i2},\texttt{v}_{\sigma_i(3)}); \\ \dots \\ U_{i|\sigma_i|-1}\texttt{m}_{i|\sigma_i|-1} \ \texttt{=} \ \texttt{getOrCreate}_{i|\sigma_i|-1}(\texttt{m}_{i|\sigma_i|-2},\texttt{v}_{\sigma_i(|\sigma_i|-1)}); \\ addaspect; \end{cases}$$

$$addaspect = \begin{cases} \texttt{m}_{i|\sigma_i|-1}.\texttt{put}(\texttt{v}_{\sigma_i(n)},\ \texttt{this}) & |\sigma_i| = n \\ U_{i|\sigma_i|}\ \texttt{m}_{i|\sigma_i|}\texttt{=}\ \texttt{getOrCreate}_{i|\sigma_i|}(\texttt{m}_{i|\sigma_i|-1},\texttt{v}_{\sigma_i(|\sigma_i|)}); & |\sigma_i| < n \\ \qquad\qquad\qquad \texttt{m}_{i|\sigma_i|}.\texttt{add(this)} \\ \texttt{v}_{\sigma_i(1)}.\texttt{\_aspects}_i\texttt{=}\ \texttt{this} & |\sigma_i| = 1 \end{cases}$$

Fig. 9. Rules for generating `associate` method

```
aspect A perobjects(T1, T2, T3) {
  before(T2 v2, T3 v3): call(* *.*(..))
      && args(v2, v3) && associated(*, v2, v3) { ... }
  before(T1 v1, T2 v2, T3 v3): call(* *.*(..))
      && args(v1, v2, v3) && associated(v1, v2, v3) { ... }
}
```

Fig. 10. An example aspect definition

instance into a sequence of maps for each σ_i. Therefore, the compiler adds the statements of Fig. 9 for each σ_i in the associate method.

$\texttt{getOrCreate}_{ij}(m, v)$ in the $install_i$ statements in Fig. 9 returns a value of type U_{ij} for key v in `Map` m if it is registered. If not, it creates an empty map of type U_{ij}, registers it in m with key v, and returns the created object. The last line of the $install_i$ registers the aspect instance depending on the length of σ_i.

For example, assume we have an aspect definition shown in Fig. 10 and the compiler uses sequences of indices $\sigma_1 = \langle 2, 3 \rangle$ and $\sigma_2 = \langle 1, 2, 3 \rangle$ for the first and second `associated` pointcuts, respectively. It inserts field declarations `_aspects1` of type `Map<T3,List<A>>` into type T2 and `_aspects2` of type `Map<T2, Map<T3,A>>` into type T1. It then generates the `associate` method in Fig. 11 into A.

```
void associate(T1 v1, T2 v2, T3 v3) {
    Map<T3, List<A>> m1_1 = v2._aspects1;
    List<A>          m1_2 = getOrCreate1_2(m1_1, v3);
    m1_2.add(this);

    Map<T2, Map<T3, A>> m2_1 = v1._aspects2;
    Map<T3, A>          m2_2 = getOrCreate2_2(m2_1, v2);
    m2_2.put(v3, this);
}
```

Fig. 11. associate method generated for Fig. 10

```
static void _dispatch( T_{σ_i(1)} v1, T_{σ_i(2)} v2,...,T_{σ_i(l)} v_l) {
    if(!⟨parameterless dynamic conditions⟩) return;
    U_{i1} m_{i1}=v1._aspects_i; if(m_{i1}==null)return;
    U_{i2} m_{i2}=m_{i1}.get(v2); if(m_{i2}==null)return;
    ...
    U_{il-1} m_{il-1}=m_{il-2}.get(v_{l-1}); if(m_{il-1}==null)return;
    U_{il} m_{il}=m_{il-1}.get(v_l); if(m_{il}==null)return;
    for (U_{il+1} m_{il+1} : m_{il}.values()) {
        for (U_{il+2} m_{il+2} : m_{il+1}.values()) {
            ...
                for (U_{i|σ_i|} m_{i|σ_i|} : m_{i|σ_i|-1}.values()) {
                    invokebody
                }
            ...
} } }
```

$$
invokebody = \begin{cases} \text{for}(A \text{ a} : m_{i|σ_i|}) \text{ a._abody}(v_1,...,\ v_l); & |σ_i| < n \\ m_{i|σ_i|}._abody(v_1,...,\ v_l); & |σ_i| = n \end{cases}
$$

Fig. 12. Rules for generating dispatching method for pointcut p_i

Dispatching Advice Execution. The compiler realizes advice dispatching by inserting a call to a method that dispatches advice execution at each joinpoint shadow that statically matches the pointcut. The dispatching method receives l parameters from the context (i.e., the joinpoint),[6] finds all aspect instances associated to those parameters, and calls method _abody on each aspect instance. The _abody is the method translated from the advice body, which first checks conditions due to dynamic pointcuts (e.g., if and type tests), followed by the body of the advice.

For brevity, we here explain the cases for before and after advice declarations. The case for around advice is explained in the Appendix.

The rules for generating the dispatching method, which is shown in Fig. 12, depend on the parameter sequence $σ_i$. Due to the sharing of parameter sequences

---

[6] Actually, thisJoinPoint and other arguments used in pointcuts other than associated should be passed to the advice body.

```
aspect A perobjects(T1, T2, T3, T4) {
  before(T1 v1, T2 v2): call(void m1(T1, T2))
     && args(v1,v2) && associated(v1,v2,*, *) {
    System.err.println("m1 with " + v1 + "," + v2);
  }
}
```

Fig. 13. An example aspect definition

```
static void _dispatch1(T1 v1, T2 v2) {
  Map<T2, Map<T3, List<A>>> m1 = v1._aspects1; if(m1==null) return;
  Map<T3, List<A>> m2 = m1.get(v2);              if(m2==null) return;
  for (List<A> m3: m2.values()) {
    for (A a : m3)
      a._abody(v1, v2);
  }
}
```

Fig. 14. Dispatching method generated for Fig. 13

$$S \leftarrow \{\}$$
$$\textbf{while } P \neq \{\}$$
$$\quad \tau_{min} \leftarrow \min_{|\tau|}\{\tau | \tau \in P\}$$
$$\quad P \leftarrow P \backslash \{\tau_{min}\}$$
$$\quad \sigma_{max} \leftarrow \max_{|\sigma|}\{\sigma | \sigma \in S \cup \{\langle\rangle\}, \tau_{min} \text{ contains } \sigma\}$$
$$\quad S \leftarrow S \backslash \{\sigma_{max}\} \cup \{append(\sigma_{max}, \tau_{min})\}$$
$$\textbf{end}$$

Fig. 15. Algorithm to compute a set of parameter sequence S for sharing maps

among pointcuts (which will be explained later), σ_i can be longer than the number of parameters available at the joinpoint. The dispatching method therefore consists of two parts: the first half looks up the maps by using the parameters, and the latter half iterates over all the elements in the maps. For example, with the aspect declaration in Fig. 13, the rules in Fig. 12 generate the _dispatch1 method in Fig. 14.

Sharing Maps. The compiler minimizes the number of map types that record associations by sharing maps among different associated pointcuts. This avoids the inefficiency of using redundant data structures when associated pointcuts use different parameters for dispatching advice.

Normally, an advice declaration can reuse a map object if its parameter sequence appears in the head of a parameter sequence of another advice declaration. Take the example in Fig. 10 again. When the compiler uses the sequences $\sigma_1 = \langle 2, 3 \rangle$ and $\sigma_2 = \langle 1, 2, 3 \rangle$ for the two pointcuts, we have to have two maps. When $\sigma_1 = \langle 2, 3 \rangle$ and $\sigma_2 = \langle 2, 3, 1 \rangle$, a field in T1 of type Map<T3, Map<T1,A>> is sufficient for dispatching those two advice declarations.

In order to share maps among pointcuts, the compiler computes a set of sequences S that cover all parameter combinations P in an aspect declaration by applying the algorithm in Fig. 15.

In the algorithm, τ contains σ if $\forall k \in \{\sigma(1), \ldots, \sigma(|\sigma|)\}$. $k \in \tau$, and $append(\sigma, \tau) = \sigma'$ is a shortest sequence that has the same first $|\sigma|$ elements to σ, and has all the elements in τ; i.e., $\forall j \in \{1, \ldots, |\sigma|\}.\sigma(j) = \sigma'(j)$ and $\forall k \in \tau. \exists j \in \{1, \ldots, |\tau|\}. \sigma'(j) = k$. When $P = \{\{1\}, \{2\}, \{3\}, \{1, 2\}, \{1, 3\}, \{2, 3\}, \{1, 2, 3\}\}$, one of the solutions of the algorithm is $S = \{\langle 3, 1 \rangle, \langle 2, 3 \rangle, \langle 1, 2, 3 \rangle\}$. After computing the set of sequences S, σ_i for τ_i is selected as the shortest sequence in S whose first $|\tau_i|$ elements have all elements in τ_i.

5   Performance Evaluation

We carried out microbenchmark tests for comparing run-time efficiency between (1) programs with association aspects, (2) programs with singleton aspects that manually manage associated states, and (3) programs with per-object aspects in AspectJ.

All benchmark tests were executed by Java HotSpot Client VM version 1.4.2, running on a PowerPC G4 1.25-GHz MacOS X 10.4 machine with 512-MB memory. Each execution time was measured by averaging the execution time, which is obtained through `currentTimeMillis`, of a loop that runs more than one second.

5.1   Performance of Basic Operations

We measured the costs of the basic operations, namely object creation, aspect instantiation and association, and method invocation with before advice execution. They are measured by executing programs with aspect declarations associated to n objects. The programs perform each of the following operations:

1. **OBJ:** create objects that can be associated to aspect instances
2. **ASSOC:** create an aspect instance and associate it to the n objects, and
3. **BEFORE:** invoke the empty method on an object

In the aspect declarations, there are advice declarations that use the `associated` pointcut with 1 to n bound variables:

```
aspect Test perobjects(C,...,C) {
    int x1, x2, x3, x4, x5;
    Test(C o1,...,C on) {
        associate(o1,...,on);
    }
    before(C o1, ...,C on): callEmptyMethod()
        && args(o1,...,on) && associated(p1,...,pn) {
        x1++; x2++; x3++; x4++; x5++;
    }
} }
```

where p_i is either o_i or $*$.

We compare the following three aspect implementations:

AA: that uses association aspects (shown above).
SNG: that uses singleton aspects in AspectJ with inner-class objects stored in collections for associated states (see below).
PO: that uses per-object aspect in AspectJ (namely `pertarget`). This is used only for $n = 1$.

SNG uses the same collection structures to those in the AA. For example, the SNG aspect declaration for $n = 2$ with one bound variable looks as in Fig. 16.

```
aspect Test {
 static class Relation {
   int x1, x2, x3, x4, x5;
   C o1; C o2;
 }
 HashMap C.relations;
 static void associate(C o1, C o2) {
   Relation r = new Relation();
   r.o1 = o1; r.o2 = o2;
   HashMap m1 = o1.relations;
   if (m1 == null) {
     m1 = new HashMap();
     o1.relations = m1;
   }
   m1.put(o2, r);
 }
 before(C o1): callEmptyMethod() && args(o1, *) {
   if (o1.relations == null) return;
   for (Iterator i = o1.relations.values().iterator();
     i.hasNext(); ) {
     Relation r = (Relation) i.next();
     r.x1++; r.x2++; r.x3++; r.x4++; r.x5++;
} } }
```

Fig. 16. Declaration of an SNG aspect

Table 1 shows the execution times of those basic three operations for different n and different variations of `associated` pointcuts. The column p shows the parameters of the `associated` pointcuts. Since our current implementation uses the same set of map structures, OBJ denotes the time for generating one object. OBJ and ASSOC give the same figures for the same n. The rightmost column shows the relative execution times of AA with respect to SNG. We omit the cases for (*,*,o3) and (*,o2,o3) because they are identical to the cases for (*,o2,*) and (o1,*,o3), respectively.

As we can see, AA poses at most 19% overheads compared to the manual implementation, SNG, except for the aspects associated to one object (i.e.,

Table 1. Execution times (in μs) of basic operations

	n	P	AA SNG PO	AA/SNG
OBJ	1		0.068 0.068 0.068	0.994
	2		0.133 0.140	0.946
	3		0.264 0.267	0.988
ASSOC	1		0.135 0.113 0.163	1.194
	2		1.762 1.719	1.025
	3		5.454 5.404	1.009
BEFORE	1	(o1)	0.050 0.032 0.072	1.566
	2	(o1, *)	0.382 0.379	1.009
		(*,o2)	0.326 0.322	1.012
		(o1,o2)	0.139 0.117	1.191
	3	(o1, *, *)	0.743 0.721	1.031
		(*,o2, *)	0.683 0.667	1.023
		(o1,o2, *)	0.476 0.464	1.025
		(o1, *,o3)	0.416 0.404	1.030
		(o1,o2,o3)	0.229 0.201	1.135

$P = ($o1$))$.[7] Those numbers are reasonable as the compiled code for AA basically does the same operations as SNG does, yet in much more concise descriptions.

5.2   Performance of Bit Integration

We also compared the performance by running the `Bit` integration example in AA and SNG implementations (as shown in Figs. 3 and 4, respectively). The benchmark programs first create 100 `Bit` objects, which are randomly connected via n equality and trigger relations, and then invoke `set` or `clear` methods on randomly selected objects for 1000 times.

Table 2. Execution times (in ms) of bit integration with n relations

n	AA SNG	$\frac{AA}{SNG}$	n	AA	SNG	$\frac{AA}{SNG}$
10	0.345 0.330	1.046	50	3.450	3.183	1.084
20	0.525 0.504	1.041	60	21.081	18.612	1.133
30	0.804 0.742	1.084	70	62.731	57.124	1.098
40	1.338 1.197	1.118	80	347.120	287.047	1.209

The overall execution times are shown in Table 2. As seen in the rightmost column on the table, the relative execution times of AA with respect to SNG

---

[7] The relative overheads are increased from our previous measurement, which was 14%[12]. We presume that the additional overheads are introduced by the guard code in the implementation of the association aspects that guarantees safe addition and deletion of associations during advice dispatching. Since the guard code adds constant overhead to each method invocation, we predict the ratio AA/SNG will not change significantly for the cases $n > 3$, though we have not measured.

range 1.0 to 1.2, depending on the density of the relations. We conjecture that the differences in the implementation details caused those differences. In particular, we presume that the major overheads come from the guard code in the AA implementation that allows safe addition and deletion of associations during advice dispatching.

6   Expressiveness Evaluation

In this section, we illustrate a practical application program built with association aspects. We then compare the implementation of the application against the same application implemented differently, namely with Java and with pure AspectJ. The comparison illustrates the advantages of association aspects.

6.1   An Application: Integrated Development Environment

We developed a simple integrated development environment(IDE) by integrating existing application programs. Note that we used major open source software as the applications to be integrated, rather than toy programs. Figure 17 shows a screenshot of our developed IDE, consisting of:

- jEdit[8] text editor on the left window.
- Apache Ant building system[9] with our own simple GUI called `AntManager`, whose role is to list source files in a project description file `build.xml` and to launch the Ant process with the project file, on the bottom right window
- our own IDE front- end that starts the `AntManager` after letting the user choose a `build.xml` file, and coordinates between the `AntManager` and jEdit.

The IDE front end uses association aspects called `AutoBuild` in order to build a project after saving a file in the jEdit text editor, and in order to save jEdit buffers before building a project.

The IDE instantiates an `AutoBuild` aspect when a user selects a source file from `AntManager` or opens a file with jEdit. The instantiated aspects are associated to a `Buffer` object in jEdit and the `AntManager` object itself. The `Buffer` object contains a copy of the text in the opened file. It has a method `save` to write the modified text to the file. The `AntManager` object is instantiated on a per-definition file of a project (`build.xml`) basis. Its method `build` calls Ant with the build file.

When an aspect `AutoBuild` observes a call of method `save` to an associated `Buffer` object, it invokes the method `build` of the associated `AntManager` object. Moreover, when method `build` is called, the aspect `AutoBuild` invokes `save` method to an associated `Buffer` object so that Ant can build the project with the latest files.

---

[8] http://www.jedit.org
[9] http://ant.apache.org/

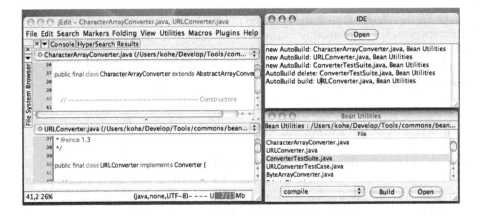

Fig. 17. Screenshot of a tiny IDE system built with association aspects

6.2   Implementation of Integrated Development Environment

The code of the aspect `AutoBuild` from the design that was described in the previous section is represented by Fig. 18. We implemented the same IDE in Java and in AspectJ without using association aspects. By comparing those implementations against the implementation in AspectJ with association aspects, we observed the following problems:

The Pure Java Implementation. In the pure Java Implementation, the code for integration crosscuts the underlying applications. We had to define a generic `Listener` interface and to modify the `Buffer` and `AntManager` classes to implement the interface, and to insert code fragments to notify the `Listener` into several methods of those classes.

AspectJ Implementation Without Association Aspects. Figure 19 shows an implementation of `AutoBuild` in AspectJ without using association aspects. It basically follows an implementation technique discussed in Sect. 2.3. The implementation adds the fields that store references to `Relation` objects into `Buffer` and `AntManager` by means of intertype declarations.

The implementation even tries to modularize the code for managing associations by declaring an abstract aspect `Association` and by letting `AutoBuild` inherit from `Association`. The reusability of this approach is, however, limited as we have to define `Relation` inner class in `AutoBuild` and to explicitly write loops over `Relation` objects in each advice body.

6.3   Comparison of Code Size

Table 3 compares implementations in AspectJ with and without association aspects in terms of code size. In the table, the AALOC column shows the lines of code of the implementation with association aspects on a per-file basis.

```
aspect AutoBuild perobjects(Buffer, AntManager) {
  private int busy;

  after(Buffer buffer, AntManager project):
    execution(public boolean Buffer.save(..))
    && target(buffer) && associated(buffer, project) {
    if (busy > 0) return;
    busy++;
    project.build();
    busy--;
  }

  before(final Buffer buffer, AntManager project):
    execution(public void AntManager.build())
    && associated(buffer, project)
    && target(project) && if(buffer.isDirty()) {
    if (busy > 0) return;
    busy++;
    SwingUtilities.invokeLater(new Runnable() {
      public void run() {
        if (buffer.save(jEdit.getLastView(), null, false)) {
          buffer.setDirty(false);
          jEdit.getLastView().getEditPane()
              .getBufferSwitcher().updateBufferList();  }
        busy--;
    } });
  }
  //...advice delete AutoBuild when file is closed,
  //    and so on, goes here
}
```

Fig. 18. Code of AutoBuild with association aspects

The AJLOC column shows the numbers without association aspects, in which
AutoBuild is defined by two aspects: AutoBuildAj.aj and Association.aj.
The two implementations share the Java classes AntFile.java, AntManager.
java and IDE.java that define GUI for ant and IDE.

As we can see, AALOC of AutoBuild.aj is 50, and AJLOC of
AutoBuildAj.aj is 83. In other words, the implementation with association aspects has merely 60% code size when compared against the implementation
without association aspects.

The difference in the code size can be observed as the additional lines in the
implementation without association aspects. The comments in Fig. 19 classify
the additional lines into the next three groups:

+**REL:** code for Relation class declaration
+**LOOP:** code for loops to access all relations
+**GET:** code for retrieving states in Relation objects

```
public aspect AutoBuildAj extends Association {
  private static class AutoBuildRelation extends Relation { //+REL
    private int busy;                                        //+REL
    ... //following getter and setter of busy definitions    //+REL
  }                                                          //+REL
  protected Class getRelationClass() {                       //+REL
    return AutoBuildRelation.class;                          //+REL
  }
  after(Buffer buffer):
    execution(public boolean Buffer.save(..))
    && target(buffer)  {
    for (Iterator iter = (Iterator) associated(buffer, ANY); //+LOOP
        iter.hasNext();)  {  // writing explicit loop by hand //+LOOP
      AutoBuildRelation r = (AutoBuildRelation) iter.next();  //+LOOP
      AntManager project = (AntManager) r.getRight();         //+GET
      int busy = r.getBusy();                                 //+GET
      if (busy > 0) return;
      r.setBusy(busy+1);
      project.build();
      r.setBusy(busy-1);
  } }
  ... //following other advice definitions
}
```

Fig. 19. Code of AutoBuild by the original AspectJ

Conversely, the advantages of association aspects are to provide language constructs for those operations.

The advantages of association aspects would become more significant when we develop more practical IDEs. This is because such an IDE would have more integrated operations not only between Buffer and AntManager, but also among multiple projects (e.g., build depending projects before building a project), between a text editor and a source file versioning system, between a text editor and a compiler for handling error messages, and so on. Implementing those additional features by using association aspects would be good for assessing extensibility and adaptability of aspects. We would like to explore this in future work.

Table 3. The result of comparing code size

File name	AALOC	File name	AJLOC	AALOC/AJLOC
AutoBuild.aj	50	AutoBuildAj.aj	83	0.60
		Association.aj	77	
AntFile.java	85		85	
AntManager.java	128		128	
IDE.java	132		132	
Total	395		505	0.78

7 Discussion

7.1 Comparison with Eos

As the work on the association aspects is based on the work on Eos [4], we here discuss the differences in detail. The most notable difference is that Eos implicitly uses the current target object when selecting aspect instances at advice execution. In contrast, association aspects can use arbitrary objects that are explicitly specified by pointcuts. The mechanism in Eos is less flexible for the following situations: (1) when aspect instances should be selected by using a nontarget object, e.g., when advising a call to a class method, and (2) when aspect instances should be selected by using more than one object, e.g., when a security concern is to prevent method calls from object A to B, it can be realized by an aspect instance associated to A and B. When a call from A to B happens, all the aspect instances associated to B run an advice body in Eos, even though the caller object A could be used for selecting aspect instances.

Both association aspects and Eos can distinguish roles of associated objects. Eos, however, distinguishes by introducing additional role constructs around advice declarations, which might make it difficult to reuse aspects. For example, even though `Trigger` and `Equality` aspects in Sect. 2.1 only differ in what objects should be used at advice dispatching, the declarations in Eos have different program structures, since the former has to enclose advice declarations in a role construct. Since association aspects distinguish roles of objects by the parameter positions in the `associated` pointcuts, the declarations of those aspects can only differ in the pointcuts. Our approach, in which advice dispatching is governed by pointcuts, would fit the other language features in AspectJ, as it usually reuses aspects through the abstraction mechanisms of pointcuts (i.e., the named pointcuts and the abstract pointcuts).

Both Eos and association aspects should be careful about the performance penalty for the objects with no associated aspect instance. For the `Bit` integration example, a `set` call to a `Bit` object that has no associated `Equality` instances should not have significant overhead. On this regard, there are two possible dimensions to the overhead.

The first is the number of aspect instances. A naive implementation (which is called the first work-around [4]) would significantly degrade its performance to look up a systemwide table of aspect instances. Both Eos and association aspects avoid this problem by having a list of associated aspects in each object.

The second is the number of advice declarations that statically match to the call. Association aspects would linearly degrade the performance as each advice declaration adds a getting a field and null checking into the method call expression. Eos avoids this problem by having a list of thunks for each method call expression. However, the approach in Eos requires more memory and more operations for associating/unassociating aspect instances.

Those differences in implementation would result in the differences in performance characteristics. However, we would need more programs written with association aspects in order to carry out quantitative comparison. This is because the difference in performance depends on the number of advice declarations at a joinpoint shadow and the number of joinpoint shadows that are advised by different sets of aspect instances.

7.2   Other Related Work

Prior to the proposal of AOP, there have been studies on language mechanisms that support the evolution of collaborative behavior for object-oriented languages, namely the contracts by Helm and Holland [13], and the context relations by Seiter et al. [14, 15]. Those languages rely on different mechanisms from pointcut and advice. Although there are many commonalities between those language mechanisms and association aspects, there are also differences when compared more closely. For example, a context relation can be associated to an arbitrary number of objects, while an association aspect can be associated to, at most, one object for each parameter position. Conversely, an association aspect can be associated to an object pair in the same type, which does not seem to be possible in the context relations.

There are AOP languages that have similar mechanisms to association aspects, namely CarsarJ proposed by Mezini and Ostermann [16, 17, 18], EpsilonJ proposed by Tamai et al. [19], and ObjectTeams proposed by Herrmann et al. [20, 21]. Those language models can support integration concerns by using role objects and collaboration contexts.

In CaesarJ, a `cclass` object corresponds to an aspect instance, which can be instantiated with several `cclass` instances that wrap objects as role members. However, CaesarJ has no mechanism to associate a `cclass` instance to a group of objects and to find associated instances. Supporting integration concerns would need manual management of wrapper instances. A more recent version of CaesarJ supports variable management implementations by a mixin-like reuse mechanism.

EpsilonJ and ObjectTeams have a construct to define a context that encloses several role definitions. A context (or a team in ObjectTeams) can be instantiated explicitly and can bind a role to an arbitrary object. EpsilonJ realizes one-to-many relations by introducing a mechanism that broadcasts calls to all role objects of a specified type in a context; ObjectTeams can generalize the mechanism by using an abstract team.

JAsCo [22] is an aspect-oriented language for component-based software development. JAsCo introduces new language constructs such as a hook and a connector. Although they have different granularity from the module system of the association aspects (or AspectJ), we think that association aspects are useful to connect(integrate) existing components as well as JAsCo.

Ostermann et al. proposed an expressive pointcut language ALPHA based on logical queries over dynamic properties of a program execution [23]. Unlike other extensible AOP languages that can query over static structures of a program, ALPHA is so powerful that it can define pointcuts that examine a past state in a program execution with individual object references. As a result, it is possible to write a pointcut like "when called `set` or `clear` to a target `bit1`, there was a call `associate(bit1,bit2)` in the past, then bind the second parameter to `bit2`". However, it is not clear whether such a pointcut can be as efficiently implemented as association aspects.

Colman and Han developed the ROAD framework [24] using association aspects for defining a coordination system that manages an organizational system. In the ROAD framework, objects are modeled as the roles in a specific organization. Association aspects act as the stateful contract between role objects. When an association aspect picks up a message between the role objects, the advice of the aspect coordinates the role objects

The current version of association aspects is implemented by modifying the `ajc` compiler [10]. There is another AspectJ compiler named `abc` developed by de Moor et al. [25]. `abc` is an extensible compiler for implementing new language constructs such as association aspects. We expect that association aspects for the `abc` compiler can be achieved by applying the same compilation strategy as that described in Sect. 4.

8   Conclusion

We presented association aspects as an extension to in AspectJ. They are based on the notion of instance-level aspects in Eos [4], and extended with the pointcut-based advice dispatching mechanisms that enable flexible yet concise descriptions of aspects whose instances are associated to more than one object. As a result, the association aspects can give straightforward representations of crosscutting concerns that have stateful behavior with respect to a particular group of objects.

We developed a compiler for association aspects by modifying the AspectJ compiler (`ajc`). The compiler employs an optimization strategy that reduces the number of data structures. The benchmark tests exhibited that the slowdown factors of the programs using association aspects with respect to the regular AspectJ programs are 1.0 to 1.2.

As an application of association aspects, we developed an tiny IDE by integrating existing applications in a nonintrusive way. Although this is merely one particular example, we observed that the use of association aspects reduced the code size of the core integration aspect in the IDE to approximately 60% from the one defined without association aspects. Our future plan is to quantitatively evaluate association aspects by using software metrics other than code size. In particular, evaluation criteria used for comparing GoF Design Pattern implementations in Java and AspectJ [26] would be useful.

Bridging between design level concepts and association aspects at the implementation level is also left for future work. Association aspects would be a suitable vehicle to implement many design-level concepts such as relation objects in UML, roles in the collection designs, and composites of concepts in CoCompose [27]. It would be useful to investigate methodologies to design these concepts by assuming association aspects and to derive proper implementations from those concepts.

Acknowledgments

We would like to thank the anonymous reviewers for their valuable comments that helped us to clarify discussion and to fix English problems in an early drafts of the paper. We also would like to thank Kevin Sullivan and Hridesh Rajan for the detailed information on Eos, Alan Colman for the feedback from his experience in using association aspects, the members of the TM Seminar and the Kumini project at University of Tokyo and the members of Komiya's Laboratory at Shibaura Institute of Technology for valuable comments and suggestions.

References

[1] Kiczales G., Hilsdale E., Hugunin J., Kersten M., Palm J., and Griswold W.G. An overview of AspectJ. In: *ECOOP '01: Proceedings of the 15th European Conference on Object-Oriented Programming*, Springer, pp. 327–353, 2001

[2] Ossher H. Multi-dimensional separation of concerns: The Hyperspace approach. In: *Proceedings of Software Architectures and Component Technology*, Springer, 2000

[3] Sullivan K., Gu L., and Cai Y. Non-modularity in aspect-oriented languages: Integration as a crosscutting concern for AspectJ. In: *Proceedings of the 1st International Conference on Aspect-Oriented Software Development*, ACM, pp. 19–26, 2002

[4] Rajan H. and Sullivan K. Eos: Instance-level aspects for integrated system design. In: *ESEC/FSE-11: Proceedings of the 9th European Software Engineering Conference Held Jointly with 11th ACM SIGSOFT International Symposium on Foundations of Software Engineering*, ACM, New York, pp. 297–306, 2003

[5] The AspectJ Project at Eclipse.org. http://www.eclipse.org/aspectj/. Cited 30 January 2006

[6] Sullivan K. Mediators: Easing the design and evolution of integrated systems. *PhD Thesis*, Department of Computer Science, Unversity of Washington published as TR UW-CSE-94-08-01 (1994)

[7] Sullivan K.J., Notkin D. Reconciling environment integration and software evolution. *ACM Trans. Softw. Eng. Methodol.*, 1:229–268, 1992

[8] Gamma E., Helm R., Johnson R., Vlissides J. Design patterns. Addison-Wesley, 1995

[9] Hannemann J. and Kiczales G. Design pattern implementation in java and AspectJ. In: *Proceedings of the 17th ACM SIGPLAN Conference on Object-Oriented Programming, Systems, Languages, and Applications*, ACM, pp. 161–173, 2002

[10] Hilsdale E. and Hugunin J. Advice weaving in AspectJ. In: *Proceedings of the 3rd International Conference on Aspect-Oriented Software Development*, ACM, pp. 26–35, 2004

[11] Masuhara H., Kiczales G., and Dutchyn C. A compilation and optimization model for aspect-oriented programs. In: *Proceedings of the 12th International Conference Compiler Construction 2003*, Springer, pp. 46–60, 2003

[12] Sakurai K., Masuhara H., Ubayashi N., Matsuura S., and Komiya S. Association aspects. In: *Proceedings of the 3rd International Conference on Aspect-Oriented Software Development*, ACM, pp. 16–25, 2004

[13] Helm R., Holland I.M., and Gangopadhyay D. Contracts: Specifying behavioral compositions in object-oriented systems. In: *OOPSLA/ECOOP '90: Proceedings of the European Conference on Object-Oriented Programming on Object-Oriented Programming Systems, Languages, and Applications*, ACM, New York, pp. 169–180, 1990

[14] Seiter L.M., Palsberg J., and Lieberherr K.J. Evolution of object behavior using context relations. In: Garlan, D. (ed.) *Proceedings of the 4th ACM SIGSOFT Symposium on Foundations of Software Engineering*, ACM (SIGSOFT), pp. 46–57, 1996

[15] Seiter L.M., Palsberg J., Lieberherr K.J. Evolution of object behavior using context relations. *IEEE Transactions on Software Engineering*, 24:79–92, 1998

[16] Mezini M. and Ostermann K. Conquering aspects with Caesar. In: *AOSD '03: Proceedings of the 2nd International Conference on Aspect-Oriented Software Development*, ACM, New York, pp. 90–99, 2003

[17] Mezini M. and Ostermann K. Integrating independent components with on-demand remodularization. In: *OOPSLA '02: Proceedings of the 17th ACM SIGPLAN Conference on Object-Oriented Programming, Systems, Languages, and Applications*, ACM, New York, pp. 52–67, 2002

[18] Mezini M. and Ostermann K. Variability management with feature-oriented programming and aspects. In: *Proceedings of the 12th ACM SIGSOFT Twelfth International Symposium on Foundations of Software Engineering*, ACM, New York, pp. 127–136, 2004

[19] Tamai T., Ubayashi N., and Ichiyama R. An adaptive object model with dynamic role binding. In: *ICSE '05: Proceedings of the 27th International Conference on Software Engineering*, ACM, New York, pp. 166–175, 2005

[20] Veit M. and Herrmann S. Model-view-controller and object teams: A perfect match of paradigms. In: *AOSD '03: Proceedings of the 2nd International Conference on Aspect-Oriented Software Development*, ACM, New York, pp. 140–149, 2003

[21] Herrmann S., Hundt C., Mehner K., and Wloka J. Using guard predicates for generalized control of aspect instantiation and activation. In: *DAW '05: Dynamic Aspects Workshop (held in conjunction with AOSD 2005)*, Chicago, Illinois, pp. 93–101, 2005

[22] Suvée D., Vanderperren W., and Jonckers V. JAsCo: An aspect-oriented approach tailored for component based software development. In: *AOSD '03: Proceedings of the 2nd International Conference on Aspect-Oriented Software Development*, ACM, New York, pp. 21–29, 2003

[23] Ostermann K., Mezini M., and Bockisch C. Expressive pointcuts for increased modularity. In: *ECOOP '05: Proceedings of the 19th European Conference on Object-Oriented Programming*, Springer, 2005

[24] Colman A. and Han J. Coordination systems in role-based adaptive software. In: *COORDINATION 05: Proceedings of the Seventh International Conference on Coordination Models and Languages, LNCS vol. 3454*, Springer, pp. 63–78, 2005

[25] Avgustinov P., Christensen A.S., Hendren L., Kuzins S., Lhoták J., Lhoták, O., de Moor, O., Sereni, D., Sittampalam, G., and Tibble, J. abc: An extensible AspectJ compiler. In: *AOSD '05: Proceedings of the 4th International Conference on Aspect-Oriented Software Development*, ACM, New York, pp. 87–98, 2005

[26] Garcia A., Sant'Anna C., Figueiredo E., Kulesza U., Lucena C., and von Staa A. Modularizing design patterns with aspects: A quantitative study. In: *AOSD '05: Proceedings of the 4th International Conference on Aspect-Oriented Software Development*, ACM, New York, pp 3–14, 2005

[27] Wagelaar D. and Jonckers V. A concept-based approach to software design. In: *SEA 2003: Proceedings of the 7th IASTED International Conference on Software Engineering and Applications*, Cambridge, MA, 2003

Appendix

Generating Code of Dispatching with Around Advice

The compilation rules of around advice are slightly different from those of before and after advice due to the proceed mechanism in around advice. Figure 20 shows the skeletons of the methods and an auxiliary class, namely the _dispatch and _abody methods and the _Closure class.

When an around advice is to run, instead of directly running the advice body, the compiled code first creates a _Closure object with a list of associated aspects that match the pointcut. The _Closure object serves as a continuation of advice body. When called, it runs the advice body in the context of the next aspect instance, or performs the original operations of the joinpoint.

Assume the declaration of aspect A in Fig. 21. As shown in Fig. 22, the Compiler generates the _dispatch1 and _abody1 methods in to class A and an auxiliary class _Closure. The compiler replaces every call to m with a called to _dispatch1, which in turn runs the body of advice in the context of an aspect instance or runs method m when no more matching aspect instances are found. Note that the former case creates a new _Closure object for handling proceed in the advice body. This is needed to cope with AspectJ's language design that allows around advice declarations to call proceed more than once.

Performance of Around Advice. The implementation of around advice in association aspects has some overheads when compared against before advice. The overheads include collecting n aspect instances and dispatching n closures with proceed. Table 4 illustrates differences in execution times between around and before advice with n aspect instances. Those figures are insensitive to the number of associated objects and the number of bound parameters in associated pointcuts.

From the figures in the table, we can approximate the overhead of around advice execution by the following formula:

Table 4. Execution times (in μs) of around advice

n	AROUND	BEFORE	AROUND-BEFORE
0	0.786	0.029	0.757
1	2.016	0.327	1.689
25	11.986	3.578	8.408
50	24.103	6.948	17.155
75	39.369	10.268	29.101
100	56.223	13.642	42.581

$$AROUND(n) = 0.375n + 0.757 + BEFORE(n),$$

where $AROUND(n)$ and $BEFORE(n)$ are execution times of around and before advice with n instances, respectively.

This suggests that the around advice has overheads of approximately 0.757 μs for each joinpoint and 0.375 μs for running an advice body in the context of an aspect instance.

```
static Tjp _dispatch( Tσi(1) v1, ...,Tσi(l) vl) {
    if(!⟨parameterless dynamic conditions⟩) return _jp(v1,...,vl);
    Ui1 mi1=v1._aspectsi; if(mi1==null)return _jp(v1,...,vl);
    Ui2 mi2=mi1.get(v2); if(mi2==null)return _jp(v1,...,vl);
    ...

    Uil mil=mil-1.get(vl);
    if(mil==null)return _jp(v1,...,vl);
    List as = new ArrayList();
    for (Uil+1 mil+1 : mil.values()) {
        ...

            for (Ui|σi| mi|σi| : mi|σi|-1.values()) {
                collecting
            }
        ...

    }
    return new _Closure(as, 0).run(v1 ,...,vl);
}


Tjp _abody(Tσi(1) v1, ..., Tσi(l) vl, _Closure c) {
    if (!⟨dynamic conditions⟩) return _jp(v1,...,vl);
    //statements in the advice body...
    //proceed are translated to c.run(...)
}

class _Closure {
    List as; int i;
    _Closure(List as, int i) { this.as =as; this.i =i; }
    Tjp run(Tσi(1) v1,...,Tσi(l) vl) {
        if(i < as.size()) {
            return ((A)as.get(i))._abody(v1, ..., vl, new _Closure(as, i+1));
        } else { return _jp(v1,...,vl); }
} }
```

$$collecting = \begin{cases} \text{as.addAll(m}_{i|\sigma_i|}\text{);} & |\sigma_i| < n \\ \text{as.add(m}_{i|\sigma_i|}\text{);} & |\sigma_i| = n \end{cases}$$

Fig. 20. Code for around advice dispatching and body

```
aspect A perobjects(T1, T2, T3, T4) {
 int around(T1 v1, T2 v2): call(int m(T1, T2))
    && args(v1, v2) && associated(v1,v2,*,*) {
   return proceed(v1, v2);
} }
```

Fig. 21. An example aspect with an around advice declaration

```
static int _dispatch1(T1 v1, T2 v2) {
 Map<T2, Map<T3, List<A>>> m1 = v1.aspects1;
                             if(m1==null) return m(v1,v2);
 Map<T3, List<A>> m2 = m1.get(v2);  if(m2==null) return m(v1,v2);
 List as = new ArrayList();
 _Closure c = new _Closure(as, 0); //create a closure
 for (List<A> m3: m2.values())      //collect all matching
    as.addAll(m3);                 //   aspect instances
 return c.run(v1,v2);              //run the first advice
}

static int _abody1(T1 v1, T2 v2, _Closure c) {
  return c.run(v1, v2);               //the body of advice
}

class _Closure {
  List as; int i;
  _Closure(List as, int i) { this.as = as; this.i = i; }
  int run(T1 v1, T2 v2) {
    if (i < as.size()) {
      A a = as.get(i);                     //run advice body
      return a._abody1(v1,v2, new _Closure(as, i+1));
    } else {
      return m(v1,v2);
    }
} }
```

Fig. 22. Generated methods and class for around advice

abc: An Extensible AspectJ Compiler

Pavel Avgustinov[1], Aske Simon Christensen[2], Laurie Hendren[3],
Sascha Kuzins[1], Jennifer Lhoták[3], Ondřej Lhoták[3], Oege de Moor[1],
Damien Sereni[1], Ganesh Sittampalam[1], and Julian Tibble[1]

[1] Programming Tools Group, Oxford University, United Kingdom
[2] BRICS, University of Aarhus, Denmark
[3] Sable Research Group, McGill University, Montreal, Canada

Abstract. Research in the design of aspect-oriented programming languages requires a workbench that facilitates easy experimentation with new language features and implementation techniques. In particular, new features for AspectJ have
been proposed that require extensions in many dimensions: syntax, type checking and code generation, as well as data flow and control flow analyses. The
AspectBench Compiler (*abc*) is an implementation of such a workbench. The
base version of *abc* implements the full AspectJ language. Its front end is built
using the Polyglot framework, as a modular extension of the Java language. The
use of Polyglot gives flexibility of syntax and type checking. The back end is
built using the Soot framework, to give modular code generation and analyses.
In this paper, we outline the design of *abc*, focusing mostly on how the design
supports extensibility. We then provide a general overview of how to use *abc* to
implement an extension. We illustrate the extension mechanisms of *abc* through a
number of small, but nontrivial, examples. We then proceed to contrast the design
goals of *abc* with those of the original AspectJ compiler, and how these different
goals have led to different design decisions. Finally, we review a few examples
of projects by others that extend *abc* in interesting ways.

1 Introduction and Motivation

The design and implementation of aspect-oriented programming languages is a
buoyant field, with many new language features being developed. In the first instance,
such features can be prototyped in a system like the Aspect Sand Box [17] via a
definitional interpreter. Such interpreters are useful in defining the semantics and in
explaining the compilation strategy of new language features [32]. The acid test for
new language features is, however, their integration into a full, industrial-strength
language like AspectJ. That requires a highly flexible implementation of AspectJ that
can be extended in a clean and modular way.

The purpose of this paper is to present *abc*, the AspectBench Compiler for AspectJ,
which supports the whole of the AspectJ language implemented by *ajc* 1.2, and which
has been specifically designed to be an extensible framework for implementing AspectJ
extensions. *abc* is freely available under the GNU LGPL [1].

Challenges. An AspectJ compiler is already a complex piece of software, which, in
addition to the normal front-end and back-end components of a compiler, must also

A. Rashid and M. Aksit (Eds.): Transactions on AOSD I, LNCS 3880, pp. 293–334, 2006.
© Springer-Verlag Berlin Heidelberg 2006

support a matcher (for name patterns) and a weaver (both for intertype declarations and for advice). Furthermore, the kinds of extensions that have been suggested for AspectJ vary from fairly simple pointcut language extensions to more complex concepts which require modifications in the type system, matcher and weaver. To make the challenges explicit, we briefly review some previous work by others that has motivated our design.

At one end of the spectrum, there are fairly small extensions that require changes primarily to the syntax. An example of this kind is the *name pattern scopes* proposed by Colyer and Clement [12], which provide an abstraction mechanism for name patterns. To support this type of extension, our workbench needs an easy way of extending the syntax, as well as introducing named patterns into the environment.

A more involved extension is the *parametric introductions* of Hanenberg and Unland [23]. These are intertype declarations that depend on parameters evaluated at weave time. Their integration into AspectJ requires substantial changes to the type system as well as the intertype weaver. This kind of extension thus motivates a highly flexible implementation of types.

Most proposals for new features in AspectJ are, however, concerned with the dynamic join point model. Sakurai et al. [39] propose *association aspects*. These provide a generalisation of per-object instantiation, where aspect instances are tied to a group of objects to express behavioural relationships more directly. This requires not only changes to the front end, but also substantial changes to code generation. Making such code generation painless is another design goal of our workbench.

The community as a whole is concerned with finding ways of singling out join points based on semantic properties rather than naming. For instance, Kiczales has proposed a new type of pointcut, called *predicted cflow* [29]. **pcflow**(p) matches at a join point if there may exist a path to another join point where p matches. It is correct to let **pcflow**(p) match everywhere, but that would lead to inefficient programs. An efficient implementation of **pcflow**(p) needs substantial, interprocedural program analysis. Our workbench needs to provide a framework for building such analyses.

In fact, examples where efficient implementation necessitates an analysis framework abound. Particular instances include the *data flow pointcuts* of Masuhara and Kawauchi [31], and the *trace-based aspects* of Douence et al. [14], as well as the *communication history aspects* of Walker and Viggers [45].

All of the above are additions to the AspectJ language, but, of course, restrictions can be equally important in language design. One promising example is the proposal of Aldrich to restrict the visibility of join points to those that are explicit in the interface of a class [2]. We aim to support the implementation of such restrictions, and this requires a flexible implementation of the type system and the pointcut matcher.

Finally, we note that the implementation of advanced static checking tools for aspect-oriented programs, such as those investigated by Krishnamurthi et al. [30], require all types of extensions discussed above, ranging from simple variations in syntax to making advanced analyses such as escape analysis take into account the effects of advice.

In summary, we can see that an extensible AspectJ compiler must be able to handle a wide variety of extensions, possibly touching on many components of the compiler, including the front-end scanner and parser, the type checker, the matcher and weaver, and potentially requiring relatively sophisticated program analysis to ensure correctness and efficiency.

Design Goals. One approach to implementing a language extension is to modify an existing compiler. However, this is not always the best approach, since existing compilers may not have been designed with extensiblity as one of the main goals. Furthermore, they may be constrained to work with infrastructures which themselves are not easily extensible. In the case of AspectJ, the only pre-existing implementation is *ajc*, which is designed to support fast and incremental compilation and also to interact closely with the Eclipse toolset.

Our approach was to design and implement *abc*, the AspectBench Compiler, with extensibility as its primary design goal. We also aimed for an optimising implementation of AspectJ, and we briefly summarise that perspective in our comparison with *ajc* in Sect. 6.5. To support extensibility, we distilled the following requirements from the above discussion of the challenges involved:

Simplicity. It must be relatively simple to develop new extensions. Users of the framework should not need to understand complicated new concepts or a complex software design in order to implement their extensions.

Modularity. We require two kinds of modularity. First, the compiler workbench itself should be very modular, so that the different facets of each extension can be easily identified with the correct module of the workbench. Second, the extension should be modular (separate from the workbench code). Users of the workbench should not need to change existing code; rather, they should be able to describe the extensions as specifications or code that is separate from the main code base.

Proportionality. Small extensions should require a small amount of work and code. There should not be a large overhead required to specify an extension.

Analysis capability. The compiler workbench infrastructure should provide both an intermediate representation and a program analysis framework. This is necessary for two reasons. First, some extensions may require relatively sophisticated analyses to correctly implement their semantic checks and weaving. Second, some extensions may lead to a lot of run-time overhead unless compiler optimisation techniques are used to minimise that overhead.

The *abc* Approach. To meet these objectives, we decided to build on existing, proven tools, namely the Polyglot extensible compiler framework for the front end [37], and the Soot analysis and transformation framework for the back end [43]. [The McGill authors of the present paper are the authors of Soot.] Indeed, Polyglot has been shown to meet the criteria of simplicity, modularity and proportionality on a wide variety of extensions to the syntax and type system of Java. By the same token, Soot has been shown to meet all the above criteria for code generation, analysis and optimisation.

Given the success of these building blocks, we felt it extremely important to design *abc* so that both are used *as is*, without any changes that are specific to *abc*, in order to allow easy migration to new releases of those frameworks. As explained in Sect. 2, this has dictated an architecture where the front end separates the AspectJ program into a pure Java part and a part containing instructions for the back end.

Contributions. In general terms, the contributions of this paper are the following:

Comprehensive account of an AspectJ compiler. While *ajc* has been in use for eight years or more, there are few publications that give a comprehensive account of its main design decisions, a notable exception being the description of its advice weaver in [27]. The present paper aims to provide a general overview of how to build an AspectJ compiler, while pointing out the structure that is common to *ajc* and *abc*. We also examine the consequences of the different design goals of *ajc* and *abc*, in particular how *abc* places more emphasis on extensibility and optimisation.

Extensible workbench for AOP research. We have identified the requirements for a workbench for research, in aspect-oriented programming languages by analysing previous research in this area. We show how *abc* meets these requirements, and validate our architecture with a number of small but nontrivial examples. Furthermore, we present an overview of extensions to *abc* that have been implemented by other researchers.

Experience with Soot and Polyglot. *abc* builds on Polyglot and Soot without making any changes to these two components. As such, *abc* is one of the largest projects undertaken with either Soot or Polyglot. This paper is therefore also an experience report, assessing the suitability of Polyglot and Soot for building aspect-oriented programming tools.

At a more technical level, the contributions of *abc* with respect to extensibility are these:

Pass structure. *abc* has a carefully designed pass structure, where each compiler pass achieves exactly one task, so that it is never necessary to split an existing pass when inserting a new one required by an extension. Designing such a pass structure that processes all types in the right order is quite hard, as witnessed, for example, by a bug concerning ITDs on inner classes in *ajc* [5]. Another example is the need for three separate passes that evaluate classname patterns. The pass structure is outlined in Sect. 2, and then further detailed as necessary for our examples.

Separator. *abc* includes a *separator* pass that splits the original AspectJ abstract syntax tree (AST) into a pure Java part and the aspectinfo; by enforcing that separation very strictly, extensions never need to modify the code generation pass, which is used unchanged from the Soot framework. The separator is explained in Sect. 2.3.

Use of Jimple. *abc* implements the use of a typed, stackless, three address intermediate representation, namely Jimple, to significantly simplify doing a good job of writing a new weaver for new join point types. The advantages of Jimple (versus bytecode) for weaving are discussed in Sect. 6.3.

Regular IR for pointcuts. *abc* also includes an intermediate representation of pointcuts that is more regular than at source level. This representation makes it easier to represent new pointcut primitives, and we shall illustrate this with the example of local pointcut variables. The intermediate representation includes reducing complex pointcut expressions to disjunctive normal form. An added benefit is that it sorted out some nettly problems with the treatment of disjunction (||) in *ajc* [4]. Our intermediate representation for pointcuts is presented in Sect. 3.6.

Reweaving. An explicit representation of residues via a metalanguage that can be optimised based on further analysis of woven Jimple; and a re-entrant design of the weaver to exploit such opportunities via a weave-analyse-weave cycle. This re-weaving architecture enables easy plug-and-play of complex optimisations. This architecture is first introduced in Sect. 2.4, and we present some numbers that demonstrate its advantages in Sect. 6.5.

Paper Structure. The structure of this paper is as follows. In Sect. 2, we first give an overview of the main building blocks of *abc*, namely Polyglot and Soot, and show their role in the overall architecture of *abc*. Next, in Sect. 3 we sketch the main points of extensibility in *abc*. We then turn to describe some modest but representative examples of AspectJ extensions in Sect. 4, and their implementation in Sect. 5. The design goals of *abc* are contrasted with those of the original AspectJ compiler *ajc* in Sect. 6, and we examine how the different goals have led to different design decisions. A particular topic highlighted in Sect. 6 is the use of Jimple in a weaver, why it is good for extensions and for implementing optimisations. In Sect. 7, we review a few examples by other researchers who have extended *abc*. Also in Sect. 7, we discuss a number of similar projects that share *abc*'s goals. Finally, in Sect. 8 we draw some conclusions from our experience in building *abc*, and we explore possible directions for future research.

This paper is an enhanced, updated version of [6]. New material includes: the architecture of the weaver in Sect. 2, a detailed qualitative comparison to *ajc* in Sect. 6, a discussion of other projects that build on *abc* in Sect. 7, and many small improvements throughout.

2 Architecture

As stated in the introduction, *abc* is based on the Polyglot extensible compiler framework [37] and the Soot bytecode analysis and transformation framework [43]. Using Polyglot as an extensible front end enables customisation of the grammar and semantic analysis; in the back end, Soot provides a convenient intermediate representation on which to implement the weaving of extensions, as well as tools for writing any program analyses that extensions may require.

Input classes can be given to *abc* as source code or class files, and *abc* is able to weave into both. Source files are processed by the Polyglot front end, whereas only the signature part of class files are read by Polyglot in order to perform type checking of the source code. In both cases, weaving is performed on Jimple, Soot's intermediate representation.

Because *abc* works with an unmodified Soot and Polyglot, it is easy for us, as the developers of *abc* itself, to update to the latest versions of Soot and Polyglot as they are released. By the same token, authors of AspectJ extensions can upgrade to new versions of *abc* without difficulty. This independence was achieved mainly by separating the AspectJ-specific features in the code being processed from standard Java code. In the front end, *abc* generates a plain Java AST and a separate aspect information structure containing the aspect-specific information. We call the aspect information structure the *AspectInfo*. The unmodified back end can read in the AST (because it is plain Java), and *abc* then uses the *AspectInfo* to perform all required weaving. A simplified diagram of the architecture of *abc* is shown in Fig. 1. In many respects, this architecture is similar to that of *ajc*. At this level of abstraction, the main difference is the strict use of a

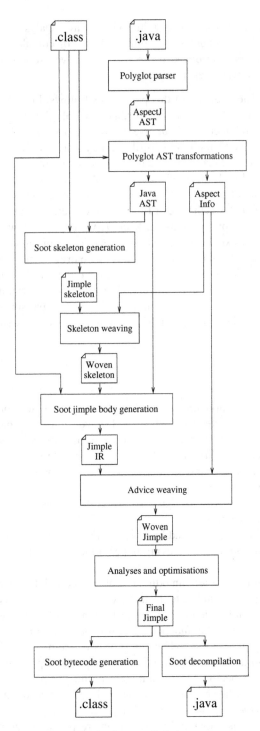

Fig. 1. *abc* overall design

separator pass (labelled "Polyglot AST transformations" in the figure) for splitting the pure Java from any aspect-specific information. This separation process is described in more detail below.

In the following subsections, we describe Polyglot and Soot in the context of *abc*, with a focus on how they contribute to extensibility. Finally, we discuss in some more detail how the two parts are connected.

2.1 Polyglot

Polyglot [37] is a front end for Java intended for implementing extensions to the base language. In its original configuration, Polyglot first parses Java source code into an AST, then performs all the static checks required by the Java language in a number of passes which rewrite the tree. The output of Polyglot is a Java AST annotated with type information, which is written back to a Java source file. Polyglot is intended to perform all compile-time checks; when a class has passed through all of the passes in Polyglot, the resulting Java file should be compilable without errors by any standard Java compiler. When Polyglot is used as a front end for Soot, the *Java-to-Jimple* module inside Soot compiles the final AST into the Jimple intermediate representation instead of writing it out to a Java file. Therefore, in *abc*, the final Polyglot passes separate the AspectJ program into pure Java (which is passed to the Java-to-Jimple module in Soot) and instructions for the backend.

Several features of Polyglot make it well-suited for writing extensions, and also help to make those extensions themselves extensible. Polyglot allows a new grammar to be specified as a collection of modifications to an existing grammar, where these modifications are given in a separate specification file, not in the original grammar file. The AspectJ grammar we developed for *abc* is specified as an extension of the Java grammar, and the grammars for extensions are in turn specified as modifications to the AspectJ grammar.

Polyglot makes heavy use of interfaces and factories, making it easy to extend or replace most of its parts, such as the type system or the scope rules, as well as the list of rewrite passes that are performed on the AST. Each pass in Polyglot nondestructively rewrites the input tree. As a result, it is easy to insert new passes in between existing ones, and each pass typically performs only a small amount of work compared to traditional compiler passes. In *abc*, we have added many AspectJ-specific passes, and it is easy for extensions to add further passes of their own. The ordering of passes must be chosen carefully, since the semantic analysis of Java source code might depend on changes to the program introduced by aspects.

Each AST node in Polyglot uses a mechanism of *extensions* and *delegates* to allow methods to be replaced or added in the middle of the existing class hierarchy, achieving an effect similar to what can be done in AspectJ using intertype declarations, but in plain Java. This mechanism is commonly used by extensions of *abc* to modify existing AST nodes.

2.2 Soot

Soot [43], which is used as the back end of *abc*, is a framework for analysing and transforming Java bytecode. The most important advantage of using Soot as the back end, both for developing *abc* itself and for extending the language, is Jimple, Soot's intermediate representation. Soot provides modules to convert between Jimple, Java bytecode and Java source code. It furthermore includes implementations of standard compiler optimisations, which *abc* applies after weaving. We have already observed significant speedups from these optimisations alone [7]. In addition to already implemented analyses and transformations, Soot has tools for writing new ones, such as control flow graph builders, definition/use chains, a fixed-point flow analysis framework and a method inliner. These features are useful for implementing extensions that need to be aware of the intraprocedural behaviour of the program, such as pointcuts describing specific points in the control flow graph.

The Jimple intermediate representation is a typed, stackless, three-address code. Rather than representing computations with an implicit stack, each Jimple instruction explicitly manipulates specified local variables. This representation simplifies weaving of advice, both for standard AspectJ features and for extensions. If it were weaving into bytecode directly, the weaver would need to consider the effect of the woven code on the implicit execution stack, and generate additional code to fix up the stack contents. None of this is necessary when weaving into Jimple. Moreover, when values from the shadow point are needed as parameters to the advice, they are readily available in local variables; the weaver does not have to sift through the computation stack to find them.

As input, Soot can handle both class files and Java source files. To convert bytecode to Jimple, Soot introduces a local variable to explicitly represent each stack location, splits the variables to separate independent uses of the same location and infers a type [20] for each variable. To convert source code to Jimple, Soot first uses Polyglot to construct an AST with type information, and then generates Jimple code from the AST. This process does not need to be modified in *abc*, because *abc* passes Soot a plain Java AST, keeping all the aspect-specific information in the separate aspect information structure. Normally, after all processing, Soot converts the Jimple code into bytecode and writes it to class files, but it also includes a decompiler, *dava* [33], which is very useful for viewing the effects of aspects and AspectJ extensions on the generated code.

2.3 Connecting Polyglot and Soot

We conclude the discussion of *abc*'s architecture by examining in closer detail how Polyglot and Soot interact. A key component of this interaction is the separation of the AspectJ AST into a pure Java AST and the auxilliary *AspectInfo* structure. This transformation enables *abc* to use the existing facility in Soot for translating a Polyglot AST into the Jimple IR. This is an important design decision in *abc*, as it implies that extension writers never need to modify the existing code generator. Other aspect-oriented systems that use a similar separation pass include AspectWerkz and Hyper/J [8, 38].

The Java AST is basically the AspectJ program with all AspectJ-specific language constructs removed. The *AspectInfo* structure contains complete information about these constructs. In cases where these contain actual Java code (advice bodies, **if** pointcut conditions, intertype method/constructor bodies, intertype field initialisers), the code is placed in placeholder methods in the Java AST.

The Java AST only contains Java constructs, but it is incomplete in the sense that it may refer to class members which do not exist or are not accessible in the unwoven

Java program. More specifically, the Java AST will in general not be compilable until all *declare parents* and intertype declarations have been woven into the program. The first of these can alter the inheritance hierarchy, and the second can introduce new members that the pure Java parts may refer to. Since both of these features may be applied to class files (for which we do not have an AST representation), it is not possible to perform this part of the weaving process on the Polyglot representation before passing the AST to Soot.

Fortunately, Soot allows us to conduct the conversion from Java to Jimple in two stages, and the application of *declare parents* and intertype weaving can happen in between. In the first stage, Soot builds a class hierarchy with mere stubs for the methods: it is a skeleton of a full program in Jimple, without method bodies. In the second stage, Soot fills in method bodies, either by converting bytecode from class files, or by compiling AST nodes.

This setup permits both static weaving and advice weaving to work on the Jimple IR, largely independent of whether the Jimple code was generated from source code or bytecode. And since the skeleton that is filled out in the second stage has the updated hierarchy and contains all intertype declarations, all member references in the code are resolved correctly in the translation into Jimple.

The two-stage weaving (static and advice) is shared with *ajc*. Indeed, the two stages are dictated by the AspectJ language design: static weaving only affects the type hierarchy, whereas advice weaving affects run-time behaviour. Furthermore, one cannot generate code without first adjusting the type hierarchy.

2.4   The Advice Weaver

The job of the advice weaver is to modify the Jimple code according to the instructions in the *AspectInfo* such that advice bodies are executed whenever the corresponding pointcuts match the currently executing join point.

The architecture of the advice weaver is shown in Fig. 2. The first step of advice weaving is to identify all *join point shadows*, that is, all places in the Jimple code that could potentially correspond to a join point in the execution of the program. Each of these is then matched against all pointcuts in the program. If it is determined that a pointcut might match a join point at a particular shadow, the matcher emits a weaving instruction telling the weaver to weave the advice body at that shadow. Since a pointcut can contain terms that depend on the run-time state of the program, it cannot always be fully determined at compile time whether a particular pointcut matches at a shadow. A weaving instruction thus consists of three parts: the shadow at which to weave, the advice to weave in and a *dynamic residue* specifying what additional run-time checks must be inserted to check that the pointcut actually matches the current join point. The dynamic residue also contains information about how to bind the values that are to become the arguments to the advice.

When all weaving instructions have been generated, the actual weaving is performed. The result is a Jimple program whose behaviour includes all advice bodies executing at the appropriate times. This program is then translated into bytecode by the Soot bytecode generator, and the result is written out to the target class files.

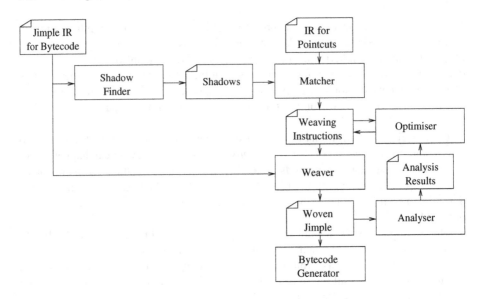

Fig. 2. Design of the *abc* advice weaver

Some extensions might require some sophisticated analysis to be done on the Jimple code. These fall roughly into two categories: *preweaving analysis*, where the analysis is performed on the original Java code before the advice are woven in, and *postweaving analysis*, where the analysis is performed on the woven code. Preweaving analysis is typically employed when the analysis results are needed by the pointcut matcher, for instance when implementing a new kind of pointcut. Postweaving analysis is used when some property of the final code is desired, for instance when doing optimisations on the final code or checking behavioural properties of the program.

In some cases, such as the **cflow** optimisation mentioned in Sect. 6.5, the analysis needs to be performed on the woven code, but the result is needed by the weaver. To facilitate such analyses, *abc* includes a mechanism for *reweaving*, which can throw away the woven code and revert to the unwoven code while retaining the analysis results obtained from analysing the woven code. This is also illustrated in Fig. 2. The results of the analysis are channelled back into an optimisation pass which modifies the weaving instructions to be used in a subsequent weaving pass. This process can be repeated as many times as necessary.

3   Defining an Extension

We now outline the basic steps needed to create an extension, in a general manner. This description is intended to give the reader an impression of the extension mechanisms available in *abc*, without delving into excessive detail. After this generic description, we shall introduce some concrete examples in Sect. 4, and show how the basic steps are instantiated in Sect. 5.

This section serves two purposes. First, we outline how we build on the existing extension mechanisms of Polyglot and Soot to achieve extensibility in *abc* (Sects. 3.2, 3.3, 3.4 and 3.8). Second, we wish to present some design decisions that are unique to *abc*, which address specific issues regarding the extension of AspectJ (Sects. 3.1, 3.5, 3.6, 3.7 and 3.9).

3.1 Syntax

The first step in implementing a new extension is usually defining what additional syntax it will introduce to the language. Making *abc* recognise the extended language involves changing the lexer and the parser that it uses. Polyglot already handles extending grammars in a very clean and modular fashion. However, the standard Polyglot lexer is not extensible—extensions are expected to create their own lexer by copying it and making appropriate modifications. Thus, in this section we describe our approach to making an extensible lexer in some detail, and then briefly summarise the Polyglot mechanism for extending grammars.

Lexer. We have designed the lexer for *abc* to support a limited form of extensibility that has been sufficient for the extensions we have written so far. Specifically, the set of keywords recognised by the lexer can be modified by an extension, and the actions taken by the lexer when encountering one of these keywords are customisable. More complex extensions can still be achieved by reverting to Polyglot's approach of copying and modifying the lexer definition. This is in agreement with the principle of proportionality which was stated as a design goal—small extensions are easy, and complex ones are possible.

The lexical analysis of AspectJ is complicated by the fact that there are really several different languages being parsed: ordinary Java code, aspect definitions and pointcut definitions. Consequently, the *abc* lexer is stateful—it recognises different tokens in different contexts. The following example illustrates one kind of problem that is dealt with by the introduction of lexer states:

if*.*1.Foo+.new(..)

The expected interpretation of such a string as Java code and as part of a pointcut will be very different; for example, in Java, we would expect "1." to become a floating point literal, whereas in the pointcut language the decimal point would be viewed as a dot separating elements of a name pattern. Similarly, "*" in Java should be scanned as an operator, while in pointcuts, it is part of a name pattern. Note also the use of what would be keywords in Java mode (**if** and **new**) as part of a pattern.

An important part of designing a stateful lexer is specifying when the lexer should switch to a different state without adding too much complexity. The general pattern we use is to maintain a stack of states, and recognise the end of a state when we reach an appropriate closing bracket character for that state. For example, normal Java code is terminated by the '}' character. Of course, braces can be nested, so we need to recognise opening braces and also count the nesting level. For more details regarding the lexer states in *abc*, see Sect. 5.2.

Parser. The *abc* parser is generated by PPG [9], the LALR parser generator for extensible grammars which is included in Polyglot [37]. PPG allows changes to an existing

File **X**	File **Y**
$S ::= a$ $\| \quad b$ $\| \quad c$	$include$ **X** $extend\ S ::= d$ $\| \quad e$

File **Z**	**Result**
$include$ **Y** $drop\ S ::= b$ $\| \quad d$	$S ::= a$ $\| \quad c$ $\| \quad e$

Fig. 3. Grammar extension mechanism

grammar to be entered in a separate file, overriding, inheriting and extending productions from the base grammar. This results in modular extensions, which can easily be maintained should the base grammar change.

The example in Fig. 3 (using simplified nonPPG syntax) demonstrates the basic principles. An existing grammar can be imported with the "*include*" keyword. New production rules can then be specified, and one can change existing rules using the keywords "*extend*" and "*drop*" to add and remove parts of the rule. More advanced changes, such as modifying the precedence of operators, are also possible. For further details on the specification of grammar, see [9].

3.2 Type System

Polyglot provides convenient facilities for extending the type system. As a minimum, this involves introducing a new kind of type object and lookup functions for these new entitites in the environment. The new type of environment is then invoked by overriding the environment factory method in a subclass of *AJTypeSystem*, which describes the type system of AspectJ itself.

To illustrate, consider the introduction of named class pattern expressions [12]. We would need to introduce a new type object to represent such names, say *NamedCPEInstance* (in Polyglot, it is convention that identifiers for type classes end with ...*Instance*). The environment then maps (possibly qualified) names to objects of type *NamedCPEInstance*.

The semantic checks for named patterns must enforce the requirement that there be no cycles in definitions, since recursively defined named patterns do not make sense. A similar check has already been implemented for named pointcuts, and it involves building a dependency graph. Such data structures necessary for semantic checks are typically stored in the type objects (here *NamedCPEInstance*): because Polyglot operates by rewriting the original tree, it is not possible to store references to AST nodes.

Examples such as the parametric introductions of Hanenberg and Unland [23] would require more invasive changes in the type system, for example, by subclassing *InterTypeMethodInstance* (the signature of a method introduced via an intertype declaration) to take account of the parameters that are to be evaluated at compile time.

3.3 Semantic Checks

New semantic checks are usually implemented by overriding the appropriate method on the relevant AST nodes. The most obvious place for simple checks is in the *TypeChecker* pass; every AST node implements a *typeCheck(TypeChecker)* method. The type checker is run after all variable references are resolved; all checks that do not require further data structures are typically put in the *typeCheck* method.

Later passes use data flow information to check initialisation of local variables and the existence of **return** statements. Again, each AST node implements methods to build the control flow graph for these purposes. In the base AspectJ implementation, these are, for example, overridden to take into account the initialisation of the result parameter in **after returning** advice, and extensions can make variations of their own.

AspectJ is somewhat unusual in that some semantic checks have to be deferred to the weaver. For example, it is necessary to type-check the results of **around** advice at each point where it is woven in. Because *abc* maintains precise position information throughout the compilation process, such errors can still be reported at the appropriate locations in the source.

3.4 Rewriting

The normal use of Polyglot is as a source-to-source compiler for extensions to Java, where the final rewriting passes transform new features into an equivalent pure Java AST. *abc* is different in that most of the transformation happen at a later stage, when weaving into Jimple. It is, however, often useful to employ Polyglot's original paradigm when implementing extensions to AspectJ that have an obvious counterpart in AspectJ itself.

For example, consider again the feature of named class pattern expressions. A simple implementation would be to just inline these after appropriate semantic checks have been done, so that nothing else needs to change in the compiler. Such inlining would be implemented as two separate AST rewriting passes, one to collect the named pattern definitions and the other to inline them—the two would then communicate via an explicit data structure that is common to both passes. As said, it is not recommended to store pieces of AST explicitly unless they are immediately transformed away.

abc does extensive rewriting of the AST prior to conversion to Jimple. This consists of introducing new placeholder methods (for instance, for advice bodies), and storing instructions for the backend in the *AspectInfo*. Extensions can participate in this process by implementing methods that are called by the relevant passes.

3.5 Join Points

Introducing new pointcuts will often involve extending the set of possible join points. For example, implementation of a pointcut that matches when a cast instruction is executed would require the addition of a join point at such instructions.

Many new join points will follow the pattern of most existing AspectJ join points and apply at a single Jimple statement. These can be added by defining a new factory class that can recognise the relevant statements and registering it with the global list of join point types.

For more complicated join points, it will be necessary to override the code that iterates through an entire method body looking for join point shadows. The overriding code can do any required analysis of the method body to find instances of the new join points (for example, one might want to inspect all control flow edges to find the back edges of loops [25]), and then call the original code to find all the "normal" join point shadows.

3.6 Pointcuts

As pointed out in the introduction, there are many proposals for new forms of pointcuts in AspectJ. To meet our objective of proportionality (small extensions require little work), we have designed an intermediate representation of pointcuts that is more regular than the existing pointcut language of AspectJ. This makes it easier to compile new pointcut primitives to existing ones.

Specifically, the back-end pointcut language partitions pointcuts into the four categories listed below. Some of the standard AspectJ pointcuts fit directly into one of these categories and are simply duplicated in the back end, while others must be transformed from AspectJ into the representation used in *abc*.

- Lexical pointcuts are restrictions on the lexical position of where a pointcut can match. For example, **within** and **withincode** fall into this category.
- Shadow pointcuts pick out a specific join point shadow within a method body. The **set** pointcut is an example.
- Dynamic pointcuts match based on the type or value of some runtime value. Pointcuts such as **if**, **cflow** and **this** are of this kind.
- Compound pointcuts represent logical connectives such as &&.

The motivation for this categorisation is that it allows the implementation of each back-end pointcut to be simpler and more understandable, which in particular makes it easier for extension authors to define new pointcuts.

An example of an AspectJ pointcut that does not fit into this model directly is the **execution**(⟨*MethodPattern*⟩) pointcut, which specifies both that we are inside a method or constructor matching *MethodPattern* and that we are at the execution join point. The back-end pointcut language therefore views this as the conjunction of a lexical pointcut and a shadow pointcut.

To add a new pointcut, one or more classes should be added to the back end, and the front-end AST nodes should construct the appropriate back-end objects during the generation of the *AspectInfo* structure.

The key class of the *AspectInfo* is the *GlobalAspectInfo* class—this is a singleton (it has precisely one instance during a compiler run), and it contains lists of advice declarations, intertype declarations, and so on. It also contains mappings to retrieve the precedence of two aspects, to find the nonmangled name of a private intertype declaration, and many similar mappings. The front end inserts the appropriate information into these data structures via the accessor functions provided by *GlobalAspectInfo*. The *AspectInfo* also contains classes for the intermediate pointcuts, and the class hierarchy for these closely follows the above description.

The back-end classes are responsible for deciding whether or not the pointcut matches at a specific location. If this cannot be statically determined, then the point-cut should produce a *dynamic residue* which specifies the generation of the required run-time code.

3.7 Advice

It appears that there are few proposals for truly novel types of advice: most new pro-posals can be easily rewritten to the existing idioms of before, after and around. For example, the proposal for "tracecuts" [14,45] reduces to a normal aspect, where a state variable tracks the current matching state, and each pattern/advice pair translates into after advice. Such new types of advice are thus implemented via rewriting, in the stan-dard paradigm of Polyglot.

Nonetheless, adding a new kind of advice that follows the AspectJ model of advice is straightforward: simply implement a new class and define how code should be gen-erated to call that piece of advice and where in the join point shadow this code should go. For example, the bookkeeping required for **cflow** is implemented as a special kind of advice that weaves instructions both at the beginning and end of a shadow.

3.8 Optimisations

The straightforward implementation of a new extension may result in inefficient run-time code. Even in the basic AspectJ language, there are a number of features that incur significant runtime penalties by default, but in many cases can be optimised. *abc* aims to make it as easy as possible to implement new optimisations, whether for the base language or for extensions. In particular, it is straightforward to transform the AST in the front end and the Jimple intermediate code in the back end.

Taking an example from the base AspectJ language, construction of the **thisJoin-Point** is expensive because it must be done each time a join point is encountered at run time. *abc* (like *ajc*) employs two strategies for mitigating this overhead. First, some advice bodies only ever make use of the *StaticPart* member of **thisJoinPoint**, which only needs to be constructed once. A Polyglot pass in the front end is used to identify advice bodies where this is the case and transform the uses to **thisJoinPointStaticPart** instead.

Second, the run-time code generated delays construction until as late as possible in case it turns out not to be needed at all; this is complicated by the fact that *if* pointcuts as well as advice bodies may make use of it, so construction cannot simply be delayed until the advice body runs. *abc* generates code that instantiates the **thisJoinPoint** variable where needed *if it has not already been instantiated*, using *null* as a placeholder until that point. The Jimple code is then transformed to remove unnecessary checks and initialisations, using a variation of Soot's intraprocedural nullness analysis, which has special knowledge that the **thisJoinPoint** factory method cannot return *null*.

3.9 Run-Time Library

The run-time library for AspectJ serves two purposes. First, it contains bookkeeping classes necessary for the implementation of language constructs such as **cflow**.

Extensions such as data flow pointcuts [31] would require a similar run-time class in order to store dynamic data about the source of the value in a particular variable.

Second, the run time provides the objects accessible through the *thisJoinPoint* family of special variables; these make information about the current join point available to the programmer via reflection. Any new pointcut introduced is likely to have unique signature information which would be accessible to the user via an extension of the *Signature* interface. For example, the standard AspectJ runtime contains, amongst others, *AdviceSignature*, *FieldSignature* and *MethodSignature*.

4   *eaj*: An AspectJ Extension

This section describes a few particular extensions to the AspectJ language that we have implemented. These extensions have been chosen to illustrate the most salient of the mechanisms that were described in the previous section. The full source code for these examples is included with the standard distribution of *abc* [1]. For ease of reference, the extended language is named *eaj*; one compiles *eaj* programs with the command "*abc -ext abc.eaj*". This is the usual way of invoking extensions with *abc*.

4.1   Private Pointcut Variables

In AspectJ, the only way to introduce new variables into a pointcut is to make them explicit parameters to a named pointcut definition or advice. It is sometimes convenient, however, to simply declare new variables whose scope is only part of a pointcut expression, without polluting the interface of the pointcut. For example, it might be desired to check that the value of an argument being passed has certain properties, without actually using that value in the advice body. The new keyword **private** introduces a locally scoped pointcut variable. For instance, the following pointcut could be used to check that the argument is either a negative *int* or a negative *double*:

```
pointcut negativefirstarg() :
        private (int x) (args(x)  &&  if(x < 0))
    || private (double x) (args(x)  &&  if(x < 0));
```

4.2   Global Pointcuts

It is very common for many pieces of advice to share a common conjunct in their pointcut. The idea of a *global* pointcut is to write these common conjuncts only once. An example use is to restrict the applicability of every piece of advice within a certain set of aspects. For example, we might write:

```
global : * : !within(Hidden);
```

This would ensure that no advice within any aspect could apply within the *Hidden* class.

As another example, it is often useful to prevent advice from an aspect applying within that aspect itself. The following declaration (for aspect *Aspect*) can achieve this more concisely than putting the restriction on each piece of advice:

```
global : Aspect : !within(Aspect);
```

In general, a global pointcut declaration can be put anywhere a named pointcut declaration can be (i.e., directly within a class or aspect body). The location of such a declaration has no effect on its applicability, except that name patterns within such a declaration will only match classes and aspects visible from the scope of that declaration.

The general form of a global pointcut declaration is as follows:

global : ⟨*ClassPattern*⟩ : ⟨*Pointcut*⟩ ;

It has the effect of replacing the pointcut of each advice declaration in each aspect whose name matches *ClassPattern* with the conjunction of the original pointcut and the global *Pointcut*.

4.3 Cast Pointcuts

The purpose of the *cast* pointcut is to match whenever a value is cast to another type. A corresponding new type of join point shadow is added which occurs at every cast instruction, whether for reference or primitive types, in the bytecode of a program.

To illustrate, the following piece of advice can be used to detect run-time loss of precision caused by casts from an *int* to a *short*:

```
before(int i):
        cast(short) && args(i)
    && if(i < Short.MIN_VALUE
        || i > Short.MAX_VALUE)
{
    System.err.println("Warning: loss of " +
                " precision casting " +
                i + " to a short.");
}
```

In general the syntax of a **cast** pointcut is **cast**(⟨*TypePattern*⟩); this will match at any join point where the static result type of the cast is matched by *TypePattern*. In keeping with the pattern of other primitive pointcuts, the value being cast from can be matched by the **args** pointcut, and the result of the cast can be matched by the optional parameter to **after returning** advice (and is returned by the **proceed** call in **around** advice).

4.4 Throw Pointcuts

The **throw** pointcut is introduced in the developer documentation for *ajc* [28], and we have implemented it in *eaj* to compare the ease-of-extension of both compilers. It matches a new join point shadow which occurs at each throw instruction.

The following example demonstrates how extended debugging information can be produced in the event of a run-time exception, using a piece of advice:

```
before(Debuggable d):
    this(d) && throw() && args(RuntimeException)
{
    d.dumpState();
}
```

5   Implementing *eaj* Using *abc*

We have given a broad outline of how extensions are constructed and discussed some specific extensions that we have implemented. We now show in detail how this was done, both to provide a guide for others and to enable a realistic assessment of the work involved.

5.1   Road Map

As we do not wish to hide any of the difficulties involved in writing an *abc* extension, the presentation in the next few subsections is necessarily somewhat technical, so let us first outline a generic road map of an *abc* extension. This will provide readers with a high-level structure for the detailed explanations that follow.

Extension Packages. An extension typically consists of five Java packages, plus two new "driver" classes that bind the extension to the existing base compiler. The five relevant packages are shown in Fig. 4. The first of these is concerned with syntax and serves to introduce new keywords and grammar rules: these will be discussed in Sects. 5.2 and 5.3 below. Next, one needs to write new classes for AST nodes. In Sect. 5.4 we give an overview of what this involves for the example *eaj* extension. It is quite common that new language features require new compiler passes. For the running example, that is the case with global pointcuts, as it is necessary to collect all of these to make appropriate modifications to advice declarations. In Sect. 5.5 we show how to write a new pass for this purpose. This also requires subclassing the existing AST representation of advice declaration: such subclasses reside in the *extension* package. For the simple examples in this paper, it is not necessary to extend the AspectJ type system. All extensions to the back end of the compiler occur in subpackages of *weaving*. Readers may wish to glance back at Fig. 2, which depicts the architecture of *abc*'s weaver. For the example in hand, one needs to extend the intermediate representation for pointcuts (in *aspectinfo*), and then make appropriate changes to the shadow finder and shadow matcher (in *matching*). More complex extensions may also introduce new kinds of residue or

abc.⟨extension⟩	
parse	new lexer and grammar rules
ast	new ast classes
visit	new compiler passes
extension	overrides of existing ast behaviour
types	new types in typechecker
weaving	
aspectinfo	new IR for pointcuts
matching	finding new shadows, matching shadows to pointcuts
residues	new residue kinds
weaver	changes to the weaver

Fig. 4. Package structure of *abc* extensions

directly modify the weaving process, but for the examples discussed here, that is not needed.

Driver Classes. Apart from extending the packages in Fig. 4, an extension author must bind all the new functionality together, so that it can be invoked (via reflection) by the base compiler. There are two driver classes for this purpose in *abc*, which any extension must subclass.

The first of these is the *AbcExtension* class. An extension can be specified when abc is invoked by passing its core package name to *abc* with the *-ext* flag. The *AbcExtension* class from this package is then loaded by reflection. All the extensibility hooks in *abc* are passed through this class. There is a default implementation of this class in the *abc.main* package, which extensions must subclass.

Another driver class is *ExtensionInfo*. This is part of the extensibility mechanism of Polyglot; all front-end extensions (except for the lexer) are registered by subclassing this class. New instances of this class are returned by the subclassed *AbcExtension*.

Runtime. Some extensions need support in the AspectJ run time. Indeed, to access reflective information about a new type of join point, we need to make sure the run time is extended, so this is usually the last step required in implementing a new extension. We shall discuss a concrete example in Sect. 5.8.

Sources of Extensibility. It may be helpful to point out at this stage what extensibility is unique to *abc*, and what extensibility has been inherited from the components we built on. We now briefly discuss that, going through the packages in Fig. 4. Polyglot provides syntax extensibility; we have added an extensible lexer in *abc*. The way AST nodes are extended in *abc* is based on the principles of Polyglot. Of course, the specific interfaces, say for implementing pointcuts, are unique to *abc*. Furthermore, more than half of the passes in *abc* are specific to AspectJ, and therefore the extensibility for introducing new aspect features is in large part determined by our design for those passes. The very small number of overrides of existing AST classes in Polyglot (in the *extension* package) is testament to the extensibility of Polyglot's Java compiler itself. All parts of the weaver are particular to *abc*, although (as further discussed in Sect. 6) it shares a lot of common structure with *ajc*. A particular feature that enables the extensibility of *abc*'s weaver is the use of the Jimple intermediate representation. Because this is so much easier to analyse and manipulate than either Java source code or bytecode, extenders will find it much easier to implement crucial components like a new shadow matcher.

5.2   Extending the Lexer

As described in Sect. 3.1, *abc*'s lexer is stateful. There are four main lexer states for dealing with the different sub-languages of AspectJ: JAVA, ASPECTJ, POINTCUT and POINTCUTIFEXPR. The first three are used in Java code, AspectJ code and pointcut expressions, respectively. The POINTCUTIFEXPR state must be separate from the normal JAVA state because the **if** pointcut allows a Java expression to be nested inside a POINTCUT, but whereas the JAVA state is terminated by a '}', we need to return to the POINTCUT state when reaching a matching closing ')' character.

Keywords for each state are stored in state-specific *HashMaps* that map each keyword to an object implementing the *LexerAction* interface. This interface declares a method

public *int getToken(AbcLexer lexer)*

which is called when the corresponding keyword is recognised. Its return value is turned into a parser token and passed to the parser for further analysis. A reference to the lexer instance is passed as a parameter to *getToken(...)*, so that side effects that affect the lexer (like changing the lexer state) are possible. A default implementation of this interface is supplied, which offers sufficient functionality to associate keywords with parser tokens and (optionally) change the lexer state; custom implementations of *LexerAction* can provide more flexibility. The default implementation provides functionality sufficient for all but 5 (out of more than 90) Java and AspectJ keywords.

Implementing the *eaj* extensions required adding several new keywords. In particular, "*cast*" was introduced as a keyword in the POINTCUT state, and "*global*" as a keyword in all four lexer states. Both "*private*" and "*throw*" are already keywords in all states, and so do not need to be introduced specifically for the private pointcut variables and throw pointcut extensions. Here is the code that adds the keywords to the respective states:

```
public void initLexerKeywords(AbcLexer lexer)
{
    // keyword for the "cast" pointcut extension
    lexer.addPointcutKeyword("cast",
        new LexerAction_c(new Integer
            (abc.eaj.parse.sym.PC_CAST)));

    // keyword for the "global pointcut" extension
    lexer.addGlobalKeyword("global",
        new LexerAction_c(new Integer
            (abc.eaj.parse.sym.GLOBAL),
                new Integer(lexer.pointcut_state()))));

    // Add the base keywords
    super.initLexerKeywords(lexer);
}
```

Both keywords use the default implementation of *LexerAction*, i.e., the *LexerAction_c* class. We see the one-argument and two-argument constructors for that class. The first argument is always the parser token that should be returned for the keyword; the second argument (if present) is the lexer state that should be selected after the keyword. As stated above, further logic can be implemented by subclassing *LexerAction_c*.

5.3   Extending the Parser

The grammar fragment below shows how two new productions are added for private pointcut variables and the cast pointcut, which can appear anywhere a normal pointcut could:

extend *basic_pointcut_expr* ::=
    PRIVATE:x LPAREN *formal_parameter_list_opt:a* RPAREN
    LPAREN *pointcut_expr:b* RPAREN:y
    {:
        RESULT =
            parser.nf.PCLocalVars(parser.pos(x,y), a, b);
    :}
   | PC_CAST:x LPAREN *type_pattern_expr:a* RPAREN:y
    {:
        RESULT =
            parser.nf.PCCast(parser.pos(x,y), a);
    :}
 ;

The fragment closely resembles code one would use with the popular CUP parser generator, apart from the **extend** keyword, which signifies that these two productions are to be added to the rules that already exist for the nonterminal symbol *basic_pointcut_expr*.

The first new production is for private pointcut variables. As will be apparent from this example, terminal tokens are indicated by capitals. Note that it is possible to bind the result of parsing each grammar symbol to an identifier, indicated by a colon and a name. For instance, we bind the result of recognising the token PRIVATE to x, and the result of recognising a *pointcut_expr* to b. These named results can then be used in the parser action associated with a production. This action is delineated with curly braces and colons. Here we use the results of the first and last symbol in the right-hand side of the production to compute the position (via the call $parser.pos(x, y)$) of the whole private pointcut variable declaration. Positions in Polyglot are always a start location (source file, line number, column number) together with an end location. Throughout *abc*, great care is taken to preserve such position information, so that it is possible to track the origin of every piece of code, even after optimisations have been applied. The second grammar production in the above code fragment is for cast pointcuts, and as it is simpler than the first production, we do not discuss it further.

Apart from extending the alternatives for existing nonterminals (as we did above), the Polyglot Parser Generator PPG [9] also allows you to drop productions, transfer productions from one nonterminal to another and override the productions of a particular nonterminal.

5.4 Adding New AST Nodes

As mentioned above, *abc*'s front end is built on the Polyglot extensible compiler framework [37]. In fact, from Polyglot's point of view, *abc* is just another extension. This means that *abc* "inherits" all the extensibility mechanisms provided by Polyglot.

In particular, adding new AST nodes is common when writing compiler extensions, and thus it is important to provide an easy and robust mechanism for doing so. All four extensions discussed above required new AST nodes. For the sake of brevity we will only present the node introduced by the global pointcut extension here; the other cases are handled very similarly.

In order to write a clean Polyglot extension, one has to adhere to the rigorous use of factories and interfaces to create nodes and invoke their members, respectively. The first step is therefore to define an interface for the new AST node, declaring any functionality it wants to present to the outside world:

```
public interface GlobalPointcutDecl extends PointcutDecl
{
        public void registerGlobalPointcut(GlobalPointcuts visitor,
                                            Context context,
                                            EAJNodeFactory nf);
}
```

We provide a method to insert the pointcut into a static data structure keeping track of the global pointcuts defined in the program (cf. Sect. 5.5). Note that the interface extends *abc*'s *PointcutDecl* interface, so it provides all the functions relevant to a pointcut declaration.

The next step is to write the class implementing that interface. Some boilerplate code is required (a constructor and methods to allow visitors to visit the node), and, of course, the method *registerGlobalPointcut*() is given a concrete implementation.

In order to make sure we can instantiate this new node type, we subclass *abc*'s default node factory (which, in turn, is derived from Polyglot's node factory) and create a method for obtaining an instance of *GlobalPointcutDecl*:

```
public GlobalPointcutDecl
        GlobalPointcutDecl (
                Position pos,
                ClassnamePatternExpr aspect_pattern,
                Pointcut pc, String name,
                TypeNode voidn )
{
        return new GlobalPointcutDecl_c(pos, aspect_pattern,
                                        pc, name, voidn);
}
```

Now the extended parser can produce *GlobalPointcutDecl* objects when it encounters the appropriate tokens (cf. listing in Sect. 5.3).

Note that all changes are local to new classes we created (in fact, these classes are in a completely separate package). The fact that *abc* itself did not have to be changed at all makes the extension robust with respect to *abc* upgrades. Also, since the new AST node extends an existing node, very little functionality needs to be reimplemented. The associated interfaces only have to declare the methods specific to the new node's particular functionality.

In the same way, interfaces *PCLocalVars* and *PCCast* were defined, along with implementing classes, for the private pointcut variables and **cast** pointcut extensions. Corresponding factory methods were added to the extended AspectJ node factory.

5.5   Adding New Front-End Passes

Implementing the "global pointcuts" extension described in Sect. 4.2 requires two new passes. First, all global pointcuts need to be collected, and then each pointcut must be replaced with the conjunction of the original pointcut and all applicable global point-cuts.

Polyglot's visitor-based architecture makes implementing this very easy. We add two new passes. The first stores all global pointcuts in a static variable, and the second applies that pointcut to the relevant code. For reasons of code brevity, these two passes are implemented by the same class, *GlobalAspects*. It uses a member variable called *pass* to distinguish which of the two functions it is performing.

The traversal of the AST is performed by the *ContextVisitor* Polyglot class. The new pass extends *ContextVisitor* with a method that performs the required action when it encounters a relevant AST node.

The following code fragment illustrates the behaviour of the new visitor upon entering an AST node:

```
public NodeVisitor enter(Node parent, Node n) {
    if (pass == COLLECT
        && n instanceof GlobalPointcutDecl) {
        ((GlobalPointcutDecl) n).
            registerGlobalPointcut(this, context(), nodeFactory);
    }
    return super.enter(parent, n);
}
```

As mentioned above, both new passes are implemented by the same class, and hence the check that *pass==COLLECT* makes sure that we do the right thing. If the current node is a *GlobalPointcutDecl* (one of the new AST nodes defined in Sect. 5.4), we call its special method so it registers itself with the data structure storing global pointcuts. Then we delegate the rest of the work (the actual traversal) to the superclass.

The implementation of the *leave()* method, which is called when the visitor leaves an AST node and has the option of rewriting the node if necessary, is very similar. If *pass==CONJOIN* and we are at an appropriate node, we return the conjunction of the node and the global pointcut.

The sequence of passes that the compiler goes through is specified in the special singleton *ExtensionInfo* class. By subclassing it and inserting our new passes in an overridden method which then calls the original method, we make sure the original sequence of passes is undisturbed. Note that this mechanism makes the extension robust with respect to changes in the base *abc* passes—we can add and rearrange passes without breaking the extension.

5.6 Adding New Join Points

To implement the cast and throw pointcuts, we first need to extend the list of join point types. This is done by adding to a list of factory objects which the pointcut matcher iterates over to find all join point shadows. The *listShadowTypes* method is defined in the *AbcExtension* class and is overridden for *eaj*: (here and elsewhere, the element type of a collection is indicated by a comment of the form /*<*ShadowType*>*/)

```
protected List /*<ShadowType>*/ listShadowTypes()
{
    List /*<ShadowType>*/ shadowTypes =
            super.listShadowTypes();
    shadowTypes.add(CastShadowMatch.shadowType());
    shadowTypes.add(ThrowShadowMatch.shadowType());
    return shadowTypes;
}
```

The definitions of *CastShadowMatch* and *ThrowShadowMatch* are very similar and we therefore limit ourselves to discussing the former. The *CastShadow-Match.shadowType()* method just returns an anonymous factory object that delegates the work of finding a join point to a static method in the *CastShadowMatch* class. This method, *matchesAt(...)*, takes a structure describing a position in the program being woven into and returns either a new object representing a join point shadow or *null*. The code for it is given in Fig. 5.

The purpose of the *MethodPosition* parameter is to allow *abc* to iterate through all the parts of a method where a join point shadow can occur, and ask each factory object whether one actually does. There are four types of *MethodPosition* for normal AspectJ shadows:

- whole-body shadows: execution, initialization, preinitialization
- single-statement shadows: method call, field set, field get
- statement-pair shadows: constructor call
- exception-handler shadows: handler

```
public static CastShadowMatch
                matchesAt(MethodPosition pos)
{
    if (!(pos instanceof StmtMethodPosition))
        return null;

    Stmt stmt = ((StmtMethodPosition) pos).getStmt();

    if (!(stmt instanceof AssignStmt))
        return null;
    Value rhs = ((AssignStmt) stmt).getRightOp();

    if (!(rhs instanceof CastExpr))
        return null;
    Type cast_to = ((CastExpr) rhs).getCastType();

    return new CastShadowMatch(
                pos.getContainer(), stmt, cast_to);
}
```

Fig. 5. The CastShadowMatch.matchesAt(...) method

Most shadows either fall into the category of "whole body" or "single statement". Two are special, namely constructor call join points and handler join points. In both cases, the special nature derives from the representation of their shadows in Java bytecode, and consequently their representation in Jimple. In Java bytecode, a constructor call is not a single instruction, but instead it consists of two separate instructions: *new* creates a new instance, whereas *invokespecial* initialises it. A constructor call join point therefore encompasses both of these instructions. Handler join points can only be found by looking at the exception handler table for a method, rather than its statements. If a new join point requires an entirely new kind of method position, then the code that iterates over them can be overridden.

The first job of the *matchesAt(...)* method is to check that we are at the appropriate position for a **cast** pointcut, namely one with a single statement. Next, we need to check whether there is actually a **cast** taking place at this position. The grammar of Jimple makes this straightforward, as a **cast** operation can only take place on the right-hand side of an assigment statement. If no such operation is found, we return *null*; otherwise we construct an appropriate object.

Defining the *CastShadowMatch* class also requires a few other methods, connected with defining the correct values to be bound by an associated **args** pointcut, reporting the information required to construct a *JoinPoint.StaticPart* object at runtime, and recording the information that a pointcut matches at this shadow in an appropriate place for the weaver itself to use. The details are straightforward, and we omit them for reasons of space.

5.7 Extending the Pointcut Matcher

Again, we describe the implementation of the **cast** pointcut and omit discussion of the almost identical **throw** pointcut. Once the corresponding join point shadow has been defined, writing the appropriate back-end class is straightforward. The pointcut matcher tries every pointcut at every join point shadow found, so all the **cast** pointcut has to do is to check whether the current shadow is a *CastShadowMatch*, and if so verify that the type being cast to matches the *TypePattern* given as argument to the **cast** pointcut:

```
protected Residue matchesAt(ShadowMatch sm)
{
    if  (!(sm instanceof CastShadowMatch))
         return null;
    Type cast_to = ((CastShadowMatch) sm).getCastType();

    if  (!getPattern().matchesType(cast_to))
         return null;

    return AlwaysMatch.v();
}
```

The *AlwaysMatch.v()* value is a *dynamic residue* that indicates that the pointcut matches unconditionally at this join point. For those pointcuts where matching cannot be statically determined, this is replaced by one which inserts some code at the shadow to check the condition at runtime.

5.8   Extending the Run-Time Library

AspectJ provides dynamic and static information about the current join point through *thisJoinPoint* and associated special variables. For the **cast** pointcut extension, this run-time interface was extended to reveal the signature of the matching cast. For example, the following aspect picks out all casts (except for the one in the body of the advice) and uses run-time reflection to display the type that is being cast to at each join point:

```
import org.aspectbench.eaj.lang.reflect.CastSignature;

aspect FindCasts
{
    before():
        cast(*) && !within(FindCasts)
    {

        CastSignature s = (CastSignature)
            thisJoinPointStaticPart.getSignature();

        System.out.println("Cast to: " +
            s.getCastType().getName());

    }
}
```

Implementing this requires changes both in the back end of the compiler (where the static join point information is encoded for the run-time library to read later), and the addition of new run-time classes and an interface.

Static join point information is encoded in a string which is parsed at run time by a factory class to construct the objects accessible from *thisJoinPointStaticPart*. This happens just once, namely in the static initialiser of the class where the join point shadow is located. The alternative, which is to directly generate code to construct these objects, would be expensive in terms of the size of the bytecode produced; using strings provides a compact representation without too much run-time overhead.

The static information for a **cast** pointcut is encoded as follows. To allow us to easily reuse the existing parser for such strings, a fair amount of dummy information is generated, corresponding to properties that cast join points do not have. For example, modifiers such as **public** are important for join points that have a method or field signature associated with them, but make no sense for the cast join point. The string for the **cast** pointcut is constructed from four parts:

- modifiers (encoded as an integer—0 for a cast)
- name (usually a method or field name, but for a cast it is just "cast")
- declaring type—class in which the join point occurs
- type of the cast

For example, a cast join point within a method in the class *IntHashTable* which casts the value retrieved from a *HashMap* to an *Integer* would produce the following encoded string:

```
"0-cast-IntHashTable-Integer"
```

The run-time factory is subclassed to add a method that creates an object implementing the new *CastSignature* interface for appropriate join points. The aforementioned *AbcExtension* class has a method which specifies which run-time class should be used as a factory for **thisJoinPointStaticPart** objects, which is overriden so that run-time objects are created with the new factory:

```
public String runtimeSJPFactoryClass()
{
      return
            "org.aspectbench.eaj.runtime.reflect.EajFactory";
}
```

5.9   Code Measurements

To enable the reader to assess the amount of effort involved in implementing each of these new features, we have summarised some statistics in Fig. 6. The table shows the size of the whole parser, and of the boilerplate for factories in the top and penultimate row, respectively. The most interesting part is the breakdown by construct in the middle. For private pointcut variables, all the work goes into defining new AST nodes, and there is no need to define new passes or to touch the weaver in any way. By contrast, global pointcuts require the introduction of new Polyglot passes, which reduce the new construct to existing AspectJ constructs. Finally, for cast and throw pointcuts, there is substantial work in the weaver, because these introduce a new type of join point.

eaj measurements		Files	Lines of code
Parsing		1	74
Private pointcut variables	AST nodes	2	130
	Passes	0	0
	Weaver	0	0
	Run time	0	0
Global pointcut declarations	AST nodes	4	64
	Passes	1	77
	Weaver	0	0
	Run time	0	0
Cast pointcuts	AST nodes	2	46
	Passes	0	0
	Weaver	2	94
	Run time	2	27
Throw pointcuts	AST nodes	2	46
	Passes	0	0
	Weaver	2	91
	Run time	2	16
Extension information and shared classes		7	205
Total		27	870

Fig. 6. Code measurements for *eaj*

It is pleasing to us that the distinction between the examples is so sharp, as it gives good evidence that the aim of modularity has been achieved. This claim is also backed up by the fact that none of the extensions required any change to the code of the base compiler: the extensions are clearly separated plug-in modules. We believe that the amount of code that needs to be written also meets the criterion of proportionality that was introduced at the beginning of this paper. The criterion of simplicity is more difficult to measure, but we hope that the sample code in this section suffices to convince the reader that we have succeeded in this respect as well. The examples presented here do not demonstrate analysis capability: in Sect. 7 we do, however, discuss some more substantial case studies done by others which make essential use of the analysis framework in *abc*.

6   Detailed Comparison to *ajc*

The de facto standard workbench for research into variations and extensions of AspectJ is the *ajc* compiler. It has served this purpose admirably well, and, for example, [31,39] report on the successful integration of substantial new features into *ajc*.

We believe that, in view of the explosion of research into new features and analyses, the time has now come to disentangle the code of the base compiler from that of the extensions. The benefits are illustrated by the table in Fig. 7. It compares the implementation of the **throw** pointcut in *abc* and *ajc*. In the case of *ajc*, we have to modify a large number of existing files, thus tangling the new extension with the existing compiler base. At the cost of some subclassed factories (and thus some more lines of code), *abc* disentangles the two completely: there is no need to modify any part of the base code, and *abc* extensions are clearly separated plug-in modules.

Throw pointcut statistics	*ajc*	*abc*
Core compiler/run-time files modified	8	0
throw-specific files created	2	6
Factory subclasses created	-	5
Total files touched	10	11
Lines of code written[1]	103	187

Fig. 7. The **throw** pointcut in *ajc* and *abc*

These differences follow directly from the design goals of *ajc*, which are quite different from those of *abc*: it aims to be a production compiler, with very short compile times and full integration with the Eclipse IDE. More information about *ajc*, including a detailed description of its weaver, can be found in [27]. By contrast, *abc*'s overriding design goals are extensibility and optimisation, as well as a complete separation from the components it builds on. In the remainder of this section, we make a detailed comparison between the architecture of *ajc* and *abc*, in particular examining where the different design goals led to different design decisions.

---

[1] Note that the numbers in Fig. 7 for *abc* take into account the relevant lines of files, which are listed under "Extension information and shared classes" in Fig. 6.

6.1 Separation from Components

To examine the way *ajc* and *abc* use their respective building blocks, we first measured their size in lines of code, making a distinction between the front end and back end. The overall size of *ajc* and *abc* are comparable, as shown in the following table. These numbers were obtained in consultation with the authors of *ajc*, using the SLOCcount tool:

	ajc	*abc*
Front end	10,197	16,444
Back end	23,938	17,397
Total	34,135	33,841

At first glance it appears that *ajc*'s front end is much smaller than that of *abc*. As we shall see shortly, this is achieved at the cost of making numerous changes in the source of the Java compiler it builds on—and these changes are not listed here. Furthermore, *abc* uses Polyglot, which encourages the use of many tiny classes and requires a fair amount of boilerplate for visitors and factories. Another notable point in the above table is the small size of the back end of *abc*, which performs the most complex part of the compilation process (weaving). This is explained by the use of a clean intermediate representation, Jimple (which we present in more detail below in Sect. 6.3), as well as the rich set of analyses available in the Soot framework. We now examine in some detail how well *ajc* and *abc* are separated from the components that they build on.

Separation from Base Compiler: *ajc*. *ajc* builds on the Eclipse Java compiler. This compiler has been written for speed: for example, it eschews the use of Java's collection classes completely, in favour of lower-level data structures. It also uses dispatch on integer constants in favour of inheritance whenever appropriate.

Unfortunately, the architecture of the Eclipse compiler implies that *ajc* needs its own copy of the source tree of that compiler, to which local changes have been applied. These changes are by no means trivial: 44 Java files are changed, and there are at least 119 source locations where explicit changes are made. Furthermore, the grammar from which the Eclipse parser is generated has been modified. For pointcuts, the new parser simply reads in a string of "pseudotokens" that are then parsed by hand (using a top-down parser) in the relevant semantic actions.

The 119 changes have complex dependencies. For example, the class that implements Java's scope rules needs to be changed in eight places. It is because of such changes to the Eclipse source tree that it can be fairly painful to merge *ajc* with the latest version of the Eclipse compiler.

Separation from Base Compiler: *abc*. By contrast, *abc* does not require any changes to the source of its base compiler, which is Polyglot. Polyglot has been carefully engineered to be extensible, and indeed *abc* is just another Polyglot extension. The changes to the scope rules are handled by introducing a new type for environments and a new type system. These are implemented as simple extensions of the corresponding classes in Polyglot. It is thus very easy to upgrade to new versions of Polyglot, even when substantial changes are made to the base compiler.

There are 14 types of AST nodes in Polyglot where it is necessary to override some small part of the behaviour. This is necessary, for example, because **this** has a different semantics in AspectJ when it occurs inside an intertype declaration. However, since Polyglot has been designed to allow changes of this nature to be made by subclassing, rather than by changing the source of Polyglot itself, no extra work is required when updating to a new version of Polyglot.

Finally, as we have described earlier, *abc* provides a clean LALR(1) grammar, presented in a modular fashion thanks to Polyglot's parser generator, which allows a neat separation between the Java grammar and that of an extension such as AspectJ.

Separation from Bytecode Manipulation: *ajc*. *ajc* uses BCEL, a library for directly manipulating bytecode, in order to perform weaving and code generation. As in the case of the base compiler, however, a special version of this library is maintained as part of the *ajc* source tree. Originally this was regularly synchronised with the BCEL distribution, using a patch file of about 300 lines. The specialised version is now developed as part of *ajc*, as BCEL is no longer actively maintained. The modified BCEL consists of 23,259 lines of code.

Separation from Bytecode Manipulation: *abc*. *abc* is completely separate from the Soot transformation and code generation framework; no changes to Soot are required whatsoever.

We conclude that *abc* is the first AspectJ compiler to achieve a clean-cut separation between the components it builds on. It seems likely that it will be possible to port the ideas that helped achieve this to extending other programming languages with aspect-oriented features.

6.2 Compile Time

It is natural to inquire what the impact of using aspects is on the time taken to compile a program: an AspectJ compiler does a lot more work than a pure Java compiler. To assess this issue, we decided to compare four different AspectJ compilers: normal *ajc*, *ajc* plus an optimisation pass of Soot over its output (*ajc + soot*), *abc* with all optimisations turned off (*abc -O0*), and *abc* with its default intraprocedural optimisations (*abc*). We measured compile times for six benchmarks from [16], as shown in Fig. 8. Our experiments were done on a dual 3.2-GHz Xeon with 4-GB RAM running Linux with a 2.6.8 kernel. We compiled using *abc* 1.0.1, *Soot* 2.2.0, *ajc* 1.2.1 and *javac* 1.4.2. The first column shows the benchmark name. We then give the size of the source in lines (as counted with *sloccount*) and the number of times advice needs to be woven into a shadow. The remainder of the columns show the four different compilers, plus *javac* where applicable.

The first three AspectJ benchmarks (bean, figure, sim-nullptr) have Java equivalents, where the weaving has been performed by hand (bean-java,figure-java,sim-nullptr-java). As expected, aspect weaving has a significant impact on compile times. The main reason is that an AspectJ compiler needs to make a pass over all generated code to identify shadows and possibly weave in advice. It may be possible to curtail such a pass, for example, by determining from information in the constant pool that no pointcut can match inside a given class. We plan to investigate such ways of reducing the extra cost

Benchmark	SLOC	APPS	*ajc*	*ajc* + *Soot*	*abc-OO*	*abc*	*javac*
bean	124	4	1.77	4.00	3.30	3.59	-
bean-java	104	0	1.43	3.21	3.05	3.03	0.54
sim-nullptr	1474	138	2.96	12.00	10.38	10.69	-
sim-nullptr-java	1547	0	1.75	6.52	7.45	8.64	0.76
figure	94	12	1.62	3.43	2.95	3.07	-
figure-java	98	0	1.25	2.83	2.63	2.65	0.51
LoD-sim	1586	1332	4.10	29.87	36.47	46.14	-
dcm	1668	359	3.37	17.07	14.74	17.43	-
tetris	1043	29	2.88	8.42	8.40	8.93	-

Fig. 8. Compile times using *ajc*, *abc* and *javac* (seconds)

of aspect weaving in future work. The last three benchmarks (LoD-cflow, dcm, tetris) make heavy use of aspects so there are no hand-woven Java equivalents.

Overall, the compile times indicate that *abc* is significantly slower than *ajc*. This is no surprise, as *abc*'s code has not been tuned in any way for compile-time performance, whereas short compile times are an explicit design goal for *ajc*. The sim-nullptr benchmark is typical: the difference between *abc* and *ajc* for programs of a few thousand lines is usually a factor of about 4. For examples where *abc* does a lot of optimisation, such as LoD-sim, the gap can be slightly larger. For very large inputs, such as *abc* compiling itself, the difference can be a factor of 14.

The compile times of *abc* reflect the cost of its powerful optimisation framework. In particular, an appropriate comparison is not with *ajc* (which lacks such optimisation capabilities), but with *ajc* + soot. This comparison shows that the compile times of *abc* and *ajc* + soot are quite similar, which is encouraging.

It is furthermore pleasing that a research compiler such as *abc* can cope with very sizeable examples (such as compiling itself); we believe that one natural use of *abc* would be for optimised builds of programs whose day-to-day development is carried out with *ajc*.

6.3 Weaving into Jimple (*abc*) Versus Weaving into Bytecode (*ajc*)

We illustrate the advantage of weaving into the three-address Jimple representation (as *abc* does) compared to weaving directly into bytecode (as *ajc* does) with a simple example of weaving a piece of advice before the call to method bar in the Java code shown in Fig. 9a. The results of weaving into this code both directly on bytecode and through Jimple are shown in Fig. 9b–d. In all cases, the instructions inserted in weaving are shown in boldface.

Figure 9b shows the bytecode for the method after the call to the before advice has been woven by *ajc*. Note that of the inserted bytecodes, only those at offsets 12 through 17 implement the lookup of the appropriate aspect and the call to the advice body. All of the remaining bytecodes are stack fix-up code that must be generated to fix up the implicit bytecode computation stack.

```
public int f(int x,int y,int z)
{
    return bar(x, y, z);
}
```

(a) base Java code

```
public int f(int x,int y,int z)
0:  aload_0
1:  iload_1
2:  iload_2
3:  iload_3
4:  istore %4
6:  istore %5
8:  istore %6
10: astore %7
12: invokestatic
        A.aspectOf ()LA;
15: aload  %7
17: invokevirtual
        A.ajc$before$A$124 (LFoo;)V
20: aload %7
22: iload %6
24: iload %5
26: iload %4
28: invokevirtual Foo.bar (III)I
31: ireturn
```

(b) direct weaving into bytecode (*ajc*)

```
public int f(int,int,int)
{ Foo this;
    int x, y, z, $i0;
    A theAspect;

    this := @this;
    x := @parameter0;
    y := @parameter1;
    z := @parameter2;
    theAspect = A.aspectOf();
    theAspect.before$0(this);
    $i0 = this.bar(x, y, z);
    return $i0;
}
```

(c) weaving into Jimple (*abc*)

```
public int f(int x,int y,int z)
0:  invokestatic A.aspectOf ()LA;
3:  aload_0
4:  invokevirtual
        A.before$0 (LFoo;)V
7:  aload_0
8:  iload_1
9:  iload_2
10: iload_3
11: invokevirtual Foo.bar (III)I
14: ireturn
```

(d) bytecode generated from Jimple (*abc*)

Fig. 9a–d. Weaving into bytecode versus weaving into Jimple

Figure 9c shows the Jimple code for the same method after the call to the before advice has been woven by *abc*. The key difference is that Jimple does not use an implicit computation stack. Instead, all values are denoted using explicit variables. Prior to weaving, the Jimple code is as in Fig. 9c, but without the three lines in boldface. To weave, *abc* needs only declare a Jimple variable, then insert the two lines to look up the aspect and call the before advice. No additional code to fix up any implicit stack is needed.

Figure 9d shows the bytecode that Soot generates from the Jimple code from Fig. 9c. This bytecode has the same effect as the *ajc*-generated code in Fig. 9b, but it is significantly smaller because of Soot's standard backend optimisations. In addition, it uses only three local variables, compared to seven required by the *ajc*-generated code. We have observed that, even with modern JITs which perform register allocation, the excessive number of local variables required when weaving directly into bytecode has a significant negative impact on the performance of the woven code.

6.4 Using Soot Optimisations in Weaving

The use of Soot as a back end for *abc* enables it to leverage Soot's existing optimisation passes to improve the generated code. This simplifies the design of the weaver, but also enables aspect-specific optimisations that would be difficult or impossible to apply directly during weaving. In these cases, the Java optimisations are typically augmented with AspectJ-specific information.

For example, AspectJ makes a special variable named *thisJoinPoint* available in advice bodies. This variable contains various reflective information about the join point that must be gathered at run time and is relatively expensive to construct, so both *abc* and *ajc* implement "lazy" initialisation for this variable. This means that it is only constructed when it will really be needed by an advice body, but that it is never constructed more than once even if more than one piece of advice applies at a join point. This is done by first setting the variable to *null*, then initialising it with the proper value just before advice is called, but only if it still contains *null*.

In *ajc*, the implementation does not work if there is any around advice at the join point (for technical reasons), and it is special-cased to avoid the unnecessary laziness if there is only one piece of advice at the join point. In *abc*, the lazy initialisation is used in all cases, and a subsequent nullness analysis is used to eliminate the overhead of the laziness in most cases (including the one where there is only one piece of advice). The analysis is a standard Java one, which has been given the extra information that the AspectJ run-time library method which constructs the *thisJoinPoint* object can never return *null*. Thus, the implementation is simpler and more robust than the *ajc* version.

6.5   Performance of Object Code

It is beyond the scope of the present paper to do a detailed comparison of the efficiency of code generated by *ajc* and *abc*. In earlier work, in preparation for the construction of *abc* itself, we conducted a detailed study of the dynamic behaviour of aspect-oriented programs [16]. Through a specially constructed set of measurement tools, we were able to confirm the common belief that in many AspectJ programs the overhead introduced by aspects is negligible. However, we were also able to identify common cases where the overheads are surprisingly high. Motivated by these results, we made it an explicit goal of *abc* to be able to experiment with new aspect-specific optimisations.

Because optimisations are an explicit design goal of *abc*, it is important that such experiments are thorough and realistic. In a companion paper [7], we provide a detailed account of the most important optimisations in *abc*, and of their effect on run times. The reader is referred to that paper for a detailed technical account aimed at compiler writers; below we review the most salient points that are relevant to the present comparison with *ajc*.

The first kind of optimisation is an improved implementation of **around** advice, giving a six fold speedup on some benchmarks. In certain cases, *ajc* reverts to generating closures in order to implement **proceed**. When this happens, a lot of heap space is used, leading to very significant overheads. By contrast, in *abc* we are able to avoid the construction of closures in all but very rare pathological cases. In cases where *ajc* does *not* generate closures, it performs a great deal of inlining. This can result in significant code bloat, especially where the advice is woven at many different join point shadows. Again, the compilation strategy employed by *abc* strikes a careful balance between code size and speed. This is illustrated in Fig. 10. Further details of the benchmarks can be found in [7, 16].

Benchmark	Time (s) abc	ajc	Size (instr.) abc	ajc
sim-nullptr	21.9	21.4	7893	10186
sim-nullptr-rec	23.6	124.0	8216	10724
weka-nullptr	19.0	16.0	103,018	134,290
weka-nullptr-rec	18.9	45.5	103,401	130,483
ants-delayed	17.5	18.2	3688	3785
ants-profiler	22.5	21.2	7202	13401

Fig. 10. Execution times and code size

Benchmark	abc					ajc	
	no-opt	sharing	sharing+ counters	sharing+ counters+ reuse	+inter-proc	1.2 (no-opt)	1.2.1 (sharing+ counters)
figure	1072.2	238.3	90.3	20.3	1.96	450.5	167.7
quicksort	122.3	75.1	27.9	27.4	27.3	123.5	28.9
sablecc	29.0	29.1	22.8	22.5	20.4	29.7	24.2
ants	18.7	18.8	18.7	17.9	13.1	33.0	32.9
LoD-sim	1723.9	46.6	32.8	26.2	23.7	4776.2	35.3
LoD-weka	1348.7	142.5	91.9	75.2	66.3	2349.2	113.5
Cona-stack	592.8	80.1	41.2	27.4	23.1	1107.4	56.0
Cona-sim	75.8	75.3	73.8	72.0	73.6	76.8	69.0

Fig. 11. Optimisations of **cflow**

The second kind of optimisation is a set of intraprocedural improvements to **cflow**. In *ajc* 1.2, the implementation of **cflow** used expensive manipulations of a stack, where a simple counter would have sufficed. Also it retrieved the same thread-local state multiple times in a single procedure body, and it did not share work between multiple occurrences of the same **cflow** pointcut. All these problems were eliminated in *abc*, and compared to version 1.2 of *ajc*, these small optimisations yield improvements of 182× (the LoD-sim benchmark). The simplest of these optimisations (counters and sharing) were incorporated into *ajc* 1.2.1.

In earlier work, prior to the start of the *abc* project, we showed how an interprocedural analysis can be used to completely eliminate the cost of **cflow** [40]. This is a good example where the full analysis capabilities of *abc* come into play. The essential idea is to construct a static approximation of the dynamic call graph, so that for each shadow, we can determine at compile time whether it will be in the **cflow** of a given pointcut. Such call graph construction is notoriously hard [21], and thus it is important that we do not need to construct a new analysis from scratch for AspectJ, or indeed for every extension of AspectJ.

We would therefore like to leverage existing analyses for pure Java. To that end, *abc* provides the technique of *reweaving*, which we briefly touched upon in Sect. 2, in particular Fig. 2. The compiler does a first pass over the program, weaving advice naively. The result of this process is a representation of the complete program as pure Jimple code, without any aspect-oriented features. This is then analysed in the usual manner. The results of the analysis are fed back into an optimiser of the *advice-lists*, which can be viewed as little metaprograms that contain instructions to the weaver. The optimisations usually consist of turning a piece of dynamic residue (like updates of the **cflow** stack) into a no-op.

The effectiveness of our optimisations of **cflow** is shown in Fig. 11. The message for researchers who wish to implement their own advanced extensions to AspectJ is that *abc* provides the necessary infrastructure to overcome the challenge of implementing these new features efficiently. It is our belief that new proposals for robust semantic pointcuts (e.g., [15, 45]) necessitate the same type of optimisations and analyses that we have used to make **cflow** efficient.

7 Related Work

The related work falls into two parts. First of all, others have made an independent assessment of the extensibility of *abc*, by implementing extensions of their own. We first discuss some of these. Second, we review a number of alternative proposals for building an AOP language workbench, and we contrast them with the approach taken in *abc*.

7.1 Users of *abc*

Harbulot and Gurd apply aspect-oriented techniques to parallelise scientific code [25]. For these applications, it is imperative to be able to define join points for loop iteration. The alternative is to refactor the code to expose such join points via spurious method calls. It is, however, not an easy task to define a robust notion of loop join points that does not depend on the syntactic presentation of the code. This problem is addressed in [26], and solved by a language extension that is implemented in *abc*.

To illustrate, suppose that we wish to advise loop iterations over a given array. Say we want to intercept the loop

```
for (int i = 0; i < array.length; i + = 1) {
    Object item = array[i];
    . . .
}
```

In the proposed extension of Harbulot and Gurd, this can be achieved with the pointcut

```
pointcut arrit(Object[] array, int min, int max, int stride) :
    loop() && args(min, max, stride, array);
```

Note, however, that it is highly nontrivial to detect the relevant patterns in bytecode. Their implementation first recovers loop structure by computing dominators, and then it does a flow analysis of the loop body to determine the loop variable, its lower and upper bound (0 and *array.length* above), as well as the stride (1 in the above example). The join point shadow matching depends on the precision of these analyses: there may be loop iterations for which the correct *min*, *max* and *stride* cannot be statically determined. The implementation described by [26] does however work independent of whether the user employed **while** or **for** to express a computation.

This case study thus provides a good example of the need for strong analysis capabilities in an extensible compiler for AspectJ. Similar examples abound in the literature, such as Kiczales' *predicted cflow*. The analysis capabilities of *abc* are also indispensable to efficiently implement advanced pointcuts such as the *dataflow pointcut* of [31].

Stolz and Bodden propose to use aspect-orientation for the run-time verification of temporal properties. They define an extension of AspectJ where the user can specify properties as LTL formulae [42]. The implementation is an extension of *abc*.

The atoms of the LTL formulae are pointcuts; and a formula as a whole is translated into an alternating automaton, coded as a regular AspectJ aspect. The translation is thus done entirely using Polyglot, and no changes to the backend are needed. This illustrates one of the advantages of our architecture: it has a gentle learning curve, and there is no need to enter into the complications of generating Jimple if that is not desired.

Experience seems to suggest that many beginning users of *abc* start by implementing an extension as a source-to-source transformation very early on in the compiler, even prior to name disambiguation. Then, when more sophisticated error checking is required, the transformation is moved later and is delayed until all checking is complete. Indeed, such is the intended use of the Polyglot framework.

In the case of these novel features for runtime verification, however, there would be a clear benefit to delaying at least part of the code generation even further, so that it is possible to take advantage of the analysis framework in the backend to examine control flow. Again, *abc* provides all support necessary for making such a step from the implementation described in [42].

Aotani and Masuhara. It is natural to seek language-level mechanisms to enhance the expressive power of pointcuts. A particularly promising approach is put forward by Aotani and Masuhara [3], and they have implemented it with *abc*. Here the idea is to use **if** pointcuts and join point reflection to conveniently express pointcuts such as "all calls where the declared type of the receiver is an interface":

```
pointcut interfaceCall() :
    call(* *(..)) && if(isInterface(thisJoinPoint));

static boolean isInterface(JoinPoint tjp) {
    return tjp.getSignature().getDeclaringType().isInterface();
}
```

When used directly in AspectJ, this would lead to quite inefficient code. Instead, Aotani and Masuhara adopt the perspective of *partial evaluation*, evaluating **if** pointcuts at compile time. Strictly speaking, this is therefore not an extension of the AspectJ language, but rather a change in compilation strategy. Again both the Polyglot-based front end and the Soot-based back end lend themselves very well to implementing such transformations.

Other Extensions of *abc*. The overview above is not exhaustive, and many other researchers are actively developing extensions of *abc*. Examples include DJCutter (a distributed AOP language) [36], Cona (a tool for checking contracts) [41], trace-based aspects [15, 45], a model checker for aspects [30], and tools to perform tasks such as slicing [46]. We are very encouraged by all these developments, and we believe it provides fairly strong independent evidence of the claims for *abc*'s extensibility made in this paper.

7.2 Other Workbenches for AOP Language Research

Of course, we are not the first to realise the need for a workbench to conduct aspect-oriented programming language research, and below we review some earlier approaches put forward by others.

Javassist. Javassist is a reflection-based toolkit for developing Java bytecode translators [11]. Compared to other libraries such as BCEL, it has the distinguishing feature that transformations can be described using a source-level vocabulary. Compared to *abc*, it provides some of the combined functionality of the Java-to-Jimple translator plus the advice weaver, but its intended applications are different: in particular, it is intended for use at load time. Consequently, Javassist does not provide an analysis framework like Soot does in *abc*. In principle, such a framework could be added, but it would require the design of a suitable intermediate representation akin to Jimple.

Josh. Josh is an open implementation of an AspectJ-like language based on Javassist [10], and as such it is much closer in spirit to *abc*. Indeed, the primary purpose of Josh is to experiment with new pointcut designators, although it can also be used for features such as parametric introductions. Because of the implementation technology, there is no special support for the usual static checks in the frontend, which is provided in *abc* by the infrastructure of Polyglot. Josh does not cover the whole of AspectJ, which limits its utility in realistic experiments.

Logic Metaprogramming. A more radical departure from traditional compiler technology is presented by *logic metaprogramming*, as proposed by [13, 22]. Here, program statements where extra code should be woven in are selected by means of full-fledged Prolog programs. This adds significant expressive power, and, like Josh, the design makes it easy to experiment with new kinds of pointcuts. The system operates on abstract syntax trees, which are not a convenient representation for transformation and analysis—many years of research in the compilers community have amply demonstrated the merits of a good intermediate representation. A further disadvantage, in our view, is the lack of static checks due to the increased expressive power. The success of AspectJ can partly be explained by the fact that it provides a *highly disciplined* form of metaprogramming; some of that discipline is lost in logic metaprogramming, because the full power of Prolog precludes certain static checks. Nevertheless, a system based on these ideas is publicly available [44], and it is used as a common platform by a number of researchers.

Pointcuts as Functional Queries. Eichberg, Mezini and Ostermann have very recently suggested an open implementation of pointcuts, to enable easy experimentation with new forms of pointcuts [18]. Their idea is closely related to that of logic metaprogramming, namely to use a declarative query language to identify join point shadows of interest. A difference is that they opt for the use of the XML query language XQuery instead of a logic language. Furthermore, [18] only deals with static join points. As argued in the introduction, several recent proposals for new pointcut primitives require data flow analyses. We believe that it is not convenient to express such analyses via queries on syntax trees. It is, however, quite easy to transfer some of the ideas of [18] to *abc*, by letting the queries range over Polyglot ASTs. A challenge, then, is to define appropriate type rules to implement as part of the frontend.

8   Conclusions and Future Work

We have presented *abc*, and its use as a workbench for experimentation with extensions of AspectJ. Our primary design goal was to completely disentangle new features from the existing codebase, and this goal has been met. In particular, extensions need not make any changes to the code of the base compiler: they are truly separated plugin modules. We hope that such disentangling will enable yet more rapid developments in the design of aspect-oriented programming languages, and the integration of ideas from multiple research teams into a single system, where the base can evolve independently of the extensions.

This project has also been an evaluation of the extensibility of Polyglot and Soot, from the perspective of aspect-oriented software development. We now summarise their role in the extensibility of our design, and identify possible improvements.

Polyglot. Polyglot turned out to be highly suited to our purposes. Its extension mechanisms are exactly what is needed to implement AspectJ itself as an extension of Java, with only minimal code duplication. This in turn makes the development of *abc* relatively independent of further improvements to Polyglot.

As we have remarked earlier, the Polyglot mechanism of *delegates* mimicks that of ordinary intertype declarations, whereas *extension nodes* roughly correspond to what an AspectJ programmer would naturally do via **declare parents** and interface intertype declarations. Polyglot achieves this effect by cunningly creating a replica of the inheritance hierarchy in code, which then provides the hooks for appropriate changes. Arguably that mechanism is somewhat brittle, and it is certainly verbose, replicating the same information in multiple places of the code.

We thus face the question whether it would be possible to extend *abc* using AspectJ, or indeed any other dialect of Java that features open classes. The answer is in the positive, as *abc* is written in pure Java. Todd Millstein has used Relaxed MultiJava [35] in precisely this way, using open classes in lieu of Polyglot's delegate and extension nodes, to implement his recent work on predicate dispatch [34]. It follows that users who prefer to use AspectJ to extend *abc* can do so without further ado.

Would the result be more compact and understandable code? Unfortunately, a significant proportion of Polyglot's extensions is taken up by boilerplate code for generic visitors in each new AST node. To generate that automatically, one would need reflection or a feature akin to parametric introductions [23]. The reflection route has been used with much success, in a framework by Hanson and Proebsting [24] that is very similar to Polyglot.

On the whole we feel our choice of Polyglot has been justified. To further assess its merits, we are now engaged in a comparative study of Polyglot's extension mechanism and more advanced technologies such as aspect-oriented reference attribute grammars [19]. In particular, we would like to investigate how multiple, independent extensions can be composed.

Soot. The choice of Soot as the basis for our code generation and weaver has had a fundamental impact not only on the quality of the code that is generated, but also on the ease by which the transformations are implemented. The Jimple intermediate representation of Soot has been honed on a great variety of optimisations and analyses before we applied it to *abc*, and we reap the benefits of this large body of previous work.

Equally important has been the use of the Dava decompiler that is part of the Soot framework. This makes it much easier to pinpoint potential problems, and to communicate the ideas about code generation to others. It also opens the way to exciting new visualisations, for example to indicate at source level exactly what dynamic residue was inserted at a join point shadow.

In the comparison with *ajc* we demonstrated the importance of the analysis framework in Soot: it is indispensable to eliminate the overheads of advanced language features such as **cflow**. The need for such optimisation is likely to increase with new proposed extensions such as predicted control flow [29], data flow pointcuts [31] and trace cuts [14, 45]. Apart from optimisation, Soot's analysis capabilities are also crucial in the robust implementation of new pointcuts, for instance, those for loop iteration [26].

In summary, we have demonstrated (both through experiments of our own and by reviewing work of others) that *abc* provides an extensible framework for experiments in the design of aspect-oriented programming languages, meeting the criteria of *simplicity, modularity, proportionality* and *analysis capability* set out in the introduction. The next step in its development, namely the upgrade to Java 1.5, will provide a further opportunity to hone these characteristics. Soot is ready for this transition, but Polyglot still needs to be updated to Java 1.5.

Acknowledgments

This work was supported, in part, by NSERC in Canada and EPSRC in the United Kingdom. Our thanks to Chris Allan for his comments on a draft of this paper. Adrian Colyer gave helpful advice on how to collect relevant statistics regarding the source of *ajc*.

References

[1] abc. The AspectBench Compiler. Home page with downloads, FAQ, documentation, support mailing lists, and bug database. http://aspectbench.org. Cited 1 February 2006

[2] Jonathan Aldrich. Open Modules: Modular Reasoning about Advice. In Andrew Black, (ed.) *ECOOP 2005: 19th European Conference on Object-Oriented Programming, LNCS vol. 3586*, Springer, Berlin Heidelberg Newyork, pp. 144–168, 2005

[3] Tomoyuki Aotani and Hidehiko Masuhara. Compiling conditional pointcuts for user-level semantic pointcuts. In *Proceedings of the SPLAT workshop at AOSD 2005*, http://www.daimi.au.dk/ eernst/splat05/. 2005

[4] AspectJ bug database. Wrong variable binding in || pointcuts. https://bugs.eclipse.org/bugs/show_bug.cgi?id=61568, 2004

[5] AspectJ bug database. ITD on inner class: missing accessor method. https://bugs.eclipse.org/bugs/show_bug.cgi?id=73856, 2005

[6] Pavel Avgustinov, Aske Simon Christensen, Laurie Hendren, Sascha Kuzins, Jennifer Lhoták, Ondřej Lhoták, Oege de Moor, Damien Sereni, Ganesh Sittampalam, and Julian Tibble. *abc*: An extensible AspectJ compiler. In: Peri Tarr, (ed.) *AOSD 2005: 4th International Conference on Aspect-Oriented Software Development,* ACM, pp. 87–98, 2005

[7] Pavel Avgustinov, Aske Simon Christensen, Laurie Hendren, Sascha Kuzins, Jennifer Lhoták, Ondřej Lhoták, Oege de Moor, Damien Sereni, Ganesh Sittampalam, and Julian Tibble. Optimising AspectJ. In: Vivek Sarkar and Mary W. Hall (eds.) *PLDI 2005: ACM SIGPLAN Conference on Programming Language Design and Implementation,* ACM, pp. 117–128, 2005

[8] Jonas Bonér. AspectWerkz — dynamic AOP for Java. http://codehaus.org/ jboner/papers/aosd2004_aspectwerkz.pdf, 2004

[9] Michael Brukman and Andrew C. Myers. PPG: a parser generator for extensible grammars, www.cs.cornell.edu/Projects/polyglot/ppg.html. 2003

[10] Shigeru Chiba and Kiyoshi Nakagawa. Josh: an open AspectJ-like language. In: Karl Lieberherr (ed.) *AOSD 2004: 3rd International Conference on Aspect-Oriented Software Development,* pp. 102–111, 2004

[11] Shigeru Chiba and Muga Nishizawa. An easy-to-use toolkit for efficient Java bytecode translators. In: Frank Pfenning and Yannis Smaragdakis (eds.) *GPCE '03: 2nd International Conference on Generative Programming and Component Engineering, LNCS vol. 2830,* Springer, pp. 364–376, 2003

[12] Adrian Colyer and Andrew Clement. Large-scale AOSD for middleware. In: Karl Lieberherr (ed.) *AOSD 2004: 3rd International Conference on Aspect-Oriented Software Development,* ACM, pp. 56–65, 2004

[13] Kris de Volder. Aspect-oriented logic meta-programming. In: Pierre Cointe (ed.) *2nd International Conference on Meta-level Architectures and Reflection, LNCS vol. 1616,* Springer, Berlin Heidelberg New York, pp. 250–272, 1999

[14] Rémi Douence, Pascal Fradet, and Mario Südholt. Composition, reuse and interaction analysis of stateful aspects. In: Karl Lieberherr (ed.) *AOSD 2004: 3rd International Conference on Aspect-Oriented Software Development,* ACM, pp. 141–150, 2004

[15] Rémi Douence, Pascal Fradet, and Mario Südholt. Trace-based aspects. In: Robert Filman, Tzilla Elrad, Siobhan Clarke, and Mehmet Akşit (eds.) *Aspect-Oriented Software Development,* Addison-Wesley, 2004

[16] Bruno Dufour, Christopher Goard, Laurie Hendren, Oege de Moor, Ganesh Sittampalam, and Clark Verbrugge. Measuring the dynamic behaviour of AspectJ programs. In: *Proceedings of the 19th ACM SIGPLAN conference on Object-oriented programming, systems, languages, and applications,* ACM, pp. 150–169, 2004

[17] Chris Dutchyn, Gregor Kiczales, and Hidehiko Masuhara. Tutorial: AOP language exploration using the Aspect Sand Box. In: Gregor Kiczales (ed.) *AOSD 2002: 1st International Conference on Aspect-Oriented Software Development,* ACP, 2002

[18] Michael Eichberg, Mira Mezini, and Klaus Ostermann. Pointcuts as functional queries. In: Wei-Ngan Chin (ed.) *APLAS 2004: Second ASIAN Symposium on Programming Languages and Systems, LNCS vol. 3302,* Springer, Berlin Heidelberg New York, pp. 366–381, 2004

[19] Torbjörn Ekman and Görel Hedin. Rewritable reference attributed grammars. In: Martin Odersky (ed.) *ECOOP 2004: 18th European Conference on Object-Oriented Programming, LNCS vol. 3086,* Springer, Berlin Heidelberg New York, pp. 144–169, 2004

[20] Etienne Gagnon, Laurie J. Hendren, and Guillaume Marceau. Efficient inference of static types for Java bytecode. In: Jens Palsberg (ed.) *Static Analysis Symposium, LNCS vol. 1824,* Springer, Berlin Heidelberg New York, pp. 199–219, 2000

[21] David Grove, Greg DeFouw, Jeffrey Dean, and Craig Chambers. Call graph construction in object-oriented languages. In: Toby Bloom (ed.) *OOPSLA: ACM Conference on Object-Oriented Programming Systems, Languages and Applications,* ACM, pp. 108–124, 1997

[22] Kris Gybels and Johan Brichau. Arranging language features for more robust pattern-based crosscuts. In: Mehmet Akşit (ed.) *AOSD 2003: 2nd International Conference on Aspect-Oriented Software Development,* ACM, pp. 60–69, 2003

[23] Stefan Hanenberg and Rainer Unland. Parametric introductions. In: Mehmet Akşit (ed.) *AOSD 2003: 2nd International Conference on Aspect-Oriented Software Development,* ACM, pp. 80–89, 2003

[24] David Hanson and Todd Proebsting. A research C# compiler. *Software — Practice and Experience,* 34(13):1211–1224, 2004

[25] Bruno Harbulot and John R. Gurd. Using AspectJ to separate concerns in parallel scientific Java code. In: Karl Lieberherr (ed.) *AOSD 2004: 3rd International Conference on Aspect-Oriented Software Development,* ACM, pp. 122–131, 2004

[26] Bruno Harbulot and John R. Gurd. A join point for loops in AspectJ. In: Curtis Clifton, Ralf Lämmel, and Gary T. Leavens (eds.) *FOAL 2005: Foundations of Aspect-Oriented Languages,* pp. 11–20, 2005. Technical report 05-05, Department of Computer Science, Iowa State University. http://www.cs.iastate.edu/ leavens/FOAL/index-2005.shtml

[27] Erik Hilsdale and Jim Hugunin. Advice weaving in AspectJ. In: Karl Lieberherr (ed.) *AOSD 2004: 3rd International Conference on Aspect-Oriented Software Development,* ACM, pp. 26–35, 2004

[28] Jim Hugunin. Guide for developers of the AspectJ compiler and weaver, 2004. http://dev. eclipse.org/ viewcvs/index.cgi/ checkout / org.aspectj/ modules/ docs/ developer/ compiler-weaver/ index.html? rev=1.1& content-type=text/html& cvsroot=Technology_Project

[29] Gregor Kiczales. The fun has just begun. Keynote address at AOSD. aosd.net/archive/2003/ kiczales-aosd-2003.ppt. 2003

[30] Shriram Krishnamurthi, Kathi Fisler, and Michael Greenberg. Verifying aspect advice modularly. In: Richard N. Taylor and Matthew B. Dwyer (eds.) *ACM SIGSOFT International Symposium on the Foundations of Software Engineering,* pp. 137–146, 2004

[31] Hidehiko Masuhara and Kazunori Kawauchi. Dataflow pointcut in aspect-oriented programming. In: Atsushi Ohori (ed.) *1st Asian Symposium on Programming Languages and Systems, LNCS vol. 2895,* Springer, Berlin Heidelberg New York, pp. 105–121, 2003

[32] Hidehiko Masuhara, Gregor Kiczales, and Chris Dutchyn. A compilation and optimization model for aspect-oriented programs. In: Görel Hedin (ed.) *12th International Conference on Compiler Construction, LNCS vol. 2622,* Springer, Berlin Heidelberg New York, pp. 46–60, 2003

[33] Jerome Miecnikowski and Laurie J. Hendren. Decompiling java bytecode: problems, traps and pitfalls. In: R. Nigel Horspool (ed.) *11th International Conference on Compiler Construction, LNCS vol. 2304,* Springer, Berlin Heidelberg New York, pp. 111–127, 2002

[34] Todd Millstein. Practical predicate dispatch. In: John M. Vlissides and Douglas C. Schmidt (eds.) *OOPSLA 2004: Conference on Object-Oriented Programming, Systems, Languages and Applications,* ACM, pp. 345–364, 2004

[35] Todd Millstein, Mark Reay, and Craig Chambers. Relaxed MultiJava: Balancing extensibility and modular typechecking. In: Ron Crocker and Guy L. Steel Jr. (eds.) *OOPSLA 2003: Conference on Object-Oriented Programming, Systems, Languages and Applications,* ACM, pp. 224–240, 2003

[36] Muga Nishizawa, Shigeru Chiba, and Michiaki Tatsubori. Remote pointcut—a language construct for distributed AOP. In: Karl Lieberherr (ed.) *AOSD 2004: 3rd International Conference on Aspect-Oriented Software Development,* ACM, pp. 7–15, 2004

[37] Nathaniel Nystrom, Michael R. Clarkson, and Andrew C. Myers. Polyglot: An extensible compiler framework for Java. In: Görel Hedin (ed.) *12th International Conference on Compiler Construction, LNCS vol. 2622,* Springer, Berlin Heidelberg New York, pp. 138–152, 2003

[38] Harold Ossher and Peri Tarr. Hyper/J: multi-dimensional separation of concerns for java. In: *22nd International Conference on Software Engineering,* pp. 734–737, 2000

[39] Kouhei Sakurai, Hidehiko Masuhara, Naoyasu Ubayashi, Saeko Matsuura, and Seiichi Komiya. Association aspects. In: Karl Lieberherr (ed.) *AOSD 2004: 3rd International Conference on Aspect-Oriented Software Development,* ACM, pp. 16–25, 2004

[40] Damien Sereni and Oege de Moor. Static analysis of aspects. In: Mehmet Akşit (ed.) *AOSD 2003: Proceedings of the 2nd International Conference on Aspect-Oriented Software Development,* ACM, pp. 30–39, 2003

[41] Therapon Skotiniotis and David H. Lorenz. Cona: aspects for contracts and contracts for aspects. In: *OOPSLA '04: Companion to the 19th Annual ACM SIGPLAN Conference on Object-Oriented Programming Systems, Languages, and Applications,* ACM, pp. 196–197, 2004

[42] Volker Stolz and Eric Bodden. Temporal Assertions using AspectJ. In: *Fifth Workshop on Runtime Verification (RV'05),* Electronic Notes in Theoretical Computer Science, Elsevier Science, 2005

[43] Raja Vallée-Rai, Etienne Gagnon, Laurie J. Hendren, Patrick Lam, Patrice Pominville, and Vijay Sundaresan. Optimizing Java bytecode using the Soot framework: Is it feasible? In: David A. Watt (ed.) *CC 2000: Compiler Construction, 9th International Conference,* pp. 18–34, 2000

[44] Kris De Volder. The TyRuBa metaprogramming system. http://tyruba.sourceforge.net/

[45] Robert Walker and Kevin Viggers. Implementing protocols via declarative event patterns. In: *FSE-12: ACM Sigsoft International Symposium on Foundations of Software Engineering,* pp. 159–169, 2004

[46] Jianjun Zhao. Slicing aspect-oriented software. In: *10th IEEE Workshop on Program Comprehension,* pp. 251–260, 2002

Author Index

Lecture Notes in Computer Science

For information about Vols. 1–3802

please contact your bookseller or Springer

Vol. 3846: H. J. van den Herik, Y. Björnsson, N.S. Netanyahu (Eds.), Computers and Games. XIV, 333 pages. 2006.

Vol. 3845: J. Farré, I. Litovsky, S. Schmitz (Eds.), Implementation and Application of Automata. XIII, 360 pages. 2006.

Vol. 3844: J.-M. Bruel (Ed.), Satellite Events at the MoDELS 2005 Conference. XIII, 360 pages. 2006.

Vol. 3843: P. Healy, N.S. Nikolov (Eds.), Graph Drawing. XVII, 536 pages. 2006.

Vol. 3842: H.T. Shen, J. Li, M. Li, J. Ni, W. Wang (Eds.), Advanced Web and Network Technologies, and Applications. XXVII, 1057 pages. 2006.

Vol. 3841: X. Zhou, J. Li, H.T. Shen, M. Kitsuregawa, Y. Zhang (Eds.), Frontiers of WWW Research and Development - APWeb 2006. XXIV, 1223 pages. 2006.

Vol. 3840: M. Li, B. Boehm, L.J. Osterweil (Eds.), Unifying the Software Process Spectrum. XVI, 522 pages. 2006.

Vol. 3839: J.-C. Filliâtre, C. Paulin-Mohring, B. Werner (Eds.), Types for Proofs and Programs. VIII, 275 pages. 2006.

Vol. 3838: A. Middeldorp, V. van Oostrom, F. van Raamsdonk, R. de Vrijer (Eds.), Processes, Terms and Cycles: Steps on the Road to Infinity. XVIII, 639 pages. 2005.

Vol. 3837: K. Cho, P. Jacquet (Eds.), Technologies for Advanced Heterogeneous Networks. IX, 307 pages. 2005.

Vol. 3836: J.-M. Pierson (Ed.), Data Management in Grids. X, 143 pages. 2006.

Vol. 3835: G. Sutcliffe, A. Voronkov (Eds.), Logic for Programming, Artificial Intelligence, and Reasoning. XIV, 744 pages. 2005. (Sublibrary LNAI).

Vol. 3834: D.G. Feitelson, E. Frachtenberg, L. Rudolph, U. Schwiegelshohn (Eds.), Job Scheduling Strategies for Parallel Processing. VIII, 283 pages. 2005.

Vol. 3833: K.-J. Li, C. Vangenot (Eds.), Web and Wireless Geographical Information Systems. XI, 309 pages. 2005.

Vol. 3832: D. Zhang, A.K. Jain (Eds.), Advances in Biometrics. XX, 796 pages. 2005.

Vol. 3831: J. Wiedermann, G. Tel, J. Pokorný, M. Bieliková, J. Štuller (Eds.), SOFSEM 2006: Theory and Practice of Computer Science. XV, 576 pages. 2006.

Vol. 3830: D. Weyns, H. V.D. Parunak, F. Michel (Eds.), Environments for Multi-Agent Systems II. VIII, 291 pages. 2006. (Sublibrary LNAI).

Vol. 3829: P. Pettersson, W. Yi (Eds.), Formal Modeling and Analysis of Timed Systems. IX, 305 pages. 2005.

Vol. 3828: X. Deng, Y. Ye (Eds.), Internet and Network Economics. XVII, 1106 pages. 2005.

Vol. 3827: X. Deng, D.-Z. Du (Eds.), Algorithms and Computation. XX, 1190 pages. 2005.

Vol. 3826: B. Benatallah, F. Casati, P. Traverso (Eds.), Service-Oriented Computing - ICSOC 2005. XVIII, 597 pages. 2005.

Vol. 3824: L.T. Yang, M. Amamiya, Z. Liu, M. Guo, F.J. Rammig (Eds.), Embedded and Ubiquitous Computing - EUC 2005. XXIII, 1204 pages. 2005.

Vol. 3823: T. Enokido, L. Yan, B. Xiao, D. Kim, Y. Dai, L.T. Yang (Eds.), Embedded and Ubiquitous Computing - EUC 2005 Workshops. XXXII, 1317 pages. 2005.

Vol. 3822: D. Feng, D. Lin, M. Yung (Eds.), Information Security and Cryptology. XII, 420 pages. 2005.

Vol. 3821: R. Ramanujam, S. Sen (Eds.), FSTTCS 2005: Foundations of Software Technology and Theoretical Computer Science. XIV, 566 pages. 2005.

Vol. 3820: L.T. Yang, X.-s. Zhou, W. Zhao, Z. Wu, Y. Zhu, M. Lin (Eds.), Embedded Software and Systems. XXVIII, 779 pages. 2005.

Vol. 3819: P. Van Hentenryck (Ed.), Practical Aspects of Declarative Languages. X, 231 pages. 2005.

Vol. 3818: S. Grumbach, L. Sui, V. Vianu (Eds.), Advances in Computer Science - ASIAN 2005. XIII, 294 pages. 2005.

Vol. 3817: M. Faundez-Zanuy, L. Janer, A. Esposito, A. Satue-Villar, J. Roure, V. Espinosa-Duro (Eds.), Nonlinear Analyses and Algorithms for Speech Processing. XII, 380 pages. 2006. (Sublibrary LNAI).

Vol. 3816: G. Chakraborty (Ed.), Distributed Computing and Internet Technology. XXI, 606 pages. 2005.

Vol. 3815: E.A. Fox, E.J. Neuhold, P. Premsmit, V. Wuwongse (Eds.), Digital Libraries: Implementing Strategies and Sharing Experiences. XVII, 529 pages. 2005.

Vol. 3814: M. Maybury, O. Stock, W. Wahlster (Eds.), Intelligent Technologies for Interactive Entertainment. XV, 342 pages. 2005. (Sublibrary LNAI).

Vol. 3813: R. Molva, G. Tsudik, D. Westhoff (Eds.), Security and Privacy in Ad-hoc and Sensor Networks. VIII, 219 pages. 2005.

Vol. 3812: C. Bussler, A. Haller (Eds.), Business Process Management Workshops. XIII, 520 pages. 2006.

Vol. 3811: C. Bussler, M.-C. Shan (Eds.), Technologies for E-Services. VIII, 127 pages. 2006.

Vol. 3810: Y.G. Desmedt, H. Wang, Y. Mu, Y. Li (Eds.), Cryptology and Network Security. XI, 349 pages. 2005.

Vol. 3809: S. Zhang, R. Jarvis (Eds.), AI 2005: Advances in Artificial Intelligence. XXVII, 1344 pages. 2005. (Sublibrary LNAI).

Vol. 3808: C. Bento, A. Cardoso, G. Dias (Eds.), Progress in Artificial Intelligence. XVIII, 704 pages. 2005. (Sublibrary LNAI).

Vol. 3807: M. Dean, Y. Guo, W. Jun, R. Kaschek, S. Krishnaswamy, Z. Pan, Q.Z. Sheng (Eds.), Web Information Systems Engineering - WISE 2005 Workshops. XV, 275 pages. 2005.

Vol. 3806: A.H. H. Ngu, M. Kitsuregawa, E.J. Neuhold, J.-Y. Chung, Q.Z. Sheng (Eds.), Web Information Systems Engineering - WISE 2005. XXI, 771 pages. 2005.

Vol. 3805: G. Subsol (Ed.), Virtual Storytelling. XII, 289 pages. 2005.

Vol. 3804: G. Bebis, R. Boyle, D. Koracin, B. Parvin (Eds.), Advances in Visual Computing. XX, 755 pages. 2005.

Vol. 3803: S. Jajodia, C. Mazumdar (Eds.), Information Systems Security. XI, 342 pages. 2005.